M

BENEATH A RUTHLESS SUN

ALSO BY GILBERT KING

Devil in the Grove: Thurgood Marshall, the Groveland Boys,
and the Dawn of a New America

The Execution of Willie Francis: Race, Murder,
and the Search for Justice in the American South

BENEATH A RUTHLESS SUN

A TRUE STORY OF VIOLENCE, RACE,
AND JUSTICE LOST AND FOUND

GILBERT KING

RIVERHEAD BOOKS • NEW YORK • 2018

RIVERHEAD BOOKS
An imprint of Penguin Random House LLC
375 Hudson Street
New York, New York 10014

Library of Congress Cataloging-in-Publication Data
Names: King, Gilbert, author.
Title: Beneath a ruthless sun : a true story of violence, race, and justice
lost and found / Gilbert King.
Description: New York : Riverhead Books, 2018. | Includes bibliographical references.
Identifiers: LCCN 2017053110 | ISBN 9780399183386 (hardcover) |
ISBN 9780399183430 (ebook)
Subjects: LCSH: Daniels, Jesse Delbert, 1938– . |
Discrimination in criminal justice administration—Florida.
Classification: LCC HV9955.F6 K56 2018 | DDC 364.15/32092 [B]—dc23
LC record available at https://lccn.loc.gov/2017053110
p.   cm.

Printed in the United States of America
1   3   5   7   9   10   8   6   4   2

BOOK DESIGN BY LUCIA BERNARD

For Mary Jane Miles
and in memory of Dorothy King

To gain these fruits that have been earned,
To hold these fields that have been won,
Our arms have strained, our backs have burned,
Bent bare beneath a ruthless sun.

—*James Weldon Johnson*, "Fifty Years (1863–1913)"

Racism has never been a "simple" story. Ever.

—*Ta-Nehisi Coates*, on Twitter

CONTENTS

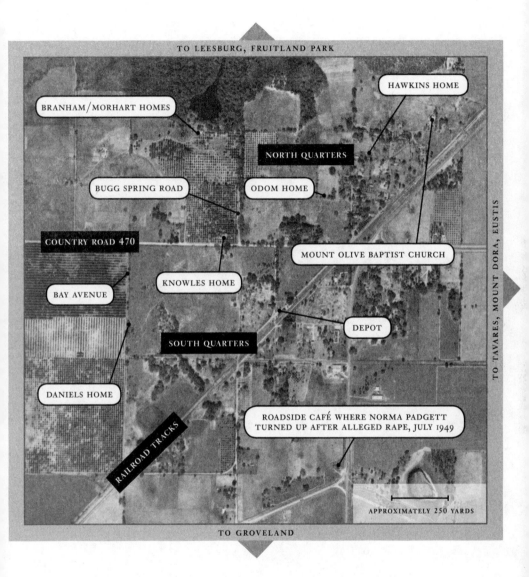

TO LEESBURG, FRUITLAND PARK

HAWKINS HOME

BRANHAM/MORHART HOMES

NORTH QUARTERS

BUGG SPRING ROAD

ODOM HOME

COUNTRY ROAD 470

MOUNT OLIVE BAPTIST CHURCH

KNOWLES HOME

BAY AVENUE

DEPOT

SOUTH QUARTERS

DANIELS HOME

ROADSIDE CAFÉ WHERE NORMA PADGETT
TURNED UP AFTER ALLEGED RAPE, JULY 1949

RAILROAD TRACKS

APPROXIMATELY 250 YARDS

TO GROVELAND

TO TAVARES, MOUNT DORA, EUSTIS

Aerial view of Okahumpka

PART ONE

Okahumpka teen Jesse Daniels

A Killing Freeze

In Okahumpka he was known as the boy on the bike. Most any afternoon, as soon as he heard the Atlantic Coast Line train blow its whistle on its approach to the depot a few miles south of Leesburg, he would be pedaling his way to pick up the afternoon post. At Fate Merritt's grocery, Mayo Carlton might grab hold of the store fiddle and play "Mary Had a Little Lamb" for him while postmaster Sallie Reeves sorted the mail in the next room. Buster Beach would be there, too, well before the West Coast Champion arrived, to share the day's gossip or to tell the boy a corn-fed tale. The men of Okahumpka spoke kindly to him. They'd offer him a wedge of tangerine and tousle his uncombed hair with their meaty, sunbaked hands. They were sure to ask about his daddy.

Some days the boy would linger at the grocery, a nickel in his palm, his eyes on the penny treats, until Mr. Merritt would hand him his favorite Black Cow candy and patiently narrate the financial transaction. The boy would smile and say thank you, but the arithmetic lesson would be lost on him by the time he reached the door.

Other boys and girls his age had finished high school, but Jesse

Delbert Daniels had fallen behind early. It had taken him four years to pass the third grade, and by the age of sixteen he had advanced only two more. He was "not educable," the fifth-grade teacher at Leesburg Elementary School told his mother, and although he'd been granted a social promotion, it came with the condolatory recommendation that he be withdrawn from further schooling.

The mail pocketed in his baggy trousers, and the trousers tucked into his socks so they'd not catch in the bike's greasy chain, the boy would pedal back toward home. The way took him by the fishing hole where he often passed his days. Often Jesse would dawdle, mail in pocket, with no notice of the hours passing, until he found himself caught in a summer downpour. The torrential afternoon rain soaking his hair and clothes, he would stand up on the pedals and lean into the blustery wind while the clay kicking up from the tires spattered his pants and shirt. His mother, Pearl, would rush him inside their humble wooden house, take the wet mail, and dry him briskly with a towel. She'd remind him to pedal home fast when the sky over Sumterville began to darken, and Jesse would say, "Sorry, Mama." But he'd be no more mindful the next time he saw cascades of black and gray clouds billowing in the west, and he'd hear no alarm in the volleys of distant thunder.

Jesse's rides almost always took him past the fifty-four-acre Knowles estate off Bugg Spring Road. The imposing two-story Georgian frame house with two white columns on its front porch stood grandly among oaks and palm trees and a small grove of Florida pines that towered over the surrounding fields and scrub. Joe Knowles sometimes hired Jesse for seasonal work there. In summer it was watermelons. The fifty-pound Garrisons and Tom Watsons demanded more strength to pick, load, and pack without bruising than a scrawny boy could offer, however. While some Lake County farmers hired white football players from Leesburg High, who took the opportunity to bulk up their muscles "pitchin' melons," Jesse usually worked with black laborers, trailing behind the "cutters." Alongside pint-sized Negro boys, brush in one hand and in the other a jar of thick copper sulfate paste, he'd paint the freshly cut stems to reduce the threat of parasitic fungi. Or he'd glue labels on melons before they were stacked in the railcars. When spring came around, Jesse got hired on to drop seeds for a new crop and to fertilize the young vines for eighty-five cents an hour.

The money was needed. Jesse's father, Charles, was an illiterate sixty-nine-year-old veteran of World War I with a long history of arthritis as well as a debilitating heart condition that, for the past decade, had rendered him unemployable. His meager monthly welfare benefits and Army pension could not keep pace with the family's rent increases, and almost yearly, they'd had to relocate from Okahumpka to ever smaller houses in ever more remote corners of Lake County—Yalaha, Howey-in-the-Hills—until they'd settled, once again, in rural Okahumpka.

Jesse's mother, Pearl, was twenty-six years younger than her husband, but likewise debilitated by a weak heart. She had had four miscarriages before Jesse was born in 1938, and would go on to suffer two more. During her pregnancy with Jesse she'd been stricken with malaria, which devastated large swaths of the American South in the 1930s, as a growing number of poor people built shacks in swampland. Doctors had therefore advised Pearl to wean the newborn quickly, but Jesse's health was precarious, too. In infancy he contracted whooping cough, and in childhood he suffered three bouts of rheumatic fever. The second attack, at age ten, left him "slow to think," as Pearl put it, and the last, at sixteen, left him with a stammer and perhaps damage to his heart valves.

In 1956, Pearl had applied to have Jesse admitted to the Florida Farm Colony for Epileptic and Feeble-Minded Persons in Gainesville, a state-funded facility that had been established in 1919 to habilitate children with mental deficiencies. Pearl saw the Colony as an opportunity to give her son a more independent and productive adult life. Using Intelligence Quotient testing developed by the French psychologists Alfred Binet and

Theodore Simon in 1905, the institution adhered to a classification system for the "feeble-minded." Jesse was an "imbecile," with an IQ in the 25–55 range, not as high-functioning as the "morons," whose IQs measured in the 55–75 range, but capable of being trained to perform repetitive tasks. By 1956, however, the Colony had become congested with bedridden "idiots"—persons with IQs below 25, who had "difficulties communicating and [were] often incontinent"—and as their discharge was infrequent, no bed was available for Jesse. Pearl had had to accept that her boy would have to make do with eighty-five-cent hours in the citrus groves and melon patches of Lake County.

By the spring of 1957, the Danielses were renting an unpainted, weather-beaten four-room wood-frame house that stood on pilings amid a cluster of similar homes on tiny lots along Bay Avenue. With a corrugated metal roof overhanging a short front porch outside and a tin wood-burning stove inside, such Florida Cracker houses had become as familiar as any feature in the rural landscape of northern and central Florida. Only clay County Road 470 separated them from the even smaller, vertical-boarded shacks of the Negro families on North Quarters Road—a vestige of slavery times when blacks lived in clusters of cabins often called "the quarters."

The Danielses "kept to themselves and didn't interact with others much," a neighbor recalled. "They were quiet and depressed-looking. Like those Dust Bowl photographs of migrants from the Depression. Their lives were hard." Another neighbor, Carlton "Red" Fussell, remembered the family as "near starvation." Red's father, Lewis, had hosted weekly fish fries to feed Okahumpka's poor during the Depression, and in the winter, when he killed a hog, he'd have his son deliver a shoulder of fresh pork to Pearl, along with some homemade cane syrup stored in old whiskey bottles. "My daddy would help anyone if they looked like they needed it," Red recalled. Summers, too, were oppressive for workers who toiled in the shadeless melon patches of Lake County. Mr. Knowles would admonish Jesse and the other pickers about the dangers of sunstroke. "Don't let the bear get you," he'd say. None of them could afford to be treated in local hospitals, and if severely afflicted, they might be unable to work for a week or more—an economic hardship on their families. Pearl continually reminded her son to drink plenty of water, especially in the sweltering afternoon heat. From season to season, her worries about the boy never abated.

SINCE THE FALL OF 1957, there had been constant rumblings in the skies over Cape Canaveral, eighty miles to the east of Lake County. Ballistic missiles with names like Thor and Jupiter and Snark glowed like Roman candles as they soared over the groves of Okahumpka and ripped through the ragged clouds above. America's Space Race with the Soviet Union had hit full throttle, and as the two nations battled for aeronautic supremacy, unannounced launches on the coast had become a part of everyday life in east central Florida. Not all of the American rockets ascended with grace. Many failed spectacularly, their engines losing thrust at liftoff or exploding on the pad or bursting into flames over the Atlantic. One long-range missile, failing to respond to controls, was last seen "headed for the jungles of Brazil." Another crashed fifty miles to the south, just outside a popular Vero Beach restaurant, blowing out its windows. Undeterred, scientists and engineers kept trying. By day and by night, the giant, liquid-fueled cylinders, shaking the earth along Florida's coastline as they shot skyward like flaming white arrows, afforded irrefutable evidence that a new age had begun.

"The character of east central Florida is changing nearly as fast as the rockets that streak across the sky from Cape Canaveral," the *New York Times* reported. Governor LeRoy Collins had prioritized Florida's commitment to the space industry, and the military, as well as aviation and defense corporations like Northrop, Douglas, Boeing, and Martin, had been flocking to the region. Relocated engineers and their families made temporary households in the roadside hotels that had sprouted up along highway A1A in the booming town of Cocoa Beach. Market centers were mushrooming in the scrubland and swamp, and luxury hotels, real estate, and banking were booming as the population swelled. New schools were needed, and new highways, airports, and waterways.

Scores upon scores of the missile industry's support workers were packed into blistering-hot trailer offices that one newspaper deemed to be "the worst sweatshops this side of New York's garment jungle." The workers and their families lived in overcrowded trailer courts, and their low wages pushed more and more of them inland, where ultimately they took refuge in makeshift homes at the edge of undrained, mosquito-infested swamps.

Orlando, long the epicenter of Florida's thriving citrus business, was deep in "the grip of a giant fist of change" by 1957. But all evidence of central Florida's transformation halted at the Lake County line. The citrus elite cared not to trail the flaming paths of missiles in the sky, and on the ground they were spared the unsightly sprawl generated by the aerospace "glamour" industries. Indeed, as the *Times* reported, "some of the old-line citrus growers, financially secure, resent the thrust of industrialization." For while cattle ranching still counted as a major industry across central Florida, it was agriculture—particularly the profit from millions of orange trees—that made and kept the area so independently prosperous that it needed no help from Governor Collins and his cadre of out-of-state investors. Lake County alone took in nearly $25 million from citrus in 1956, more than the entire state of California. The county finished construction on the 226-foot-tall Florida Citrus Tower in Clermont that same year, in which half a million tourists would ascend to the observation deck to gaze over miles of orange groves in every direction. It was a time and place, one journalist observed, when "citrus was king, and Lake was where the princes lived."

Secure in their cocoons of wealth and privilege, the citrus princes barely felt the crisis in confidence that shook the country when, despite the best efforts of the U.S. military and Florida's burgeoning defense industry, America failed to outstrip its Cold War competitor in the Space Race. On October 4, 1957, the USSR succeeded in placing the first artificial satellite, Sputnik 1, into orbit. A month later, the Russians launched Sputnik 2, and Laika, a stray dog from the streets of Moscow, became the first animal to orbit the earth.

President Eisenhower had pinned the nation's best hopes of demonstrating primacy in the Space Race to the Cape Canaveral launch of the first Vanguard rocket on December 6. It proved to be a disaster. The flight, broadcast live on national television, lasted barely two seconds after liftoff. Four feet from the ground, the rocket crashed back onto the launchpad, toppled over, and exploded. Across east central Florida, in their cramped homes at the edge of swamps, thousands of Florida's "space itinerants" stared in horror and disbelief at their black-and-white screens, wondering what future this strange, unforgiving wasteland held for them.

The princes of Lake County, meanwhile, continued to thrive. With kingdoms of orchards, they had no desire to conquer the skies, and no suspicion that from them would soon arrive an unimagined misfortune.

On December 10, 1957, a blast of Arctic air bore down on the American Midwest. In Okahumpka, farmers and citrus growers prepared for battle as high winds forced the cold front south. They lit smudge pots and built bonfires—fat pine, diesel fuel, and old tires set aflame in pyres a hundred yards long—to keep the orchards and citrus groves warm. Attended by black-eyed "smudgers," the fires smoldered all night, reeking of scorched rubber and spewing thick black soot into the groves.

Farmers with crops near canals raised the water table in an effort to keep the ground warm. Others flew crop dusters at low altitude to douse the groves with water; extra water in the soil would store more heat from the sun, which would help neutralize the chill at night. Ice, as every Florida grove owner was keenly aware, begins to form in citrus tissue at 28 degrees Fahrenheit, and more than four hours at or below that temperature would irreversibly damage the fruit.

By Wednesday, December 11, Lake County farmers, eyeing their thermometers, were bracing for the inevitable. Warren Johnson, head of the Florida Frost Warning Service, had issued a statement as dour as it was discouraging: "Hard freeze in North and Central Districts and frost and freezing temperatures in Southern districts Thursday morning." Snow was falling in Jacksonville, and the coldest front of the season was moving rapidly to the south with winds gusting 20 to 35 miles per hour. Twenty-five people had been killed in fires caused by overheated stoves, and the national death toll from exposure had already reached fifty.

Florida vegetable farmer W. E. Tyler took one final, stoical glance at his forty-five-acre tomato crop and decided to go hunting. "The freeze killed the whole crop," he lamented. "That's the chance you take when you plant in the fall. I never had time to go hunting before, but now I don't have to worry about the tomatoes."

Still, at the peak of the holiday shipping season, Okahumpka's citrus men clung to the hope that they might somehow salvage enough fruit to meet the demand. In advance of the freeze, they dispatched armies of pickers into the groves with twenty-four-foot ladders, to attempt to pick as much of the crop as possible. More vital than saving the crop, however, was saving the trees themselves. With the freeze looming, everyone in the community was expected to pitch in. For two straight days, from sunup to sundown, Jesse Daniels, his nostrils blackened and burning from the oily soot in the air, worked alongside other locals, including women and children, building banks—cone-shaped piles of sand two to three feet high—around the bottoms of the trunks. "It was hard work," Jesse recalled. "Made my whole body ache."

With each hour after the sun set on Thursday, December 12, the farmers' hopes dwindled. The temperature dropped to 12 degrees overnight, and the following morning Warren Johnson's office tersely declared the freeze a "major disaster" for the state. Temple oranges and tangerines had been especially hard hit, and scores of citrus shippers and juice-concentrate plants across the state closed for the day to assess the damage. The product to fill an estimated ninety million boxes had gone unharvested.

That Friday, Jesse Daniels again got up at dawn to prepare for another long day's labor in the groves. At least he'd not be soil-banking. Instead, he'd join the fruit pickers at local groves, where they'd harvest a crop of mid-season Parson Brown oranges. The Parson Browns not only offered sweetness but also tolerated cold, even into the teens, and citrus growers like Joe Knowles were trusting that the frozen oranges would still be acceptable for the production of concentrate. They would have to be picked immediately, however, and the juice would have to be squeezed from the fruit within days. Pressed for time, grove owners competed for available workers, who, under such circumstances, could count on receiving a little more than the usual twenty cents per box of picked oranges.

Pearl Daniels made sure her son was properly dressed for the weather. Jesse didn't own a pair of gloves, so she protected his hands with two pairs of socks. At the grove, Jesse helped in the "cleaning out": gathering the fruit that hung inward on the frosty branches or that hung low on the trees but was obscured by the pickers' ladders. With the harvest from the injured trees, Joe Knowles was striving to cut his losses against the impact of the freeze as well as a rumored statewide citrus embargo by the Florida Citrus Commission, which would prohibit the use of freeze-damaged oranges in producing concentrate. Should damaged oranges go to market, the commission reasoned, consumers and dealers were likely to be wary of Florida fruit for years to come. The state had not imposed an embargo since the freeze of 1948, however, and Knowles was determined to ship as much product as possible before the ban took effect.

The next few days brought a return of moderate temperatures to the region—too moderate, in fact, up into the mid-seventies. With the rapid warming the leaves on even the strongest trees turned brittle; then they took on the burnt reddish cast every grower feared: the unmistakable indicator of severely freeze-damaged trees. Early surveys from the state's Agriculture Disaster Committee estimated the losses to citrus growers at fifty to a hundred million dollars. The governor's forecast was even more dire; he told his cabinet that as much as 75 percent of the state's orange crop had been lost. He was therefore planning to meet, on the evening of December 17, with citrus-industry leaders who were arriving in nearby Ocala to discuss emergency federal loans and other assistance. "I do not know what we can do," Collins said, "but we should do everything possible."

LATE IN THE EVENING OF THE 17TH, in a ranch house east of Eustis, Noel Griffin Jr. was lying asleep in bed with his wife, June, when the telephone rang, startling them both. It was Sheriff Willis McCall, with an urgent ten-eight that put his twenty-nine-year-old deputy into immediate service. A woman had been raped in Okahumpka—a woman "from an important family." Still groggy, Griffin was thinking he should ask the street address when the sheriff spluttered the victim's name. Griffin no longer needed to ask the address.

The deputy jumped into his uniform and holstered his revolver. Okahumpka lay twenty-five miles southwest of Griffin's ranch, but at this late hour, with Griffin's much-reputed lead foot applied to the accelerator of his 1956 Plymouth Belvedere, it wouldn't take long to get there. Cherry top flashing, he ran the red light past the courthouse in Tavares, then raced west on U.S. Route 441 toward Leesburg, where so many of the state's citrus barons lived. On the outskirts of town, he sped by the vibrant neon sign announcing the BIG ASS MOTEL. Local kids with air rifles had so unfailingly shot out the sign's second neon-tubed B that the motel's owner had finally given up on fixing it. Few people in Lake County knew it as the Big Bass, anyway.

Minutes away from Okahumpka, Griffin picked up the radio crackle of McCall's voice. All deputies converging on the scene were receiving the sheriff's command: "Round up every nigger you see." Griffin followed the flashing red lights of the other cruisers into North Quarters, a pocket of small unpainted shacks. His high beams cut into the dazed eyes of black women roused from bed in the middle of the night, standing silent outside their homes or bouncing sleepy babies in their arms as they paced. Griffin stepped out of his Plymouth. Up and down the road, harried deputies were shuttling shirtless young black men away in handcuffs. Barking hounds were pulling their white handlers into homes yet to be searched.

"Evvie!"

Griffin turned at the sound of his nickname, a relic of his childhood inability to pronounce a shortened version of his middle name, Edward. It was Doug Sewell, tugging a cuffed Negro by the arm. "Take in every swinging dick," Sewell told him.

The cacophony continued through daybreak. Griffin thrust three young men into the back of his Plymouth and hauled them off to the jail in Tavares, where two other deputies were interrogating suspects. Curious white neighbors from South Quarters ventured onto the scene and stood in the gray light, speculating, nodding and gossiping as the last of the deputies' cars packed with the black boys of Okahumpka lurched into gear and sped north through boundless acres of rotting citrus.

JESSE DANIELS WOKE on the morning of Wednesday, December 18, to the sound of a car churning sand outside. "Uh-oh," he said to his mother, who was busy fixing breakfast for Charles, "there's a deputy car."

"Jesse," Pearl said, "I need some things at the grocery. Why don't you bike down there for me, and maybe you'll hear what happened."

"Okay, Mama," Jesse replied. "Maybe I can get to talk to a deputy—"

"No, son," Pearl interrupted—she always tried to protect Jesse from "unkind" people, strangers who might mock him for his stutter and childlike speech—"you just listen."

In minutes Jesse was on his way down to Merritt's. He spotted a deputy's Plymouth parked in front. He laid down his bike, went inside, and sidled up to the lawman.

Half an hour later, Jesse returned home from the store with the flour his mother had wanted. He looked shocked and embarrassed, and he was hesitant to speak.

"I found out," he stammered. "A Negro raped a white woman." And added, "I think I know what that means."

FOR MABEL NORRIS REESE, Wednesdays had a special routine. Wednesday was the day the *Mount Dora Topic*, the weekly newspaper that she and her husband, Paul, owned and ran, went to press. The alarm clock would go off at four a.m. in their house on Morningside Drive in Sylvan Shores, a small, upscale community of Mediterranean Revival and ranch homes along the west side of Lake Gertrude. Within the hour, Mabel would be barreling along the few miles to the *Topic*'s office in downtown Mount Dora. There she'd go over that week's edition, making corrections in the lead galleys, before heading back home to cook breakfast for Paul and their daughter, Patricia.

Once Patricia had been seen off to school, Mabel would return to the office with Paul for the long hours ahead. Side by side, they would dress up the pages of the newspaper together. Harold Rawley, who ran the Linotype machine, would set the pages one metal line of type at a time, to be inked and printed later that night on the Old Topper, the *Topic*'s big press. Mrs. Downs, a seventy-two-year-old widow who had taken over the print work from her late husband, would stand in the hot air atop the press platform, feeding sheets of paper into the jaws of the loud, cranky machine that birthed the "inky babies," as Mabel called them.

In addition to covering meetings, writing stories and weekly editorials, taking photographs, and selling ads, Mabel worked the arm on the wing mailer and slapped name stickers on each freshly printed copy until, as she liked to tell Patricia, "the pile on the left goes way down and the pile on the right climbs to a mountain." (Patricia herself attended to the wrapping and stamping of the papers, and Paul and his brother delivered the lot of them to the post office.)

Mabel had performed this strenuous Wednesday routine more than five hundred times in the ten years that she and Paul had been publishing the *Topic.* She'd missed only two issues—once when she'd been briefly hospitalized and once the previous summer, when she'd traveled to Illinois to accept a journalism award.

Sturdy and still stylish at forty-three, Mabel favored printed cotton shirtwaist dresses, which she sometimes wore with pearls, and with her bebopper's cat-eye glasses she was easily spotted out and about in old-fashioned Mount Dora. This week, she had wrapped herself as well in the warm winter coat she'd had few opportunities to wear since she'd left Akron, Ohio, a decade before and headed out to sites around Lake County to see how people had been affected by the freeze.

Mount Dora had not been spared, as many of its wealthier residents had lost their own small groves. But in the camps for seasonal laborers on the outskirts of town, conditions were far worse, ensuring, Mabel observed, "misery for the men, women and children who annually make their way to Florida to seek a living as laborers." Lured by ads in local newspapers across the country, promising an abundance of winter work picking fruit in sunny Florida, they'd come to the citrus groves and vegetable farms of Lake County in droves, "on the proverbial shoe-string,"

Mabel wrote. The events of the past week had shattered their hopes. The Florida Citrus Commission had imposed the threatened embargo on all fresh fruit, virtually wiping out the one remaining employment possibility for itinerant pickers. There would be no celery to cut, no tomatoes to harvest, no budding trees to nurse, and no fruit to pick—not even freeze-damaged fruit.

Most of the laborers had arrived in Lake County without money for a return trip, and they had depended on their first week's wages to cover their rent and living expenses. Local police, overwhelmed by requests for food, pointed the desperate itinerants to the King's Daughters, a charitable organization. Mabel was moved both by the workers' plight and by the "quiet work" of the charity, which provided bus fares and gasoline for stranded families, as well as mattresses for workers who were sleeping on the bare floors of houses without electric light or heat.

But as the weather had quickly returned to more-than-seasonable temperatures, what would become known as the 1957 Freeze was almost as rapidly receding from newspaper headlines into history. So when, in the wee hours of December 18, only a couple of hours before her normal Wednesday routine would have begun, rumors of a white woman's rape began to circulate, Mabel was free to follow her reportorial instincts. They took her to Okahumpka, where she'd heard that residents of North Quarters were being harassed. There she found that Sheriff McCall's deputies were not only terrorizing the residents but also arresting on suspicion virtually every young black male in the neighborhood. One of them described how Negro suspects were being rounded up and taken in by up to five carloads at a time. "They woke me up at two a.m. and told me I would get the electric chair if they didn't kill me beforehand," he said. Another Okahumpka resident told Mabel, "They took in thirty-three of our menfolk. Not just men, but boys, too . . . A body couldn't do anything but wait for 'em to come pounding on the door."

By daybreak, Mabel had pages of notes to transcribe, and they reverberated with fear—fear that, once again, the Lake County Sheriff's Department was indiscriminately rounding up young black men, and that, once again, violence would come of it. "A restlessness began to run through the quarters," Mabel wrote, "and it mounted steadily."

Meanwhile, over at the county courthouse in Tavares, deputies James Yates and Leroy Campbell were interrogating an endless stream of suspects. Ethel Cope, a fifty-three-year-old maid from Okahumpka, showed up for work that Wednesday morning after a sleepless, uneasy night, worried that her nephew, eighteen-year-old Sam Wiley Odom, was one of them. She described to her employers how all night long deputies had ransacked black homes, busting in and throwing furniture around in the name of the law. One of the young men they'd picked up in the initial sweep was Sam.

Ethel Cope had good reason to worry about her nephew. The victim was not just any white woman. She was Joe Knowles's thirty-one-year-old wife, Blanche Bosanquet Knowles—mother of three young children. Later on Wednesday, Deputy Yates began eliminating some of the suspects who'd been hauled off to jail for questioning. Sam Wiley Odom was not among them. Yates hadn't liked some of the Odom boy's answers, and he'd cast a hard eye on the teenager sitting so calmly behind bars. He persuaded McCall to engage the services of Lieutenant William Donaldson, a polygraph examiner from the Hillsborough County Sheriff's Department in Tampa, to aid in the interrogations. Meantime, Sam Wiley Odom wouldn't be talking to any lawyers or receiving any family visitors. The boy was going to have to be more cooperative. He was going to have to start telling Yates the truth.

The Knowles family, December 1957

CHAPTER TWO

Real Sunshine

IN THE MINUTES after her attacker fled the scene, Blanche Knowles, alone in the house with her children—her husband, Joe, was out of town—sprang into action. Still in her nightgown, still trembling in terror, she rushed into the bedroom where her two boys, eight-year-old David and six-year-old Steve, were sleeping. Trying to remain calm, she roused them from their beds and hurried them back to her bedroom, where one-year-old Mary still lay sleeping in a crib. Blanche bolted the door, then picked up the phone. She dialed Joe's brother, Tim. No one answered. Shakily, she tried the family attorney, W. F. ("Red") Robinson. A few rings brought him to the phone. When she told him what had happened, he instructed her not to do a thing and said that he'd be there straightaway. It was Robinson, not Blanche, who called the police.

Blanche huddled with her children in the dark. With the flashlight on the bedside table she read the time on the clock: It was 1:25 a.m. Less than half an hour later, Robinson arrived in Deputy James Yates's car; they were followed by other deputies from the Lake County Sheriff's Department. Blanche carried Mary down the stairs and out onto the front porch, the two boys, still in their pajamas, trailing after her. The wail of the police cruisers' sirens pierced the night and the glow from their flashing red lights danced across a canopy of Spanish moss. Yates pulled Blanche aside to take her statement, with Robinson standing by. Without hesitation, she provided him with an account of the incident and a description of her attacker. She told him she had been "raped by a Negro"—a young Negro, "with bushy hair." After leaving her bedroom, she said, the man had taken a tumble down the staircase and busted out of the house through the back screen door.

Immediately Yates radioed McCall, who in turn put out the call to his deputies to sweep the Quarters. On McCall's orders, too, Yates assumed the lead in the investigation. In light of the information taken from the victim, he headed to the rear of the Knowles home. There, flashlight in hand, squatting in the sandy soil, he located diamond-shaped heel prints that he followed to a set of tire tracks in the clay on the north side of County Road 470. Already confident that the tracks had been laid by the perpetrator's getaway car, Yates was eager to have them cast in plaster. The piece of evidence that most drew Yates's attention, though, was discovered by his longtime partner, Deputy Leroy Campbell: A pair of "soiled" men's undershorts, size 34, lay to the south of the front door. The scent on the undershorts excited the hounds at the scene, and they pulled deputies in the direction of the Quarters. As more deputies appeared on the scene, Yates dispatched them to the Quarters as well.

Red Robinson arranged to have Blanche and the Knowles children driven in a police car to his house in the Palmora Park section of Leesburg, to spend the night. Once they arrived, Robinson summoned the Knowles family physician, Dr. Durham Young. Upon observing that Blanche was "highly nervous and quite upset," he gave her a "tablet to settle her nerves." Then he accompanied her to the local hospital in Leesburg, where, at around 2:45 a.m., he performed an examination that revealed evidence of "sexual intercourse within a twenty-four-hour period preceding" the exam. He also observed "no bruising or other physical injury and none was complained of," and went on to note that Blanche "was a rather stoic type of person and was not hysterical and was quite herself and very well composed under the circumstances." His examination complete, Young gave Blanche a shot of sedative, and Robinson drove her back to his home in Palmora Park. Efforts were being made to locate her husband, the attorney assured her. With that solace and the sedative, Blanche was finally able to fall into a deep sleep.

The family's Christmas card that year had shown the Knowleses posed formally at the window of their Okahumpka living room. Blanche, in dress and heels, and dark lipstick, is sitting with Mary propped on her lap; David stands on the right and Steve on the left, both of them in pin-striped blazers and bow ties. Behind them hulks Joe, in a business suit and crisp white shirt and a tie. In that same room, with the cold front descending on Florida, the family had gathered to decorate their Christmas tree in front of a crackling fire. The boys had helped Blanche hang ornaments while Joe treated them to the holiday croonings of Frank Sinatra and Nat King Cole on the record player. Outside, on the dozens of acres of citrus where, in warmer weather, the boys climbed trees and hauled a little wagon packed with sandwiches and fruit that Blanche prepared for their picnics, smudgers, their faces black with soot, were attempting to ward off the worst of the cold by "firing the groves" off Bugg Spring.

On the morning of December 18, though, the Knowles boys awoke in strange beds in a strange house, its windows offering no familiar view of the citrus groves, and their mother told them they would not be going home. By then she had been informed by Robinson that Sam Powell, her husband's close friend, had driven to Tampa to locate Joe and bring him back to Lake County. Meanwhile, the sheriff's department, Robinson had also reported, was leaving no stone unturned in its efforts to apprehend the young Negro who had raped her.

The lives of the family in the Christmas portrait had been altered, irreversibly.

THE ELDEST OF FIVE CHILDREN, Blanche Bosanquet had grown up in a proud, tradition-steeped family on Fair Oaks, a grand estate in the small citrus town of Fruitland Park, just ten miles north of Okahumpka and only a few miles north of Robinson's Leesburg home. The Bosanquets' house, by far the largest in a town of fewer than five hundred people, was a sprawling eleven-room mansion that had been built by Blanche's British ancestors when the site of the estate was the colony of Chetwynd.

The Bosanquets traced their pedigree back to seventeenth-century France. As Huguenots, they had been driven from their Catholic homeland to Protestant England. By the nineteenth century, they had established a generations-long dynasty of bankers and merchants with close ties to the British crown and the East India Trading Company. Blanche's grandfather Louis Percival Bosanquet left London in 1888, at the age of twenty-three, to join his older brother, Augustus, in central Florida. Like dozens of other wealthy young English bachelors in the area, the Bosanquet brothers were seized by "citrus fever." Together, they purchased one hundred acres of land bordering Zephyr Lake in Chetwynd from a freed slave. Relying on skilled black laborers, they set about building Fair Oaks from the rosin-rich cores of the region's plentiful yellow pines, because rosin deterred termites. They dedicated twenty acres of the land to citrus, mostly oranges and mandarins; the rest they cultivated with seeds imported from their native England and thus introduced to Florida fruit like the Red Ceylon, a tropical peach that would become widely popular.

In her novel *Golden Apples*, Marjorie Kinnan Rawlings dubbed such young Englishmen "remittance men"—black sheep who were provided a monthly remittance by their wealthy families back in England so long as they stayed out of the country. Blanche's father, Alfred Bosanquet, did not view settlers like his father and uncle as ne'er-do-wells or irresponsible adventurers, however, and in a speech he gave to Chetwynd descendants, he set the record straight: "The young men who came here were interested in grove culture, travel, and a new country, and were sons of good English families." They worked and studied hard; no doubt they played hard, too, and always they maintained their "English pride," never more so than on Sunday mornings when, handsome in their "white riding breeches, white jackets and red scarfs," they'd ride through the woods to Holy Trinity Episcopal Church, which the Bosanquets had been instrumental in founding and constructing.

Bosanquet family lore had it that twenty-five-year-old Ellen Lewis Hall of Marietta, Ohio, riding past Fair Oaks on a visit to her mother's Fruitland Park home in the fall of 1891, caught Louis's eye from an upstairs bedroom window—although, in another version of their first encounter, it was he who was riding by the Hall house when he spotted the young Ellen, possibly dressed only in her nightgown, at her bedroom window. However their courtship started, it ended in what was, in Chetwynd at least, a scandalous marriage, for the Bosanquets vaunted their ties with English royalty, and Ellen Lewis Hall was a descendant of Betty Washington Lewis, a sister of George Washington, "who stole the United States from Great Britain."

When Augustus Bosanquet departed Florida to assume the post of secretary of the Royal British Club in Lisbon, Portugal, Louis claimed Fair Oaks as his own. With a staff of black caretakers, he and Ellen maintained the mansion, the citrus groves, a vegetable garden, livestock, chickens, and a stable on the property. Louis proved to be a "horticulturist extraordinaire," cultivating around the mansion more than a thousand varieties of trees, including camphors from India and hibiscus from Hawaii—to say nothing of "14 varieties of bamboo; at least 14 varieties of palms; 100 varieties of fancy-leaf caladium; 75 varieties of roses; 16

varieties of cranium lilies along with citrons, which bore a heavy crop annually"—and amassing what was reputed to be the most extensive horticultural library in the state. He would in time hybridize a magenta lily, *Crinum* "Ellen Bosanquet," named for his wife, as well as a small lavender one, the *Crinum* "Louis Bosanquet"—both of which would be introduced commercially.

Chetwynd exposed the English citrus arrivistes to environmental challenges they hadn't encountered before. The heat could be relentless, the humidity oppressive, the rains torrential—not to mention the abundance of mosquitoes, alligators, panthers, snakes, and other "wild animals that roamed the land and ate their crops." The climate forced the young Brits to abandon at least some of their boarding school formalities, Eton and Cambridge be damned. "This is a nether region," wrote one of them. "Because of it we have not been obliged to adapt civilized manners such as wearing coats and ties at dinner." By the end of the decade, however, with their businesses burgeoning and their fortunes growing, Chetwynd seemed to them less a netherworld than a tropical paradise.

"The Blizzard" changed all that. Much as would happen more than sixty years hence, as 1894 was nearing its end a brutal cold front from the north descended on Florida. Temperatures dropped as low as 13 degrees, and within three days an entire year's citrus crop had been destroyed, most of it on the tree. An unseasonably warm, wet January subsequently engorged the trees with an abundance of sap, and when a second, equally bitter freeze—"The Blizzard"—arrived in central Florida a few weeks later, it caused the sap-filled trees to literally explode, "the sounds of their cracking and splitting limbs and boughs echoing over the desolate landscape."

"The disaster is overwhelming," one Lake County resident entered in his diary. "Don't know how we will come out of it. No Sunday School. Too cold. Everyone feels about as blue as can be." Another local walked into the middle of his hundred-acre grove, "looked at what was the end of all his dreams and hopes for the future," and put a gun to his head. Growers in Mount Dora referred to the calamity as "Florida's Funeral." With no government or state aid to be had, it was "root, hog or die" for the farmers and growers. The value of their land and homes collapsed. The erstwhile carefree young Brits were trying now to survive on turtles, rabbits, cabbage—on anything they could scavenge that unsparing winter. Many of them had no choice but to abandon Chetwynd. The Bosanquets stayed on; their income-producing properties in London ensured their solvency.

In 1897, with three young daughters toddling about Fair Oaks, Louis and Ellen Bosanquet welcomed a son, Alfred, into a more hopeful world. Two years later, though, another "Great Blizzard" wreaked havoc across the South, the fourth hard freeze to strike the grovelands in just two decades. (Freezes of such devastating magnitude were generally reckoned to occur in Florida just once every forty years.) The freeze of 1899 was estimated to have killed more than 90 percent of the state's citrus trees. Most of the remaining Chetwynd colonists fled. Alfred recalled seeing, as a child, abandoned houses years after the freeze, the tables still set and blankets still on the beds. Virtually overnight Chetwynd became a ghost colony; the name disappeared from maps. By the turn of the century, only fifteen Chetwynd families remained, among them the Bosanquets. They diversified their crops to limit their exposure to future freezes. In the nearly twenty years it took for the citrus industry to fully recover, they kept Fair Oaks and Holy Trinity Church free from debt.

By then, Alfred had come of age. In 1925, accompanying his indefatigable brother-in-law, David Newell, on a hunting trip in Missouri, he met Ruth Marion Ward, the daughter of an English-born coffee salesman. After a brief courtship and a wedding in St. Louis, the newlyweds moved into Fair Oaks with Alfred's parents. Although Ruth was not wealthy, she was educated and drawn to the refined sensibilities and social rituals that defined Chetwynd colony life. The following year, Blanche was born. Four more children followed.

By all accounts, Ruth ruled the roost while Alfred pursued his botanical interests. "An English gentleman always has a garden," he was fond of saying, and he took great pleasure in importing plants from around the world. Ruth sustained Fair Oaks' most venerated tradition, hosting Sunday-afternoon high tea. Dozens of tables would be set up on the front lawn to serve finger sandwiches and dainty cakes to the parishioners who, dressed in their finest, arrived by horse and buggy after the church service. Ruth would pass on the tradition to Blanche and her two sisters and their Newell cousins, all of whom continued it well into the twentieth century.

Verbal and vivacious as a child, Blanche—or Bampy, as she was known—crossed proper English manners with native Southern sass. On her first day of school at Leesburg Elementary, when Ruth presumed to answer the questions with which the teacher peppered her new pupil, Blanche interrupted. "Who's going to kindergarten," she asked, "you or me?" She was remembered not only as a "chatterbox," but also as a calm, sweet, gregarious, independent child, who was as bright—in the words of her first-grade teacher—as *real* sunshine."

For Blanche and her siblings, Fair Oaks was an idyllic place, albeit the idyll was redolent of a bygone, paternalistic American South. The family still employed various black caretakers, including Sam and pipe-smoking Lilla, an older married couple who lived just up the road and served as handyman and cook. A handful of other neighbors did the laundry, milked the four cows, and made sure the household ran smoothly. After the deaths of Louis (in 1930) and Ellen (in 1931), Alfred inherited the Bosanquet real estate interests, which included forty-one rent-rich flats in London.

But the prosperity did not last. It may have been the case that "Daddy wasn't a good businessman," as Blanche's brother Bud recalled, but, in any event, the Bosanquet interests could not withstand the cataclysmic effects of oncoming world events. After World War II broke out in Europe, it was difficult to get money out of England. To maintain Fair Oaks, the family was forced to go into business. Converting Alfred's formal English garden into a commercial enterprise that grew flowers for sale rather than for show, they opened a flower shop in Leesburg. Everyone pitched in. The boys helped with deliveries and the girls assisted Ruth in the shop. Fancying herself the "floral designer" helped Ruth come to terms with running the till.

Then, in December 1941, the Japanese bombed Pearl Harbor, and the United States entered the war. Fear of another sneak attack by air took hold of the nation, especially in Florida with its thousand-plus miles of vulnerable coastline. In conjunction with the national Aircraft Warning Service, twenty-four-hour plane-spotting stations situated atop tall buildings and towers sprouted up across Florida. They were staffed in shifts by volunteers like Alfred Bosanquet, who made note of any visible plane's specifics—its altitude, direction, speed, and number of engines—and transmitted them by radio to a military base in Tampa.

"Swear to secrecy," Alfred bade his daughter, and she promised never to tell anyone—not her brothers or sisters; not even her mother—where she went so many evenings. She'd park the family's Chevrolet convertible by Earle Fain's theater and glance about to make sure she hadn't been followed. Then she'd begin to climb the fire escape at the rear of the four-story First National Bank, known as "Leesburg's skyscraper," with her father's dinner in tow—Lilla's roast pork with his favorite black-eyed peas and biscuits, still warm from the stove. Blanche wasn't good with most secrets, but this one, couched in the demands of patriotism, she took seriously. "I was honored," she recalled, to be trusted with keeping her father's location secret and to be allowed to assist him. While he settled into his supper, she'd lie back on the blanket spread out on the tar-and-gravel roof and train the binoculars on the night sky. Friendly plane or shooting star? Whatever Blanche did, she did it diligently.

The bombing of Pearl Harbor brought the war to Leesburg in other unmistakable ways. Gas rationing limited travel by car, and Blanche's horseback rides around Fruitland Park and bicycle rides to Leesburg became a necessity rather than an afternoon's diversion. To boost morale for servicemen, the United Service Organizations set up clubs in abandoned buildings, barns, and even train stations across America. Alfred served on the approval committee for the Leesburg USO on Main Street, and when Blanche turned sixteen, she volunteered as a junior hostess at the Saturday-night dances. "There was one short serviceman, and he could polka," she recalled. "The minute they'd start up a polka, he'd come over and get me, and we'd be the only two dancing. I'd never done the polka before, but, boy, we had a good time . . . The soldiers would start clapping their hands and say, 'Yeah, Sergeant! Yeah, Sergeant! Yeah, Sergeant!'"

As the war went on, Blanche became a volunteer plane spotter in her own right, as did her cousins. She and Priscilla Newell often shared shifts on the roof of the bank. Late one afternoon, they caught sight of the Ku Klux Klan parading down Main Street in their white hoods and robes. The girls crept up to the edge of the bank's façade and peeked over, "scared silly that somebody would look up and see us and come after us," Priscilla remembered.

As a result of the Lend-Lease Act of 1941, by which foreign allies were provided U.S. military aid, cadets from England's Royal Air Force had been arriving at Lodwick Field in Lakeland, Florida, about sixty miles south of Fruitland Park, to receive pilot training. In Florida, the cadets were spared Britain's foul weather, chronic shortages of fuel and aircraft, and Luftwaffe bombings. Thinking that they might enjoy some English hospitality and the variety and abundance of an American larder, Alfred made arrangements for seven RAF pilots-in-training to visit Fruitland Park whenever a leave or time off allowed them the opportunity.

At Fair Oaks, the cadets sat down to Lilla's generous Southern meals and the high teas now held in their honor on the Bosanquets' lawn. They enjoyed, too, the attentions of Blanche and her cousins, and entertained their hosts in turn with tales of youthful derring-do: how, high in the skies over Florida, they'd discovered some prankster had planted live snakes in the cockpit; or how, stealthily, in low-glide approaches, they'd spied on college girls sunbathing nude on rooftops, risking that the coeds might catch the numbers on their planes and report them to the base.

On occasion, cadets would get a week's break between class sessions, which would allow them a more leisurely visit with the Bosanquets. So it happened that Ted Bennett and Fred Mitchell came to stay. And to woo. Blanche was amused to discover that both pilots seemed to be interested in her and jealous of each other, and even more amused that her mother confused one with the other, determined though each was to make a singular impression.

It was Ted, the nineteen-year-old son of a shipping company secretary from the East End of London, who captured Blanche's affections. The photo album she kept, chronicling the wartime experience in Lake County, included photos of various cadets posing or horsing around with Blanche and her sisters and cousins at Fair Oaks, but the fellow it featured most was Ted. There he was, reclining in a rowboat on nearby Zephyr Lake; having Blanche straighten his tie; riding shotgun in the convertible, with Blanche at the wheel; walking hand in hand with her down a dirt road in Fruitland Park; kissing her as she leaned against the open door of the Chevy, her hands clasped around his neck.

From time to time, Blanche and her sisters and cousins, accompanied by Ruth, visited the pilots at Lodwick Field in Lakeland, and in August 1942, she and her mother made the six-hour drive to Napier Field in Dothan, Alabama, for Ted's graduation ceremony. He was initially stationed to Montgomery, but he and Blanche still managed to see each other on the occasional weekend, and for her birthday, he sent her flowers from the family's shop. Ruth herself took down the accompanying message: "Hello, Darling, wish we could spend this leave together. Miss you very much, all my love, Edward."

Come September, Blanche began her freshman year at Florida State College for Women in Tallahassee, and Ted was sent to the European Theater. By late September, he had successfully completed nineteen bombing operations, most of them over France, in support of land forces, and a few over Germany that targeted weapons and fuel facilities. One day soon thereafter, Ruth arrived unexpectedly in Tallahassee, saying she thought Blanche might like to come home to Fruitland Park for the weekend. At home, Blanche learned that Ted was missing in action. On September 24, he and six crew members had set out across the English Channel toward Calais, when they encountered heavy German anti-aircraft fire from the ground. In a letter Ted had written before the ill-fated mission, he urged her not to lose heart if ever he were reported to be missing in action. According to Bud, the letter said, "I might be alive in Germany," and in it, the Englishman went on to explain that it wasn't uncommon for RAF pilots and their crews, after they'd been shot down, to be taken as prisoners of war. It could be many months, Ted cautioned, before news of their survival made it back to loved ones. So instead of grieving, Blanche abided by Ted's urging and chose to believe that he was alive in a German camp, and that soon the war would end and she'd move to England and marry him. She'd always wanted to travel by ship to England.

Blanche's English pilot did not make it through the war, as she learned in December. Enemy fire had taken down his plane over Calais. The news of Ted's death left Blanche despondent. Still, she carried on at school in Tallahassee. When she came back home for Christmas, she savored the spirit of the holiday and took comfort in its familiar routines. Once again she'd waited in the kitchen while Lilla packed a sack of roast pork and black-eyed peas and biscuits. Then she'd drive into Leesburg, park by Earle Fain's theater, and climb the fire escape of the bank to deliver her father his dinner. Lying on the blanket, she'd scan the sky for a passing shadow or a flicker of light—for any sign of a plane in lonely, ghostly flight up among the stars.

It was Ruth who took notice of a picture of another pilot, Joe Knowles, in the *Daily Commercial*. The accompanying story reminded readers that Joe had been a football star at Leesburg High School before attending Rollins College on an athletic scholarship, where he'd also been a member of the basketball, wrestling, boxing, and rowing teams. He'd spent four years of the war at bases throughout the South, serving as a flight instructor in the Army Air Corps. Now he was back in Lake County, where he would be going to work in the family business.

What a catch this handsome, square-jawed bachelor looked to be—and from one of Leesburg's most successful families. Ruth figured she knew just the girl for him. Susanna Ward, Ruth's twenty-six-year-old niece from Webster Groves, Missouri, was spending the summer of 1947 at Fair Oaks, after a stint in the U.S. Naval Reserve. When Joe stopped by the flower shop one afternoon to pick up a corsage for his mother, Ruth seized the opportunity and invited him to dinner at Fair Oaks.

Joe had been born in 1916 in North Dakota. His father, William G. Knowles, was a potato farmer. But when times got tough during the Great Depression, William announced that the family would be moving south. "We may starve to death in Florida," he told them, "but we are not going to freeze to death in North Dakota." After careful consideration, he had decided to take his chances in the citrus business. He sold the potato farm, and he and his wife and three young sons packed everything they owned and moved to Leesburg.

Besides being an exceptional athlete in high school and college, Joe was a hard worker, and he'd considered following in the career footsteps of his brother Harold, a physician in Orlando. But when the war broke out, Joe had enlisted in the Army Air Corps, and after his discharge he'd followed his other brother, Tim, into the family business.

At thirty, Joe still carried the swagger of a star football player, and at Fair Oaks he gave Bud and Gogo, Blanche's brothers, some pointers. He impressed Susie Ward, too, with his self-possession and what seemed a promising future in his family's commercial ventures; at the time he was working in his father's watermelon business. By the end of the evening, Susie was smitten.

A few nights later, Joe called the Bosanquet house. Ruth answered, and Susie, hovering expectantly, waited for her chatty aunt to pass her the phone. She waited in vain. It was Blanche, home from college for the summer, with whom Joe wanted to speak. She had not been vying with Susie for Joe's attention—"She was just being Bampy," Bud recalled—but Susie, indignant and aggrieved, accused Blanche of stealing her boy-friend and returned to Missouri.

Bampy and Joe became a couple, and Joe became a fixture at the Bo-sanquet house for the rest of the summer. He frequently played big brother to Bud and Gogo, not always to happy effect. He took issue with the boys' juvenile, freewheeling approach to Monopoly. "He wanted to play by the exact rules," Bud said. "He took the fun out of the game." They never played it with him again. When he gave twelve-year-old Gogo coaching in how to block, he'd get a little rough. "He had this big ring," Bud said, "and Gogo would end up with all these bruises. Joe thought Gogo was a big baby. He said my mother babied him, and Gogo soured on Joe after that."

Still, when Blanche returned to college for what would be her final semester, Bud recalled her as being the happiest she'd been in some time, and soon thereafter she and Joe were engaged. They set a wedding date for three weeks after Blanche's graduation in 1948, and Ruth set herself to planning the ceremony—at Holy Trinity Church, of course—and reception. "It was a big, big deal in town," Priscilla remembered, uniting not just the photogenic couple but also two prominent Lake County families. As befit such a union, the couple planned to honeymoon in style. They took a driving tour to Niagara Falls and back, with stops in Charleston, Richmond, Philadelphia, New York, Buffalo, Toronto, Cleveland, St. Louis, and Birmingham, in a brand-new car, Joe's surprise wedding gift to Blanche.

After the marriage, Joe quickly began to establish himself as one of the princes of Lake County. He and his friend Syd Herlong—Albert S. Herlong Jr., of A. S. Herlong Packing Company—became founding members of Leesburg's Quarterback Club. Quarterback Clubs were popular throughout the South, each chapter serving as a social network that knit together the city's most powerful men in banking, politics, and business. Every spring, the Leesburg members, many of them alumni of the University of Florida and its College of Law, would hold a banquet at the local Elks Lodge. A Florida Gators or other conference coach would address them, and the membership would pick a Gators road game from the next season's schedule to attend. Come that autumn night, all the prominent men of Leesburg would pack their bags and gather at the city's downtown train depot. On board, they'd drink scotch, smoke cigars, and play high-stakes poker as the train rolled through the night. The following morning, the sleeper cars would be detached from the train and parked in the depot. The club members would sleep all day Friday, rise in time for dinner and drinks, and carouse all night, retreating to the sleeper cars for naps. On Saturday, donning their orange Quarterback Club fedoras, they'd head out to the stadium to cheer on their beloved Gators. "What a trip," was about the most they'd say upon being met back in Leesburg by their wives and children. But as their sons grew older, they'd later get a private rendition of the lively particulars of the weekend, effectively guaranteeing the Quarterback Club another generation of exclusive membership.

A LITTLE MORE THAN A YEAR after the wedding, at a Sunday dinner with the Bosanquets and the Newells, Blanche announced that she was pregnant. The words were barely out of her mouth when her mother blurted out, "Well, I knew that!"—a pronouncement that scuttled any celebratory toast and prompted an aggravated response from her son-in-law.

"How did you know it?" Joe demanded. "Did Blanche tell you?"

Proudly, Ruth announced that she'd figured it out herself when a friend stopped by the flower shop and divulged that she'd recently run into Blanche at Dr. Holland's office. Since Blanche had chosen not to mention the doctor visit to her mother, Ruth had surmised that her eldest daughter must be pregnant.

"She didn't like anybody to put anything over on her," Bud said of Ruth. "She ought to have kept quiet and said, 'Oh, good.' Instead, it got to be a little heated there with Joe. The two of them were very strong-willed."

Ruth had not had to surmise about her handsome son-in-law's willful behavior or the reputation it had earned him. As far back as his high school days, Joe Knowles's popularity with the ladies was no secret around Leesburg. Nor was the fact that now and again, as it pleased him, he enjoyed extramarital companionship.

"Everybody knew Joe had affairs," said Priscilla Newell. "Women kind of flocked to Joe." Certainly Ruth knew, and although she as certainly disapproved, she had not been about to risk jeopardizing her daughter's prospects over Joe's philandering. "Ruth practically pushed them together," Priscilla said. "Ruth's ambition was to make sure that all three of her daughters got married. Joe was the catch and Aunt Ruth was bound—just determined—to get him."

Neither before nor after the marriage did Ruth ever broach the subject of Joe's infidelity with either her son-in-law or her daughter, at least not to anyone's knowledge, but she frequently locked horns with Joe for control over what each purported to be Blanche's best interests. Ruth envisioned her daughter, elevated in wealth and status by her marriage, at the center of the Leesburg social scene Ruth herself so admired. Once the children came, however, Joe decided that he and Blanche should move into the big house by Bugg Spring in Okahumpka (which he pronounced "Okeehumpkee," the Seminole word for "deep waters"), next to his father's orange groves. He had fond memories of his rugged outdoor upbringing in rural North Dakota, he said, and he wanted to raise his children in a similar environment, away from the social milieu of the Leesburg citrus elite. He wanted acreage, horses, and cattle rather than suburban living among the tony houses of Palmora Park.

Bud Bosanquet, for one, wasn't so convinced by Joe's ruralist nostalgia. The house cost Joe nothing, Bud knew, having been included in the purchase price of the property when Joe's father bought it, and since then it had stood empty. Whatever Joe's reasoning, his decision vexed Ruth. In Okahumpka, Blanche would be removed not only from the social scene in Leesburg but from most other company as well. With Joe constantly traveling to bolster his watermelon and citrus business, she would often be alone with small children. Blanche assured her mother there was nothing to worry about.

And for a number of years, there didn't seem to be, at least judging by the family's fortunes. Joe continued to work hard and play hard with the Leesburg elite, forging social bonds that paid them back in countless ways. Syd Herlong had become a U.S. congressman, and to further advance his political career, he hosted an annual golf tournament—the Herlong Hassle, as it came to be known—at Silver Lake Country Club, where the city's well-to-do played alongside celebrities and politicians from Washington, D.C. Guests enjoyed the Florida sunshine by day almost as much as they did the legendary gin games at night. They might also be inclined to take in an amateur theatrical performance by the local Melon Patch Players, especially if handsome Joe Knowles was performing.

The owners of the largest groves, Joe and Syd Herlong among them, maintained their own packinghouses in downtown Leesburg, thus allowing them to realize even more substantial returns on their citrus operations. Joe also took on the responsibility of procuring thousands of watermelons each year for the city's Watermelon Festival, where he bestowed the coveted Knowles Trophy to the grower of the season's largest melon. Jesse Daniels was one of nearly sixty thousand people who attended the 1957 festival, pedaling his Schwinn five miles north from Okahumpka to eat hot dogs and watch the fireworks over Lake Harris.

That year the Quarterback Club had traveled to Auburn, where the Gators were taking on the undefeated Auburn Tigers at their homecoming game. The train left on Halloween, long after trick-or-treating children and their mothers had turned in for the night. But the real highlight of the year was the ten-day celebration of Leesburg's centennial. During it, Joe starred as the detective in the Melon Patch Players' production of the murder mystery *Laura*, earning praise from the *Leesburg Daily Commercial* for his tasteful but "believable" handling of the romantic scenes with the young actress in the title role. "Joe taught me how to kiss for the stage," the actress recalled, impressed by his confidence both onstage and off.

The centennial also included the antics of the "Keystone Kops," who'd haul perpetrators of such offenses as wearing makeup (women) or shaving (men) without a permit before a "Kangaroo Kourt," an "unjust body" that meted out "such punishments as pies in the face and dunkings in a pool" with uncharacteristic evenhandedness. Willis McCall, whose father was a Lake County dirt farmer but who had garnered the support of the big citrus men while working as a fruit inspector for the Florida Agriculture Commission, and had gotten them to back him for sheriff in 1944—and every election since—was a member. So were such power brokers as circuit judge Truman G. Futch and state attorney Gordon Oldham. State senator J. A. "Tar" Boyd, a Quarterback Club stalwart, was found guilty of gross malfeasance "for his failure to display facial foliage," and was given a choice between "walking up and down Main Street in his underwear" and paying a five-dollar fine. A political career to consider, Boyd chose the latter, but the Kourt deemed the senator's lawyer— no other than Red Robinson—incompetent and made a cartoonish show of branding him with a supposedly red-hot iron. Kourt proceedings culminated in a vigilante committee that "swarmed over the judge's stand and made off with the Keystone Kops in revenge for past humiliation of citizens," carting Judge Futch off to jail for contempt and throwing state attorney Oldham and Sheriff McCall "body, boots and britches" into the waters of Lake Harris. A tongue-in-cheek letter to the editor of the *Commercial* commended the vigilantes: "I say keep up the good work boys and we will run the whole lawless gang out of gas."

IT HAD BEEN a banner year for Joe Knowles in another way as well. Through Syd Herlong's secretary, Carole Weatherly, he'd met a congressional aide named Mary Ellen Hawkins. Alabama-born-and-bred, Hawkins had moved to Washington in 1950 to work as an aide, "but the congressman was a drunk and wasn't re-elected." She'd then switched to New York representative Kenneth Keating's office, and at a meeting of the House Labor Committee, a young congressman from Massachusetts had caught her eye. "Oh my goodness," she'd thought at the time. "Who is that?" She had apparently also caught the young congressman's eye, which was how Mary Ellen Hawkins had begun having movie and dinner dates with her Georgetown neighbor John F. Kennedy.

Through Weatherly, Hawkins was introduced to Joe when he came to town to discuss business with Herlong, his old friend and congressman. She found Joe to be agreeable and well educated, "a good old boy and a gentleman," and the two discovered shared interests in politics and art. He sent her fruit from Florida, and they dined together when he visited D.C. Joe was no JFK, but before long Hawkins grew infatuated. They began an affair. At the end of 1957, Hawkins resigned her position in Washington. She'd decided to relocate to Naples, Florida, and she let Joe know that in mid-December she'd be making the move south.

So it wasn't an urgent business matter that had called Joe out of town on December 17, as he'd told Blanche on the phone in the hours before her rape. Instead, he had driven to a Leesburg service station in the afternoon, then waited patiently for Mary Ellen to arrive in a car packed with her belongings. After greeting her, Joe got back in his car, and Mary Ellen followed him for eighty miles south to Tampa under the darkening sky. The couple went to dinner, then spent the night together in a hotel room—the same pitch-black night that a prowling man broke through a screen door at the Knowles home in Okahumpka and crept up the stairs to the bedroom where Blanche was sleeping.

Early the next morning, Joe and Mary Ellen left the hotel parking lot in their separate cars, with Joe leading the way to show her the route to Naples. In trying to keep up with him, Mary Ellen ran through a caution light. A policeman stopped both cars and escorted Joe and Mary Ellen to a Tampa police station. There the police delivered the message Sam Powell had left for Joe. Without saying why, they made it clear that he was to return to Lake County immediately. The couple said hasty goodbyes. Then Mary Ellen continued south to Naples while Joe sped north, back to Leesburg, where Sam and a close circle of fellow Quarterback

Clubbers awaited him, ready to convene, if not a Kangaroo Kourt, at least a loyal council to weigh in on how to deal with the terrible blow that had befallen one of their own.

And in nearby Mount Dora, a reporter with a fondness for bebop glasses and a history as a troublemaker for the powers-that-be was about to begin a long and ruinous crusade to run the whole lawless gang out of gas.

The Platt family at their Pistolville home in Lake County

CHAPTER THREE

Smoked Irishman

As the morning grew bright, new rumors swirling around Lake County were threatening to further upend Mabel's Wednesday routine. But while the reports of the previous night had emanated from the black community, immediate and shot through with fear, this second wave of rumor was coming from the white sections of Okahumpka and Leesburg, and it was steeped in innuendo. It centered on the conjecture that the victim's husband, Joe Knowles, had been out of town on business at the time of the incident. And hadn't Mrs. Knowles been seen earlier that evening at the Rotary Club in Leesburg, out drinking with some men? And was it true that after the alleged attack, instead of calling the police immediately, she'd first called the Knowles family lawyer? People speculated. Maybe the "rape" was no rape at all.

After ten years, Mabel was no stranger to the stark contrasts entrenched in Lake County, and her own appreciation of the reasons for them had been hard-earned. Mount Dora had charmed her at first sight, even though Patricia—"Punky," in those days—had come down with measles on the drive south from Akron. "I thought it was a bit of heaven when I first came here," Mabel recalled. Towering oak trees draped in Spanish moss shaded the downtown streets, which were lined with Victorian-era Queen Anne homes, Craftsman bungalows, and conch houses. Its gardens lush with azaleas and hibiscus, and its lawns like carpets of deep green St. Augustine grass, the quaint lakeside town hardly bore comparison to the planate pastures, clay roads, and dilapidated shacks that dotted the landscape of Okahumpka, twenty miles to the west.

From the outset of her residence in Mount Dora, Mabel worked hard night and day at her career. Many were the occasions that her tired little daughter napped on the stacking table in the pressroom while Mabel attended to the business of getting out her weekly edition of the *Mount Dora Topic*. During the paper's first few years, Mabel's news stories and editorials had for the most part reflected an idyllic view of Lake County. She diligently reported city council votes and Little League baseball scores; she breezily profiled locals like Elmira Lodor, the city's only "flying saucer expert," and seasonal residents like Elwood Bancroft, who arrived from the Midwest each autumn to congregate with the other snowbirds on the bowling greens and shuffleboard courts of quiet downtown Mount Dora. All of that changed with the case of the Groveland Boys.

In the summer of 1949, a seventeen-year-old white girl named Norma Padgett accused four young black men of kidnapping and raping her. One of the four was killed by a mob before he was even jailed. The other three were found guilty in a sham of a trial; one of them was sentenced to life in prison, while the other two—Sam Shepherd and Walter Irvin— were sentenced to death. In November 1951, however, the U.S. Supreme Court overturned the guilty verdicts of Shepherd and Irvin. In his opinion, Justice Robert Jackson described their trial in the hostile atmosphere of Lake County as "one of the best examples of one of the worst menaces to American justice."

On the eve of the retrial, Lake County sheriff Willis McCall, incensed by the Court's decision, drove the hundred-plus miles north to Raiford State Prison, purportedly to transport the two defendants back to Lake County. Instead, McCall took a detour down a quiet clay road. Moments later, shots rang out, and two handcuffed men were lying in a roadside ditch next to the sheriff's Oldsmobile. Samuel Shepherd had been killed instantly, but his best friend, Walter Irvin, had somehow survived three bullet wounds—two of them inflicted by the sheriff, the third by a deputy, James Yates—and played dead until witnesses arrived on the scene. The sheriff claimed that he'd shot the two men in an escape attempt. What Irvin described hours later, however, was the cold-blooded murder of one man and the attempted murder of another by two officers of the law.

McCall was cleared by a coroner's jury, which concluded that the sheriff had fired on the prisoners in self-defense. Judge Futch, who was known as "the whittling judge" for his custom of paring down hickory sticks while sitting on the bench through a long day's testimony, declined to impanel a grand jury on the grounds that the investigation by the coroner's jury had been so thorough as to obviate the need for further inquiry. No federal charges were brought against either McCall or Deputy Yates. Meanwhile, Irvin was retried and, to no one's surprise, reconvicted.

The shooting of the Groveland prisoners effected an awakening in Mabel and marked a turning point in her career. Until then, she and the *Topic* had sided unequivocally with McCall and the prosecution, publishing as fact virtually any notion or bias that the sheriff cared to convey to the public about the case. Like most of the county, she'd allowed herself to get swept up in the outrage over Padgett's allegations, and even before the trial began, she'd called for the defendants' execution by electric chair to avenge Padgett's honor. When Justice Jackson, in his opinion, cited the "prejudicial influences" of newspaper stories published in Lake County, there was no doubt as to whose stories he meant. "I probably needed to be stepped on," Mabel acknowledged later.

Now convinced that McCall had decided to take the law into his own hands by executing the Groveland defendants before they could be re-tried, and regretful of her own role in facilitating the initial convictions and death sentences, Mabel resolved to do henceforth what few journal-ists in the county dared. She resolved unfailingly and aggressively to report on violations of civil rights, particularly the injustices suffered by blacks in Lake County at the hands of Willis McCall, and on any other action she believed to be an abuse of power on his part. "He hated me from then on," Mabel noted. Indeed, McCall took to ridiculing her as "Red Mabel" and missed no opportunity to accuse her of dangerous "leftist leanings" in the press. But that was the least of it, as the events of the next few years would bear out.

In May 1954, Mabel wrote an editorial defending the Supreme Court's decision in *Brown v. Board of Education* by urging tolerance and a gradual move toward school desegregation in the South. She took issue with Mc-Call's public letter to the Ford Motor Company, in which he threatened to boycott its cars because the Ford Foundation had financially sup-ported a study on the harms of segregation. In August, she again took to the press to deplore a spate of cross-burnings in Mount Dora, where the Klan had been mostly dormant for the previous six years.

Not long after, one night when Paul was working late at the *Topic*'s office, Mabel had just kissed Patricia good night when she heard a car idling in front of a neighbor's house. She peeked through the blinds of her bedroom window and saw several figures in white silhouetted in the glow of the taillights; one of them began moving toward her front gate. Cubby, the family's large and aggressive Chow mix, snarled as Mabel headed into the living room. That was when the darkness outside ex-ploded into hot yellow light.

Flames whipped high above Mabel's sight line as she stared out the window, paralyzed with fear that the fire would catch the Spanish moss hanging over the rooftop. She heard an engine roar as the car sped away.

Cubby was barking loud enough now to wake Patricia, but it was another sound that captured Mabel's attention: a rustling that seemed to be coming from the roof. At first she thought that the Spanish moss had indeed ignited—the roof would be next, and after that the entire house—but then she realized what she was hearing wasn't the crackle of fire but the splash of rain, the kind farmers call heaven-sent. The flames from the gasoline-soaked cross in her front yard began to sputter and die out.

Later, unable to sleep, Mabel lay in bed pondering how actions like these could be tolerated in a nation that "seeks to be the guiding light for freedom and against terrorism." She turned to her bedside Bible and found a Psalm that afforded her some comfort: "Return unto thy rest, O my soul; for the Lord hath dealt bountifully with thee."

The next morning Mabel sat down at her Royal typewriter to compose her weekly column. "I shall not take it as a signal that I must lapse into silence," she wrote. "I will continue to speak as one who hopes to inject a small voice of reason and sanity into a situation which could divide our nation further in this, her most trying hour." Her courage and resolve grew as she typed, and remembering the rain that had poured down from the skies and saved her house, she wrote, "See why I shall not become mute with fear?"

Mabel's story, with Patricia's photo of the fiery cross accompanying it, garnered ample attention around Lake County, and newspapers across the country ran notices of the Florida editor who'd had a Klan cross burned in front of her home. Mabel and Paul took down the cross and put it in the garage to hold for the police, but the police never came. Two days later, when Mabel arrived at the *Topic* office, half a block from the Mount Dora police station, she discovered that a blood-red "KKK" had been crudely painted on the front windows as well as on the concrete sidewalk by the front door. Neither the police nor the Lake County Sheriff's Department saw fit to investigate.

On September 16, Mabel's weekly column again commented on the attempts of the KKK to silence her and noted that her trusted watchdog would "make mincemeat of crossburners." One night a month later, when the Reeses returned home from the office, they found Cubby lying motionless on the floor. The killing of the family pet "cut much deeper than did the ridiculous act of burning a cross in front of my home, or painting my office windows with red crosses and KKKs," Mabel wrote in the *Topic*, hoping to address the man responsible so that he might "enjoy the full taste" of his deed. Cubby, she wrote, "died in agony—a death as lingering and painful as if you had nailed her to one of your crosses. I hope you are now thoroughly happy."

An autopsy performed by a Lake County veterinarian concluded that the dog had consumed meat laced with strychnine, but Sheriff McCall refused to accept the finding and ordered the veterinarian to send the dog's organs to the State Board of Health for further testing. A week later, McCall obtained the state's toxicological analysis, which, he claimed, showed no traces of strychnine "or any form of poisoning." The veterinarian, standing by his original report, pointed out that the dog's organs had been sitting in a garbage can for nearly a week, and thus rendered useless for any analysis. That did not stop McCall from asserting, in a letter to the *Topic*, "I was glad to learn that the dog was not poisoned, as I despise dog poisoners almost as much as I do a communist."

Mabel had no doubt about who was behind the ongoing intimidation. "We had telephone calls day and night. No one identified themselves, but they would threaten." One night she and Paul were awakened by the sound of a slamming door and footsteps. Someone had broken into the garage. "I guess they wanted their cross back," Patricia recalled. The lack of interest on the part of law enforcement in such episodes reinforced Mabel's conviction that the sheriff's department and police essentially sanctioned the burgeoning presence of the Ku Klux Klan in Mount Dora.

For Mabel and the *Topic*, official indifference was cause for community concern. Two months later, Bryant Bowles, a white supremacist

from Tampa who'd founded the National Association for the Advancement of White People in response to the Supreme Court's ruling in
Brown, accepted Sheriff McCall's invitation to speak at the Lake County
Courthouse in Tavares. At a recent rally, adamant that integration would
lead to miscegenation, Bowles had held up his three-year-old daughter,
shouting, "Do you think that my daughter will ever attend schools with
Negroes? Not while there's breath in my body and gunpowder will
burn—and gunpowder *will* burn! If the Negroes go to your children's
school, let your conscience be your guide . . . I know what I would do!" At
another rally, Bowles had charged, "The Negro will never be satisfied
until he moves into the front bedroom of the white man's home." By this
point the group's rallies and intimidation tactics, under Bowles's inflammatory direction, had succeeded in terrorizing and ostracizing school
officials and districts that had begun the process of integration in accordance with the Supreme Court's ruling.

In a *Topic* editorial, Mabel rebuked Bowles for bringing his tour of
"hate-mongering and rabble-rousing" to Lake County. She also implicated McCall's son Malcolm, who had been photographed collecting
new membership fees for the NAAWP at an event at the Lake County
Courthouse. "By whatever name it is called," Mabel wrote, "the Ku Klux
Klan smells the same." She lamented that "no public official protested
the use of the taxpayers' property as a soap box for increasing tension in
an area where calm and reason is so desperately needed."

The sheriff, who had sponsored the event, declined to respond directly to Mabel's attacks, beyond commenting that she was "just cussing
me for being a white man." He did affirm his support for the NAAWP,
declaring, "If it goes down, I'll go with it. Bowles is a Florida cracker and
he's on the level." However, Bowles, who had boasted that the event had
recruited a thousand new members to the NAAWP's Lake County chapter, including "six county and three circuit judges," marched into the
Topic office brandishing Mabel's column, with the word "LIE" scrawled

across it. "I will get even by some means or other," he told Paul, who was working there alone, "even if I have to stay in this county for two years."

A week later, Mabel began investigating a new story. She had learned that five children from a family named Platt had been expelled from school in Mount Dora because of complaints from white parents who suspected they might be Negroes. She visited Allen and Laura Platt at their simple three-room home on the outskirts of town in Pistolville, where clapboard shacks housed a small community of "poor Southern crackers" who had migrated to Lake County to work the citrus groves and melon fields. They explained to Mabel that they were not colored but Irish-Indian—a line of descent they could trace back to 1587, when Sir Walter Raleigh's "lost colony" intermarried with Croatan Indians. They had recently moved from South Carolina, where they had lived in an Indian community and belonged to a white church; their children had attended schools that admitted both whites and Indians. They had marriage documentation and birth certificates to prove that they were white. Mabel spoke with the Platt children and found them to be exceedingly polite and curious, plainly "exhibiting the fruits of parental training."

The Platts recounted how Willis McCall, summoned by principal D. D. Roseborough to Mount Dora's Fifth Avenue School, had had the children line up for examination. Tall, with a round face and thick, meaty hands that he liked to lay on a man's shoulder to make a point, the sheriff was an intimidating presence. That evening, he'd arrived unannounced at the Platt family home along with a deputy, whom he instructed to photograph the children. "Denzell favors a nigger," he'd proclaimed, pointing at the seventeen-year-old, and of thirteen-year-old Laura Belle, he commented, "I don't like the shape of that one's nose."

"He like to gave my wife a heart attack," noted Allen, who had not been at home. "He made her cry with the things he said." Once McCall had dispensed with the Platt children, one by one, in his crude "lesson in anthropology," Principal Roseborough had no choice but to prohibit them from attending school "until the sheriff is satisfied."

On Thanksgiving Day, the *Topic* ran front-page photographs of Allen and Laura Platt and their school-aged children above the caption "These Children Were Evicted." Mabel's article described the family's ordeal: After meeting with hard times in drought-plagued South Carolina, they had been forced to sell their small farm and relocate to Mount Dora, where their children were now being ostracized. "If you are a parent," Mabel wrote, "look at your own child and think what it would mean to you if an adult said: 'I do not like your child's nose' and thereby decreed that your child cannot associate with other children."

That morning, policemen and deputies appeared in front of the *Topic*'s office. Mabel spotted the bespectacled sheriff on the street, standing by his black Oldsmobile. Approaching cautiously, she asked what he and his deputies were doing outside her office. "I'm protecting this town from left-wingers," McCall told her.

"Well, you're missing a lot of sleep, aren't you, Sheriff?"

"Yeah," McCall grumbled, "and I'm missing a hunting trip."

"Isn't that too bad," Mabel replied.

McCall kept up his attacks on the Platts. "There must have been a smoked Irishman in the woodpile," he jeered at yet another NAAWP rally, ridiculing their claim of Indian-Irish ancestry. And Mabel continued to attack McCall, as a man who "deliberately pierces a soul with cruel words and with the arrows of blind hate."

By December, the feud between the "lady editor" and the sheriff had become a national story in itself, and *Time* and *Life* both dispatched reporters and photographers to Lake County to cover it. Mabel tried to keep the focus on the Platts, and criticized the *Miami Herald*, which was also covering the story, for shedding "not a tear about the . . . children who were not allowed to go to school." She spoke at length to the *Life* reporters, with whom McCall then refused to meet. "I know what company you've been keeping, so I don't want to talk to you," he said. He turned away the reporter from *Time* as well.

In mid-December, the case was attracting out-of-town television crews, and the social stresses were taking a toll on the Reeses. They could no longer attend the local yacht club's lakeside gatherings. "Everyone would have a few drinks and first thing I know, someone would be blasting me for my editorials," Mabel recalled. Soon the family stopped going out altogether. More seriously, the threats and anonymous phone calls continued. Mabel was already at the *Topic* office one day at four a.m. when Patricia telephoned from home. She'd just received a call saying that the Platts' house was on fire and that Mabel was needed on the scene. Mabel, suspicious, in turn called her friend Jesse Hunter, the former state attorney in Lake County who had twice prosecuted the Groveland Boys case. Like Mabel, Hunter, though an avowed segregationist, had soured on the sheriff after the shootings of Samuel Shepherd and Walter Irvin. He'd also become one of Mabel's most trusted sources. "Don't you dare go out on that highway," he told her now. "You'd be gotten sure as anything." Instead, Mabel telephoned the Platts and awoke the entire household; they were fine.

Despite Mabel's efforts, *Time*'s story focused as much on the feud between her and McCall as on the Platt family's dilemma. "The Platts," the story concluded, "had moved into a cabin out of town, their children were out of school and as far as anyone could tell, no one besides Editor Reese seemed to care." But to judge from the hundreds of letters that soon poured into the *Topic* offices, from all over the country and from abroad as well, people did care. With only two exceptions, Mabel claimed, all "expressed anger over the treatment of the Platt children." It was a letter from a local girl, though, that particularly captured Mabel's attention. It had been written by fifteen-year-old Mardie Bardwell, an honors student. "We would like to correct that statement," it read, referring to the *Time* story's conclusion. "WE CARE."

Mardie Bardwell had been present in the school hallway when Sheriff McCall examined the frightened Platt children, and she distinctly remembered him announcing, "I smell niggers." Outraged by what she had witnessed, she had brought up the plight of the Platt family in her Sunday-school class at the Methodist church. It was after one such class that she'd sat down to pen her letter, and she set her sights on Willis McCall. "The Constitution says all persons are innocent until they are proven guilty," she wrote, "and that a man is to be considered truthful until he is proved to be a liar. We feel the Platt children got a raw deal. Their right to an education has been taken away because of the opinion and prejudices of one man." Drawing a distinction between such opinions and the law, she continued, "To be expelled for violation of Florida segregation laws is one thing: to be expelled because of an unfounded suspicion is another. Therefore, we believe the Platt children should be permitted to remain in school until the sheriff can prove they don't belong here. That is our position and we want the world to know it."

The "we" referred to the more than sixty fellow students Mardie had subsequently enlisted to sign the letter. After they had done so, however, Mardie began to question the wisdom of sending it to a national magazine. If published, it was bound to cause an uproar in Mount Dora, with unhappy consequences for the students she had involved. So she decided not to send it but to keep it, and to keep it a secret among herself and the students who'd signed it. "We weren't supposed to tell our parents," Mardie said, "but Pat Reese, the loudmouth, told her mother."

Acting on her daughter's tip, Mabel called the Bardwell home and asked to speak with Mardie. "I've been doing this by myself," the reporter said, in tears. "I've gotten no response, and this is the first time anyone's supported me." She pleaded with Mardie to let her publish the letter in the *Topic*. Finally the girl relented and, without consulting the others who had signed, granted Mabel permission.

The impact of publication was immediate. Mabel's headline—"We

Care! Students Demand Reentry of Children in School"—affronted Mardie. "There was no demand in my letter," she pointed out. "The letter was about due process, and a protest against the authority of one man. It had not been proved that the Platts were black." Mabel admitted that her headline was "unfortunate," but argued that it was "based upon the presumption that for the children to 'remain' in school, as the letter requested, they would first have to be readmitted." She later defended her decision to publish "because it was Good News, and that Good News was needed in Mount Dora as much as it was in the offices of *Time* magazine."

The publication of the letter exposed the signers to their parents' wrath. Some, like June Bowie's father, claimed that their children hadn't understood what they were signing, but June was grounded for two months nonetheless. No parent was more irate than Mardie's father, Robert Bardwell. The president and manager of the Lake County Fuel Company as well as the president of the local Lions Club, Bardwell hunted on occasion with Willis McCall. Shortly after the letter's publication, a cross was burned on the front lawn of the family home. "People canceled gas business with my father," Mardie recalled. "It hit him where it hurt. I tried to do good, but I made a mess."

Mardie found herself ostracized by her friends. A chalk line appeared down the center of the sidewalk outside the school, one side marked for "White People," the other for "Nigger Lovers." One morning an angry crowd gathered at the school, and when Mardie attempted to enter someone threw a bottle at her. She was handed a paper bag bearing the inscription "For Nigger Lover Bardwell." Inside was a black doll.

Mardie's parents decided it would be best that she leave town as soon as possible. Prestigious private Stephens College, in Columbia, Missouri, agreed to accept her even before she graduated from high school. And so, at sixteen, Mardie left Lake County for good.

Not everyone was unhappy with Mabel, however. With Christmas approaching, a grateful Allen Platt wrote to thank her for all her support in the *Topic* as well as for the money and clothing her readers had been sending their way. "My wife and I and our children were very lost until our case was taken up by your newspaper," Platt wrote. "We felt sure God would see us through, but we had no other place to turn but to prayer. We are beginning to think now that our prayers are being answered."

Increasingly frustrated in his attempts to gain justice for his children, Platt wrote an open letter to Governor Collins that Mabel published. "I have no other course than to appeal to you," it read. "I have no money to hire a lawyer or pay the expenses of witnesses from South Carolina. Being thrown out of school is not the most important thing. To have my family branded as niggers is even worse."

The governor ordered an investigation into the case, but he responded to Platt only in general terms: "You are getting a look at prejudice, perhaps the most tenacious and blinding of all human emotions. Prejudice dethrones reason and justice and prospers in the atmosphere of the fear it spawns."

Frustrated that her reporting alone could not gain "reason and justice" for the Platts, Mabel decided to press Jesse Hunter into service. At her urging, he agreed to represent the Platts in a lawsuit against the Lake County School Board. He traveled to South Carolina at his own expense in order to acquire pertinent and necessary documentation—U.S. Army records, the Platts' marriage and driver's licenses—and to take depositions from various teachers and school officials. Hunter's involvement in the Platt case seemed to many Lake County residents to be a remarkable about-face, given his firm anti-desegregation stance. To Willis McCall, it was a personal affront: Jesse Hunter, the state prosecutor with whom he had worked so closely to prosecute the Groveland Boys, was now working with Mabel Norris Reese in a suit to allow coloreds to attend school alongside whites. The school board countered by hiring one of McCall's longtime allies—the former U.S. attorney and staunch segregationist Herbert S. Phillips, who, Mabel reported, attempted to drag out the case indefinitely by throwing up "one technical objection after another."

The Platts' landlady informed them they would have to pack up and move out, since she'd been getting threats that the "house might catch fire" if the Platts didn't leave. The family moved to Apopka, in neighboring Orange County, but the school board there would not admit the children until the Lake County case was settled. Teachers from Mount Dora's Christian Home and Bible School visited to tutor them until admission could be arranged, but private schooling would cost money. The *Topic* took up the cause, and outraged citizens from around the country sent in contributions totaling more than twelve thousand dollars. Admission of the Platt children got chancy, however, when the president of the Bible school was visited one evening by a group of Klansmen with a message for him—that "there would be trouble if the Platt kids were taken into his school," as Mabel reported. Willis McCall delivered his own message less subtly, and in person: "This school will be burnt down if those niggers attend another day."

In October 1955, in what the *St. Petersburg Times* described as "a surprise move," Judge Futch, who had presided over both trials in the Groveland case, ruled in favor of the Platts on the grounds that the Lake County School Board had failed to prove that the children were of Negro descent. Jesse Hunter had forced Futch's hand by requesting a bench trial, whereby a judge, rather than a jury, would determine the verdict. A jury, Hunter reasoned, would almost surely have felt compelled to maintain segregation in their community, taking into account the effect of Willis McCall's intimidating presence. "Much as I hate it," Futch declared, "it becomes my duty to determine the facts without a trial by jury."

"The Lord be praised," said Allen Platt upon hearing the court's decision. "I feel like I am living in America again." Except it was Willis McCall's America in Lake County, and Jesse Hunter, being entirely familiar with the sheriff's history of meting out his own extrajudicial justice, was fearful of violence. The former state attorney, who had recently taken to keeping guns in his office, warned Mabel about protecting herself and her family. "I swore I would never have a gun in my house," Mabel said, "but he scared me into having guns at my front door." Hunter advised the Platt family to be exceedingly careful as well.

McCall was as livid with Futch's "disgraceful" ruling as he'd been with Hunter's involvement in the case. Hunter in turn called McCall's attack on Futch "outrageous." When asked whether he, too, had been receiving threats, Hunter replied, "The only person who has threatened me has been Sheriff McCall."

Governor Collins had personally contacted Mabel to say how pleased he was with the outcome of the case, and to assure her that she and her family would have no more trouble with McCall. Still, Mabel had lived in Lake County long enough to know that on the rare occasions when a court ruled against the interests of Willis McCall, those cases were often resolved to his satisfaction by other means.

A few days after Jesse Hunter's courtroom victory, McCall spoke at a Lions Club dinner where he received a standing ovation for his efforts to keep the Platt children out of Lake County schools. Mabel covered the event for the *Topic*. Hesitant though McCall was, he said, to make a speech before the press, "especially one that handles the truth carelessly," he proceeded, because he didn't want to be called chicken. "I've been raised among Negroes and whites—I was raised on a farm," McCall told his audience. "I can tell a stalk of yellow corn from white corn; rutabagas from turnips; sweet potatoes from Irish potatoes; a Hereford bull from a Black Angus bull. Only way to know is by looking at them. I've been called a racial expert, but you don't have to be a racial expert to tell— unless you're prejudiced and have some reason to look at it another way. I looked at these people, and I listened to people in business and with children in school. I looked at them and just fairly agreed that they have Negro blood. In my book they were mulattoes and they still are."

With the lawsuit resolved in their favor, the Platts rented a house back in Lake County so that their children could resume their education at the Mount Dora Christian Home and Bible School. They'd been attending classes only a few days when, at midnight on Friday, November 11, a band of nightriders descended on their house and tossed flaming jugs of gasoline at the windows. The sound of broken glass and the screams of the youngest children awakened Platt and his wife. One wall of the house was already on fire. Platt acted quickly; he got his wife and daughters safely out of the house and then attended to extinguishing the fire. His sons meanwhile grabbed their hunting rifles, leapt through flames, and started firing into the groves where the marauders had disappeared.

Sheriff McCall himself arrived on the scene with deputies. He concluded that the footprints indicated that seven or eight "hoodlums" had been responsible. Even after Platt pointed out a crude cross drawn in the sand near one set of prints, the sheriff stuck to his story, positing that the Klan wasn't likely involved, but rather some high school boys who might not "want to go to school with burrheads." To the reporters on the scene, who included Mabel, McCall opined ominously, "I'm afraid the trouble is just starting." Still, he was making no plans to guard the Platt home. "I haven't got enough men," he said, "and I can't babysit with those people." Then he berated Platt for telephoning Mabel before calling the sheriff's office. "I've got more justice from Mrs. Reese than I have from you," Platt replied.

When McCall and his deputies departed, Platt showed Mabel the trail of footprints that led from the grove to the back of his house. Exasperated, he lamented his family's situation: "My boy, Denzell, is due to register for the draft—to be ready to go and fight for freedom. My wife sometimes gets so upset about this she wants to pack up and run, and I tell her, we have sons that are ready to fight for the United States of America—why should they have to run in fear of their lives in America?

They haven't done anything. They haven't hurt anyone." But the family didn't have "any way to run." The struggle had drained their finances, and they had no money to start again somewhere else.

The experiences of the past year had also altered Platt's sympathies. If he had originally felt, as he had written in his letter to Governor Collins, that "having my family branded as niggers is even worse" than having his children thrown out of school, the indignities his family had endured had opened his eyes to the violence and injustice suffered by generations of blacks. Indeed, he had shared their plight; in effect, he'd been forced to live his life in Lake County as a black man. "I saw the suffering they all had to put up with," Platt said. "We've just got to learn we've got to treat everybody alike."

CONVERSION EXPERIENCES LIKE PLATT'S—and Mabel's—remained a rarity in Florida. Its newspapers, like most in the South, had responded to the 1954 *Brown* decision with venom and assurances that the state would refuse to comply with the Supreme Court's directive. The press effectively declared war on desegregation, and blacks suffered the eventual violence. After more than a thousand cases in which black students applied for admission to all-white colleges or universities, the first concussive, campus-wide instance of violence related to the ruling occurred on February 6, 1956: riots broke out on the University of Alabama campus as its first black student, Autherine Lucy, began to attend classes there.

The riots charged the racial atmosphere of the South, especially in Florida, which nearly two years after the *Brown* ruling still retained all the "Jim Crow aspects of the Deep South," and remained one of only four states that had "no public school integration at any level." Segregationists, capitalizing on their political momentum, sought to devise legislative methods that would circumvent the Supreme Court's ruling. Senator

Strom Thurmond of South Carolina drafted a "Declaration of Constitutional Principles," a congressional resolution condemning the *Brown* decision as a "clear abuse of judicial power" that the South would "fight to the end." The resolution, which became known as the Southern Manifesto, stepped up the pressure on politicians with more moderate positions on race to declare themselves for or against segregation. The few Southern congressmen who refused to sign became casualties in the 1956 elections. As one newspaper reporter observed at the time, "The middle ground is dwindling between the never and the now."

On the radical shift in race relations wrought by the *Brown* decision, historian C. Vann Woodward observed, "Something very much like panic seized many parts of the South toward the beginning of 1956, a panic bred of insecurity or fear. Race relations deteriorated in many areas, and as both races recoiled, old lines of communication between them snapped or weakened. On the white side, resistance hardened up and down the line, and in places stiffened into bristling defiance."

The Southern outcry against *Brown* gave birth to the White Citizens Council of America, which boasted some three hundred thousand members in eleven states—the NAACP's Thurgood Marshall tagged these politically mainstream councils "the uptown Klan." The downtown Klan, meanwhile, throbbed with new life, especially in rural, agricultural central Florida, where the deterioration in race relations was palpable. A Gallup poll in 1956 indicated that four out of five whites in Florida opposed integration, and the Association of Florida Ku Klux Klan collected more than fifty thousand signatures on a petition condemning *Brown*, which it attempted to present to Governor Collins.

Collins had come into office in 1955, in a special election after the sudden death of the previous governor. The son of a neighborhood grocer from Tallahassee, Collins was only twenty-five when he was elected state representative in 1932; in 1940, he was elected state senator. A gifted communicator, tall and handsome, with an equally attractive wife and four photogenic children, Collins was seen as a rising star in an increasingly cosmopolitan Florida. The state had prospered under his tenure, as both the population and the economy had boomed. Collins aligned himself with the state's progressive forces on issues like education, women's rights, and funding for the disabled. On the issue of segregation, he had attempted to maintain a relatively moderate stance—far too moderate to satisfy the Pork Chop Gang, the coterie of conservative lawmakers from North Florida who had succeeded in gaining dominance in the state legislature through malapportionment.

Among Collins's moderate stances was his opposition to the death penalty. When Jesse Hunter, despite having twice successfully prosecuted the Groveland Boys case, wrote to him to express serious doubts about Walter Irvin's guilt, Collins appointed an independent investigator whose report convinced him that the state had failed to establish Irvin's guilt "in an absolute and conclusive manner." In his first year in office, swayed by Hunter's urging, the investigator's report, and pressure from the NAACP and religious leaders, Collins had commuted Walter Irvin's death sentence to life in prison.

The white citizenry of Lake County was outraged. One hundred twenty-one residents of Lake County, including the alleged victim, Norma Padgett, signed a petition opposing the commutation. McCall was so incensed at the very possibility the governor was considering such a move that he sent him a furious letter, in which he charged that "irresponsible people" were "sticking their noses in our affairs" and that any leniency shown to a convicted rapist would only demonstrate that criminals can "ravish our fair womanhood without proper and severe punishment." Two weeks later, four hooded members of the Ku Klux Klan fired shotguns into the Negro Masonic lodge in Umatilla, the sheriff's hometown, where a union meeting of the United Packinghouse Workers was taking place. Twelve black men were wounded, one seriously. Sheriff McCall, who had left town earlier that afternoon with his wife, Doris, for a three-day boating trip to celebrate their twenty-fifth wedding anniversary, informed reporters that although he personally would investigate the shootings, his office didn't have "any leads—not the first one." Mabel reported that in the aftermath of the shooting, hundreds of Klansmen had gathered in Lake County, one of whom was overheard at a gun store in Leesburg promising that blacks shouldn't expect merely buckshot in the future. "Next time, we'll make it count," he'd said.

Collins indicated that he had sent investigators to Lake County and was "fully conscious of an unsatisfactory atmosphere surrounding law enforcement" there, but he refrained from suspending the sheriff. Mabel, however, did not hesitate to take aim. "Disgrace before the rest of the state, before the nation, and before the world, continues to be the lot for Lake County," she wrote in an editorial. Ridiculing the excuses offered by the sheriff's department, who complained that local blacks would not "cooperate" with them in their investigation, she observed pointedly, "They were speaking of the frightened Negroes who were the targets of the shotgun pellets, and who know what kind of law enforcement, what kind of justice there is in Lake County." Assuring her readers that the good people of Lake County—"the grove owner, the banker, the hotel owner, the merchant . . . cannot want the county to maintain its reputation for lawlessness and violence," she voiced the hope that "the bloody pages of recent Lake County history will be closed emphatically by the citizens in next year's election."

The racially charged atmosphere in the state ensured that Collins would face a bitter political battle. The Supreme Court of Florida determined that, given the circumstances in which he had come into office, he was eligible to seek reelection in 1956. (Florida's Constitution precluded sitting governors from running for consecutive four-year terms.) Most formidable among Collins's primary opponents was Sumter Lowry, a veteran of both world wars who had served as lieutenant general of the Florida National Guard. As the avowed "white supremacy candidate,"

Lowry saw integration as a policy enmeshed in the "International Communist conspiracy . . . to destroy our Christian Church through infiltration; and to destroy our race by mixing it with the blood of the Negro race." He knew how to command attention with scare tactics that played to the electorate's greatest fear. In his campaign speeches and print ads, he constantly invoked Walter Irvin's name and face and he barely acknowledged questions regarding his plans or positions on any other issue besides race.

Collins kicked off his reelection campaign at a joint ladies-night banquet for the Mount Dora and Tavares Kiwanis and Lions Clubs on February 21, 1956. Days before, Judge Futch had ordered a grand jury investigation into the actions of the governor and the state pardon board regarding the Walter Irvin commutation. In a statement to the press, Collins had maintained there was nothing to investigate other than his conscience, which was "beyond control or coercion of a grand jury," and declared his decision to be subject only to review "by God and the people of Florida." Still, he had no choice but to attempt to make his case politically in his speech at the banquet. "I have serious questions about the guilt of Walter Lee Irvin," he said. "I cannot take his life." The *Ocala Star-Banner* observed that Collins's explanation garnered merely "scant applause" from the two hundred fifty ladies in his audience.

Mabel was among them. In addition to giving public support to his "calm approach to the integration problem," she had been offering private support in correspondence with the governor throughout the Platts' troubles and the Irvin case. Collins, in turn, had written to express his gratitude for her ongoing support of his commitment to racial decency and justice, and she had published his letters in the *Topic*. Now she lingered at the end of the evening banquet, hoping for a brief conversation with the governor before her five-mile drive back to Sylvan Shores.

Mabel's neighbor Herbert K. Beiser was home watching television that night, but he was not too absorbed in his program to notice when the noisy, light-colored sedan turned down Morningside Drive. The automobile slowed, and had barely passed the Reese home when it came to a stop. Its engine idled. Then a loud "whistling sound" brought more of Mabel's neighbors to attention. Seconds later, a bright flash of light and a tremendous explosion rocked the tranquillity of Sylvan Shores. The blast echoed across Lake Gertrude and reverberated for miles in every direction. Beiser's television "blanked out." He called the sheriff's office. Other neighbors lost telephone service. Alarmed, they rushed out to the street and toward the Reese house. Frantically they called for Mabel and Paul, but neither one answered, and the house was dark. Another neighbor, a Mrs. Charles Hener, would later report that she had spoken to a "strange" man who'd asked if she'd heard the explosion and then run back to his car. He'd driven hastily away, she said, and was dressed in attire "akin to riding clothes or some manner of uniform."

The neighbors felt helpless. Afraid to approach the Reese house for fear of another blast, they stood about on the street, waiting. Where were the police?

This was the scenario that greeted Mabel when she arrived home from the banquet at about 9:30 p.m. Paul arrived around the same time; he'd been at the office. Patricia was staying overnight with a friend. Fortunately for the Reeses, the bomb had exploded in the front yard, far enough away from the house not to cause significant structural damage. Still, Mabel was distraught, especially as no officer of the law materialized. Two nights later, Paul Reese returned home from the office a little after nine at night to discover that "a load of fish heads, whole dead fish and other garbage" had been dumped on the lawn in front of the house. He'd just carted the debris to the rear of the house when he noticed a light-colored car approaching. The explosion this time was only about a quarter as strong as the first. Mabel, who had been inside the house with Patricia, immediately telephoned Futch, who was scheduled to hear testimony the next morning in the grand jury investigation of Walter Irvin's commutation. Futch invited Mabel to relate her story to the grand jury.

She arrived in Tavares with a paper sack full of bomb fragments she'd recovered on her property. She complained of Sheriff McCall's failure to investigate the bombings, thereby denying the people of Sylvan Shores their rightful protection. State attorney A. P. Buie also called to the stand Herbert Beiser, who affirmed that he had received "no satisfaction" upon calling the sheriff's department. As Beiser was leaving the courthouse, McCall summoned him into his office. "The only thing wrong with your neighborhood is the Reeses," he said. At Futch's urging, though, McCall did eventually dispatch two deputies, one of them his son Malcolm, to Mount Dora to investigate the incident. Malcolm McCall concluded that the devices were Army-issue simulated bombs, which "would cause damage and possible injury if thrown into a home or near a person."

While in Lake County, LeRoy Collins had been scheduled to ride in the annual George Washington's Day parade in nearby Eustis, a county event second only to the Leesburg Watermelon Festival and the perfect setting for a ceremonial campaign appearance. McCall, however, had for the past decade fancied himself to be the star of the parade, leading the floats and marching bands from atop his Palomino, Pretty Boy, and sporting his trademark white Stetson. And this year McCall was running for reelection. He enjoyed the advantages that incumbency afforded him, like posting himself at the head of a well-attended parade. What he did not enjoy was Collins's encroachment on his territory, or remarks like those the governor had recently made about the "unsatisfactory atmosphere surrounding law enforcement" in Lake County.

In view of the bombings at the Reese house, Collins's staff had made arrangements for additional security in Eustis as well as back home in Tallahassee, where a highway patrolman was stationed at the Collins home. So he was caught off guard when, just as he prepared to position himself in the backseat of a parade car, Norma Padgett herself stepped forward from the crowd of people lining the street. Defiantly she jeered, "You're the one who let out the nigger that raped me. Suppose I was your sister, would you have done that?" Collins mumbled something to the effect that he'd come to Lake County not for political reasons but to "be with the community," and Norma was led away, but the confrontation was duly noted by the press, with one paper expressing outrage that "Sheriff Willis V. McCall's deputies served as escorts . . . and assisted her in approaching Gov. Collins on a crowded street." Unsurprisingly, the sheriff denied any involvement on the part of his department. Collins, however, had no doubts. "McCall had set her up for that," he said later.

Concerns about Willis McCall and Lake County were by now circulating far beyond the state borders. Adlai Stevenson, then the Democratic presidential aspirant, was touring the state. When Mabel inquired of a Chamber of Commerce officer about the possibility of arranging for him to make a campaign stop in the Mount Dora area, he replied that Stevenson wanted to steer clear of Lake County because of its "reputation for lawlessness." The candidate had said, "That's one part of the state of Florida I'd rather not visit."

WHILE MABEL CONTINUED her efforts at "vanquishing the threat of a dictatorship in Lake County," she had to acknowledge that the town had hardly rallied behind her. Despite the region's robust population growth, circulation of the *Mount Dora Topic* had been steadily declining since Bryant Bowles of the National Association for the Advancement of White People had declared that he'd "get even" with Mabel for her unflattering articles.

Get even he did, with help from powerful quarters. In May 1955, Thomas P. Dwyer of LaGrange, Illinois, the former Midwest advertising and sales director for Conover-Mast Publications in Chicago, had decided to establish a second local newspaper, the *Mount Dora Herald*, on Mabel's turf. Why was not clear, the *Orlando Sentinel* noted, as the town was barely big enough to support a single newspaper, although it went on, insinuatingly, "There are those who believe the new paper was not started ... principally because the town is such a flourishing one that its merchants need a second advertising medium."

The paper set up its office directly across the street from the *Topic*. Mabel soon discovered that its backers had funded her rival with enough advertising to support the *Herald*'s publishing efforts for a full year. The first issue of the *Herald* made its mission clear. "We wish to state unequivocally that we are heartily in accord with the South's deeply grooved traditions," stated its editors, and that "we here in the South will not be bullied easily into a way of life alien to us." Over the next few months, the paper's political objectives became obvious. First and foremost, it strove to delay or stall desegregation by promoting states' rights. It published a letter to the editor that provided contact information for the establishment of a Florida "Citizens' Council" like those already working in Mississippi, Alabama, and Georgia to provide a "unified front in opposition to public school integration." It regularly afforded guest-column space to blacks who were opposed to desegregation, and ran news stories with headlines like "Negroes Do Not Want Integration." Second among the *Herald*'s objectives was its resolve to defend any actions taken by Willis McCall. He was routinely praised for his commitment to law and order in Lake County. His local speeches received full coverage, especially when they targeted a certain newspaper as a "propaganda machine" run by "the kind of people" who "cram their way of life down the throats of the American people." Third, the *Herald* set its sights on "that other newspaper" as a target and seized any opportunity to embarrass and harass its co-owner and editor with veiled threats and accusations of communist leanings.

Mabel watched from the *Topic* offices as McCall went in and out of the *Herald*'s offices to confer with the new publisher. And she watched as she lost previously steady advertisers to the competition. She and Paul were feeling the pinch, and Mabel began to question the wisdom of the choices she had made in a career that had focused on journalism less as a business than as a means of seeking social justice—a course that had certainly "interfered with the cash register." Those with more savvy in media and business had advised her to heed the economic pitfalls of taking stands on controversial issues. "I refused to listen," Mabel admitted, "and so I am badly bruised by all the plunges I have taken."

She had expected that she would somehow triumph. "I blasted the sheriff to the next county," Mabel wrote later of her coverage of the Platt case. "It looked as if I had him. It looked as if he was finally impaled upon my editorial pen. I went out on my next advertising rounds fully expecting the powers that be to say—'Well, I guess you had him pegged all along.' Instead, the shoulders were much colder; the advertisers were all so very busy; the customers were all well stocked with printing." Nevertheless, she and Paul "tightened [their] belts and waded deeper into the fight." She made her usual advertising rounds and "picked up the crumbs" here and there, while Paul printed "scratch pads and tablets in lieu of the printing orders we no longer had."

Mabel Norris Reese at her *Mount Dora Topic* office

CHAPTER FOUR

Make Tracks

By the early evening of December 18, 1957, many of Okahumpka's black residents had gathered in the small, concrete-block Mount Olive Baptist Church on North Quarters Road. Most of their men and boys had been released, but some were still being held in police custody as possible suspects in the rape of Blanche Knowles. The community was on edge. Those who'd made their way to the church turned to Brother Melvin Hawkins Sr. for comfort and guidance. The Quarters residents at the gathering had barely begun to share the worry and distress they were experiencing when about ten lawmen led by Deputy Yates barged into the church. Yates said that they would be taking names—that a number of the young men present had already been questioned by the police didn't seem to matter.

A tall, athletic-looking teen caught the deputies' attention. One of them asked his name. The boy answered, "Bubba Hawkins." His given name was Melvin Jr., and he was Brother Hawkins's son.

Immediately the reverend stepped forward, but a deputy grabbed Bubba's arm. "You're coming with us," he said, and he began leading the boy out toward his car. His father protested: Bubba had been at home with the family all night. That Melvin Jr. was a good boy, a quiet, church-going boy; that he attended all-black Carver Heights High School in Leesburg, because his father "wanted his kids to focus on school" rather than work in the groves and melon patches like most other eighteen-year-olds; that he was a star football player; that he was funny and well liked; that he sang regularly in the church choir—none of that would have mattered to the deputies. They were set on their purpose.

The deputies escorted Bubba back to his family's small house, where they ordered him to produce the shoes he'd been wearing the night before. The boy complied. The deputies then informed the elder Hawkins that they'd be taking his son to Tavares for questioning. Helplessly, in the oak-canopied darkness of Okahumpka, Bubba's parents watched as a convoy of green-and-white Plymouth Belvederes retreated into the night. Inside one of them was their frightened son.

A few minutes outside Okahumpka, somewhere around Yalaha, the convoy stopped. The deputies yanked Bubba Hawkins from the car transporting him. They walked him into a dark grove. With pistols holstered butt-forward on their belts, they formed a semicircle around him. They accused him of the rape; roughly they prodded him to confess. Intimidated, terrified, Hawkins denied any involvement. The victim had "scratched the nigger who raped her," one deputy snarled, and he ordered Hawkins to take off all his clothes. Meekly, shivering in a sea of leafless trees, the soil littered with split orange rinds reeking of rot, the boy obeyed. When he had dropped his undershorts, several deputies brandishing long-handled flashlights stepped forward. Beams of light darted back and forth across Hawkins's face, his arms, his legs, illuminating a popular, funny, churchgoing eighteen-year-old boy's naked fear but no scratches. The deputies ordered him to turn around; nothing on his back or rear. Still, they aimed to menace him into a confession. Terrified though he was, Hawkins repeated his denial. One of the deputies ordered him to get dressed. Then they shuffled him off to the jail above the Lake County Courthouse.

Hawkins spent the night in jail with a few other boys from the Quarters who were still being held by the sheriff's department for questioning in the Okahumpka rape case. One of them was Sam Wiley Odom—or Wiley Sam Odom, as he was known in the Quarters—who'd been seized in the initial sweep.

The next morning, Deputy Yates awakened Hawkins. They were going for a little ride, he said, and he told the boy to put on the shoes he'd been wearing on the night of the rape. The road was familiar. Yates and his partner Leroy Campbell were driving him to Okahumpka, but they weren't taking him home. The squad car stopped at the Knowles place. Yates had Hawkins "walk around and make tracks" in the soil outside the house. The deputy told the boy that he "wanted to check his shoe prints." That done, Campbell drove Hawkins back to Tavares. Yates stayed behind to examine the prints. The deputy's preoccupation with this sort of evidence had earned him some measure of notoriety around the county. The efforts that had won the initial convictions of the three black defendants in the Groveland case had included his plaster casts of footprints— never mind that a leading forensic expert for the FBI had testified that Yates had faked them.

Meanwhile, anxiety in the Hawkins family ran high. They'd had not a word from the sheriff's department, and could only conclude that Bubba was spending a second night in jail. Melvin Sr. turned to his brother Virgil in Daytona for guidance.

It was Virgil, not Melvin Sr., who'd seemed destined for a life in the church. Their father, Virgil W. Hawkins, had settled in Okahumpka at the turn of the twentieth century, when the region still resembled the "vast, untamed wilderness, plentifully stocked with wild cattle" that government reports had described back in 1821, when the United States took possession of Florida from Spain. The Indian Removal Act of 1830 had allowed cattlemen to enlarge their holdings as the Seminoles were pushed out of North Florida and down into the "thick, impenetrable flat woods and deep bogs" around Okahumpka. In that refuge, or what was designated their "zone of confinement," they harbored Africans who had been freed by Spain as well as fugitive slaves who were fleeing their white masters in cotton-belt states. While some of the fugitive blacks indentured themselves as servants or labored as slaves to the Seminoles, others allied themselves with the Native Americans and took up arms beside them in their wars against the United States, thus to be known as Black Seminoles. Though they maintained separate cultures, the Seminoles, native and black, coexisted as allies in Okahumpka, more particularly in Bugg Spring, an area that Florida governor William P. DuVal considered "the poorest and most miserable region I ever beheld."

By 1900, most of the Seminoles had been wiped out in battle, succumbed to disease or starvation, or been relocated to Indian territory west of the Mississippi. The population of Florida, at slightly more than half a million residents, was the smallest of any state in the South. In what was essentially still "pioneer country," settlers dwelt largely in rural homesteads that stretched from the plantation belt in the Panhandle down to the swamps of the Everglades. In central Florida, cow hunters still roamed the swamps and prairies. Hardy men, they abided the swampy, mosquito-infested terrain and defied the frequent hurricanes, not to mention the indigenous bears, panthers, alligators, and wild boars. To protect themselves against the sun and rain, they wore thick, slouched wool hats and wide pants tucked into tall leather lace-up boots that shielded them from the razor-sharp leaves of saw grass and the plenteous rattlesnakes. What most notably identified them, though—and was said to give them and this rural "cracker country" their names—were the long, braided rawhide whips they cracked to drive cattle from the scrub to the trails and thence to the coastal markets that had been carved out over the past century.

A day laborer in the grueling turpentine camps of Lake County, Virgil W. Hawkins worked alongside blacks who were being exploited by a convict-lease system that thrived in the decades following the Civil War and ensured cheap labor for the industry. Hawkins managed to avoid falling victim to debt slavery and saved enough money to purchase, for two hundred dollars, a ten-acre homestead in Okahumpka, on which he built a modest wood-frame house. He married Josephine Brown, and with her he joined the African Methodist Episcopal (AME) Church. Together they set out to build an independent family farm, while Virgil took seasonal work as a citrus picker or as a laborer in the nearby kaolin pits. They started a family.

Their life together took some of the sting out of the oppression suffered by blacks in Florida, but they could not ignore it. Between 1882 and 1930, Florida had the highest per capita lynching rate of any state in the nation. Like many Southern political leaders of the time, Florida governor Napoleon Bonaparte Broward considered his white voting constituency to be unconcerned with the economic plight of blacks, but the lynching did concern him, as a threat to "civilization and Christianization." He therefore proposed that the United States purchase some "foreign territory" where blacks could be deported, in order "to protect the white man from his own temper."

To increase the opportunities for his children to advance in and beyond their community, as well as to elevate his own stature, Virgil W. Hawkins served for years as a deacon at Okahumpka's Bethel AME Church. Bright and verbally adept, Virgil Jr. seemed the best suited of his sons to follow him into the clergy, once he'd finished his schooling. But it was law that interested Virgil Jr. Accompanying his father to the Lake County Courthouse, he observed the patent fear and helplessness of poor black defendants who were paraded before a judge without understanding the legal proceedings or their rights. "At that tender age," Virgil Jr. would remember, "I didn't know what a lawyer did, but I knew I had to do something." He promised God he would someday defend "those who don't even know what the word 'guilty' means."

When he let slip his ambitions, Virgil Sr. exclaimed, "This child is going to hell for lying. Says he's going to be a lawyer!" The revelation afforded the family a good laugh, yet they and other relatives were soon turning to Virgil Jr. when legal matters arose. "Go get Virgil," Josephine would say. "He'll know what to do. He's going to be a lawyer." His father began referring to him as "my little lawyer." When he finished tenth grade—the final year of public education for blacks in Lake County—Virgil Sr. and Josephine decided to send him on to complete a high school curriculum at the AME-run Edward Waters College in Jacksonville. Though heavy on Bible studies, the school's rich curriculum included courses on the history of civil rights, which accounted for its reputation as a site for future "race leaders." No less vital than the classroom experience were the freedoms Virgil Jr. enjoyed in being part of Jacksonville's thriving black community.

After graduating in 1930, Virgil headed north to Lincoln University in Pennsylvania, whose alumni included Thurgood Marshall and Langston Hughes. But the Great Depression made it impossible for him to continue, and he returned to Lake County. There he met and married Ida Frazier, a schoolteacher from nearby Ocoee. They settled in Ocala, and for years Virgil commuted more than fifty miles a day from there to Groveland's dilapidated black elementary school as he worked himself up from a lowly teaching position to principal.

At the age of thirty-seven and still without even a baccalaureate degree, Virgil Hawkins Jr. chanced upon an opportunity to keep his dream of a legal career alive when he was offered a position as director of public relations at Bethune-Cookman College in Daytona Beach. There, he was able to attend classes and continue his education. His engagement with the intellectual community reawakened his passion for the study of law, and he resolved to honor the promise he'd made to God. The University of Florida in Gainesville had the only public law school in the state; however, it admitted only whites. Relocation might have been an option, but he and Ida, both of them Florida-born-and-bred, neither wanted nor could afford to live up North.

A Daytona Beach attorney, Horace Hill, knew the NAACP was looking for plaintiffs to challenge discriminatory policies in public education, and he believed Virgil Hawkins—married but without children, and with a good job at a respected black institution—would be an ideal candidate. So, in 1949, along with four other black aspiring law students, Hawkins applied to the University of Florida College of Law, and the NAACP started preparing their case. Predictably, the State of Florida denied them admission, and the Legal Defense Fund filed suit. No one in the plaintiff's camp anticipated the fallout that followed.

The Florida Board of Control, the government agency first in line to respond to the suit, did so by offering Hawkins a full scholarship—on the condition that he agree to attend an out-of-state law school. Bethune-Cookman College meanwhile received notice that the school's business loans would not be renewed unless they fired Virgil Hawkins. Stores where Ida shopped in Daytona Beach refused to issue her any further credit, and banks called in their loans. Threatening letters arrived regularly in the Hawkinses' mail. Their neighbors were harassed. The State of Florida moved to institute a law school at Florida A&M, the black college in Tallahassee.

The measures being taken to keep blacks out of the University of Florida College of Law began to take their toll on Virgil and Ida both. They decided to publicly feign a marital separation in order to remove Ida from the malign eye of harassers. She returned to Lake County, where she taught at Carver High School and lodged with Virgil's family in Okahumpka. To escape detection, Virgil would drive the seventy-plus miles to Okahumpka in the middle of the night and sneak into his parents' house by crawling under the floorboards. "We're older than you," his brother Melvin would tease him. "Why is your hair whiter than ours?" Virgil had a quick reply: "While you're in your beds sleeping at night, I'm running, ducking, dodging and hiding under houses."

In June 1950, the Supreme Court ruled unanimously in *Sweatt v. Painter*, another of Thurgood Marshall's cases, that a black applicant, Heman Marion Sweatt, must be admitted to the University of Texas School of Law, a decision that would pave the way for the landmark segregation case *Brown v. Board of Education* four years later. The State of Florida had filed an amicus brief in support of the State of Texas in the case, so the ruling was in effect a rejection of Florida's arguments. Except that Florida dug in; the state defied the Court's order by writing an opinion that upheld its plan to establish, as the University of Texas had attempted to do, a law school for blacks at Florida A&M. The Florida Supreme Court, meanwhile, delayed issuing a final order in the Hawkins case. Thurgood Marshall lambasted Florida's contempt for the U.S. Supreme Court's ruling as the Fort Sumter of "an undeclared second civil war." But the Court itself was not disposed to consider Hawkins's case, as *Brown v. Board of Education* was already in the pipeline. Virgil Hawkins had no choice but to wait.

In May 1954, the U.S. Supreme Court handed down its unanimous ruling in *Brown*, thereby declaring racial segregation in public schools to be unconstitutional. One week after the ruling, the U.S. Supreme Court granted Hawkins's writ of certiorari: In light of the *Brown* decision, the Florida Supreme Court's judgment was vacated. Thurgood Marshall assigned the case to Constance Baker Motley, a thirty-four-year-old attorney who'd graduated from Columbia Law School and was working at the Legal Defense Fund in New York. On the drive down to Tallahassee, her toddler son was denied use of a bathroom because of the color of the family's skin, a precursor to the racial antagonism the black female attorney from New York would encounter in Florida when arguing before "a group of stone-faced white male judges." Of the Florida Supreme

Court in the 1950s, one journalist later observed, "It is doubtful that any institution in the South was more resolutely racist. No Southern court fought desegregation longer or harder." Baker Motley was nonetheless astounded when the Florida Supreme Court finally rendered its opinion that the U.S. Supreme Court's decision to clarify further the federal enforcement of school desegregation (in what became known as *Brown II*) allowed the University of Florida to defer admission to Hawkins for whatever length of time the State might require to "evaluate the potential harm to the public" that he might pose.

Once again Hawkins was denied his dream of a legal education and career, but he drew strength from three significant women in his life— his wife, Ida; Constance Baker Motley; and Mary McLeod Bethune, a founder of Bethune-Cookman College, who urged him "to fight until it's over. Never stop. If you stop now, it might be a generation before somebody else comes along to take up the fight. Why not this generation?" So once again, Hawkins had rooted in.

It would be nearly two more years before the Supreme Court—on the same day that Strom Thurmond unveiled in the U.S. Senate his Southern Manifesto against public racial integration—handed down a per curiam (unanimous) decision in regard to Virgil Hawkins. The Court determined that Hawkins was within his rights to attend the University of Florida College of Law and was "entitled to prompt admission under the rules and regulations applicable to other qualified candidates."

The Supreme Court's decision "horrified whites throughout Florida," and it affected the 1956 Democratic primary election even more profoundly than had Governor Collins's commutation of Walter Irvin's sentence. With Sumter Lowry now calling all the more vehemently for the state to resist integration by any means necessary, Collins felt compelled to issue a statement. "Every legal recourse will be followed to avoid integration," he promised. He offered to argue against Hawkins's admission before the Supreme Court. In a hastily assembled "State Conference to

Stop Integration," he brought the issue before his cabinet, legislators, and state university presidents in Tallahassee. The conference produced a message to President Eisenhower that Collins himself drafted. It emphasized that the State of Florida was committed to the "tradition and customs of segregation, which are as rooted in this state as in any other Southern state," even as it warned that Florida was "experiencing a serious deterioration of racial relations." It pledged formally to "use every legal means to avoid integration in the schools."

Sumter Lowry's campaign mocked the assembly as a "meeting of the integrationists" by which Collins strove to mask his true intention: to abide by a Supreme Court decision that would enable Virgil Hawkins to attend the University of Florida College of Law. As if to prove it, Lowry distributed brochures that featured photographs of the governor shaking hands with members of the Florida Negro Teachers' Association. Another candidate, former governor Fuller Warren, depicted Collins as that "curly-haired boy up in Tallahassee—the friend of the N-double-A-Cee-P" and accused Hawkins of brutally beating two schoolchildren—one with an auto fan belt, the other with a palmetto stick—at the Lake County school in Yalaha, where he had taught in the early 1940s. The beatings, Warren contended, would "legally and morally" bar Hawkins from admittance to the University of Florida College of Law. Although two former school officials stated they had no recollection of any such incidents and Warren could point to no other substantiation, Hawkins was forced to respond. "It is regrettable," he said, "that a man who has been so greatly honored by this state, as has Ex-Governor Fuller Warren, should be capable of descending to such depths as to falsely assail one of the state's humblest citizens."

As the Florida primary drew near, the rhetoric, already intense, was amplified by coverage across the state and in national publications such as the *New York Times* and the *Atlanta Constitution*. The Florida State University student newspaper published a letter from the chairman of the steering committee of the Sumter Lowry Student Organization. "A Negro is now sitting on the doorstep of the University of Florida waiting for admittance," the letter advised. "The time for action has past [sic], yet the Governor does nothing. It is no wonder that the NAACP has chosen LeRoy Collins as their standard bearer . . . On May 8, the voters of Florida will say whether they want to maintain segregation or let professional politicians sell out their children."

Meanwhile, Virgil Hawkins's long battle was still far from over. His case would return to the Florida Supreme Court and then to the United States Supreme Court, where his victory again would prove to be in vain. The State of Florida simply refused to obey the mandate of the highest court in the nation and sought to make an example of Hawkins by steadfastly blocking his admission to the University of Florida College of Law. In the meantime, Hawkins once again rooted in, unaware that another case entirely would bring him and his family into the crosshairs of Sheriff Willis McCall.

On December 19, 1957, state attorney Gordon Oldham made a public statement about the Okahumpka rape case and the suspect. Not yet out of his twenties, Oldham was believed to be the youngest man ever elected state attorney in Florida. His baby face, though, belied a razor-sharp mind, which won him regard as a legal luminary, destined for higher office. The son of a prominent citrus man and a member of the Leesburg Quarterback Club, Oldham moved comfortably among the Lake County elite, including Sheriff Willis McCall, who was standing at his side during the hastily assembled press conference. Oldham first disclosed that the victim in the case had been assaulted in bed "by a young Negro who had gained entrance to the woman's home by slashing a screen and unlatching the front door." He indicated that, the rape notwithstanding, "the woman was not harmed otherwise." He then announced that an "unnamed Negro," who "would be identified only if he is charged in the case," was currently being held for questioning. Further leads were meanwhile being investigated, he said, and he noted that a mobile unit from Orange County had been brought in to lift fingerprints from the victim's home, prints that were now "being checked against the suspect."

Beyond that, the authorities had nothing to add about the circumstances surrounding the attack, and McCall refused bluntly to answer any questions from reporters. But later that evening, both Melvin Hawkins Jr.'s name and the news of his arrest by Sheriff Willis McCall were released. It was also confirmed that the heel prints Deputy Yates had discovered outside the victim's home matched the bottoms of Hawkins's shoes.

The next day's local newspapers linked the rape directly to Melvin's notorious uncle, "Florida's most publicized integrationist," and soon newspapers around the country were carrying the story with inflammatory headlines like "Attack Charge for Nephew of Fla. Integrationist" and "Hawkins Kin Held by McCall in Rape Case." Although, as one story pointed out, the governor had not had to call out the National Guard, as he had in the Groveland case, to restrain a mob of Klansmen from torching black homes, something more quietly sinister seemed to be afoot in Lake County. For one thing, now days after his jailing, eighteen-year-old Sam Wiley Odom had still not been released; for another, the sheriff's department was also refusing Bubba Hawkins his right to an attorney. All Virgil Hawkins could learn on a visit to Oka-humpka was that his nephew was being held "incommunicado" in an undisclosed jail. When Mabel pressed the sheriff's office as to why Hawkins wasn't being arraigned, the department imposed a news blackout. When, on a courtroom plea day, county judge W. Troy Hall asked specifically that Hawkins appear before the circuit court, Deputy Yates curtly declined. Hawkins had been moved to an "undisclosed location," Yates told the judge, and "we're not ready to produce him yet."

More days passed with no further information on Bubba Hawkins's whereabouts. Mabel, unaware that Hawkins had been moved from Tavares, wrote, "For a week now, an 18-year-old Okahumpka Negro has been lodged in Lake county jail, with no warrant filed to certify his arrest, and with no appearance of the man before any magistrate." She cited statute 901.23 of the Florida Criminal Code, which states that a person arrested without warrant must, "without unnecessary delay," be taken before the nearest magistrate with an official complaint describing the offense for which the person was arrested. Furthermore, McCall had "unofficially" charged Hawkins with rape and discussed the evidence against him publicly while continuing to hold him incommunicado and without representation. Mabel also criticized McCall for inflaming Melvin's connection to his uncle.

The Hawkins family was terrified. They knew all too well what might be the fate of an eighteen-year-old black boy not only under suspicion of raping a white woman but also in the custody of Willis McCall. They feared that the sheriff's imposition of a news blackout might be a delaying tactic; that perhaps his department's interrogation of Bubba had turned violent, and they needed time for the boy's injuries to heal. Four days after Bubba was locked up, Virgil Hawkins notified the FBI office in Ocala of the situation and set up a meeting for his brother with Robert Saunders, an attorney with the NAACP in Tampa. Melvin Sr. told Saunders that someone he knew had overheard Sheriff Willis McCall order his deputies to arrest "young nigger Hawkins," because he was the nephew of "that nigger who was trying to get into the University of Florida."

A black man who grew up in Tampa, Saunders didn't need to be briefed on the reputation of the sheriff of Lake County. Six years earlier, on Christmas night, 1951, shortly before the second Groveland trial was set to begin, a bomb had exploded beneath the home of Harry T. Moore, executive secretary of the NAACP in Florida, killing him and his wife,

Harriette. As the bombing bore all the earmarks of a Ku Klux Klan assassination, and because Moore had been relentless in his public denunciations of Willis McCall, the NAACP and the FBI suspected that the Lake County sheriff must have been involved, at least tangentially. Moore's killing had left the NAACP in Florida rudderless. Saunders, who had volunteered with the NAACP while attending college in Detroit, suddenly found himself being interviewed for the job by the top brass, including Thurgood Marshall himself. He accepted on the spot. "I did not think about the danger at all," he recalled. "I just could not believe that these fine and courageous men had entrusted me with so precious a mission." As Saunders was leaving, one of the leaders had tendered him a few parting words of advice: "Stay out of the little towns."

When Saunders returned to Tampa to set up his office, he was dismayed to learn not only that the Florida organization was verging on bankruptcy but also that blacks in the state were still terrified by the fact of the bombing. In the years since, Saunders had grown keenly aware of the personal terror that Virgil Hawkins had been living with every day since he'd filed his 1949 suit. So when Melvin Hawkins arrived with his daughter Gloria at Saunders's Tampa home for their initial meeting, the NAACP executive took their fears seriously. "We needed to move fast," Saunders remembered, "and only the governor possessed enough power in the state to restrain McCall."

LeRoy Collins was living in the Grove—an antebellum plantation house in Tallahassee, owned by his wife, Mary Call—while waiting for the construction of the new Florida Governor's Mansion to be completed. Largely due to overwhelming support from black voters, Collins had managed to hold off Sumter Lowry and the rest of the field in the highly contentious Democratic primary of 1956. He had then cruised to victory over his Republican opponent and become the first Florida governor to serve two consecutive terms. It was close to midnight when Saunders telephoned Collins. Mary Call answered the phone. Informed that the governor was asleep, Saunders requested that she wake him for an urgent matter. Once Saunders had briefed him, the governor—alarmed but hardly surprised, given his own history with McCall—spoke for nearly an hour with the elder Hawkins. The governor gave Hawkins his word that young Bubba would be located and protected.

On December 23, true to his word, Collins wired McCall, ordering the "inhumane roundup" to cease. He then contacted Gordon Oldham, who assured the governor that "the Negro youth was being held lawfully at this stage of the investigation of the crime and being treated properly" at a jail in Tampa. The governor asked Oldham to pass on the information to the Hawkins family. "I assume this has been done," Collins told a reporter, and deemed that no further intervention in the case by his office was necessary.

"We're still in the middle of the investigation," McCall responded to a reporter's questioning, reserving further comment. As for the news that the NAACP had contacted Collins and was seriously considering taking Hawkins's case, the sheriff said, "They've blasted me before, and I've still got nothing to say."

Was it the news blackout and the fact that a rape suspect was being held incommunicado without being charged that made the case feel so strange?

It certainly struck Mabel as odd that McCall and Oldham weren't moving more aggressively to charge Hawkins in front of a courtroom full of reporters, if only to reassure the public that a rapist wasn't running loose. Perhaps another sheriff might have seen silence as a means of allaying racial tensions, but not McCall. In fact, nothing was more likely to infuriate the notoriously short-fused and rabble-rousing McCall than the idea, let alone the practice, of interracial sex, consensual or otherwise, as he'd evidenced the previous year in a case that had made headlines across the state.

Evvie Griffin had been on the job for about a year on October 3, 1956, when Willis McCall informed him that he'd be needed on a stakeout in the Big Scrub of Ocala National Forest. "Bring a camera," the sheriff told him.

On the ride up to the Scrub, Eustis police chief Andy Groves briefed Griffin more fully on the case. Emily "Apache" Brown, a rail-thin, petite white nineteen-year-old from Lake County, had been regularly attending dances at the American Legion Hall in Orlando, where one evening she became friendly with a white girl her age, a tall bleached blonde named Marlene Taylor. After the dance, when the two of them stopped at a drive-in, Marlene had waved genially to a carload of black men whom she apparently knew. Apache was curious. "I'm dating a Negro," Marlene confided.

Originally from Miami, Marlene Taylor had married and given birth to a daughter by the time she was sixteen. At eighteen, after her divorce, she'd moved with her baby to her father's home in Orlando. There, she'd met an airman stationed at Pinecastle Air Force Base. They'd married in March 1956, but within a few months her husband had been transferred to a base in Europe. By September, Marlene had quietly begun a sexual relationship with Maxie Thomas Deckard, a twenty-one-year-old black airman from Palestine, Texas. Marlene shared these bits of her history with Apache, and then, to Apache's surprise, asked her if she might like to go out on a "sex thrill date" with a Negro. Laughing, playing along with what she assumed was a joke, Apache said yes.

Later that night, after she'd left her new friend and driven back to her parents' home in Lake County, Apache made a telephone call to Chief Groves.

Apache was in "some kind of trouble," Griffin recalled, and he surmised that she might have been using the information she passed on to the Eustis Police Department to help extricate herself from her own legal predicament. In any case, Chief Groves knew exactly whom he should talk to next. He met with Sheriff McCall, and together they put into place a plan to lure Marlene Taylor and her "thrill date" into a setting and situation where they could be arrested under a Florida miscegenation statute prohibiting "interracial cohabitation and fornication." Groves argued that McCall's cabin in the Scrub provided the perfect site for the entrapment, but the prospect of Negroes fornicating with white girls inside his own four walls did not appeal to McCall. Groves persisted, and eventually, if unenthusiastically, McCall yielded.

The night before they staged the entrapment, they rehearsed. Groves, McCall, and Lake County deputy Doug Sewell drove Apache to the sheriff's camp to familiarize her with the layout of the cabin and to outline for her the plan of attack. The following day, Apache called Marlene to tell her that she'd been thinking about what Marlene had suggested and, yes, she really would like to get together with a Negro—she even knew where they could do it. Her father was away on vacation, she said, so they could all go up to his place, a secluded cabin tucked deep in the pines.

Marlene did not need much convincing. She called Maxie Deckard, shared her excitement, asked him to find a date for Apache, and arranged to meet up with them at a gas station.

Deckard showed up around nine p.m. with a friend, twenty-six-year-old Staff Sergeant Conley Gipson Jr., from Navasota, Texas, at the wheel of his 1956 Pontiac convertible. They were waiting, cautious, the Pontiac idling, when Apache's blue Chevrolet pulled into the service station. Apache did not need to explain why it was necessary for the two black men to follow her and Marlene in a separate car; in Lake County that was obvious.

They were approaching the Scrub, Gipson and Deckard trailing at a safe distance, when Apache suddenly pulled the Chevy off the road by a phone booth and stopped to make a call. A few miles farther on, she stopped at another pay phone. Deckard, already nervous about the rendezvous, didn't like what he was seeing. "It doesn't look right," he told

Gipson, noting that they had already passed one Lake County squad car, and another, he thought, might be following them. While they waited for Apache to complete her call, Gipson peered in the rearview mirror. Slowly a green 1956 Oldsmobile from the Lake County Sheriff's Department was approaching; slowly it passed them and then, gaining speed, disappeared into the night. Probably they were looking for someone else, Gipson conjectured. His friend, though, was sufficiently spooked that he persuaded Gipson to pull off alongside a cluster of pines because he simply did not want to go any farther into the forest. Noticing that the Pontiac was no longer behind them, Apache circled back to the parked car. Flirtatiously, she assured the two men that everything was fine and they'd be able to spend the whole night together undetected in the cabin.

Marlene, too, had spotted a patrol car, and she thought that they should turn around, but Apache allayed her concerns as well.

Within minutes of each other, the Chevy and then the Pontiac pulled up to the cabin. Apache leapt from her car, and with Marlene on her heels, she rushed into the cabin and turned on all the lights. The Air Force men watched from the front seat of the convertible until the girls called them into the cabin.

Once inside, Gipson promptly produced a fifth of vodka while Apache pulled four Cokes from the refrigerator. Deckard downed a shot of the vodka and was contemplating another, but Marlene was coaxing him into the bedroom. She shut and locked the bedroom door behind them. They kissed, and the airman began peeling off her clothes. One of them turned out the light.

Gipson and Apache proceeded more awkwardly. They had barely met, and by his own admission, Gipson wasn't "very good socially." So, alone with Apache in a remote cabin deep in the Scrub, he sat opposite her at the kitchenette table and waited for her to "make the first move."

Only they weren't alone. Just after eleven p.m., in Gipson's words, "all hell broke loose." The door of the cabin burst open, and Andy Groves burst in, with Eustis police officer David Shelley behind him.

"Run!" Apache yelled to Gipson.

Rushing into the cabin behind the two policemen, Sheriff McCall and Deputy Griffin paid no heed to Apache or the alarmed Gipson. With his pistol drawn, McCall lowered his shoulder and busted through the bedroom door. Marlene Taylor screamed. Trying to cover herself, she'd managed to sit up in the bed when McCall smashed her over the head with his .38 caliber Smith & Wesson. Then, turning to Deckard, he bashed the airman across the right side of his forehead. He didn't stop there. With Deckard, like Marlene, bleeding profusely from the head wound, McCall pistol-whipped the black man repeatedly with the butt of his gun until Deckard blacked out.

Gipson, who'd watched the assault from the kitchen, would later say, "This was a real beating." Griffin, too, would recall McCall's blind rage. "Something in Willis snapped when he saw those two in his bed," he said.

By Griffin's account, McCall continued to batter Deckard even after he'd fallen unconscious. Marlene, screaming and crying, was begging the sheriff to stop. Griffin, himself frightened, reached out to grab McCall's arm. "You're going to kill him," he shouted.

McCall straightened up, but he'd not finished with the fornicators. He ordered Marlene to lie down beside Deckard so that Griffin could get some photographs. "We were clean as a white fish," Deckard said. "We did not have on a stitch." The officers kept their guns trained on the couple. Deputy Sewell handed Griffin some flashbulbs, and McCall struck Deckard's head a few more times to turn the airman's face toward the camera. Griffin snapped the photos. Her head resting back against the wall, her blond hair and pale face dripping with blood, her eyes dazed, Marlene had intertwined her legs with Deckard's, while he lay flat on his back, out cold. The flashbulbs popped; the lawmen leered.

When Deckard regained consciousness, McCall ordered the two

lovers—both of them "a bloody mess"—to get dressed and then marched them into the kitchen. There they joined Apache and Gipson, who had been searched and had readily assured the officers, "I'm not going anywhere." Nonetheless, Groves and Shelley, their guns drawn, hovered over him and Apache.

Marlene put her head under the kitchen faucet and turned on the cold water to wash the blood from her hair. Then, with a dishcloth, she attempted to stop the bleeding on Deckard's head. McCall rasped, "Look at that nigger lover helping the nigger."

At a signal from McCall, Shelley, with Gipson in tow, followed the sheriff outside the cabin, where Sewell was waiting. Inside the cabin, Deckard and the others could hear Gipson pleading helplessly with the three lawmen. "Don't . . . Please don't," he begged, but his words fell on ears deaf to the cries of a black man.

"Don't you know any better than to go out with white women?" McCall shouted. Gipson tried to answer, tried to explain that he hadn't done anything wrong, that he hadn't broken any laws, as Shelley struck him with his long-handled flashlight, and McCall—all the while growling, "Don't try to hit me, nigger!"—started swinging his gun at Gipson's head with such abandon that he lost his grip and it went flying with enough force to dent the cabin. Gipson lay sprawled in the dirt and pine needles while Shelley, merciless with his flashlight, continued to bludgeon him.

"Don't kill him!" Apache begged them. "He did not do anything!"

McCall did not reply but he paused, first to catch his breath and then to retrieve his gun. He ordered Deckard, who had regained consciousness, out of the cabin.

"Let's kill these niggers and throw them to the alligators," McCall suggested.

"No," one officer objected, figuring it wasn't worth the trouble it would cause, and asked McCall if they should handcuff the men.

After waving the officers away, the sheriff moved in close to Deckard.

"Run, nigger. Run," he dared the battered airman. "I want to get in some target practice."

Despite the numerous blows to his head, Deckard was clear-minded enough to sense the danger. "I believe the Big Man was trying to give us a chance to run so he could shoot us," he later asserted.

Bloodied and beaten, the two men were cuffed and shoved into the backseat of Gipson's Pontiac. With Evvie Griffin at the wheel and Andy Groves riding shotgun, they headed back to the Lake County jail, where Deckard and Gipson were to be arraigned on moral charges, fornication, and whatever else McCall decided they might be guilty of. Groves, though, had an idea of his own. A few minutes into the drive, he pointed to a cut on the road up ahead. Leaning in toward Griffin, he whispered, "If you run up there on that cut, I'll kill 'em."

Not in this car, you ain't goin' to, Griffin said to himself, and ignoring the police chief, he drove past the cut.

In Tavares, the court charged Maxie Deckard with illegal cohabitation and Gipson with vagrancy. Both were also charged with resisting arrest. They were confined in the Lake County jail, with bail set at a thousand dollars. They received no medical treatment for their wounds.

Only with the intervention of the Air Force were the accused airmen able to arrange bond. Escorted by the Air Police, who were armed with machine guns, as well as by troopers from the Florida Highway Patrol, they exited the Lake County Courthouse, where a crowd of angry whites was quickly gathering. The charges had been reduced to "obstructing justice," and the airmen were banned from the state.

Apache Brown escaped both injury and charges, but Marlene Taylor was charged with illegal cohabitation and denied the right to counsel. The following week the *Daily Commercial* published a closely cropped photo of her bloodied face. The accompanying article accused the Lake County sheriff's office of not only failing to safeguard pertinent crime-related evidence but also allowing nude photos to be widely circulated around Lake County for "pornographic purposes." Mabel Norris Reese joined the Leesburg paper in calling for Governor Collins to suspend McCall from office, pending a full investigation of the cabin arrests and the photographs. When McCall learned that Apache had become something of a local "celebrity" and was talking freely about the incident around Lake County, he tracked her down, handed her one hundred dollars, and personally delivered a warning: "Keep your mouth shut."

Evvie Griffin knew who was responsible for circulating the photos. "I took the damned pictures," he'd later admit, but it was Deputy James Yates who had "borrowed" the prints from him and distributed them countywide. Except Yates had not done it solely for the pornographic purposes that the *Daily Commercial* decried. "It was a message to white women," Griffin said, and the message was, "Don't fool around with niggers in Lake County."

By then the ACLU was calling for an investigation, and within days the FBI had dispatched agents to Lake County—Willis McCall was, by the fall of 1956, no stranger to J. Edgar Hoover. It was time for the sheriff to pay Marlene Taylor a visit. He needed her to corroborate a version— his version, and the version that policemen and deputies would relate to FBI agents—of what had happened at the cabin in the Big Scrub on the night of October 4. He told Marlene he was sorry that she'd been hit on the head, but it was of course an accident. And it was all because Deckard had "attacked him upon entering the bedroom" and so he'd been forced to hit him with his gun and unfortunately "the blow [had] glanced off Deckard" and had inadvertently struck, and bloodied, Marlene. McCall also persuaded her to voluntarily sign a statement that "she did not want to see any newspaper people or reporters while she was in jail as she did not want to cause any embarrassment to her family."

Over the next few days, FBI agents interviewed everyone present at the Big Scrub cabin on October 4. The statements of the law enforcement officers varied little. Their accounts included descriptions of two strong, young black men "wrestling" for guns and engaging in a "hell of a fight" with the sheriff in their attempts at "resisting arrest." None of the lawmen was willing to provide a signed statement, however, the FBI noted. (Because "that was all bullshit," according to Griffin, and as he remembered it, the two airmen never resisted arrest—"They were meek.")

As for the photographs, McCall informed the FBI agents that they "were not available," and he "refused to furnish any copies or negatives."

The FBI withdrew. The photographs disappeared from public scrutiny. The story faded into yesterday's news. McCall was elected to a fourth straight term as sheriff. As his next-door neighbor, J. E. Peacock, observed, "It gets under a Florida Cracker's skin to observe such frequent tactics as have been resorted to in efforts to break down the morale and efficiency of a man of Sheriff McCall's caliber. It seems that his County has been singled out from time to time for the ravages of negroes upon white women and girls, and because of his efficiency and untiring efforts, he has likewise been singled out as a target for those opposed to genuine law enforcement."

Groveland, Big Scrub, and now Okahumpka—the rape of Blanche Knowles was exactly the kind of crime Mabel would have expected the sheriff to close, and Oldham to prosecute, swiftly—all the more so as it afforded them the opportunity to pack off to the electric chair the nephew of one of the most hated men in Florida. Yet both the sheriff's department and the state attorney's office had gone silent, and silent they remained for the time being.

To Mabel, it made no sense.

Frampy Cope Snack Bar in Okahumpka's North Quarters

CHAPTER FIVE

Sensational Lies

THREE DAYS AFTER THE RAPE of Blanche Knowles, with Melvin Hawkins Jr. named as the lead suspect, and Sam Wiley Odom still be- behind bars at the Lake County jail, Sheriff Willis McCall and Deputy James Yates returned to Okahumpka. Their investigation was about to take a curious turn. Yates parked his cruiser at the end of Bugg Spring Road, by a one-story house once owned by a Confederate officer, and knocked on the door. The man who answered was Charles Morhart, a thin and stylish forty-nine-year-old former dental professor who had moved from Virginia to help his sister, Augusta Branham, manage the family citrus grove after the death of her husband.

In rural Lake County, Charles Morhart had been living a quiet if slightly eccentric life as "an asexual bachelor" in this house adjacent to his sister's, just off the Knowles's property. Morhart's nephew, Joseph Branham III, remembered him as "Unkie," "a jovial intellectual who loved boating." Unkie was a magnet for women, "but he didn't seem very interested in them."

The Branhams, like everyone else in Okahumpka, were aware that

Bubba Hawkins was being held for the rape of Blanche Knowles, so they were surprised when McCall and Yates showed up at Bugg Spring to ask questions about Morhart's whereabouts on the night of December 17. "They were very interested in Charles," Joseph recalled, and especially interested in his shoes—"He wore these Navy Last shoes, with no treads and flat soles, that he would buy at Getzel's Department Store in Leesburg." As he had done with Bubba Hawkins, Yates confiscated the shoes.

Charles Morhart may have been eccentric by Lake County standards, but he was also well-to-do and well connected. He knew a lawyer in Leesburg named P. C. Gorman, who moved in the same circles as the men of the Leesburg Quarterback Club. Gorman also sat on the board of the Citizens National Bank of Leesburg with Joe Knowles and Red Robinson, the Knowles family attorney. Telephone calls were made and conversations ensued in Tavares. In short order, Morhart's shoes were returned, with an apology for the "misunderstanding."

On Sunday evening, December 22, after revisiting the crime scene, deputies Yates and Campbell stopped at the small, tin-roofed Cracker house on Bay Avenue where the Daniels family lived, just a few hundred yards west of the Knowles and Branham-Morhart homes. They told Charles and Pearl that they would like to talk to their son, Jesse. Pearl and Charles knew that Mrs. Knowles had said she'd been raped by a Negro and that one of the Hawkins boys was being held for the crime. So they didn't see how Jesse, who'd learned of the rape only the morning after it occurred, could be of any help to the deputies, not to mention, as Pearl tried to explain, Jesse's "condition," which hindered his mental faculties.

Nevertheless, Pearl invited the deputies inside. On the wall in the small living room hung a framed "God Bless Our Home," and a school photograph of Jesse at eight, all smiles. It was Pearl's favorite picture of her only child, taken just before the first of his three frightening bouts with rheumatic fever.

As it happened, Jesse himself was at home, and Yates told Pearl that he wanted to take her boy to Tavares, to "ask him a few questions."

The request startled Pearl and Charles, but Jesse was not alarmed. "Sure, I'll go. I'm not afraid. I want you to get the right man," he said to Yates. "After all, my mother's a woman."

Yates promised the Danielses he'd bring Jesse back home to them later that night. It proved to be a long night. As the hours passed, increasingly anxious and unable to sleep, Pearl and Charles told themselves that one of the deputies must have taken Jesse to his own home rather than drive the boy out to South Quarters in the middle of the night.

Dawn broke. The worried parents shared a rushed breakfast before driving to the courthouse, where they waited for the sheriff's office to open. And waited. Deputies offered the Danielses little help and no information, but they refused to leave. When state attorney Gordon Oldham arrived, he informed them that there was nothing to implicate Jesse in the crime but that Sheriff McCall "wanted to hold him a little while longer." He also told them that they would not be permitted to visit with their son as long as the authorities were conducting an ongoing investigation.

Helpless and with no knowledge of what their legal rights might be under the circumstances, Charles and Pearl realized that they needed an attorney, but they couldn't afford to hire one. So they did the only thing they could do. They returned to South Quarters, where they continued to wait and to hope Yates would soon make good on his promise to bring Jesse back home to them.

ON DECEMBER 24, Melvin Hawkins Sr. did what he usually did on Christmas Eve: He chopped down a Florida holly and stood it up inside the house, the dangling red berries affording nature's own ornaments. This Christmas season, though, circumstances had cast a pall on any festivities. Melvin was alone in the house.

After being held incommunicado for five days and nights, without a warrant or a hearing, Bubba Hawkins had finally been released by the Lake County deputies. To his family's relief, he appeared to be unharmed. He related how, despite the efforts of McCall and his deputies to persuade him to confess to the rape of Blanche Knowles, he had refused; he recounted how they'd even driven him to Tampa to take a lie detector test. "They didn't hurt me," Bubba said. "Just called me a nigger." But with the story still hanging in the air, unresolved, that a local white woman had been raped by a young black man, and with fears of vigilantism still running high in the Quarters, the family had thought it wise for Melvin Sr.'s wife, Alice, and the children—including Bubba—to decamp to Alice's sister's home in Leesburg until the situation in Okahumpka quieted down.

Perhaps the phone call from the governor to Oldham had protected Bubba against a beating or worse. But for Mabel, it fell far short of the dedicated investigation into the boy's detention that the sheriff's action seemed to call for. She accused the governor of "fence straddling" and suggested that he was "either too hasty in obtaining the facts; misinformed of them, or he, like so many others, has no desire to tangle with Willis McCall." Upon releasing the boy to his parents, she noted, McCall had said nothing to exonerate him, even though such incidents "are most damaging to race relations." She expressed disappointment in the governor's inaction, given his frequently declared "promises that he will not be over in a corner—washing his hands of it all."

Mabel tracked down Alice Hawkins shortly after her son's release. Alice refused to discuss his whereabouts, but she did state that he would not be returning to Okahumpka anytime soon. "I know my boy couldn't have had anything to do with it," she said. "He was here with me all evening—we were popping corn. He's a good boy who would like very much to go to college and make something of himself."

Bubba Hawkins made it home to his family for Christmas, but Sam Wiley Odom was not so fortunate. Evidently the Lake County Sheriff's

Department wasn't quite done with the brooding, husky teenager from North Quarters. Yates held him a few more days, and then, without fanfare, the last black suspect in Blanche Knowles's rape walked free.

PEARL AND CHARLES DANIELS spent a sad Christmas Day in Okahumpka. Again they had been rebuffed by the sheriff's department. "I packed all of his Christmas presents and went to the jail but they wouldn't let me in," Pearl told Mabel in an interview for the *Topic*. The next day, Pearl tried yet again, this time with Charles; they brought clean clothes for Jesse, and Pearl had baked a batch of his favorite cookies. She said the clerk first hesitated, and then relented. "Well, I want to do the right thing," he'd said, and led the Danielses upstairs to the jailer's office. They'd been waiting there for over an hour when Willis McCall spotted them. Shaking, as if "trying to get his composure," the sheriff bellowed, "Remember what I told you yesterday—that you wouldn't see that boy? Well, that still goes!"

The Danielses' plight worsened, quickly. With McCall thwarting them at every turn, they placed all their hope in Yates's decency in his promise to bring Jesse back home. Not so decently, the deputy invaded their home. While they were attempting to visit their son in Tavares, Yates was driving back to Okahumpka. When he discovered that no one was home at the Daniels house, he decided, without a warrant, to step inside and have a look around. Inside Jesse's room, the boy's guitar and a pair of undershorts caught the deputy's attention.

On Saturday, December 28, at the sheriff's office, McCall and the state attorney held a hastily assembled press conference at which Oldham announced that they were now holding a nineteen-year-old white youth for the rape of the Okahumpka housewife ten days earlier. Jesse Daniels had confessed to the crime, McCall said, and Melvin "Bubba" Hawkins, along with the other twenty-two black suspects, had thus been "cleared of all suspicion." As for earlier reports that the attacker was a Negro—which had led to the detainment of the nearly two dozen black men—Oldham explained that because the house was dark at the time of the incident, the victim had been unable to discern the features and skin color of her attacker.

"We haven't left many stones unturned, I don't think," the sheriff broke in, and he assured the reporters that they had the right man in Jesse Daniels, as the boy had in fact confessed to the crime. He confirmed that Daniels had no criminal record and that he was "mentally retarded"; yet, reporters noted, McCall "would not disclose what led to the arrest of the young citrus worker."

"What of the diamond-shaped heel print?" asked one reporter, and another followed up with, "What about the shorts found at the scene?" The undershorts and heel print, they'd been previously told, provided evidence that linked Bubba Hawkins conclusively to the crime.

McCall was dismissive of any inconsistencies; he simply assumed the attitude, Mabel wrote, "that the case was closed." While he acknowledged that, yes, Daniels was the only white man among the twenty-three suspects, he pointed out that Daniels was also "the first man to be charged." And the right man: "We've been working day and night on this case," McCall said, and it was now solved. Jesse Daniels was being held without bond, and the sheriff was taking no more questions.

Immediately after the press conference, McCall drove to Okahumpka to inform Jesse's parents that their son had confessed to the rape of Blanche Knowles.

Pearl went numb with the news. Choking back tears, she told the sheriff, "He couldn't be guilty."

"He's guilty all right," McCall replied. "Why, he even told me the color of the rug on the staircase going up to the bedroom. And he described the furniture in the bedroom."

At that, Charles spoke up. "Look here, Sheriff," he said. "This thing was supposed to have happened in complete darkness. You said because it was dark she couldn't tell whether it was a Negro or a white man. How could my boy say what color the rug was?"

McCall merely shrugged at the logic, and then suggested that maybe Jesse had "imagined" the color of the rug after seeing a picture in a magazine—reasoning, or lack of it, that only confused Pearl more, as did his admonition that Pearl and Charles not discuss the "rug business" with anyone. "The newspapers grab hold of it and make headlines this big," McCall said, extending his hands wide, Pearl recalled, like a "bragging fisherman."

Rather than argue the point with the sheriff, Pearl begged that he let her visit Jesse, who had now been separated from his family for four days and five nights. She prayed that the deputies, aware of his condition, were protecting him while he was in their custody, but she also knew the juvenile ward where he was being held was not a safe place for a boy with Jesse's mental disability and emotional vulnerabilities.

She'd learned of the conditions suffered by juvenile offenders from Mabel, who earlier in the year had toured the boys' detention ward at the Lake County jail with her friend county judge W. Troy Hall Jr. "Lad in the Dungeon" was the headline to her exposé of the conditions under which juvenile offenders were being held. It described in painful detail five cases of "misguided humanity lolling in dreary cells," one of them a sixteen-year-old boy in solitary confinement. He "peered from out of appalling darkness . . . in a cell with no light, no window, and with precious little air available through the inch-square grill work of the great door to the cell." Convicted and jailed for auto theft, the boy had been locked in the dungeon for "extra punishment" after he'd disobeyed a jailer's command. He was badly in need of a haircut, and standing dazed beside the toilet in a urine-stenched corner of the cell, he looked "almost like something out of *Les Misérables*"—or, as Judge Hall remarked, "like the dark ages. That's the way they used to treat people hundreds of years ago."

The cell next to the "dungeon" confined a grown man who'd been judged to be insane and was awaiting an open bed at Chattahoochee, the notorious state mental hospital up in Florida's Panhandle. All night long he'd run water at full force into the basin of the cell's tiny sink, the boy told Mabel, and he'd make "strange noises" that rattled the boy so badly he couldn't sleep. "I feel like I'm going crazy in here," he said. One of the juvenile counselors had asked a deputy if the boy could be moved to another cell. "Let him sweat it out in there," was the deputy's response.

Judge Hall was in the process of explaining to Mabel that Florida wasn't supposed to even have windowless "sweat boxes" anymore, as they'd been deemed inhumane, when their tour was interrupted by the sudden appearance of Sheriff McCall. Having been tipped off by one of the jailers that his nemesis had gained access to the juvenile ward, he demanded to know how Mabel had gotten admittance. Hall replied for her; she'd asked him, he said, adding, "Someone's got to let people know about it."

In this moment of standoff, it must have struck them both, sheriff and judge, how much their long relationship had deteriorated. They'd been boyhood friends, and together they'd grown into manhood. It was Hall who'd come immediately to the sheriff's defense after the shooting of the two Groveland boys, and Hall who'd helped craft the statement, delivered to the press and the FBI, positing that the action taken by the sheriff had been one of self-defense, as the two prisoners had jumped him in an attempt at escape. Hall, too, had been in charge of the coroner's inquest that cleared McCall of any wrongdoing. Since then, however, like Jesse Hunter and Mabel herself, Hall had been increasingly offended by McCall's displays of racism and violence, and he was no longer willing to defend or enable the sheriff's brutality. The former friends had been clashing publicly and politically for the past six years, although the electorate continued to embrace both of them. (Hall liked to tell the story of a Lake County man who had informed him that he'd voted for both McCall and Hall: "I voted for Willis to protect us from the niggers. I voted for you to protect us from Willis.")

Turning his gaze away from the judge, McCall focused his wrath on Mabel. "The judge brought you here," he spluttered, "but you're not going any further. I'm not showing you anything. You wouldn't tell the truth. You just tell sensational lies." And he blocked their progress. He could not, however, prevent Hall from disclosing to Mabel that the five white teens in the ward had been jailed weeks earlier on charges ranging from auto theft to rape—no effort was made to separate first-time or minor offenders from serious criminals—and were still awaiting indictment. As for the black juveniles, they "could not be seen," Mabel had written, "because they are in with adult prisoners, and adults are under the complete jurisdiction of the sheriff."

Mabel's exposé of the failings inside the county jail, coupled with a statement from Governor Collins regarding the "deplorable conditions" in which juvenile offenders were being held, had prompted the Lake County Children's Committee to call an emergency session. But McCall had played the victim, and played the committee, asserting that some people cared more about conditions in the jail than they did about the safety of their sheriff. So it was that conditions on the ward remained as they had long been, and since Florida law defined offenders under the age of twenty-one as minors, it was here that white, nineteen-year-old Jesse Daniels was now being held for rape.

McCall decided to honor the Danielses' request for a visit, and they followed him back to Tavares. "You can see him for just one minute," the sheriff advised them as they stepped inside the courthouse elevator. "But I warn you," he added, "you can't discuss the case with him. Not one word. Do you understand?" Pearl nodded.

As they approached the cells, Pearl spotted her son almost immediately. From behind bars, Jesse "looked at us as if we were strangers."

Pearl leaned close. "Son, I hate to see you here so bad," she said. Jesse simply stared at her.

"Kiss me, Jesse," she said again, and slowly, "like someone in a trance," the boy moved forward and brushed his lips against Pearl's face. Reaching through the bars, she caressed his face, trying to give him assurance with her hands and her voice. "It's all right, son. We love you . . . and we believe you."

That motherly avowal spurred the vigilant McCall to action. He grabbed Pearl's arm and wrenched her backward so fiercely that he nearly tossed her to the floor. "That does it! That's it!" he squalled. "You broke your promise. Now you'll never see him again!"

As he hustled the Danielses from the ward, Pearl managed a glance back at her boy, who looked to be numb with fear.

A news story in the *Daily Commercial* trumpeted Jesse's arrest with the headline "Feeble-Minded Boy, 19, Held in Assault Case," while other stories noted the strange turn of events in Lake County. "A white laborer has been arrested and formally charged in a rape case here which saw a colored youth held incommunicado for five days, shattering the 'colored-man-did-it' tale of the alleged victim," read one story, which also noted the governor's intervention on behalf of Melvin Hawkins. Black newspapers ran headlines that reflected their perplexity, and that of their readers: "Victim Says 'Negro Did It,' but White Man Admits Florida Assault."

A prominent Okahumpka man volunteered to set up a Jesse Daniels Defense Fund and to act as its treasurer. In only a few days Pearl received numerous one- and five-dollar donations from blacks and whites alike. On Mabel's advice, Pearl traveled thirty miles west to Inverness, in nearby Citrus County, where she introduced herself to George Scofield, a well-respected criminal attorney affectionately known around central Florida as the Colonel. Scofield agreed to do a preliminary investigation into the case on retainer, which Pearl could cover with the defense fund donations, but she would have to raise additional money if he was to undertake Jesse's legal defense.

When news of the defense fund reached the sheriff's department, Mc-Call invited the acting treasurer to his office and played him a recording of Jesse's confession. The man withdrew his support for the fund.

To bolster the case for Jesse's defense, Pearl canvassed South and North Quarters for signatures to an affidavit declaring that Jesse was "completely harmless": that he had played with girls in the neighborhood for years and had demonstrated "no interest in sex at all." Thirty-two residents signed, including a man who ran a filling station in Leesburg and had been fired, Pearl said, for maintaining Jesse's innocence.

In his initial investigation of Jesse's case, George Scofield traveled to Tavares, where McCall played him the recording of Jesse's confession. Then he told Pearl that he estimated his fee for representing Jesse would be two thousand dollars—"not exorbitant for such capital cases," as Mabel noted, but an amount that floored Pearl. As it was, the Danielses were barely scraping by on Charles's pension of one hundred dollars a month, plus whatever extra money Pearl and Jesse might bring in. Scofield understood, but, as he apologetically explained, he could not mount an adequate defense in what would be a time-consuming death-penalty case without sufficient funds. He was able to offer Pearl one bit of good news, though: He had been able to convince McCall to permit her another visit with her son. He advised her to go as soon as possible, as Jesse was in a "critical" situation at the jail.

When Pearl tried to arrange the visit, however, McCall refused to honor his word to Scofield.

By early January, with Jesse's grand jury appearance approaching, desperation had taken up residence in the Daniels home. On Mabel's advice, Pearl appealed to Collins.

"Governor Collins," Pearl wrote, "my son is 19 years old, true—but in many ways he is like a little boy . . . who depends on us to cover him during the night, to come wake him from his nightmares." That a boy with Jesse's manifest disabilities should have suffered McCall's middle-of-the-night interrogation and relentless pressure tactics to force him to "confess to a lie" was tantamount to "brain-washing," she asserted. She herself had had a taste of the sheriff's mode of intimidation on her one brief visit with Jesse. "Am I supposed to be manhandled by him?" she asked the governor. "What law is that, Sir?"

Pearl's letter mentioned as well that Mrs. Knowles had originally claimed she'd been raped by a Negro; and that indeed the bloodhounds had led deputies to North Quarters—not to South Quarters, let alone to the Daniels house. And what had the Daniels family been doing there, on the night of the rape? They'd watched the *Late Show* on television, and at about 1:20 a.m., Pearl had put Jesse to bed. He slept in the same room as Charles, who, due to his heart condition, slept lightly, often waking four or five times a night, and was "thus able to hear the youth in the night," should Jesse be disturbed by bad dreams. Jesse simply could not have left the room without Charles knowing it, Pearl maintained. Nor was he capable of the capital crime of which he had been accused. "Gov. Collins, to do such a thing would take a very clear mind to plan and perform," she wrote. How would a boy with Jesse's mental deficiencies be able to find out where Blanche's "business-man husband would be, or how to get out of his house, go a quarter of a mile, break in and commit such and return home without some noise?" She closed by imploring Collins, "In the mercy of God, and you as a father, will you please help my boy?"

Mabel incorporated quotations from the letter in a *Topic* news story describing how deputies had "descended on Jesse Daniels, the village half-wit," and calling for an investigation into the case. The story did not please McCall, who continued to deny the Danielses access to their son and accused Mabel of authoring the letter herself but incorporating some misspellings to make it appear that the letter had been written by Pearl.

Nor was Mabel's cozy relationship with Hall lost on McCall, or on Oldham. In all likelihood she was sharing with the judge the ongoing developments in the Danielses' situation, and now she had intervened with him to postpone Jesse's preliminary hearing until Hall returned from an upcoming trip to Tallahassee. The postponement, Mabel figured, would afford Pearl and Charles at least a bit more time to secure funds for their boy's defense.

The day Hall left for Tallahassee, Oldham, forgoing a preliminary hearing, took the case directly to Judge Truman Futch and requested that a special grand jury be impaneled to hear the case. Futch complied. The end run staggered even Mabel. She got in touch with Hall, who was furious but not surprised. The case had been snatched from his hands.

Pearl contacted Oldham's office and pleaded with the state attorney that she and her husband be allowed a visit with their son. Oldham conceded that there was no reason why they shouldn't be, but said that only the sheriff could grant the request. A call to Judge Hall elicited sympathy, and a similar deferral to the sheriff. So Pearl returned to Tavares and begged McCall to permit her a visit. Again, the sheriff denied her.

She was standing on the sidewalk outside the courthouse, in tears, when from somewhere above her a painfully familiar voice called out.

"Mommie, are you coming to see me today?"

From the barred window of his cell in the juvenile quarters on the fourth floor of the courthouse, Jesse had spotted his mother on the sidewalk below. Pearl called back to him. She tried to assure him that she would see him soon and that everything would be fine.

"Mommie, I want to tell you something," Jesse said. "I want to tell you what the man did to me."

A few days later, on the morning of January 9, Jesse Daniels was "hustled before the grand jury," as Mabel put it. Joe Knowles arrived with his wife, and both were reported to be "in the courthouse but not in the courtroom" during the selection and swearing in of eighteen jurors. In his address to them, Judge Futch stated that the accused was charged with criminal assault and stressed that it was "not within your province to consider the mental condition of the person charged."

Gordon Oldham presented the case and then led several witnesses, including Sheriff McCall, Dr. Durham Young, Deputy Yates, and Blanche Knowles through their testimony. Jesse's recorded confession was entered into evidence and played for the jurors. Waiting in the corridor outside the courtroom before he himself was called to testify, Jesse was able to hear his own voice stammering on McCall's incriminating tape. Called to the witness stand, he stuttered badly as he tried to tell the jury that he was not guilty, but Oldham, in a "lashing kind of voice that would be bruising to a sensitive soul encased in a ten-year-old mind," fired questions at Jesse in such staccato fashion that he became "confused, afraid, and could not explain to them why he was not guilty—could not tell the grim-faced men staring at him why he had made a confession." His brief appearance over, a deputy escorted him back to his cell. In her coverage of the proceedings, Mabel noted that Jesse had appeared before the grand jury "without benefit of an attorney, without even consulting with his parents." He was, she wrote, "literally a ten-year-old facing a potential life and death matter alone."

Shortly thereafter, George Scofield, although he was still not officially representing Jesse, went to see McCall again and managed to persuade him to allow the boy's parents another brief visit. McCall agreed grudgingly, but again, only on their promise not to discuss the case with their son. With a guard in hearing distance, Pearl stiffened when Jesse leaned into her and whispered, "Mama, I'm not guilty." Fearful that their visit would be curtailed, she simply held Jesse close and hushed him with assurances that help would be coming soon, though from what quarter she could not say, as she and Charles could not imagine raising enough money to pay Scofield's fee.

Governor Collins did not respond directly to Pearl's letter, but he did send two investigators to Okahumpka to look into the Daniels case. Pearl and Charles explained to them how Jesse could not have raped Mrs. Knowles on the night of December 17, and how he had been languishing in jail without the benefit of a lawyer. But once again, McCall deployed the recording of Jesse's confession, and that, Mabel reported, "was the last the parents heard from the investigators."

Mabel suspected that little would come from any investigation into the matter. "The powerful sheriff has been investigated by governors before," she noted, "and has always wiggled out of it like Houdini, leaving his victims holding the bag." Indeed, he set out to do some wiggling shortly after the governor's men had quit Lake County. He invited Charles and Pearl to his office.

On their arrival, he sent a deputy to bring Jesse down from the jail upstairs. While they waited, the sheriff cautioned them neither to speak to nor to question their son at any point. Then the session commenced—as "strange in the annals of justice" as any, Mabel reported—and they were forced to witness their son confess again to a capital crime. Throughout the interrogation, McCall guided Jesse with prompts like "Now tell how you did [this]" and "Tell how you did that," as bit by bit he extracted from the "dazed" boy a stuttered admission—"like a parrot speaking"—to the rape. When it was over, Pearl and Charles watched as the deputies removed their helpless son from the sheriff's office.

As they were leaving, McCall warned them not to discuss Jesse's confession with anyone. Pearl thought she knew why. Even orchestrated as it was, there was a key point in the confession that made no sense. McCall's questions had been eliciting from Jesse responses describing how he'd snuck out of his house and walked over to the Knowles house, how he'd taken off his clothes before he'd slashed the screen door and gone upstairs, how he'd lingered for a moment in the doorway of the bedroom, how the woman in the bed had heard a noise and stirred, and then she was awake.

"What did she say?" McCall asked Jesse.

"'Is that you, Joe?'" the boy said.

"And what did you say?" McCall asked next.

"'No, it's me, Jesse Daniels.'"

Pearl could not stop puzzling over that supposed exchange. If Jesse had given Blanche Knowles his name, "why was he not picked up for the crime the next morning?" she wondered. Almost everyone in Okahumpka knew Jesse Daniels—the boy on the bike—including Blanche Knowles herself.

Disregarding McCall's warning, Pearl decided to discuss the whole matter of Jesse's confession with Mabel, who was suitably aghast at the latest goings-on in the sheriff's office, and similarly suspicious.

In a second letter to Governor Collins, Pearl detailed the meeting in the sheriff's office and again questioned the legitimacy of her son's confession. McCall, she was convinced, not only had pressured her son into admitting to acts that he was incapable of committing but also had essentially put the words describing them in Jesse's mouth. "It was given sentence by sentence," she wrote, "exactly like an obedient child reciting his well learned lesson."

Pearl wrote, too, of her visit with Jesse in his jail cell—how he had whispered to her that he was not guilty, and how she had hushed him for fear that the guard would overhear and intervene. Still, he'd managed to whisper a bit more to her. "Someone there," Pearl wrote to Collins, "is telling the poor child he's going to Raiford," to the electric chair. And even as she again hushed him and the guard approached, Jesse had returned to what he'd called down to her in January, on the sidewalk below the courthouse: A man had "done something" to him.

Sheriff Willis V. McCall

CHAPTER SIX

You Will Not Turn Us Down

On January 9, the grand jury in *State of Florida v. Jesse Daniels* handed down a true bill indicting the Okahumpka youth for assault on the grounds that in the early morning hours of December 18, 1957, Jesse Daniels, "with force and arms . . . then and there did ravish and carnally know, by force and against the will of her, the said Blanche Bosanquet Knowles."

After the indictment, McCall continued to torment Jesse's parents by capriciously limiting their visits with him. In a letter to the governor, Pearl said that she knew she had been further antagonizing the sheriff by turning to Collins for help, and that he was punishing her for it: "McCall takes great pleasure in showing his authority over poor folks he thinks cannot fight back, or know their rights." But, she said, "the child needs us." And they needed him. "His father is old and a sick man; he is permanently and totally disabled, and failing very fast. Is it right to allow a spiteful sheriff to refuse this ex-veteran visits with his only child when both lives are so short, and when a wire or call from you could solve the situation?"

Pearl had an additional concern. The sheriff's department, she claimed, was holding as evidence the pair of Jesse's undershorts that Yates had taken from their home several days after the crime. "Is this to further trap an innocent child, or to swap with those found at the assault scene?" In closing, she lamented her and Charles's inability to hire an attorney, despite their efforts. "We are poor but decent, honest, Christian people."

Collins, who had been following the case from Tallahassee, relayed to the press that he had corresponded with the mother of the accused, and had advised her that Lake County would have to provide the Danielses with a lawyer if they could not afford to hire one. The governor's involvement, amplified by Mabel, chagrined county officials. Judge Futch quickly issued two orders: McCall was to have the prisoner in court at ten in the morning on the following Monday, January 20; and Pearl and Charles were to be present to help Futch determine whether Jesse would need court-appointed counsel. When the Danielses appeared as ordered, Jesse was already seated next to McCall, who once again forbade them and Mabel to speak to the boy. Pearl spoke up only to confirm that she and her husband could not afford an attorney.

"You may rest assured that the attorneys appointed by this court will see that your son gets a fair trial," Futch told them. "I am sorry that you did not make the request sooner." Then, in open court, he took aim at Mabel, though not by name. "It is evident from items appearing in the newspapers that you people have been receiving and acting upon poor and dangerous advice," Futch said. "It is equally evident that whoever has been advising you is either ignorant on the matters where they have advised you or else that they have deliberately misinformed you." He found it regrettable that Pearl should have allowed her letter to Collins to be published, and he suggested that the local press was interested only in discrediting his court. Justice, he opined, was more often reached "by cooperation on the part of the State and the defendant, than by bickering and recrimination."

At the hearing's end, when Futch had left the chambers, Pearl rushed toward Jesse in the hope of offering him some comfort, but McCall efficiently blocked her. Then he hustled Jesse into the hallway and back up to the jail.

Still, even the sheriff could not quell the Danielses' optimism when they left the court. Finally, a lawyer would be fighting on behalf of their son. Mabel, however, was furious. She headed straight for her office and typed a letter to Futch. In it, she invoked, among other contentious cases in which they had been involved over the years, the Groveland and Platt cases and the memory of their late mutual friend Jesse Hunter:

> *Dear Judge Futch,*
>
> *One of the cardinal rules of newspaper work drilled into me as a "cub" reporter was: "Be sure you are right, then go ahead." Since we all know it is most often difficult determining "beyond a reasonable doubt" what is absolutely right, I have made my own maxim. It is, "Be on the side of right, then go ahead."*
>
> *This was my motivation in the Platt case; it is the rule I try earnestly to follow as best my conscience can direct me in all matters. That is why I remain poor, I guess.*
>
> *I certainly did not relish the idea of so soon having another Platt case. I would prefer to coast awhile. However, my interest in law and justice is deep-rooted, and it certainly did not die when I was involved in such [matters] as . . . the harassment of defenseless people. Nor could it die when I felt another was working even harder than I to uphold justice and to be on the side of right. I am most regretful now that the one who so helped me in that case—and so polished the armor of justice—is not here now to assist me.*
>
> *Your comments in the courtroom this morning cannot be interpreted any other way than as a slap at me. But believe me,*

*I am not angered over it, unjust as it was in light of the Platt case
defense, and in light of my statement to you last Friday that I did
not get the mother to write to the governor. I knew only that she
said she "thought" she would write the governor. I did not urge her
to do so, I did not ask for a copy. I knew nothing of it until the
copy came to me in the mail.*

I treated it as the news it was.

*As for other advice to the family, I have given them none
concerning your court other than to say I felt they must trust you.
I was gratified then this morning when I heard Mrs. Daniels say
to you, "We trust you."*

I do too.

Cordially,

Mabel Norris Reese

Mabel soon had reason to think that her trust might have been misplaced. Within days, Futch announced that he was appointing the highly
experienced criminal attorney Archie Patterson "Sam" Buie as counsel
for Jesse Daniels. A graduate of the University of Florida, Buie had attained some celebrity as the star end on the football team, which he cap-
tained in the 1912–1913 season—the first full season that the team took
to the field as the Florida Gators. He had begun his law career as a prosecutor after serving in the National Guard during World War I. He had
been elected to the office of state attorney for the Fifth Judicial Circuit,
then briefly served in the state assembly before returning to his prosecutorial roots. He had been Jesse Hunter's assistant until 1952 and had replaced Hunter as state attorney upon his retirement. Buie's relationship
with Hunter had ended badly, though. As assistant prosecutor in the
Groveland case, he had taken issue with Hunter's budding friendship
with Mabel, especially when Hunter, like Mabel, turned on McCall for
shooting the prisoners. (Buie, like Troy Hall, had helped the sheriff with

his statement to the FBI, claiming the shooting was in self-defense.) The rift had widened further when Hunter, having by then retired, wrote to Collins to express his change of heart regarding Walter Irvin's guilt. When the letter was made public, Buie, then state attorney, wrote a letter of his own, urging the governor to issue Irvin's death warrant and "get rid of this case once and for all." To sully Hunter's reputation, Buie conveyed to an NAACP official in Ocala a scandalous tale that implicated Hunter in a conspiracy with McCall to execute the two Groveland Boys, but when the story reached Thurgood Marshall, he recognized it for what it was: Buie's attempt to smear Hunter at McCall's bidding.

The last major case of Sam Buie's prosecutorial career had been eerily reminiscent of the Emmett Till lynching the year before. On October 27, 1956, Jesse Woods, a thirty-nine-year-old farm laborer and a GI, was standing outside an A&P grocery store in Wildwood, a dozen or so miles west of Leesburg in Sumter County, when he allegedly called out, "Hello, baby," to a white schoolteacher. He was arrested on a drunk-and-disorderly charge. Later that evening, he disappeared from his cell. A broken lock on the front door of the unattended jail, an overturned bunk, and a trail of blood indicated that a mob had carried him off, but the Sumter County sheriff claimed he had "not a lead in the world" to begin an investigation. Many feared the incident would meet, as the *St. Petersburg Times* observed, "the dead-end fate of the Mississippi Till case."

"I believe they done killed him up," said the seventy-one-year-old father of Jesse Woods. A few days later, bloody clothing belonging to Woods was discovered in a field, and investigators from the Florida Sheriffs Bureau began dragging Lake Deacon for a body, to no avail. FBI agents soon arrived, but they, like local law enforcement, made little progress. Ignoring the advice to "stay out of the little towns," Robert Saunders from the NAACP in Tampa arrived to a "chilling" atmosphere in Wildwood, where the streets were deserted and local blacks were terrified of talking to authorities. Winning the community's trust, Saunders was led to a fishing camp in the Panhandle where he'd been told Jesse Woods could be found. Relatives at the camp confirmed that a mob of shotgun-toting young white men had abducted Woods from the Wildwood jail, forced him into a car, and driven him to a wooded area, where they'd severely beaten him and left him for dead. Woods, however, had regained consciousness, and, after hiding in a sugarcane patch, he managed to crawl to the edge of a dirt road, where, in a stroke of good fortune, he was discovered by his uncle on his way to work. The uncle rolled Woods into a rug, put him in the back of the car, and drove him north to a house where he could safely recuperate. By the time Saunders arrived there, Woods had been moved to a still more remote location in Alabama, just above the Florida state line.

Saunders notified the FBI, which placed Woods into protective custody in the state prison at Raiford. Woods claimed that he'd never said anything to the schoolteacher. Nor did he recognize his assailants, he said, as he had been ordered to keep his head down during the entire ordeal. Within days, the Florida Sheriffs Bureau, with assistance from the FBI, cracked the case, and arrested nine men for the abduction and beating of Jesse Woods. All nine pleaded not guilty, and a trial date for what became known as the "Hello Baby" case was set, with Truman Futch presiding, Sam Buie leading the prosecution, and George Scofield representing the accused. However, key witnesses, despite their previous statements identifying the abductors, were reluctant to repeat their testimony on the stand. Buie claimed ignorance as to why the witnesses had changed their story, then refused to allow a statement that the Sheriffs Bureau had taken from a defendant who had admitted to being present at the abduction; the case collapsed. Futch directed the all-white jury to acquit all of the defendants, declaring that the state "had failed to present sufficient evidence for conviction." He was careful, though, not to cast aspersions on Buie, as he might be accused of protecting young white citizens who had "never been in trouble before" by failing to fight for their convictions. In fact, Futch told the jury, he had never seen a case "where a state's attorney worked harder, more sincerely, and at the same time under greater difficulties and against greater odds." Instead, Futch placed the blame on the Florida Sheriffs Bureau, stating there had been "no excuse for them to move in and take over the case," rather than assist the Sumter County sheriff. The defendants shook hands with the jurors, then posed, smiling, for a picture in the courtroom. They told reporters they intended to seek an apology from the bureau.

After Buie had served out his term as state attorney, he announced his upcoming retirement and in effect passed the prosecutor's baton to Oldham, who was elected state attorney in 1956. Buie had barely begun his retirement when he received a telephone call from Futch asking him to take on one last case.

On January 26, Buie drove from his home in nearby Ocala to the courthouse in Tavares, there to assume his entirely new role as public defender. Oldham briefed his friend and former boss on the case, and McCall supplied him with a copy of Jesse's confession. Buie was then escorted up to the juvenile ward.

The first words he spoke to Jesse were: "Why'd you do it, boy?"

"I'm not guilty!" Jesse stammered.

"You have to be guilty," Buie said. "You confessed, didn't you?"

Buie introduced himself to Pearl and Charles. He promised them that he would spare Jesse the electric chair—never mind that rape in Florida was a capital crime carrying a mandatory death sentence. He spoke confidently of his long relationships with Oldham and Futch. He confided that in court he would often "signal" to the judge the outcome he desired. "Not one of my clients has burned yet," Buie said. "We may get this one off with life."

It did not then occur to the Danielses that all of Buie's experience as state attorney was prosecutorial and that his reputation in capital cases had been built on sending defendants to the electric chair. Still, Pearl did not lose hope that their court-appointed attorney would somehow rectify the court's colossal mistake. She and Charles resolved to put their trust in Sam Buie. They had no other choice.

Three days later, Futch ordered McCall to have Jesse Daniels transported to the State Hospital for the Insane at Chattahoochee, where he was to undergo evaluation by two "disinterested qualified experts," Dr. J. T. Benbow and Dr. J. B. O'Connor. Citing "reasonable ground to believe that the defendant is insane," Futch ordered that Jesse be detained there for observation "until such time as said experts shall determine said defendant's mental condition and notify this Court of their findings."

If Sam Buie's initial tack as defense counsel for Jesse Daniels was perplexing—to confront the boy with his alleged confession, then to assure the parents he could spare their son the electric chair by negotiating a life sentence—Buie's next move was beyond puzzling. In a letter to the two doctors at Chattahoochee, Buie in essence framed the case against his client by gently affirming his expectation that Jesse Daniels be found insane and held indefinitely at the hospital. Having been imposed upon by their "mutual friend," Buie humbly acknowledged that he was now in turn "imposing on two of my mutual friends, you two gentlemen." Then he told them why: "I know that you will not turn us down."

Buie informed the psychiatrists that he had found Jesse to possess the mental functioning of a six-year-old. And while he did not believe Jesse was insane "in the strict sense of the word," he did consider him so "within the meaning of the statute," and added that he therefore could not see how Jesse could advise, consult, or assist in the preparation of his defense.

With the letter, Buie enclosed a copy of Jesse's alleged confession. Although he acknowledged that his client denied his guilt, he declared that he himself had no doubt that Jesse was the perpetrator, citing the confession's inclusion of details that no one else could have known, "even to the part where he stated his penis went down and he had to get off and get it upright and start again."

In closing, Buie commended the physicians on their expertise and emphasized that the court had set no deadline for their report or for Jesse's return. "That was done possibly to give you as much time as you need to determine his condition."

At Buie's request, Pearl sent him a detailed report on Jesse's medical history to aid in her son's evaluation, which Buie then forwarded to the doctors. Pearl, too, turned her attention to the hospital, but not simply by mail. On February 16, she and Charles traveled by bus the 250 miles north to the Panhandle, then along the Georgia border to Chattahoochee. From the outside, the hospital seemed peaceful and bucolic. Inside, however, with its big green institutional doors and gray windows with heavy, spring-steel screens that nearly blocked out the light, Chattahoochee looked and sounded like nothing so much as a loud, chaotic state prison.

The visit with their son was brief, and they were not able to meet Dr. R. C. Eaton, the senior psychiatrist and clinical director. On her return home, Pearl wrote Eaton a letter requesting that Jesse be kept at Chattahoochee "until his trial comes up." Despite the oppressive atmosphere, "everyone there seem to like the boy and feel he has no business there," and keeping him there seemed preferable to having him under the watch of Sheriff McCall. She was eager to have Eaton's report on Jesse's evaluation. "I know the boy is very slow thinking and acting, and not strong," Pearl wrote, "but I would like to know your findings which should be more thorough than a mere mother's. I do know Jesse has always been humble, gentle, and obedient." She closed her letter to Eaton with a plea for her son's cause, since she had little doubt that the court, and possibly Buie as well, had provided the doctors at Chattahoochee only with evidence that might support their presumption of Jesse's guilt. She added, "Jesse said he talked to you about this 'frame up trouble' he's in," then asked, "Doctor, I want to know from you if you think he has the strength, and clear thinking mind to act quickly enough to carry out such an almost perfect crime as this one? Although we know for certain the boy was with us, at home, and could not have gotten out without us knowing or missing him."

A few days later, Pearl received a reply not from Dr. Eaton but from Dr. Benbow, advising her that it might be weeks before Jesse's evaluations were complete and that the hospital had no power in determining the length of his stay—it would have to abide by the court's decision. He also advised that any findings or reports would be sent directly to the court; the doctors did not "feel at liberty to express to you our probable opinion regarding his ability to act as charged." Benbow did, however, inform Pearl that her son was "making a good adjustment . . . and he is eating and sleeping well."

Meanwhile, in a letter to Buie, Dr. O'Connor expressed his displeasure at the Danielses' unexpected visit to Chattahoochee. Buie assured O'Connor that he would advise them not to visit for at least thirty days, and thereafter to request permission for a visit beforehand. He added, "You may rest assured that I will be very happy to give you any further information that I can secure about this boy, who in my opinion, is not even a high type moron."

Through all these rebuffs and setbacks, Pearl continued to rely on Mabel, in whom she found sympathy for her plight as a meek but determined woman pitted against powerful adversaries in her fight to save the life of her son. Mabel not only gave voice to Jesse's quandary through the stories that she published, but also offered genuine friendship. They were an unlikely pair—the sophisticated reporter from the North with her stylish glasses, smart skirts, and fancy necklaces, who had the ear of powerful men like Governor Collins; and the dowdy countrywoman in the faded, secondhand seersucker sundresses, her hair cropped short, her hands callused from toiling in the melon fields, crafting baskets from pine needles, or canning her own fruits and vegetables to feed her family. Still, they joined together to share not just their distaste for Willis Mc-Call and the Lake County justice system but their day-to-day worries and humorous observations about husbands and children and health as well. They began to go fishing together, Pearl taking home whatever bass they caught. And they had a significant trait in common: Neither would back down from a fight.

In late February, Dr. O'Connor submitted to Judge Futch a long and detailed report on Jesse Daniels. The patient, he noted, was "extremely slow" in his learning ability and showed "much retardation of all his thought processes and conceptual thinking." While tests scored Jesse's IQ at "only 60," the psychiatrist found that his "functional intelligence is on an even lower scale than that." Jesse had "absolutely no concept of money, and very little understanding of numbers"; he had been unable to do simple calculations involving pennies and nickels. Nor could he name the months of the year in proper sequence. He lacked basic literacy skills, spelling "elephant as 'lufort,'" and his knowledge of geography, history, and current events was nil.

O'Connor reported, too, that he had read a copy of Jesse's confession and, in his opinion, "it would appear that he gave a quite descriptive account of his behavior that night which would indicate that he had performed the act with which he is charged." O'Connor did note, however, that when he questioned Jesse about the rape, "the patient denied having had anything whatever to do with the act and he would give very circumstantial and often irrelevant rationalizations as to why anyone would think he was connected with it." The rationalizations, which O'Connor dismissed, deeming them "very shallow," were Jesse's claims that he was being blamed for a crime he did not commit. The doctor then asked his subject who he thought might be the guilty party, and Jesse speculated that "perhaps it was a negro" who raped "Mrs. Nowls," and she was "trying to shield him." Or perhaps, Jesse conjectured further, it was a white

BENEATH A RUTHLESS SUN

man, and the woman was "trying to protect her husband." O'Connor determined Jesse's alternative scenarios to be "obviously defective," in that the patient was "unable to carry out such thinking to where he would sound plausible to anyone else." Jesse also told the doctor that he had been out coon hunting with a friend on the night of the crime, and O'Connor noted that Jesse "is at a loss to explain why his colleague has not verified his alibi." Indeed, Dr. O'Connor wrote, "He seems unable to realize that he must convince others of the reasonableness of his story."

Regarding Mrs. Knowles, Jesse admitted to the doctor only that he knew her and that he had once gone to her house in Okahumpka to ask for "some oranges"—adding that he also knew Mr. Knowles and the "two young boys." Jesse then asserted that "he had never had any sexual relations with any girl," although, in a "child-like" fashion, he related how, one time in Leesburg, he and a girl went to see a movie together. He also told the doctor that he still slept with a teddy bear and evidently, O'Connor remarked, "saw nothing wrong with continuing to do so." While Dr. O'Connor made note of Jesse's avowed sexual inexperience, it did not, to his mind, undermine his conclusion that Jesse "had performed the act with which he is charged."

After correlating the results of the testing and the substance of the interviews with the patient, Dr. O'Connor and another psychiatrist on staff had concluded that Jesse was "mentally deficient to such a degree that he is incapable of managing his own affairs, and also incapable of properly consulting with his counsel in his own defense." Because the patient "cannot be trusted to look after himself and his affairs without undue risk to himself and others," it was, in their opinion, necessary, "for the protection of society," that Jesse be deemed "medically mentally incompetent" and that he should be "committed to a Mental Institution for an indefinite [period] inasmuch as the prospect for any substantial improvement in the future is extremely remote and there is no specific therapy known at present for this type of mental disorder."

· 122 ·

On March 14, Pearl and Charles Daniels arrived at the county courthouse in Tavares for the hearing that would seal their son's fate. Sitting restlessly in the gallery, they could see only the back of his head at the witness table, a deputy beside him. Mabel of course was there as well, and she observed how Jesse tried not to look at McCall, his head jerking back and his eyes lowering whenever a snatch of overheard conversation drew his attention to the jury box.

Mabel had a companion at the hearing, a man in a suit whom McCall did not recognize. Convinced that the editor was up to no good, the sheriff approached the man, who identified himself as Howard Dixon, an attorney from Miami. McCall immediately turned to Futch to challenge Dixon's right to sit in on the hearing. Dixon informed the court that he would be taking no part in the proceedings; he had arrived only as an observer, which was his right as an American citizen. McCall then proceeded, in open court, to aggressively question Dixon about his background, and the lawyer admitted that he worked for both the American Civil Liberties Union and the Workers Defense League. The sheriff pulled out a bound copy of a 1948 report by the House Un-American Activities Committee, which he often carried with him, and began citing instances in which the ACLU had been accused of such subversive activity.

Dixon was taken aback, but in spite of the sheriff's grandstanding, he was allowed to remain with Mabel in the courtroom. Judge Futch handed Dr. O'Connor's report to Buie, and together with Oldham and Red Robinson, representing the Knowles family, the four men held a brief conference out of earshot of the press. Upon returning to the bench, Futch asked his secretary to bring him the "commitment order," which to Mabel's ears sounded as if a decision had already been ordained.

When the hearing formally began, Buie announced to the court that he believed it was "unnecessary to call the doctors who had examined the defendant to appear as witnesses." Tapping the papers he held, he told the court, "I have read, and studied very carefully, their report, and I join with them in the statement they have made." The former state attorney "praised the two doctors highly," and Judge Futch similarly commended Buie for his service as court-appointed counsel. The judge, wearing an eyepatch under his glasses, did not whittle; instead he proceeded to read, "in sonorous tones," the prepared ruling.

As he had in the "Hello Baby" case a year earlier, Futch commended Buie's integrity. Then he got to the point. "This court," he declared, "upon due consideration of said report finds the defendant to be incompetent and insane, and the Honorable A. P. Buie, attorney for the defendant, having waived the presence in person of the aforesaid experts and consented to proceed upon the aforesaid report, it is now therefore ordered and adjudged that the defendant Jesse Daniels, is in fact insane and incompetent to conduct his defense in this cause." Affixing his signature to the order, Futch committed Jesse Daniels to Florida State Hospital at Chattahoochee "for care and treatment for such time and term of years as may be necessary," and prescribed that he "be not released from the aforesaid institution or its custody without the consent of this Court."

The hearing had lasted scarcely more than five minutes. In disbelief, Mabel wrote, "No one asked Jesse nor his parents if they wanted the doctors called. No one asked them if they agreed or disagreed with the findings about the boy who had no chance to be heard, and who was being judged insane with no more proof of insanity than an unproven charge that he had committed a crime, and with a strange confession as the only evidence against him." The parents, she observed, were not provided with a copy of the report, nor was it read for their benefit. Apparently, Mabel noted, the need for "cooperation" between the state and the defendant to ensure justice, which Judge Futch had proclaimed in court weeks earlier, applied only to the prosecutor, the defense attorney, the sheriff, the judge, and the Knowles family's attorney—it did not extend to the defendant and his family.

Furthermore, Mabel pointed out, the commitment order on Jesse "did not refer to the charge against him, nor did it reveal the fact that a psychiatric report on the youth had found him guilty of that charge, nor did it say that nowhere in the report was there any designation of 'insanity.'" The psychiatric report on which Jesse's commitment was based was "unique in Florida law," because, without benefit of a trial by jury, "the youth was branded as guilty of the charge against him by two doctors who had neither studied the evidence nor heard any defense." Psychiatrists, Mabel reasoned, "are not legally endowed with the right of determining a man's innocence or guilt—only with the right to determine the state of his mental capacity."

Once she realized fully the implications of the judge's ruling, Pearl Daniels broke down. In tears, she watched as the sheriff slapped handcuffs on her son's wrists and told him to "come quietly." Pained by his mother's anguish, Jesse mumbled, "I don't know how quiet I'll be," as McCall led him up to the jail to await transport back to Chattahoochee. Pearl could only mouth good-bye. And so the case against Jesse Daniels was closed, and would be filed away as solved by the Lake County Sheriff's Department and the circuit court.

Deputy Evvie Griffin's Plymouth Belvedere was idling outside the courthouse. Over the past few months, in transporting Jesse back and forth to the mental hospital in Chattahoochee, the deputy had gotten to know his gentle passenger well enough to realize there was no need to keep him bound in handcuffs in the backseat. Jesse liked Griffin; he was the "nice deputy," who always had peanuts and a bottle of Coca-Cola waiting for him in the car. One time, he and the deputy had flown, just the two of them—Griffin was the only trained pilot in the Lake County Sheriff's Department—up to Chattahoochee in the department's Cessna 172 Skyhawk. It was Jesse's first ride in an airplane. On the way from Chattahoochee to Tavares the previous day, as they'd sped through the Apalachicola National Forest, Griffin had flipped on the sirens from time to time; that always brought a smile to the face of the boy. Today was likely to be their last trip together. Evvie put the Plymouth into gear.

After Griffin delivered the boy to the hospital attendants at Chattahoochee, he set out alone on the long drive south to his home in Eustis. His first year with the Lake County Sheriff's Department had been nearing its end the night of the rape. He recalled how Blanche Knowles had stated with certainty to Deputy Yates that she had been raped by a "husky Negro"; and how Griffin and his fellow deputies, with bloodhounds leading them from the Knowles house straight into North Quarters, had rounded up dozens of black men as suspects in the case. Griffin, who'd been running bloodhounds since he was a boy, had learned to trust their keen sense of smell, especially when what they smelled lay in an article of clothing freshly recovered at a crime scene. And he had seen Jesse's confession, which had been taken, he knew, by Deputy Yates after the boy had been locked up in the juvenile ward for several sleepless nights and days.

Rape case of Mrs. Joe Knowles of Okahumpka, Fla.,

Wednesday, Dec. 18, 1957, at approximately 1 a.m.

Present in the I.D. Room of the Sheriff's Department in the Court House, Tavares, Fla., were LeRoy Campbell, deputy sheriff

James L. Yates, Deputy sheriff and the defendant, Jesse Daniels.

I, Jesse Daniels, having been advised of my Constitutional Rights, and an explanation of same given to me by Deputy Sheriff James L. Yates, do hereby make the following statement of my own free will and without promise or threat of any kind.

On December 17, my father, mother and I sat up and watched TV till the station signed off the air, the station being Channel 6, Orlando. Then my father, mother and I went to bed and went to sleep.

I woke up sometime later and went outside out the back door, my father and mother still sleeping and were not awakened by me going out.

I walked around the south side of my house out onto the road, and walked north down to the Sumterville Road. There I turned east and went down to Mrs. Knowles house. There was no lights on at the house, and I walked down the south side of the house where the driveway goes and to the front walk in the front and the front door. There I stood about twenty-five minutes looking down toward Bug Springs and Okahumpka, and went up to the front screen which was fastened and shoved it open. Then I shoved the wood and glass doors open and they were stuck like a door in damp weather when it swells up. I walked on to the foot of the stairs and there I took all my clothes off except my sox. I went up the stairs and turned to the right at the top of the stairs and went into the bed room then I looked on the bed where Mrs. Knowles was laying, then back at the bedroom door.

Mrs. Knowles was waking up and she says, "Is that you, Joe," and I says "NO, it is me, Jesse Daniels and she says let me turn on the lights and see who it is." I said, "If you do I will kill you."

Then I got in bed with her and asked her to get in position which she did. I then put my penus in her and started performing a sexual intercourse, but my penus slipped out and I asked her to put it in for me because it had got soft, but I had to put it in myself.

When I was through I asked her if she enjoyed it, and she said "Yes." I then started out of the bedroom but I heard something fall on the floor that sounded like a little piece of wood and I got down on the floor to see what it was and felt around with my hands, but could not find anything. I then went back down stairs and put on my clothes all except my shorts, which I could not find because of the darkness. I walked out the front door like I come in and went home. My mother and father was still asleep and I went to bed without awakening them.

The shorts that you found at Mrs. Knowles house with the number 26 marked on the label are my shorts, the ones that I left at Mrs. Knowles because I could not find them in the dark.

This is the truth to the best of my knowledge, and I have made this statement without any threats or promises.

(Signed) s/ Jesse Daniels

Witnesses

s/ James L. Yates
s/ LeRoy Campbell

Sworn and subscribed before me this 27th day of December 1957

s/ Margaret M. Hickman
Notary Public

The confession was as confounding to Griffin as it had been to anyone else. It made plain nonsense out of the roundup of young black men and the days-long delay in apprehending Jesse. Then there was the matter of the stutter. The kid couldn't go five seconds without stuttering, but he and Blanche were supposed to have had a lengthy conversation before and after the rape?

> Then I got in bed with her and asked her to get in position which she did. I then put my penus in her and started performing a sexual intercourse, but my penus slipped out and I asked her to put it in for me because it had got soft, but I had to put it in myself.

Not likely.

"The only thing that boy knew to do with his pecker was to piss through it," Griffin said.

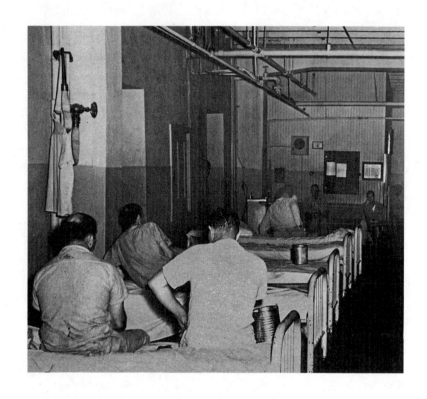

Male ward at Florida State Hospital, Chattahoochee

CHAPTER SEVEN

No Suitable Place

JESSE DANIELS ARRIVED in Chattahoochee with the words of Willis McCall echoing in his mind. Walking Jesse back to his cell in Tavares after the hearing and the signing of the commitment order, the sheriff had gleefully informed the boy that now he'd be going to the "crazy house," as that was where he belonged, after all. "You're a crazy son of a bitch," McCall had told him. "Crazier than forty hells."

"No I'm not," Jesse said. "I'm a nice guy when you get to know me."

"We know everything there is to know about you," McCall had replied, and locked the cell.

As it happened, Jesse Daniels was among a distinct minority, his parents never having threatened to send him to the "loony bin" up north. Nearly every child growing up in twentieth-century Florida had heard a parent or teacher say, "Keep acting crazy, and you'll end up at Chattahoochee." Or, in frustration, "You're going to drive me to Chattahoochee." A Florida newspaper editorial described the hospital in the 1950s as one of the most "kicked around and neglected of state institutions"—its wards overcrowded, its operation understaffed, its facilities and buildings inadequate. It was, said the paper, "a 'crazy house' for 'crazy people,' and people talked in hushed terms, if at all, if they had a relative or friend as a patient there."

It hadn't always been a crazy house.

In 1830, a decade and more after the First Seminole War, President Andrew Jackson pushed through Congress the Indian Removal Act, which authorized the president to relocate southern Indian tribes to federal territory west of the Mississippi River. The Seminoles resisted, and during the Second Seminole War (1835–1842), at a cost of twenty thousand dollars, the federal government built an arsenal strategically placed on high ground along the Apalachicola River; it became known as the Chattahoochee Arsenal. The arsenal continued to serve as a supply depot throughout the Third Seminole War, which began in 1855 and ended three years later, with most Seminoles surrendering. Those who escaped surrender, and starvation, retreated farther south to Okahumpka and beyond. Eluding capture, they proudly referred to themselves as the "Unconquered People."

In 1861, when Florida seceded from the Union, the state militia took control of the Chattahoochee Arsenal. In the aftermath of the Civil War, the structure fulfilled another purpose for the state. Florida, like the rest of the South during the Reconstruction era, strove to retain an economy based, in effect if not in name, on the practice of slavery. The legislation of the Black Codes, or Jim Crow laws, criminalized free blacks for minor infractions and activities that were deemed legal for whites. The resultant surge in arrests and inevitable convictions inundated local jails with prisoners that they soon lacked space to incarcerate. The Codes created the need for a massive expansion of the prison system. So it was that Florida governor Harrison Reed petitioned the secretary of war to have the Chattahoochee Arsenal converted into a prison. In 1868, it became the state's first penitentiary. Convict leasing was also instituted, whereby inmates were jobbed out as laborers, commonly to Florida's lumber camps and turpentine farms, so that at the same time they were serving out their sentences under the laws of the state they were generating revenue for the state.

The prison's first warden was Malachi Martin, an Irish-born carpetbagger from New York and a former colonel in the Union Army. Notoriously cruel and corrupt, he demonstrated a preference for strict military discipline and presided over what one historian described as "a horror den" of abuse and "a place of almost unrelieved brutality." Martin also skimmed personal gains off the convict-leasing system. With prison labor he not only built a luxurious, octagon-shaped house on his two-hundred-acre estate but also operated the vineyard and winery he owned a few miles outside Chattahoochee. He was believed to have made a considerable fortune.

Yet even Martin was disturbed by the nature of the offenses that were landing so many young black men and boys in his prison. In a letter to Major General George B. Carse, the adjutant-general of the State of Florida, the warden expressed his concern that the increasing number of young boys being sentenced to hard labor at Chattahoochee for what he termed "trifling crime" was forcing the prison to house them in the same areas as the most hardened criminals.

Steadily increasing, too, among the prison population were mentally ill inmates, and by 1873, their pitiful situation at Chattahoochee prompted Martin to advise the state legislature in a letter that the penitentiary was "no suitable place for such unfortunates," as it could not afford them any treatment. "I hardly know how to express my feelings on the subject," Martin wrote. "I feel that it is inhuman not to provide a suitable asylum for our insane, and that the authorities will be held responsible hereafter for a gross neglect of their official duty if such an asylum is not provided." In support of the warden's plea, the prison's surgeon, in his own letter to the legislature, implored the state to devise a plan to provide adequate care for the "lunatics" at Chattahoochee, warning, "As we sow, so we must reap." The "lunatics" soon began to outnumber the convicts, whom they ultimately replaced. In 1877, with the passage of the Lunacy Law and an allocation of ten thousand dollars for conversion and maintenance of the facility, Florida's first state penitentiary became its first mental hospital: the Asylum for the Indigent Insane.

Institutionalized mental health care in America originated in Philadelphia in 1753, when Benjamin Franklin and Dr. Thomas Bond sought to assist the growing number of "lunaticks" living on the city's streets. Their philanthropic efforts in time encouraged Pennsylvania Hospital to admit "deranged" patients, although they were relegated to cells in the hospital's dark basement, where they endured appalling negligence. Many of them were also restrained with "hand irons, leg locks, and mad-shirts," or straitjackets. They soon became curiosities for the people of Philadelphia, who'd come to the hospital to gawk at the strange, afflicted creatures in their locked cells. The hospital installed a special hatch door to ensure safe viewing, for which it charged a four-pence fee.

The treatments for mentally ill patients varied in method but not in their cruelty. Bloodletting, restraint in sensory-deprivation boxes, and subjection to "twirling wheels" or stinging sprays of water were common up to the end of the eighteenth century, when institutions like Pennsylvania Hospital adopted more humane treatments. Restraints fell out of favor, and physicians began to place an emphasis on dignity in the treatment of patients, whose curiosities, doctors now believed, could be cured. By the middle of the nineteenth century, Pennsylvania Hospital was offering swimming pools, libraries, and "occupational therapy suites" to aid in the treatment of the mentally ill. Such care was expensive, however, and thus available only to those from wealthy families.

As America became a more populous, industrialized nation in the latter part of the century, smaller, private facilities for the mentally ill began to disappear and state-run "insane asylums" started sprouting up on the outskirts of large cities. Medical staffs at these larger facilities were not only insufficient for their populations but also frequently untrained and incompetent. As individual professional attention to patients declined, neglect and abuse began to rise. Admissions protocols were vague and lacking in rigor. Although the field of psychiatry had by then become a medical specialty, cause for commitment remained highly subjective and did not always require a professional diagnosis of mental illness. In many cases, family members of the prospective patient were able to convince administrators of the need for institutionalization.

Florida's newly founded Asylum for the Indigent Insane proved to be no exception in its unexacting policies and practices. Because the determination of a person's insanity was often, as Chattahoochee historian Sally J. Ling notes, "based upon the observation of unusual social behavior," virtually any individual could be shipped off to Chattahoochee "by neighbors and/or authorities that identified [him/her] as socially abnormal or simply undesirable"—a designation that might include the senile, alcoholics, epileptics, homosexuals, and the mentally retarded. Patients committed to Chattahoochee with medical diagnoses like cigarette addiction, pregnancy, abnormal menstruation, and excessive masturbation strained the asylum's barely functional staff and contributed to the eventually massive overcrowding at the facility. Restraints at the asylum were "rigidly imposed," and "brutal force"—a carryover from the institution's recent incarnation as a prison—was meted out by attendants, often arbitrarily, as a means of establishing authority. In 1885, black males were segregated from the asylum population; at the facility that housed them, in the first year of its operation, a quarter of the forty-four black residents died, allegedly because of poor ventilation.

When, in 1896, "insanity" pleas were legitimized as a criminal defense and in many cases were employed, as Ling points out, "to deceive the jury during the commitment process," criminals with issues having nothing to do with mental illness might find themselves languishing at Chattahoochee rather than serving hard time in labor camps. Even young boys facing minor criminal charges were sent to Chattahoochee. In one case, an eight-year-old was committed, as Superintendent J. W. Trammell noted, because he was "dumb and unable to defend himself in court." By the end of the century, more than six hundred patients were resident at the facility, which had been renamed Florida State Hospital.

In the mid-1930s, the Department of Corrections established a prison facility for the criminally insane on the grounds of Chattahoochee. A subsequent investigation uncovered scandalous conditions: a lack of basic sanitary measures, a lack of privacy in shower and toilet areas, a lack of proper nutrients in the prison diet. The physician-to-patient ratio was "clearly ridiculous," and the shortage of attendants reduced treatment largely to restraint, for the most part by cuffs and chains. Among the outrages that the investigation turned up was the instance of a toddler who was living with his mother among "intensely violent and disturbed patients" in the white female department.

More hopefully, the 1930s also brought new methods of treatment to the state hospital. Insulin shock therapy, whereby intravenous delivery of the drug induced a coma, was introduced to relieve psychotic episodes among schizophrenics, as was Metrazol shock therapy, in which the drug was administered in large doses, but often with negative effects. The convulsions produced by Metrazol were in some cases—42 percent of the subjects in one study—so violent that patients sustained spine fractures during treatment. Thousands of patients at Chattahoochee underwent drug therapies daily, until the advent of electroconvulsive therapy (ECT).

Originally administered to relieve severe depression, ECT soon came to be viewed as a cure for any number of mental disorders. Through electrodes placed on the temples of the patient, who'd been strapped to a gurney, electric current was transmitted to the brain, where it triggered a grand mal seizure. The convulsions lasted for only about twenty seconds, but patients usually received a series of ECT treatments over roughly a two-week period. Memory impairment was the most common side effect of the therapy. In 1951–1952 alone, Florida State Hospital at Chattahoochee recorded nearly six thousand ECT treatments. By the 1950s, the hospital had joined a trend common to institutions across the country, in utilizing electroshock therapy not only for patients suffering from depression but also as a means of controlling behavioral problems, largely to the benefit of overtaxed hospital staff. By the mid-1950s, the abuses of ECT had become a cause for alarm.

There was, however, no treatment for mental patients more infamous than the lobotomy. The first prefrontal lobotomy in the United States was performed in 1936, in Washington, D.C., by the neurosurgeon James W. Watts, who had been engaged by the American psychiatrist Walter Freeman to operate on a female patient suffering from insomnia, anxiety, and depression and, like the majority of patients committed to asylums, facing institutionalization for life. The physicians deemed their first lobotomy a success. After performing another sixty-four procedures together, in 1941 they notoriously failed when they performed a lobotomy on Rosemary Kennedy, the "apparently retarded" daughter of the statesman Joseph Kennedy (and sister of John F. Kennedy and Robert Kennedy), who had been experiencing frequent and violent mood changes. Watts's diagnosis of "agitated depression" led him and Freeman to conclude, with some persuasion from Joseph Kennedy himself, that the twenty-three-year-old Rosemary would benefit from a prefrontal lobotomy. It was undertaken at George Washington University Hospital. Into an inch-long incision at the top of the mildly sedated patient's skull, Watts inserted a "butter knife"–like instrument, which, at Freeman's direction, he first rotated and then moved up and down before he began "slicing through the brain tissue." The procedure did not, as promised, render Rose "happy and content." In fact, it left her lethargic, partially paralyzed, incontinent, unable to communicate, and incapable of dressing herself.

Dr. James Lyerly Sr., the only neurosurgeon practicing in the state of Florida in the late 1930s, had for the most part been performing operations on hematomas and benign brain tumors in Jacksonville. The emerging field of psychosurgery, however, captured his professional interest, and an opening on the medical staff at Florida State Hospital at Chattahoochee enabled him to exercise that interest. Initially, Lyerly performed his lobotomies—slightly modified versions of Freeman and Watts's prefrontal techniques—on middle-aged patients who were suffering from severe depression and had attempted suicide. Before long, though, Lyerly was also scheduling children at Chattahoochee for his innovative surgery, among them an agitated, "feeble-minded" twelve-year-old girl who had become "a disturbance to the other children in the institution."

In the aftermath of World War II, with the return of thousands of traumatized servicemen, the population at United States mental institutions swelled. Approximately 271,000 admissions were recorded in 1946, nearly tripling the number of patients just three years before. Estimates indicated that half of the hospital beds in the country were occupied by the mentally ill and that the patient population in the nation's mental institutions had reached more than 600,000. The postwar increase in psychiatric patients, Dr. Freeman recognized, demanded a lobotomy technique more efficient than the time-consuming procedure of drilling into a patient's skull. He thus devised the "ice pick" lobotomy, in which a narrow metal pick was inserted beneath the upper eyelid and into the patient's orbital cavity until the tip reached the bony case. The pick (which was indeed taken from the doctor's kitchen) was then tapped with a hammer until it punctured the brain, at which point the surgeon twisted the pick "back and forth like a windshield wiper" to sever neural fibers. The surgery took only minutes to complete, "without surgical gloves or sterile draping," and Freeman dispensed with the need for a local or general anesthetic by immobilizing his patients with electroconvulsive shocks. Traveling in his "lobotomobile," he performed thousands of transorbital lobotomies in assembly-line fashion at state institutions across the nation.

By the mid-1950s, Dr. Lyerly, along with his partner and son, Dr. James Lyerly Jr., was driving to Chattahoochee once a month to perform two lobotomies a day. The father-and-son team was reported to have conducted more than a hundred lobotomies at Florida State Hospital, most of them, they said, with "fantastic results." Their procedures, which were designed to pacify disruptive patients by blunting their emotional distress and anxiety, became a "significant part" of treatment at Chattahoochee throughout the decade. Although the hospital reported non-prefrontal lobotomies as "other neurosurgical procedures" and categorized them as "elective surgery," they were without doubt occurring on a frequent and consistent basis at Chattahoochee, just as they were at mental institutions across the country. In effect, transorbital lobotomies mutilated a patient's brain and "permanently altered the emotional lives of tens of thousands of men, women, and children."

Another factor that drastically affected the hospital's population in the postwar decade was the Florida legislature's passage of the 1951 Child Molester Act. The act mandated that any person convicted of rape, sexual assault, or lewd and lascivious behavior against victims under the age of twelve had to be examined by two licensed psychiatrists, who were obliged to provide the court with psychiatric reports of their findings prior to sentencing. As a result, many convicted criminals who would previously have been dispatched to Florida State Prison at Raiford were sentenced instead to terms at Chattahoochee. One year after the Child Molester Act became law, the patient population at Chattahoochee had increased to 6,223, with only twelve physicians on staff, most of them untrained in psychiatry. The low salaries offered to doctors and the hospital's remote location in Florida's Panhandle made positions at Chattahoochee "unattractive to men with families."

While doctors at Chattahoochee continued to prescribe ECT, insulin shock therapy, and lobotomies in their treatment of mentally ill patients well into the 1950s, the decade would see the introduction of a therapy that psychiatrists would newly claim produced "miraculous results." Two French physicians—Henri Laborit, a surgeon, and Pierre Deniker, a psychiatrist—had been experimenting with chlorpromazine, a drug used largely as an anti-nausea medication in the United States, when they discovered that, in stronger doses, chlorpromazine worked to seda-tive effect on some of their "most agitated and uncontrollable patients." It induced "disinterest without loss of consciousness," and for long periods of time the patients would sit motionless—"often pale and with eyelids lowered," Laborit observed. That effect earned the drug—known more commonly by its trade name, Thorazine—its epithet as a "chemical lo-botomy," and it quickly gained prevalence as the therapy of choice in state institutions across the country. Difficult patients became docile and could be "moved around like puppets." Thorazine did not remedy pa-tients' disorders, but, rather, it moderated their behavior, and did it with such efficiency that the drug was dispensed indiscriminately. A patient in the white male department at Chattahoochee disclosed that the care of the wards' thirteen hundred white men was the responsibility of a single physician—the "pill-doctor," as he was called—who was "licensed by the state as an obstetrician." According to the patient, the "pill-doctor" dispensed antipsychotic medications to patients who sometimes had not been seen by a doctor for years. For doctors and attendants at Florida State Hospital, which was teeming with violent psychopaths, rapists, and murderers, Thorazine was a godsend.

In 1957, in response to the situation at Chattahoochee, with its over-crowded wards and inadequate care, the state established the Division of Mental Health, which opened two new mental hospitals to relieve some of the population stress at Florida State Hospital. Nevertheless, admis-sions at Florida State continued to rise, in large part because violent criminals who'd pleaded insanity almost invariably ended up at Chattahoochee, an institution much reputed for its function as a high-security prison for the mentally ill. More than a third of its approximately seven thousand patients in 1957 had been charged or convicted of a crime, but they were not separated from the general population. Nor was there any "segregation as to type of mental illness, age, health, or charge." As a result, the "feeble elderly were housed among teen-agers, psychopaths and criminals, ranging from forgers to rapists and even murderers."

It wasn't only the criminals that patients at Chattahoochee had to worry about. Overtaxed attendants—who themselves were sometimes jumped, beaten, and even killed by the hardened criminals—would commonly lash out at docile patients, young and old alike, often without provocation or at the slightest infractions of hospital rules. Patient abuse was rampant. The attendants favored choking and beating, and they'd enter the cause of patients' broken arms as "fall in shower" on their internal reports. "At Chattahoochee, each of us stood alone," wrote one patient who kept a diary of his stay there, "helpless to save ourselves or a friend. There were times when the horrors crowded me to the edge and all I could see was blood on a man spread-eagled on a bed; blood on a ninety-eight-pounder in a straitjacket; blood on an old man's ear. And a naked woman in a cage."

Perhaps the most famous patient at Chattahoochee at the time Jesse arrived was Ruby McCollum, a black woman from Live Oak, Florida, who in August 1952 had shot a white physician and state senator, Dr. C. Leroy Adams. She was tried and found guilty by a jury of white men (some of whom were patients of Dr. Adams's) and sentenced to death in the electric chair at Raiford. Zora Neale Hurston, while living in Florida, covered the trial for the *Pittsburgh Courier* and brought national attention to the case by reporting what the trial judge (who had been a pallbearer at Dr. Adams's funeral) had kept out of the proceedings. McCollum, whom the judge had placed under a gag order, had also been prevented from testifying at her trial as to the details of what she had written in notes and letters: that Dr. Adams had repeatedly forced her into sex over the years, and that she had given birth to a daughter by him and was pregnant with another child of his when she went to his office and shot him four times. Hurston's coverage of the trial managed to expose another ugly truth of white supremacy in the Jim Crow era—the lingering existence of "paramour rights," another unwritten law of the antebellum South, which entitled a white man to take a black woman, married or not, as his concubine and force her to bear his children.

In 1954, the Florida Supreme Court had overturned McCollum's guilty verdict on a technicality, thus forcing a retrial. This time, however, McCollum entered a plea of insanity, and after a psychiatric evaluation, she had been declared mentally incompetent to stand trial and was committed to the infamous "Florida madhouse" along the Panhandle.

AZALEAS WERE IN FULL BLOOM at Chattahoochee when Jesse Daniels stepped out of Evvie Griffin's Plymouth. Live oaks shaded the neatly trimmed lawn that abutted the redbrick pathway up to the freshly painted white administration building with grand porches on both of its two stories. The deputy left Jesse with two male attendants in white uniforms. They escorted him back inside.

Since Jesse had undergone a psychological evaluation and a dental exam a few weeks before, he bypassed the records room and proceeded to admittance, where he was weighed and measured. His height was recorded as five feet, nine inches, his weight as 133 pounds, and his vital signs as normal, except for a significantly higher blood pressure than that recorded during his February evaluation—the staff attributed the spike to anxiety. His blood was tested, and he was vaccinated for smallpox and typhus. Now patient A-27378, Jesse was given a bath, deloused, and issued institutional clothing. Attendants, meanwhile, inventoried the items on his person at the time of admittance:

1 Pocket watch with leather string

1 Billfold [money, if any, not indicated]

5 Pictures

1 S.S. Card

1 Registration Card

1 Xray Card

1 G.P. Card

1 shirt

1 Tee shirt

1 pr. Socks

1 pr. Pants W/Belt

1 pr. Shorts

1 cap

1 Holy Bible

1 Tube Cement

1 Mouth Harp

Dr. Eaton, in his evaluation of Jesse upon admission, noted that the patient "seems unconcerned, behavior co-operative . . . Wants to have his harmonica . . . Insight and judgement nil." The patient also seemed to be under the impression that he would be resident at Chattahoochee for only "two or three months," Eaton remarked, as Jesse had told him, "I'll sure be glad when this is all over and I go home with my dad and mother." In all, Eaton observed, "This boy gave the impression of being rather simple, and seemed to be obviously defective." His diagnosis—"Mental Deficiency, Moderate"—was based on an IQ of 60, which placed Jesse in the "low-grade Moron" category. While Jesse evidently understood the nature of the charge against him, Eaton noted, the boy continued to deny it and stated calmly that he'd been framed. "I didn't have anything to do with it," he said.

Jesse also told Eaton that "he had only been near the woman's place once in his life," and he was not referring to the alleged late-night visit that he had detailed, supposedly "of his own free will," in his confession. Dr. Eaton included a photostat of the typed, two-page confession that had been provided by Jesse's court-appointed counsel, Sam Buie, in his file on patient A-27378. In the file, too, was a note that Eaton had made regarding a telephone call from Sheriff McCall, who had told him that "all the investigations indicated that he [Jesse] actually did commit the act." With particulars as to the results of those investigations, Dr. Eaton was able to question Jesse more probingly about the charges against him and about his movements on the day of the attack.

Jesse's memory seemed to Eaton to be "fairly good for the immediate past, and probably is fair for the distant past," but the boy had "no idea of dates." He knew what year it was, but he could not name the month, and he seemed to think there were twenty-four months in a year. When asked how many weeks in a year, he'd replied, "There are ten weeks, isn't there?" He'd incorrectly placed the crime he'd allegedly committed in November.

Still, Dr. Eaton noted, Jesse was able to accurately relate specific details about his activities the days before and after the rape. This time, however, Jesse made no mention of coon hunting with a neighbor on the evening of December 17. He recounted for Eaton that on the night of the crime, before he'd gone to bed, he'd been watching television late, but he couldn't have left the house after his parents were asleep, he said, "because all of the doors are quite noisy." He recalled the police cars and barking dogs that overran Okahumpka in the early hours of the morning, and he recounted how he had gone on his bike to the grocery store, where he'd heard a deputy tell a woman that a Negro had raped a white woman. Jesse also said that he himself did not know a "thing-in-the-world" about the rape case, but that when the sheriff and the deputies kept asking him question after question after question, he "got mixed up at the time and admitted doing it." He couldn't "explain why the woman who was raped said that he was the one who had done it," so he guessed that maybe "she was afraid." About what, he told Eaton, he could not imagine. He related, too, how, on the one occasion he'd gone to the Knowles house to ask for some oranges to eat, Mrs. Knowles had kindly obliged. He described her as being "well-dressed, very attractive looking," and he figured she had at least a high school education.

Jesse also told Dr. Eaton that his mother, after learning that Jesse had confessed, instructed him to "tell everybody that he did not do it."

In exploring Jesse's sexual history, Dr. Eaton recorded a number of details that Jesse had shared with O'Connor. According to the patient, he had never had sexual intercourse "with any girl or woman." He had once asked a girl to a movie in Leesburg, so that he could "buy her some candy" and have "real clean talks with her," he said, and insisted to the doctor that he "treats all females with respect."

When Eaton asked Jesse if he knew why he was at the hospital, Jesse responded without hesitation. "Treatment," he said. When asked to elaborate, he told Eaton that he didn't think anything was wrong with his mind. He did have bad dreams, though. Which was why he slept with a teddy bear, as he had been doing ever since he could remember. If a bad dream awoke him in the middle of the night, his mother would comfort him; Jesse told the doctor how she'd lay a toy stuffed baby penguin on the bed beside him and whisper him back to sleep.

In his summation of Jesse's admittance interview, Dr. Eaton determined the patient's speech, aside from the stutter, to be "often quite hesitant, his comprehension extremely poor, his responses are very sluggish to commands, and his movements are inclined to be rather slow. His answers, at times, are quite irrelevant, and often very inadequate, and, obviously, quite unlearned." In concluding his report, Eaton stated that the patient had "no loss of contact with reality . . . but just seems to be a rather dull sort of person." Then, with a stroke of his pen, Dr. Eaton assigned patient A-27378 to the white male department.

An attendant escorted the new arrival down the long, foul-smelling wooden corridor—"the Tunnel of Shit," as it was commonly called—that led to the general wards. In the white male department, country music was blaring on transistor radios. In Ward 5, to which Jesse had been randomly assigned, long-timers were playing cards, their games frequently punctuated by shouting matches; the ward was reputed to be one of the more violent in the department. More recent inmates, confused or in a haze, "paraded fitfully back and forth." The new arrival looked on in bewilderment.

A guard escorted Jesse down a hallway to his new living quarters. From the doorway he surveyed the room: dozens of beds that lay beneath rows of harsh fluorescent ceiling lights; an unfamiliar device (the electroshock machine); the patients—some of them shuffling aimlessly about, some writhing in fits of agitation, others blank-eyed and rigid in catatonic stupors. The guard pointed him to his bed and turned his attentions elsewhere. That night, nineteen-year-old Jesse Delbert Daniels would be lying on the bed's thin mattress without his teddy bear or his penguin doll. His eyes wide open, unable to sleep, he'd wait for the silence to come. And after it finally did, he'd be startled awake, not by his bad dreams but by the dull moans and piercing screams around him.

In late February, Gordon Oldham drove the two hundred fifty miles to Chattahoochee for a meeting with Jesse's physicians. Dr. O'Connor followed up on the visit with a letter to Oldham, in which he stated that in addition to the copy of Jesse's signed confession already on file, "We believe that it would be of value in our present psychiatric studies in his case to have also available the testimony given by the victim, if it is possible for you to furnish same."

On March 3, Oldham responded. He informed O'Connor that "in order to clear up all possible facts, I brought Mrs. Knowles back into my office and took more testimony from her." The enclosed transcript, he noted, was a "rough draft," and he made clear that he would "appreciate it if this report would be kept completely confidential as between you and any other doctor working in this case."

According to the transcript, on the evening of December 17, Blanche and her three children had stopped by Bosanquet Florist in downtown Leesburg just after dark. She was meeting up with her parents there and the family was planning to go on to the Rotary Christmas party together. About the same time, Joe called the shop to tell Blanche that he would not be able to join the family for the festivities because he had to leave immediately for Tampa to attend to an emergency business matter. Blanche did not question what he told her. Governor Collins, after all, was currently traveling around the state to confer with citrus growers and packers in the wake of the recent devastating freeze. Still, she was disappointed. She decided she'd let her boys go to the Christmas party with her parents while she drove back to Okahumpka with one-year-old Mary.

A little before seven p.m., Blanche parked the car behind the house. She fixed herself supper, then fed the baby and put her to bed upstairs. About two hours later, Alfred and Ruth Bosanquet dropped off their grandsons but did not come inside. At nine-thirty, after watching a bit of television with the boys, Blanche took them upstairs to bed. Once they'd fallen asleep, she retired to her own room. The Knowleses slept separately in twin beds, and Mary was already sleeping in a crib at the foot of Blanche's bed.

The curtains on three of the four bedroom windows were already drawn; the fourth was partially open. Blanche changed into her nightgown, settled herself in the bed, turned out the bedside light, and "went sound asleep."

At approximately one o'clock in the morning, Blanche awoke. She'd felt the touch of a "very cold hand" on her skin beneath the bed covers. She stared hard into the darkness, toward the bedroom door, as she "had a feeling that somebody had just started out of the room" and was perhaps going to "a little hallway closet." She assumed it was her husband, back home from Tampa, and she called out his name.

"Joe, is that you?"

No response. Maybe, Blanche thought, one of the boys was not feeling well, or maybe he'd thrown off his bedclothes and gotten chilled, "since the hand that touched her was so cold."

"Come back in the room," Blanche said.

Still, no answer. Wide-awake now, she sensed the presence of someone hovering in the darkness just outside the bedroom door. A minute passed. Sitting up in her bed, she listened intently to the silence.

"Who is it?" she asked.

She sensed hesitation. Then movement. Barely discernible, a shadowy tall figure was stepping into the dark room. Certainly it wasn't either one of the boys, and it wasn't her husband, either.

"Who is it? What do you want?" she asked.

A man's voice answered; she could not see his face. "I've got a gun," said the voice, soft but tinged with unmistakable menace. "Don't turn on the lights or I'll shoot you."

Her heart pounding in fear, Blanche leapt from her bed, shielding herself with a sheet. "Get out! Get out! Get out!" she screamed.

The voice silenced her with a command. "Do as I say or I'll shoot you."

Blanche was still clutching the bedsheet when the faceless figure of a man grabbed her hand. The sheet fell from her shoulders to the floor.

"Turn loose," the man said, and motioned vaguely at the bed.

"Oh, God. Not that," Blanche said, comprehending what he meant.

"Don't say anything or I'll shoot," the man said again.

As he closed the space between them, and as Blanche extended her hands to brace herself against contact, her hands crossed with his and she realized that he wasn't holding a gun. "I told him so," she said to Oldham.

At that, the man wrapped both his hands around Blanche's neck. "You do just as I say or I'll choke you," he said.

"I felt like he meant it," Blanche recalled. "I couldn't breathe while he had his hands there. And so then he touched my hips and told me to get in position. I don't know exactly what he intended for me to do, but I didn't move."

"I can't," she told the man, and he pressed her into position himself, which was when she realized that he was already naked, except for the pair of socks she could tell he was wearing "by the way his feet hit the bedclothes." He was also, "as far as I could ascertain, exceedingly cold," and he did not have "a complete erection." His effort to perform "the act" was "very feeble and inexperienced," Blanche observed, and noted, "As far as I can figure out he never got any more of an erection." He "definitely didn't know quite what to expect several times, or what he wanted me to do, or what he wanted to do himself." He seemed confused, rattled.

Aiming to prevent a wretched violation from escalating into a violent assault, Blanche tried to calm him. She was patient and cooperative; her words were gentle. "At one time I almost felt like maybe he was a little afraid that if I kept talking I might talk him out of it," she recalled, "because he became very insistent that I be quiet."

"Don't talk," he ordered her.

The rape did not last long. "Possibly not more than one or two minutes," Blanche estimated. It ended with a question.

"Did you enjoy that?" her assailant asked.

"No," Blanche said. It was, she reflected, an act she had never experienced "with anyone except my husband."

Her reply elicited momentary silence. Then:

"Well," the man said, "in that case I'd better go."

His "almost apologetic" tone surprised Blanche. It was "like he felt I had had a dance with him and he'd stepped on my toe . . . so he'd leave me."

He rose from the bed. He was facing the doorway, but vacillating, as if there was something he needed to say. Having defused a potentially violent situation by not resisting, Blanche recalled, she didn't want to risk angering him now, not with her children sleeping nearby. So she'd hear him out, she decided, whatever he felt compelled to say.

Still, he stood silent and slightly hunched in the doorway. The pause was awkward, though it allowed Blanche the opportunity to slip back into her nightgown. Then, turning again toward her, he spoke.

"I came up here to kill you," he said.

Blanche was silent.

"During the war I got all the killing I could want. But if you ever tell anybody I was here, I'll come back and blow up the camp. There's two men waiting for me down there in the car."

Blanche hardly knew what to make of his statements, let alone how to respond to them, so she simply listened without comment.

"I was paid five thousand dollars to kill you." The words, spoken with import, hung in the air.

When Blanche failed to respond, he prodded, "Wouldn't you like to know who paid me that?"

"Yes," she said.

The man seemed to be debating with himself; and then, forgoing the question he'd raised, he asked another.

"Would you like to know where I live?"

"Whatever you want to say," Blanche answered, curt, her patience wearing thin. She immediately regretted her tone.

"Well, if you act like that . . ." the man chided her, his mood darkening. "Don't you act sly to me."

"You tell me whatever you'd like to tell me," said Blanche, hoping to repair her damage to their tenuous rapport. "If you'd like to tell me that, I'll be glad to hear it."

"Just for that I'm not going to tell you."

He did not tell her, either, what he was missing when he got down on his hands and knees and "started hunting for something on the floor." His search apparently unsuccessful, he stepped into the hallway, but in a few seconds he returned to the bedroom and resumed his quest. "It was not in a particularly intelligent manner, because he kept hunting over exactly the same spot . . . fanning out with his hand in front of him, patting the floor right hard, trying to find something that he apparently thought was there." He rose to his feet, his hands empty. What he'd been looking for—a piece of clothing? a weapon?—Blanche did not know.

She'd stood by quietly, warily, in her carefulness not to incite him, and prayed that he'd just leave. He seemed to be prepared to go when he warned her "not to tell anybody, not to turn on any lights after he left, not to phone anybody, not to ever tell anybody ever." Then he warned her again.

Finally, in a few "fast steps," he hastened to the stairway, which he'd barely begun descending when he went tumbling all the way down seventeen of the steps to the bottom. He crashed into the gate that Joe had installed to keep little Mary from crawling up the steps. "There's nineteen steps in that stairway, so he fell a good ways," Blanche noted.

The man scrambled to his feet, and Blanche heard him run to the back door. He "pulled quite violently," so violently that she thought he might have pulled it off the hinges when he exited the house. She waited three or four minutes, until she was sure he had gone, hurried to retrieve her sleeping boys, then bolted shut her bedroom door.

That was the entirety of Blanche's account of the incident itself, as provided to the doctors by Oldham. It was a much more detailed narrative than the one Blanche had given to Yates on the night of the attack. If the doctors were looking to it for confirmation that Jesse's insistence on his innocence was delusional, they could certainly have found it. There were a number of details that matched his signed confession—the perpetrator's nakedness but for his socks, his incomplete erection and fumbling in the act, his mysterious searching around on the floor. It included the detail that had caught Pearl's attention—Blanche asking, "Is that you, Joe?"—but not Jesse's self-incriminating response.

The transcript also included a striking admission. Blanche Knowles acknowledged to the state attorney that she knew Jesse Daniels, that he was the boy on the bicycle who'd pedaled past her house virtually every day—"five to ten times" a week, she estimated. "Quite often when I'd get in my car to go to town to take the maid home in the afternoon I'd see him on his bicycle stopped under, I believe it was a big oak tree, right on the edge of our property, on the edge of our grove," Blanche said. "And any times when you'd go past him when he was on the bicycle he'd always stop and pull over to the side while you went by."

She recalled one occasion, a few months before the rape, when Jesse came to the house with two younger boys and asked for some oranges— satsumas, to be precise, which, Blanche told Oldham, "are an early tan-gerine." "I told them yes," she recalled, "and I think I said to Jesse, 'Did you have some?' And he said, 'Thank you, Ma'am,' or something like that." It was the same occasion that Jesse had recalled and related in his interview with Dr. Eaton.

Not long after, Blanche "was by the 10 cent store with my little baby and a woman came up to me very, very friendly. I had no idea who she was, but she was talking about [how] she'd never seen my baby before, and then went on to talk about her baby." The friendly woman, Pearl Daniels, pointed to her nineteen-year-old son, Jesse. "That was her baby," Blanche told Oldham.

"Now after the time that the boys came up to the house, sometimes when I'd see Jesse I'd wave to him," Blanche continued. "I felt rather sorry for the boy . . . I thought that possibly it was health that was wrong with him. I felt something was. He acted strangely and never was with any other children. Except on that one occasion had I ever seen him with any other children."

Missing from the transcript, however, was one especially pertinent detail. It did not anywhere mention what Blanche had initially told Yates on the night of the rape: that the perpetrator was "a Negro," a young Negro "with bushy hair." Instead, it included Blanche's veiled disavowal—pointedly elicited by Oldham—of that earlier claim.

"Now, Mrs. Knowles," the transcript recorded him asking, "the voice that talked that night, was it a very peculiar voice to you?"

"Yes, it was," Blanche said. "I told the authorities I had never heard a voice quite like it, and I never heard a white man speak like that and that was one reason that I at first thought it possible it might have been a Negro. But it was a very distinct voice, the way he spoke, his phrasing, his pronunciation and all. They were very distinct."

"Now," Oldham asked, "did you hear that voice again after all this had taken place, in Tavares, with other voices?"

Yes, Blanche said, she had recognized the voice, first on a recording that the authorities there had played for her, and then in a room in which several people whom she could not see were asked to repeat phrases she had heard on the night of the attack. "And again I recognized the voice."

Only two suspects in the Knowles rape were being held in the jail at Tavares at the time Blanche had supposedly been asked to make a vocal identification of her attacker: Jesse Daniels and Sam Wiley Odom. Bubba Hawkins had been taken to Tampa for a lie detector test.

By the time of Blanche's interview with the state attorney, Jesse Daniels had been arrested, indicted, and delivered to Chattahoochee for evaluation. Yet Oldham did not ask her if she thought Jesse was her rapist. Neither did Blanche at any point in the interview in any way link Jesse Daniels to the attack. Nor, for all the focus on voices, did she note the most distinctive characteristic of Jesse's speech—the unmistakable stutter that impeded his every utterance.

But it was not the doctors' business to make sense of all that. Or of the perpetrator's supposed remarks about killing and war experience and the five thousand dollars, which anyone who had conversed with Jesse would surely have found difficult to imagine him saying. No, the doctors had received a transcript, just as they had requested. And once again, they did not let down their friends in Lake County.

RESTLESS AND WORRIED but ever determined—she had to do something to help her son—Pearl Daniels continued to seek signatures for her petition attesting to Jesse's good character. She wrote letters to the doctors at Florida State Hospital; she inquired about her son's health, she asked how he was adapting to his new surroundings. Daily she waited at Merritt's store in Okahumpka for replies to arrive from Chattahoochee in the afternoon's post.

She strived to raise money so she could pay the bus fare for a visit to Jesse. At an antique shop in Fruitland Park, she attempted to pawn her husband's broken timepiece; desperate though she was, she found the five-dollar offer unfair as well as unacceptable. ("It will run," she told Mabel, "if only I had a key to wind it.") To save money, she canned more beans; to make money, she picked up work in the melon patches of Okahumpka. Her body got tired and her feet were swollen; she admitted to Mabel that she was having pains in her heart. "Should go to Dr. but can't afford it," she wrote. "It's painful & weakening, but I'll probly live."

Understanding that Sam Buie had no further interest in her son's cause, and without any resources to hire an attorney, Pearl set to investigating the case herself. "Keep learning more things," she wrote to Mabel, "but if it's any help or not is the thing. Mrs. Twiss—a neighbor said [Deputy Doug] Sewell told her that he got a phone call at 5 minutes past 3 a.m. about the rape. That Mrs. Knowles had called Red Robinson's wife + the wife call'd Red, so he could call the law??? Then Red was where—I wonder??" Pearl had no other news, "but I'm trying to be all eyes + ears so to learn." She closed her letter with the hope that Mabel might drop Jesse a short note ("Do whatever you can for our darlin"). As an afterthought, she asked the reporter if she might have any "used unwanted jars."

Mabel encouraged Pearl, but she knew that Jesse's commitment order, once it had been signed by Judge Futch, had put in place legal obstacles that would be extraordinarily difficult to overcome for a family with no financial resources. She did write Jesse a short note, and she got together a few jars to help Pearl with her canning. She wanted to bolster Pearl's optimism, but Mabel's own hopes for the boy were fading.

And then something happened that changed Mabel's sentiments and Jesse's prospects. In the early morning hours of April 1, three blasts from a policeman's shotgun echoed out over the palmetto brush on South Fourteenth Street in Leesburg, just down the road from where Blanche Knowles was sleeping. A suspect had been taken into custody. Mabel soon learned of the arrest, and the charges. She knew immediately what it meant. At her office, she rolled a fresh sheet of onionskin into her old Royal and began to type the words that would bring new hope to a mother and her boy.

"And then," she tapped, "a rapist struck."

Sheriff Willis McCall, flanked by deputies James Yates and Leroy Campbell

CHAPTER EIGHT

Well-Laid Plan

Soon after daybreak on April 1, 1958, Leesburg police chief Bill Fisher received an urgent call informing him that a young black man had been caught fleeing the scene of a rape, and was shot by one of his officers. That the alleged victim was a middle-aged white Leesburg woman was enough to rouse Fisher from his bed, as his department had recently been investigating some breaking-and-entering incidents at the homes of white women in Leesburg and Okahumpka.

First, on March 11, days after Jesse Daniels had been transferred to Chattahoochee, Mrs. Amelia Rutherford awakened in the middle of the night to the sounds of someone in her Leesburg home. Her scream apparently frightened the intruder, who quickly fled the scene. Then, two weeks later, Mrs. Opal Howard, a woman in her early thirties who lived only a block away from Blanche Knowles, awakened from an uneasy sleep "to find a man bending over her" in the dark bedroom. Her scream stirred her husband from his sleep, and the "partly undressed" intruder ran from the house. Fisher had lifted fingerprints from both houses, which he'd sent to the more sophisticated crime lab at the Orange County Criminal Investigation Bureau. After interviews with both women, police investigations had focused on possible black suspects. To date, none had been apprehended. But this latest incident sounded similar, and the suspect whom Deputy Yates had taken into custody might, Fisher reasoned, be the same man he was seeking. He wanted to be present for questioning. He drove to Tavares and slipped in through the back door of the Lake County Courthouse to await Willis McCall.

The chilly relationship between the two men had grown chillier since Fisher's unsuccessful run for McCall's job in the last election. "Fisher hated Willis," Evvie Griffin recalled, adding that the bespectacled, forty-seven-year-old police chief, though a staunch segregationist himself, believed that McCall was a corrupt bully and a disgrace to law enforcement. Fisher was also well aware that the sheriff was the law in Lake County, and he would need to tread lightly in McCall's domain. When Yates and McCall arrived with the suspect in tow, he turned out to be none other than eighteen-year-old Sam Wiley Odom, who'd been detained for the rape of Blanche Knowles, then released after Jesse Daniels was apprehended. Odom's shoulder was bandaged, and his arm was in a sling. Under questioning, he stated that he was a tenth-grade night student at the Carver Heights Negro School in Leesburg, and that by day he worked in an ornamental nursery. Colorful and talkative, he freely confessed to the rape, early that morning, of sixty-year-old Kate Coker, who worked as caretaker of an invalid woman.

The night before, Odom related, he had walked from his home in North Quarters to a section of South Leesburg that was only blocks away from the home of Joe Knowles's mother, where Blanche and Joe had moved with their children after the attack in Okahumpka. He was "getting high" on moonshine when he fell asleep in an empty garage on South Sixth Street. He woke up early the next morning, and on his way back to the Quarters he got the idea to break into a house he had come upon. He took out his switchblade and was in the process of cutting the phone wires when a milkman spotted him and asked him what he was doing.

"I'm looking for my boss man," Odom told him.

A woman poked her head outside the door to see what was going on, and the milkman yelled to her, "Go get your gun!"

Odom sprinted away through an apartment property and found a spot to hide. The coast clear, he decided he'd have another try at a break-in. He chose a house on South Fourteenth Street. After he'd stripped down to his undershorts and socks, he severed what he believed to be the telephone wires, and again he got caught—not by a milkman but by a yapping white dog that pounced on him and started biting his leg. The commotion roused the household, and when Kate Coker came outside to investigate, Odom grabbed her by the arm and forced her back inside. He pushed her through the kitchen and into the living room. There, on a settee, he raped her. The invalid woman under Coker's care lay confined to her bed, unable to move.

After the attack, Odom threw on the clothes he'd left outside and raced over to the old Okahumpka Road that led back to the Quarters. When he caught sight of Deputy Yates's cruiser, though, he darted into the woods. With more police arriving at the scene, Odom attempted to hide himself in the palmetto brush. That was where Patrolman Charles Padgett spotted him. He ordered Odom to halt, but the youth made a run for it. Padgett fired, the blasts of his shotgun shattering the morning quiet. His first two shots missed; the third sprayed a load of buckshot into Odom's shoulder. The youth halted, and surrendered. Padgett and Yates took him in handcuffs back to the house where Coker claimed she had been attacked, and she positively identified Odom as her attacker. The officers then jailed him in Tavares.

"There's just one thing I want to know," Odom said after admitting to the rape. "How did they get in touch with you? I cut the phone wires so they couldn't call."

McCall shrugged; the woman had made a phone call, he said. Fisher stated the obvious: "You must have cut the wrong wires." But Odom insisted he'd cut the right wires. Then, taking a different tack, he considered, "If I had just taken another road, you never would have caught me. But I guess anybody that does this will end up getting caught."

Yates and Fisher continued their questioning, but Odom seemed unable to admit, or even to grasp, the mistakes he'd made that had led to his apprehension. Several times he recalled his post-rape conversation with the victim. "She promised she wouldn't tell no one if I didn't hurt her," he said, as indignant as he was incredulous.

McCall had worse news for Odom: Florida law invoked a mandatory death sentence for rape, he said, "unless the jury recommends mercy."

Before the close of the interview, Odom admitted to Fisher that he had been involved in other break-ins around Leesburg and Okahumpka. Indeed, the fingerprint evidence that Fisher had collected would eventually tie Odom to the incidents involving Amelia Rutherford and Opal Howard. In both cases, Odom would be charged with breaking and entering with intent to commit a felony.

Bill Fisher was pleased when he left Tavares. He was certain that Odom had cased the homes of at least two of the women he'd targeted, as their spouses traveled frequently or worked night jobs. It was only by happenstance that Opal Howard's husband was home on the evening that Odom paid his felonious visit. Also, Fisher noted, in both the Rutherford and Coker incidents, the attacker (Odom, by his own admission) had almost entirely undressed before entering the intended victims' homes.

But something nagged at Fisher. Why had neither Yates nor McCall explored the possibility that Odom might also have been responsible for the rape of Blanche Knowles back in December—a rape that had occurred barely a stone's throw from Odom's house? Hadn't Blanche told deputies that her attacker was a husky Negro with bushy hair? At least forty pounds heavier than Jesse Daniels—that description certainly matched Sam Wiley Odom. Indeed, Odom had initially been picked up and held in connection with the attack, along with Bubba Hawkins—until Jesse was apprehended, that is. But wasn't Odom interrogated about the December rape in Okahumpka? When Fisher had raised the point, McCall and Yates were quick to declare the Knowles case definitively closed. And when Fisher asked about a palm print that had been lifted from the Knowles house and sent for analysis to the lab in Orange County, McCall had brushed away the question with a flick of the wrist. Leery of seeming to play politics with the sheriff he had tried to unseat, Fisher did not persist, and he "drew away" from McCall and Yates.

Still, before he definitively closed his own book on Sam Wiley Odom, Fisher thought he'd take a ride over to the Bosanquet place and ask a few questions. He found Blanche's father at home. The two men stood together, surveying the grounds of an estate built in another century, as Alfred struggled to put words to the calamity that had befallen the Knowles and Bosanquet families.

"It would not look good in newsprint," Alfred said, more circumspect than hesitant, that Blanche "had been raped by a Negro."

The statement confirmed Fisher's suspicions, and began to make some sense of them. Blanche Knowles might have been the victim of a traumatizing rape, her father seemed to be saying, but at least Joe Knowles would be spared the indignity of having a wife who had been violated by a black man.

If it was confirmation of a theory, however, the theory was one that Fisher felt obliged to keep to himself for the moment, for the English gentleman had spoken to him in strictest confidence.

TWO DAYS AFTER Sam Wiley Odom's arrest, Mabel Norris Reese drove to Okahumpka to pick up Pearl Daniels for the long drive north to Chattahoochee. They were both eager to see Jesse, albeit for different reasons.

Mabel was eager to interview him, now that she finally had the opportunity. Pearl was simply eager to see her son.

At the hospital, they signed in and were directed to the visitation room, where they were joined by Jesse. Mabel attempted to draw from the boy an account unscripted by McCall and his crew, but Pearl kept interrupting the long pauses between Mabel's questions and her son's stuttered responses with inquiries of her own—about Jesse's health, his eating habits, his doctors, and how he was faring. Patiently, Mabel persuaded Pearl to restrain her motherly instincts until she'd managed to conduct her interview. And just as patiently, she extracted from Jesse the tale of coercion and confusion she'd suspected.

"Talking like an excited child who could no longer hold a secret," though frequently rambling to other subjects—his passion for music, his hobby of making toy cars out of wood—Jesse disclosed the details of his ordeal back at the Lake County jail. "For two hours," Mabel wrote, "I listened to him pouring out the story that had not yet been told before a bar of justice."

Jesse described how Sam Buie had visited him in his cell and waved in his face a typewritten copy of the confession. His eyes wide with plea and apology, Jesse declared to his mother, "It's a bunch of lies! Mama, they kept asking me so many questions I got confused."

McCall and Yates had taken him into a room at the jail to be interrogated. Yates was holding a piece of paper, and McCall was holding a gun, his .38 caliber Smith & Wesson—the same gun he'd used to shoot Samuel Shepherd and Walter Irvin, six years earlier. The sheriff, Jesse said, "held a pistol to my head and said I better sign my name or he was gonna pull the trigger." To drive home the threat, McCall had aimed the gun at the floor of the cell and fired a round. "He said he'd blow my brains out," Jesse said, if he did not admit to raping Mrs. Knowles. "I didn't want to but I signed my name where he said."

So that was what Jesse had so wanted to tell his mother—"what the man did to me." It wasn't the first time McCall had used such an interrogation tactic. During the Groveland case, defendant Charles Greenlee told lawyers that after he had been convicted and sentenced to life, McCall had brought him down to his office, held a gun to his head, turned on a tape recorder, and led the terrified sixteen-year-old through a series of leading questions designed, for McCall's benefit, to "set the record straight" on Greenlee's guilt. In fear for his life, Greenlee had told McCall what he wanted to hear—that he and the other defendants had raped Norma Padgett.

ON THE LONG DRIVE back to Lake County, Mabel and Pearl were newly recharged about the prospects for Jesse's case, given the news about Sam Wiley Odom's arrest, and Jesse's description of a coerced confession. Mabel pressed Pearl for details about her son—his behavior, habits, hobbies, jobs—to establish his good character. She urged Pearl, too, to recall every particular she could, no matter how insignificant or minor, about Jesse's movements on December 17, so that they could construct a timeline of his actions—a timeline that no one had ever cared to know before, since Jesse had never been allowed to defend himself in court.

That day, Pearl recalled, she and Charles had "burned off" a lot beside their home, and Jesse and three of his friends—local boys—had helped set fire to a dead tree. The blaze had caught the attention of a neighbor, Lloyd Harrison, who had invited Jesse to go coon hunting with him that afternoon. After the hunt, around 9:30 that evening, Lloyd had returned Jesse to the Daniels home, where Charles and Pearl were watching television with some of their neighbors.

Mabel wanted to know exactly what they were watching. Pearl couldn't remember, but a few days later she wrote to tell Mabel that she'd found the *TV Guide* for the night in question—they'd watched an old movie, *Turn Back the Clock*, from 11:00 p.m. to 12:30 a.m., and then the Jack Paar show until 12:45, when the neighbors left. Pearl made them sandwiches, and Jesse had eaten his from a plate on the floor, where he was working on a "plastic model car putting on spinner hub caps," while his parents talked and watched the news. After the network sign-off, Pearl had "cleaned up crumbs & ash trays," and then the three of them had gone to bed.

They'd barely gotten to their rooms—Charles and Jesse in the room with two single beds, Pearl by herself in the other—when they'd heard a loud crash outside the house. It was the dead tree falling in the vacant lot next door—at 1:18 a.m., Pearl was absolutely certain. The noise had set the neighborhood dogs to barking, but after a minute or two, "everything seemed peaceful." Pearl checked that the doors were locked and turned off the lights. The three of them were all in their beds by 1:20 a.m.

In the timeline that Mabel was piecing together, with near certainty she placed Jesse on the floor of the Daniels house with his model cars "at the very moment a man was lurking around the big house up the main road, watching to make certain a husband was not there as an intended victim returned from an evening in Leesburg." In the room where Jesse slept with his father, there was only three feet of space between the two beds. Jesse's bed, she noted, squeaked, as the Daniels family, living on a veteran's pension, couldn't afford box springs. That squeak and the fact that Charles was, as he affirmed, a light sleeper—"With my heart like it is, I'm awake a half dozen times in the night"—had Mabel convinced that, as Charles said, "If that boy had gotten out of that bed, I'd surely have heard him."

Pearl recalled a few more details that might prove Jesse had been neither absent from the Daniels house that night nor present at the scene of the crime. First, "If he had slipped out and gone up to that house, and then tried to sneak back in, our dog would have barked at him until he found out it was Jesse." Also, if he had gone out, he would have had sand on the soles of his shoes and would have tracked it into the house. And there was also the matter of the intruder's undershorts, which were supposed to have been left at the scene, a key piece of evidence. "Well, it so happens that Jesse sleeps in his shorts and puts on clean ones when he gets up in the morning," Pearl told Mabel. "He was wearing shorts when he got up that next morning, and I'd swear they were the same ones." If Jesse had done as his accusers said and left his shorts at the Knowles house, Pearl pointed out, "When he got home then, he would have had to move out the ironing board that stands against the bureau where his shorts are, opened the drawer to get clean ones—all of this in the dark, mind you. Believe me, it just wouldn't have been possible for him to do it without us hearing him—for Charlie and I have trained ourselves to hear his every move because of his sickness."

As she'd promised Pearl, Mabel had contacted Howard Dixon in an attempt to reignite the ACLU's interest in Jesse's case. A few days after she and Pearl returned from Chattahoochee, Dixon responded. He was, he said, "urgently trying to further our investigation into the McCall situation" and was hoping to return to Lake County soon, "with the prospect of achieving some results." Dixon indicated that he'd also sent a letter to LeRoy Collins, in which he urged the governor to investigate McCall and to demand the results of fingerprint evidence "that could either confirm or deny the guilt of Jesse Daniels." He informed Mabel, too, that the chairman of the ACLU in Miami would be coming to Mount Dora to discuss Jesse's case. The chairman, Dixon noted, was committed to maintaining constitutional rights, "even in the darker areas of Florida."

Vera Rony of the Workers Defense League, whom Mabel had also approached, expressed an active interest in the case as well. "I think it is most important for all of us to do what we can to get young Daniels out of the crazy house," she wrote. "From my knowledge of these places, which is not considerable, I know that if you are not crazy when you go in, you can certainly become so in short order."

Mabel tracked down Bill Fisher in Leesburg. The police chief stated he had no doubts that Sam Wiley Odom's confession to the rape of sixty-year-old Kate Coker, made before Willis McCall and his deputy, "was on the level." He noted not just the "strong similarity" between the Coker rape and the Knowles rape but the proximity of Odom's house to the Knowles residence and the attacker's having disrobed down to his socks before entering the women's homes. When Fisher confronted Odom with fingerprint evidence from the Coker house, Odom had ruefully replied, "That's the only one where I forgot to wear gloves." Even if that were true, Odom had still managed to leave behind incriminating prints at both the Rutherford and Howard houses. More important to Fisher, Odom had freely admitted to breaking into the homes of women whose husbands, he believed, were not at home.

Although Fisher had been restrained recently in his criticism of Willis McCall, the sheriff's behavior had not ceased to bother him. A reporter from the Leesburg *Daily Commercial* had been present at the sheriff's department on the morning of Odom's arrest, but since then McCall had barred the press from questioning the suspect; nor had his department released any statements. The uncharacteristic silence of an office "that gloats over the 'crime record' of Negroes," as Mabel put it, disturbed Fisher equally. So did McCall's refusal to share with him any of the evidence critical to the Knowles case, and to Jesse Daniels's fate, and his dismissiveness of the questions Fisher had raised.

Finally, Fisher admitted to Mabel that he had never believed that Jesse had committed the attack on Blanche Knowles. Still, candid as he was in his assessment of the investigations into the two rapes, he refrained from disclosing the one crucial detail he had gleaned on his visit to Fair Oaks. He did not feel he could break Alfred Bosanquet's confidence to anyone, not even the *Mount Dora Topic* reporter who despised Willis McCall as much as he did.

Fisher's disclosures took the shape of a story that, to Mabel's mind, demanded a wider audience. So, in the hope of bringing national attention to Jesse Daniels's case, she submitted an impassioned piece to both the *New York Post* and the *Christian Science Monitor.* A decade earlier, both the *Post* and the *Monitor* had covered the Groveland Boys case, and she'd maintained connections with reporters and editors at both of the papers who had become well versed in McCall's machinations.

"Has politically powerful Sheriff Willis McCall at last outwitted himself?" read the opening to her story. "The rabid segregationist Lake County sheriff is in a predicament now that could lead to serious charges being placed against him and also involve attachés of the Florida Fifth Circuit Court here," she continued. As grounds for those "serious charges," she cited McCall's successful execution of a "well-laid plan to have a 19-year-old mentally-retarded white youth committed to the state's mental hospital at Chattahoochee as 'insane' and thereby convicted without trial on a charge of raping a prominent Lake County woman last December"—all in the sheriff's "frantic effort" to protect "power citrus growers." However, this time, Mabel suggested, McCall might have "extended himself too far," as evidenced by a recent rape case that "has exploded into the news here to upset the sheriff's plans."

That article summarized the events of December 17 that had led to Jesse Daniels's institutionalization, along with the more recent, strikingly similar rape case for which Odom had been arrested. And there was a shocking new detail, too, which had been recounted by Jesse Daniels's "distraught" mother. "Fighting valiantly," Mabel reported, Pearl had been working in the watermelon fields to raise funds for Jesse's defense. It was in the melon fields, among the "hard-eyed, segregationist white workers" of Okahumpka, that Pearl had "heard the talk"—talk that "the Ku Klux Klan intends to 'get' the Negro before he is tried." Given the history of lawlessness and violence within the Lake County Sheriff's Department, Mabel did not doubt the truth of Pearl's claim.

Mabel reported that, on her advice, Pearl had "immediately wired

Governor Collins a warning, and asked that Odom be protected for his own safety as well as to permit the investigation into whether or not he is guilty of the December attack." At the same time, Mabel acknowledged that the chances of Jesse Daniels' receiving justice by gubernatorial intervention were impeded by the fact that "the family of the December victim and their attorney are politically powerful in the state."

In any event, neither paper expressed interest in publishing the story. As one historian noted, press coverage of interracial rape cases had diminished after World War II, as the editors of mainstream—white— newspapers sought "both to avert mob violence and to preserve the appearance of a law-abiding society." And the fact that blame might have landed unfairly on a white youth rather than a black one did nothing to help encourage interest. The story ended up running in the *Mount Dora Topic* alone—a pattern that would continue to ensure that hardly anyone outside its small readership had the slightest indication that something might be amiss in the increasingly strange case of Jesse Daniels.

Still, Mabel persevered. She wrote again to Howard Dixon at the ACLU, this time in hopes of convincing the experienced criminal attorney to intercede in the Odom case, and—should the rumors Pearl had heard in the melon patches prove to be true—to keep Sam Wiley Odom alive.

By a county court order on April 8, Odom was indicted for the rape of Kate Coker. He was remanded to the custody of the sheriff of Lake County and was to be held without bond. A trial date was set for May 12. The court deemed Odom's mother and stepfather, Laura and Frampy Cope, to be insolvent and thus unable to pay for his defense. Because, like Jesse Daniels, Odom had been accused of committing a crime punishable by death, he was entitled to court-appointed counsel. Judge Futch assigned his defense to Walker M. Kennedy, a sixty-six-year-old attorney from Mount Dora. Jury selection and trial testimony began that same day.

Kennedy mounted a less-than-spirited defense for a teenage client facing death by electrocution. In his opening statement he declared that he himself "did not deny the guilt of the accused," and so "we simply ask for the mercy of this Jury for this boy." Later, in tears, he'd tell Mabel that he'd expected nothing short of a guilty verdict and a death sentence in Judge Futch's courtroom. Still, Mabel had to admit, Kennedy afforded Odom more of a defense than Sam Buie had offered for Jesse Daniels. At least Kennedy had pleaded with the all-white, all-male jury to consider Odom's circumstances. He'd described how, as a boy, Odom had had to stop attending the Negro school so that he could work in the fields and groves of Okahumpka. "His lack of education and understanding of right and wrong were factors to be taken into consideration," Kennedy had argued.

Less convincing in Kennedy's closing statement was the claim that Odom had "heard older men—Negroes returning from farm work in the North—boast of white women they had known there, and the youth's impression was fixed that all white women were 'loose.'" Kennedy asserted that "these women are the ones really responsible for this crime." And he pleaded, "None of you would press the button that would electrocute this boy. Don't make it possible for someone else to do it." The tactic was not an uncommon one in rape cases in the South in that era. As historian Lisa Lindquist-Dorr points out, "Not only did some women bring their assaults on themselves, some whites seemed to believe, but some white women's characters were already so compromised that their having been violated did not represent a threat to the social order. They were not sheltered under the mantle of white womanhood with its attendant promise of protection." Although such instances were rare, Dorr notes, "White southern men . . . despite their rhetoric to the contrary, were not so willing to endow all white women with the unfettered power to accuse black men of rape."

Sam Wiley Odom did not benefit from either of Kennedy's arguments. By the end of the afternoon, state attorney Gordon Oldham was presenting his closing argument, in which he reminded the jurors that, despite Sam Wiley Odom's plea of not guilty in court, the defendant had, on the morning of his arrest for the rape of Kate Coker, confessed to the crime before Deputy Yates and Sheriff McCall. Oldham also called the jury's attention to the fact that the defendant had not taken the stand "to deny that he was guilty of the crime with which he was charged"—a seemingly blatant violation of Florida law, which stated that no prosecuting attorney shall "be permitted before the jury or court to comment on the failure of the accused to testify in his own behalf." Oldham's ploy did not elicit an objection from the defense.

With testimony and arguments complete, Judge Futch addressed the jurors with the charge that they must be convinced beyond a reasonable doubt that "there was a penetration of the private parts of the female, Kate Coker, by the private parts of the male defendant, Sam Wiley Odom . . . and that it was done by force." Futch further informed the jury that "whoever is convicted of rape shall be punished by death unless a majority of the jury return with the verdict of conviction a recommendation to the Court for mercy." In that case, Futch stated, "the punishment shall be by imprisonment for life" or less, "in the discretion of the Court."

It was early in the evening of May 12 when the jurors convened. Six minutes later, they returned to the courtroom. They found the defendant guilty, and recommended no mercy.

Odom stood. "What have you to say why the sentence of the law should not be pronounced on you?" Futch asked him. Odom offered no response.

Judge Futch ordered Odom to be transported to death row at Raiford state prison, "to be electrocuted until you be dead; and may God have mercy on your soul."

Without a recommendation of mercy, Mabel's hopes of keeping Odom alive were fading as she and Kennedy considered next steps. Despite being certain of his client's guilt, Kennedy felt strongly that "the jury was not fair to him. It was sort of a mob action." The Ku Klux Klan had so not gotten to Odom, as Pearl had heard rumored in the melon patches of Lake County. That much Mabel knew, and was grateful for. What the reporter likely did not know was that one week before Odom's trial began, there was a rally of the Lake County Citizens' Council held at Deputy Doug Sewell's ranch in Umatilla. (At the time, the FBI was monitoring white Citizens' Councils throughout the South; these organizations, despite proclamations to the contrary, were not immune to violence.) An informant in attendance told agents that the theme of the Lake County meeting was "Our Dedication to Our Fight for States' Rights, and Americanism and Justice to All." The principal speaker, he said, was the "Honorable Gordon G. Oldham Jr." There were also short speeches by Sheriff McCall and Judge Futch, and according to the informant, approximately one hundred fifty men attended and "each signed a paper that was passed through the audience." If members of the Lake County Citizens' Council had also addressed other pertinent issues of the day at Deputy Sewell's ranch, perhaps more discreetly, such conversations were not documented in the informant's report.

Kennedy promised Mabel that he would quickly prepare Odom's appeal. Mabel herself had her mind on another miscarriage of justice. Approaching Futch outside the courthouse, she asked how long the judge thought Jesse Daniels would have to be retained at Chattahoochee. "I don't know," Futch replied, "but whether he's guilty or not, that's the place for him, with that mentality."

Whether he's guilty or not? The response infuriated Mabel and prompted yet another letter to Governor Collins, pleading with him to open an investigation into the Jesse Daniels case and appealing as much to his concern for his state's image as to his sense of justice. She was already aware of "one widely circulated national magazine" that intended to publish an article about the case. "I believe there are many things that are being neglected here in carrying out the laws of the state of Florida that need attention," she wrote, "but I would so hate to see that attention forced through 'bad publicity.'"

The "widely circulated national magazine" mentioned by Mabel in her letter to Collins was *Coronet*, a general-interest publication owned by *Esquire*. The magazine was planning to publish a feature story about Sheriff Willis McCall by William Peters, a New York writer. McCall had granted him an interview, the first he'd given to an "outsider" in years. Peters had contacted Mabel as a resource as well. She had loaned him her own clippings on McCall, and when he finished his story, he'd sent a draft to Mabel for her to read and comment on.

Mabel hadn't been shocked to find herself vilified by the sheriff, but she had been appalled by the openness with which he'd displayed his racism to a reporter for a national magazine. "We haven't had any trouble except what's been stirred up by outsiders, left-wingers, most of it Communist-inspired," he'd told Peters. "My trouble here in Lake County hasn't been with the niggers. It's been with the NAACP and the Communist Party." To prove it, McCall walked over to his safe, opened it, and pulled out a trove of newspaper clippings by which he'd identified his political opponents and perceived enemies. He told Peters that he kept another set of the documents in a bank vault so as to ensure that, in the event of loss, theft, or damage to his personal files, he "can still prove that this all started as a Communist conspiracy."

Settled back at his desk, McCall expounded on the issue that had been consuming him of late: the mixing of the races, the cause of which he lodged in the black man's desire for white women. "It's just a barbarous animal instinct that a nigger has that a white man don't have," McCall asserted. "The niggers have the idea now that the NAACP will get them out of it if they rape a white woman."

McCall professed to Peters that blacks in America had evolved in the past hundred years, but only by virtue of the influence of whites, whom, as a race, they would never equal. "They've come a far way in just a hundred years from darkest Africa," he affirmed. "Why, they're still eating each other in some places over there. I think our niggers have advanced more than any race in the same amount of time. You can attribute this advancement to the influence of the white man. I don't think you'll ever make the nigger the equal of a white man. That's why desegregation will never work. It lowers the white children's standards and morals to mix with a syphilitic, immoral, diseased race. Their brains can't compare with a white man's. They don't have the same sense of achievement. They even smell different. Why, the only way I can tell a nigger is to look at him or smell him. You'll find exceptions to some of these things, but I'm talking about generally speaking. White people advance faster, grasp things easier. You've got to have separate schools or hold the whites back, that's all."

Mabel suspected that Collins would not be pleased to see the sheriff's comments. Nor did she think McCall was doing himself any favors, but that thought seemed never to have entered the sheriff's head. "You know," he summed up to the reporter, "I used to say that America was a great country: if you liked segregation, you could live in the South; if you liked integration, you could live in the North. Now they're trying to force this thing on all of us. It won't work. It just won't work."

GOING DOOR-TO-DOOR in Okahumpka and Leesburg with her petition attesting to her son's good character, Pearl was slowly collecting more than just signatures, which soon totaled more than two hundred fifty. She was also picking up interesting bits of information. Some of it was gossip, and much of it was rumor, but a lot of it concerned Joe Knowles. "Heard in Leesburg—also Fruitland Park that Joe promised the Negro boy $500 to commit that act, & to kill her if he wanted to, & if anything went wrong, he'd pay McCall $500 to squash the confession," she wrote to Mabel. "Probably that's true & reason Joe wanted his wife to not say attacker was

Negro for fear Negro boy would tattle on Joe to someone other than Mc-Call." Pearl's sister-in-law, who lived near the Bosanquets in Fruitland Park, had also told her that Blanche's father and brother were aware of Knowles's deal with the "Negro boy" and were "about to get up a lynching party for Joe." Pearl was hoping to get confirmation. "Oh how we need proof of these things!" she wrote, in exasperation and hope.

Mabel had assured Pearl that she would handle the news coverage and deal with the legal side of Jesse's case, but now she also advised Pearl to contact the FBI and plead for an official investigation. The handwritten letter, dated November 17, landed on the desk of J. Edgar Hoover himself. Along with clippings of Mabel's stories from the *Topic*, Pearl provided both an extensive summary of the facts in her son's case and the "many gossip tales that many people believe have truth in them." For one, a man she knew claimed he had seen Blanche Knowles "being loaded into her station wagon the night of Dec. 17th drunk. If she was that drunk, one of the men must have driven her home, the other came in the car to pick up the driver, therefore it could have been one of those men. There's the thread for you to unravel." For another, "the husband, Joe Knowles made a bragg [*sic*] to an old man, a friend of ours that he (Joe) put up a big bunch of money to get our boy convicted. Why? When the boy was gentle, mannerly, shy . . . Never been in juvenile trouble, never sassed a teacher, or fought as most boys."

Pearl closed her letter not with rumor or gossip but with what she believed was a fact: Sam Wiley Odom, a recently convicted rapist, had never been questioned about his possible involvement in the Knowles rape, despite there being a "great many features of the Knowles, Howard, and Coker crimes alike." And from that she drew her conclusion: "We truely feel the 18 yr. old negro did this one too; knowing full well our son sat at our feet playing with a toy till 1:20 A.M. 18th of Dec. Please in the name of God, and kindness of your heart, and justice will you please help us clear our son through the F.B.I.??"

Within a week, Hoover replied. The FBI "is not able to be of help to you in the matter involving your son," he informed Pearl, and he suggested that she contact a local bar association or legal aid society, which might "possibly offer aid without charge."

Pearl wrote back immediately with another handwritten letter. "The Bar Association is out Honorable Sir, since the Prosecuting Attorney, and Judge that my son would have to go up before belong to it, and both are too closely knit with the Sheriff. They would farther frame the boy." She again begged Hoover for help. "Christmas is almost here, and our one and only child has been shut away eleven months, so you can imagine how we feel. No joyous preparations for us. Could you please help change that Sir?"

Pearl's persistence was rewarded. Hoover wrote again, informing her that he had passed on her letters to the Civil Rights Division of the Department of Justice "for consideration and appropriate action." There, Assistant Attorney General W. Wilson White reviewed her correspondence along with all the previous complaints and reports on investigations appertaining to Lake County and its sheriff, Willis McCall. White did not hesitate. On December 22, 1958, he ordered an investigation into the Jesse Daniels case, "to be instituted immediately."

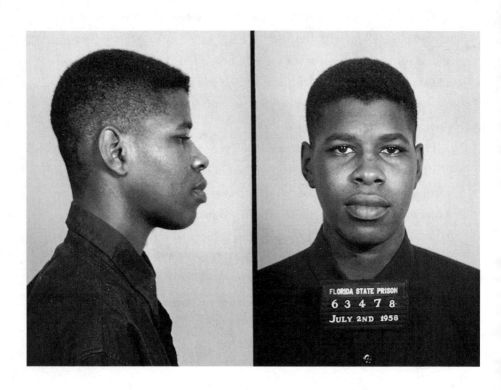

Sam Wiley Odom

CHAPTER NINE

So Much Race Pride

By THE END OF 1958, the economic impact of the previous winter's devastating freeze had been offset by the higher prices that oranges and grapefruits had commanded throughout the year, and Lake County's citrus business had made a strong recovery. The watermelon business remained in peril, but Knowles and Company nonetheless managed to prosper, as it had diversified its crops, operated its own citrus packing plant, and maintained healthy cattle holdings.

With plenty of picking to be done for the Herlongs, the Oldhams, the Knowleses, and other citrus families, the young men of North Quarters were back in the trees. No one wanted for work in harvesting season, and the boys skipped school for it. Prepared for a long day's work, the pickers would show up with coffee cans full of raccoon or possum meat for lunch, along with corn bread and the butter beans that they called "baby ears." And every crew had a gopher hook—a long pole with a stiff wire hook at its end—in case they came upon a hole burrowed by a Florida gopher tortoise in the sandy soil. Butchered, a tortoise could provide enough meat for dinner, with a leg or two left over for the next day's coffee can.

In these prosperous times, the Reese family was struggling with a different sort of freeze. Ever since Bryant Bowles of the National Association for the Advancement of White People had come bounding into the *Topic*'s office announcing that he'd get even with her, Mabel had been feeling the chill from the rival *Mount Dora Herald.* This year she'd finally been obliged to take a second job, as an editorial writer for the *Daytona Beach News-Journal*, which entailed a fifty-mile commute from Mount Dora at least twice a week. The Reeses managed to scrape by and to keep the *Topic* in print and intact, "still aiming our sights on the word 'justice.'"

Pearl Daniels, meanwhile, continued working in the fields, making her little baskets of pine straw, collecting signatures on her petition, and writing letters—letters to Jesse, to doctors at Chattahoochee, to the FBI and the Department of Justice. She continued gathering whatever information might be relevant to Jesse's case as well. It was not by accident, therefore, that one day, carrying her petition, she crossed County Road 470 into North Quarters, where she knocked on the door of Laura Cope, Sam Wiley Odom's mother.

Like Pearl, Cope had a son locked away in North Florida, and like Pearl, she had endured a year of distressing setbacks at the hands of the Lake County Sheriff's Department. In December, after the rape of Blanche Knowles, her son, Sam, had been dragged to jail in the deputies' early-morning roundup. He'd been held there, without explanation, after most of the other suspects had been released—even after Willis McCall's announcement that he was holding Bubba Hawkins, Odom's friend and neighbor, as the likely culprit. Through it all, Cope, like Pearl, had not been allowed to visit her son. Like Pearl, too, Cope knew something was rotten in Lake County.

The information Pearl gleaned from her was even more startling—and more confounding—than anything Pearl and Mabel had yet suspected. Cope told Pearl that her son had in fact confessed to the rape of Blanche Knowles. Despite that, Sam had told his mother, McCall had offered him a deal—his freedom in exchange for his "sworn statement that Melvin Hawkins raped Blanche Knowles." But her son, Cope said, had refused to finger the Hawkins boy.

Pearl learned further that, although Sam had continued to be held by the sheriff's department—beyond when not only Bubba Hawkins but Jesse as well had been taken into custody—Sheriff McCall had told Cope that the rape of Blanche Knowles would not be put on her son: "He'd see to that." And when Jesse was "finished in Chattahoochee, he'd be put somewhere else."

Even so, like Hawkins, Odom had had a brush with vigilante justice, just as Pearl had heard rumored in the watermelon fields. When Cope had visited her son on death row at Raiford, he told her that, after his arrest for the rape of Kate Coker, Willis McCall had driven him to "an isolated spot at the airport between Leesburg and Tavares," where the sheriff "threw a pocket knife to the ground and said, 'Nigger that is your knife, pick it up.'" Fearing that, had he done so, the sheriff would shoot him, Odom had refused.

Why? Pearl asked herself. Why had a convicted rapist not been prosecuted for a rape to which he had reportedly confessed? And why was her son being punished for a crime that he did not commit—could not have committed? Other questions might have disturbed her as well, such as the odd timing and sequence of events leading up to Jesse's arrest. But she was a mother; it was her son's fate that concerned her most.

"Why?" she beseeched J. Edgar Hoover, recounting these new details. "Will you *Please* in the name of *God* and *Mercy* use your Powers invested in you through the F.B.I. and the trust of the People, to see this is investigated and let us hear from you right away that it is being done."

Hoover, in his response, indicated that he had forwarded Pearl's letters to Assistant Attorney General W. Wilson White at the Civil Rights Division in the Department of Justice, where the investigation was already under way. Pearl promptly shifted her attention to White. In a letter to him, she characterized her son as an "obedient, shy boy" who had been forced to sign a confession he was incapable of reading, and explained that "the boy is not capable of inventing lies or plans for his own convenience since he is retarded, and thinks much slower than his age group." She related, too, the results of the investigation into Jesse's case by NAACP officials after Sam Wiley Odom had been arrested for the rape of Kate Coker; they "were convinced," Pearl averred, that "it was ODOM (the colored boy) and not Daniels who committed both crimes." Two weeks later, in a follow-up letter, she inquired if White had yet "made a decision in either direction" about entering the case. She wrote, "We have had no justice shown in this boy's case at all. No arrest, no trial, no witnesses," and no effectual defense, because "we were given an ex-prosecuting attorney for our son and he did not attempt to help the boy, only secretly fixed it for our boy to be sent off afterwards [and] had the nerve to tell us that is the best thing for him." But, Pearl concluded, the doctors "aren't treating the boy now that he is up there, and the Dr's told me he is not insane, just slow in thinking and acting."

Mabel's own outreach had been encouraging. She was surprised to learn that Robert Saunders in Tampa was looking into Sam Wiley Odom's case in order to decide whether or not to involve the NAACP in his appeal, particularly as some at the organization, Mabel learned, "are convinced it was Odom, and not Daniels, who committed both crimes." Contrary to its supposed policy of automatically coming to the defense of any black person accused or convicted of a serious crime, the organization was said to be considering legal steps to reopen Jesse's case.

In January 1959, FBI agents descended on Leesburg and Tavares to determine if the civil rights of Jesse Daniels had indeed been violated by the Lake County Sheriff's Department. One of those agents was Ted Tucker, who traveled to Chattahoochee to interview Jesse Daniels. Jesse told the agent he was "being kept at the hospital unjustly as a result of a confession he signed admitting the rape of Mrs. Knowles of Okahumpka,

Florida." The agent talked to Jesse about his sexual thoughts and experiences, then interviewed the assistant supervisor of Chattahoochee's white male department. The assistant supervisor claimed that Jesse had been transferred between wards in the department because he was "a close associate of other known sexual perverts and deviates." There was no record of such an accusation or transfer noted in Jesse's extensive medical records at Chattahoochee, yet the assistant supervisor felt that "for the protection of the victim and society," Jesse should continue to be confined to the mental institution, where he could be "closely supervised."

Next, Tucker visited Pearl, who had recently moved with Charles from Okahumpka to an even smaller home in nearby Yalaha. She told him, "Both my husband and I are aware of the gamble involved, if my son is declared mentally competent and able to stand trial for the rape charge. We know that our son, on the night of the rape, was in our residence, and never left the house on that particular night."

In Tavares, Tucker interviewed James Yates and Leroy Campbell. He reported that both deputies denied violating any civil rights in the Daniels case. Both also refused to furnish Tucker with a signed statement. But the agents did include in their report a signed statement from the polygrapher Bill Donaldson, whom Yates had persuaded McCall to bring in from the sheriff's department in Tampa to aid in the initial questioning of suspects. The statement indicated that Donaldson had interviewed Blanche Knowles in the sheriff's office five days after the rape, and also that he'd been present when Yates had brought Jesse Daniels in for questioning later that night. It noted that Donaldson had spoken with Jesse's parents and conversed with Jesse himself about hunting and knives before he'd administered the lie detector test. Ten minutes into the test, the statement claimed, Jesse "admitted to me he was the person who raped Mrs. Knowles," and Donaldson had advised McCall of the results. Joe Knowles, who was noted as also being present, had asked Donaldson if he thought the boy was guilty. Donaldson, the statement reported, had responded, "He [is] either guilty or crazy."

Sheriff Willis McCall played his recording of Jesse's confession for Tucker and another agent, and then proceeded to blame Mabel Norris Reese for the investigation itself, her latest attempt "to publicly discredit and embarrass him in an apparent attempt to get him out of office" by giving "the impression that Daniels is innocent of the rape charge, and that a Negro, Sam Wiley Odom, . . . is the one who committed the Knowles rape."

McCall did furnish the FBI with a signed statement, which read like a manifesto against Mabel. It accused her of having joined forces with various communist and pro-communist labor movement officials, both locally and nationally, as well as members of the NAACP in her misguided battles for justice. It also asserted that she had coopted the Danielses in her crusade by getting them to "hatch up a bunch of lies" each time they visited their son in jail, which was why, the sheriff claimed, he'd denied them further access to their son. Yet, he pointed out, he'd always allowed the boy's counsel to visit. As for the allegation of coercion, the sheriff denied that he'd fired his pistol at the floor near Jesse's feet, or that he'd given a belt to Joe Knowles so that he could beat the boy—for "Mr. Knowles being a gentleman of high standing in his community, would never have participated in any such action."

McCall's own notoriety, he asserted, put a check on his behavior as well. "There are [as] many people chasing after me as there are some beautiful movie actresses. It just happens to be for a different purpose. I am convinced at this time that my mother did not raise any completely crazy children, and if I were so inclined to violate a person's Civil Rights, which I definitely am not, and stand a defender of Constitutional Government, and a protector of people's rights, knowing that I am in the lime light and am being watched by such vultures that would cut my throat at the drop of your hat. I give myself credit for having too much sense to be trapped into a position where I might be prosecuted, thrown out of office, or disgraced." Indeed, he hoped "to see the day that the Justice Department will wake up to what is going on and quit being influenced by such individuals as is spending time and taxpayers money investigating such trumped up lies, when the Federal Bureau of Investigation and the other law enforcement officers could be busy doing their necessary jobs, without being harassed by such unjust and uncalled for problems as I have been subjected to, many times in the past." In the meantime, he would not give in to the efforts of "these left-winged elements" who were attempting "to harass and worry me to the extent that I will get mad or give up in despair." He affirmed that "as long as God lets me live . . . I will never be a *quitter* and . . . I will always be on the job when it comes to defending our American Way of Life."

On February 4, W. Wilson White informed the United States attorney in Miami that after reviewing the FBI reports on Willis V. McCall, the Civil Rights Division had "concluded that further action is not warranted." He wrote to Pearl Daniels as well, to inform her that the investigation of McCall had been completed. "It does not disclose that any violation of a federal criminal statute was committed in connection with the arrest, detention, and commitment of your son, Jesse Daniels," he wrote. "Therefore, this Department will take no further action."

Mabel Norris Reese was not surprised by the decision. She'd seen McCall survive many such investigations. In case after case, from the Groveland Boys to the Platt family to Jesse Daniels, she'd spent hours upon hours sharing details with FBI agents like Ted Tucker, only to have her efforts come to naught after they had interviewed McCall. "What are you doing believing that Communist?" was evidently all he needed to say to them, and "the investigations would stop."

Certain that a death warrant would soon be issued in the case of *State of Florida v. Sam Wiley Odom*, W. M. Kennedy filed an appeal in Futch's circuit court. In the motion, Kennedy argued that the court had erred in permitting state attorney Gordon Oldham "to comment before the jury and the Court on the failure of the accused to testify in his own behalf." Kennedy also cited the jury's failure to adequately "deliberate or consider the verdict which they returned," since they had been out of the courtroom for barely more than six minutes. By the end of the summer, Odom's case had reached the Supreme Court of Florida; oral arguments were scheduled for January 14, 1959. On Mabel's recommendation, Kennedy enlisted the assistance of Tavares attorney Walton B. Hunter, the son of Mabel's late friend and former state attorney Jesse Hunter. Together the two lawyers argued the case before the Tallahassee court, with Attorney General Richard W. Ervin representing the State.

One month later, the court upheld the circuit court verdict. In rejecting Kennedy's argument, the justices cited the fact that during the trial, Kennedy had called Odom to the witness stand and asked him his name, his age, and what grade he had reached in school. Therefore, the court ruled, Odom had appeared as a witness in the case for the defense and could not be considered a "silent defendant whose silence must be ignored."

In June, Kennedy petitioned the Florida pardon board to spare Odom's life on the grounds that the "near illiterate" boy "never had a chance before the all-white jury which condemned him" after barely deliberating. Even as he prepared his argument, he did not believe his client would stand much of a chance before the pardon board. But a few weeks earlier, a Tallahassee case had exploded into national headlines that dramatically brought before the state the issue of racial bias in the dispensation of justice.

On May 2, Betty Jean Owens, a black coed at Florida Agriculture and Mechanical University, was on her way home from the school's annual Green and Orange Ball with her date and another student couple. They had pulled off the road by a dark, wooded park when, at about one a.m., four young white men snuck up on the unsuspecting couples. One shoved a sixteen-gauge shotgun into the driver's face and ordered the black youths out of the car. The two males, tuxedoed, were forced to kneel at the roadside, while their dates in formal gowns were held at knifepoint. The white man with the shotgun ordered the two young black men to get back in their car and leave. As they started to pull away, Owens began to cry. One of the men slapped her; if she wanted to get back home herself, he warned her, she had best remain quiet. The distraction, quick though it was, lent the other young woman a chance to make it to the safety of the car before it left. Owens alone faced the four armed men. They pushed her into the backseat of their car and drove her to the outskirts of town, where they raped her multiple times.

Owens's companions, meanwhile, drove to a local police precinct and reported the incident. Joe Cooke Jr., a nineteen-year-old police intern and student at all-white Florida State, sprang into action. In a police car, he led the students on a search for their friend. Around four a.m., they spotted the assaulters' blue Chevrolet. A high-speed chase ensued until Cooke managed to pull the Chevy over. Jumping from the police car with shotgun in hand, he ordered the four young men out of their vehicle. Betty Jean Owens, in her rumpled gold-and-white ball gown, lay bound and gagged on the floor of the backseat.

A deputy arrived to assist with the arrests. The four intoxicated white men, "laughing and joking on the way to the police station," apparently figured their actions amounted to no more than horseplay. Confessions came readily. "They all admitted it," the arresting deputy said.

News of the arrests leapt onto the headlines of local newspapers and quickly spread nationwide, sowing panic, outrage, and protest. Reportedly, one white woman had to send her black maid home for the day when she showed up at the house "on the verge of hysteria" and armed with a knife "in case any white men come after me." White women in Tallahassee swore they'd never again dare to dally in a parked car "in the country moonlight lest some Negroes should be out hunting in a retaliatory mood." More productively, student protesters, encouraged by their recent victory in the 1957 Tallahassee bus boycott, urged the nation to pay attention to the case. A just decision would demonstrate that "white men could no longer attack black women without consequence." A Florida A&M student exhorted a crowd of fellow protesters, "Remember it wasn't just one Negro girl that was raped—it was all of Negro womanhood in the South." The students, though, would protest nonviolently, "unlike white men who historically used the protection of white womanhood to inspire mob violence against black men."

On May 6, hundreds of spectators crammed the Jim Crow balcony of the Leon County Courthouse while, in a secret hearing room, Betty Jean Owens and her four attackers attended grand jury proceedings. Indictments followed, and the four men were led back into the courtroom. One by one, each of the four defendants pleaded not guilty to the charge of rape. The trial date was set for June 11.

In advance of the trial, Roy Wilkins of the NAACP wrote to Governor Collins, noting pointedly that in recent lynching cases such as that of Emmett Till, the victim's race had stood in the way of justice. "Full punishment has been certain and swift in cases involving a white victim and a Negro accused," Wilkins wrote, "but the penalty has neither been very certain nor heavy in cases involving a Negro victim and a white accused." Martin Luther King Jr., speaking at Bethel Baptist Church in Tallahassee, praised the student protesters for having brought the case to national attention. It represented "a clear-cut opportunity for the South to demonstrate to the world that there are people who believe in justice," but "if the court fails now, Florida will be condemned in the eyes of the nation." Ella Baker, director of the Southern Christian Leadership Conference, put her faith in the case itself; it was so solid, she believed, that "not even an all white Florida jury could fail to convict."

On June 11, Betty Jean Owens took the stand. Speaking softly, she recounted how one of her attackers, eighteen-year-old David Beagles, held "a wicked looking foot long knife" to her neck as he forced her to the ground. The men then tugged at her dress and pulled off her underwear, slapping her repeatedly because she was crying and begging them to stop. "I couldn't do anything but what they said," Owens testified, and for several hours in the woods, the four of them took turns raping her—seven times in all, she said. When they were done, two of the men blindfolded her and pushed her back into the car. After Cooke spotted the car and initiated the chase, one of the rapists suggested "dumping the nigger." But they were forced to pull over and surrender before they did any dumping.

The defense attorneys took advantage of cross-examination to paint "the Negress" Owens as a "stereotypical black jezebel." They questioned her virginity and attempted to wrest from her an admission that she had engaged in consensual—and pleasurable—sex with the four white men. "Didn't you derive any pleasure from that? Didn't you?" the attorneys pressed.

The defense called friends and family of the four young men as character witnesses, who invariably described the defendants as "good boys." The phrase was an ill fit for twenty-four-year-old William Collinsworth, the oldest of the attackers, who'd held the shotgun on Owens during the rapes, except when he himself was perpetrating them. After his arrest he'd been sent to Chattahoochee "for tests of his sanity," as he had pleaded not guilty by reason of insanity, but he'd returned for the trial. Testifying on his behalf, his wife, Pearlie, allowed that her husband was "not himself when he was drunk," but when he was sober, she told the courtroom, "you couldn't ask for a better husband."

The defense attorneys were not short of explanations to excuse the behavior of the accused. The presence of alcohol in Collinsworth's "Indian blood," combined with his "moronic mentality," caused him to act "primitively." Sixteen-year-old Ollie Stoutamire was merely in "the wrong place at the wrong time," according to his attorney, who claimed that the prosecution of his client was the work of "outside agitators" and in his closing argument urged the jury, "Don't become hysterical like the northern press did."

When word spread that the jury, after three hours of deliberation, had reached a verdict, spectators filed back into the courtroom, while hundreds of black protesters held a vigil outside. Those watching from the Jim Crow balcony could not see the white faces below, but if they had, they would have seen most looking stunned and relieved: The jury found all four defendants "guilty with a recommendation of mercy" because they had found "no evidence of brutality." The judge set sentencing for two weeks hence, and the defendants were packed off to Raiford in the meantime. One of the defense lawyers, asked if he'd appeal the verdict, said, "You don't appeal a victory."

After the trial, Betty Jean Owens told a reporter, "I'm grateful that twelve white men finally believed the truth. But they also recommended mercy, and I wonder what they would have done if one of our boys had done it to a white girl." The verdict brought Betty Jean's grandmother to tears. "I've lived to see the day when white men would be really brought to account for what they did to Negroes," she said. Betty Jean's mother spoke more strongly. After praising the jury for "upholding my daughter's womanhood," she let it be known that "I did my best to bring my children up right. They have race pride. They have so much race pride that they wouldn't fool with no white man, trash or not. The only way they could have gotten Betty was the way they did. Take her."

Editorials in many national newspapers framed the verdict as a victory for race relations. "What happened in Tallahassee was a triumph for law and order," the *New York Times* declared. "The defendants were tried fairly and convicted. And all this happened in a Southern city. Beside those facts the recommendation for mercy is essentially a detail." Black newspapers were decidedly less commendatory. The *Baltimore Afro-American* wrote, "True-to-tradition white men made it inescapably clear at 12:35 Sunday morning that death for rape is only for colored men accused by white women." As to the jury's failure to find "evidence of brutality," the editorialist asked, "What did this jury want in the way of evidence?" The *Pittsburgh Courier* called attention to the fact that since 1924, thirty-seven black men, many of them teens, had been executed for the rapes of white women in Florida, whereas only one white man had been sentenced to death for the same crime—he'd confessed to the 1925 rape of a four-year-old girl on Thanksgiving Day. The *Chicago Defender* mocked the adulatory tone with which the "white press" greeted the jury's recommendation for mercy. "Meanwhile the wailing cries of four Negroes awaiting execution in the death row of Florida's state penitentiary—for raping white women—are drowned out by the din and hoopla over the verdict which has spared the lives of four white rapists."

With racial tensions already running high and more than a dozen segregation bills before the state legislature, the Owens case, as one Tallahasseean observed, "couldn't have happened at a worse time." It also presented Kennedy with an opportunity to buttress his legal argument for clemency for Sam Wiley Odom. Yet when he appeared before the Florida pardon board to argue for clemency, he chose not to exploit the verdict that had been issued in the Tallahassee rape. "I saw in the papers that I would use the case up here as an argument," he noted, but then announced, "I have no intention of doing that. I plead only for fairness to this boy. Each case must be considered on its own merit. All cases are different." As in the court trial, Kennedy did not question Odom's guilt; instead, he cited the convicted youth's age and limited schooling as mitigating factors. "He didn't seem to realize the severity of what he had done," Kennedy explained to the board. "He had admitted his act readily, but didn't think she would mind. He said he just wanted to try a white woman." Stories "told him by his father and Negro boys in military service of white women going with Negro men" had "inflamed" the curiosity of an impressionable boy, he said.

As for the six-minute deliberation that had convicted Odom with no recommendation for mercy, Gordon Oldham defended it and the jury, which "needed no time to decide Odom's guilt because the case was open and shut."

Nor did Leesburg police chief Bill Fisher favor Kennedy's appeal. Despite his negative feelings about Willis McCall, Fisher was unequivocal in his support of the death penalty for Odom. "I wish you could have seen the hysteria of this woman, and others," Fisher told the pardon board. "I think this type of thing—if we law enforcement officers don't do the best job we can—it will lead to lynchings."

In July, the Florida pardon board turned down Kennedy's appeal, and on August 10, Governor LeRoy Collins signed Sam Wiley Odom's death warrant. The Okahumpka youth would have just two weeks to live.

Unwavering though he was in his certainty that justice had been served in Odom's case, Fisher remained troubled by the pattern of the recent rape cases in Lake County and by the investigative work, or lack of it, done by the sheriff's department, especially with regard to the case against Jesse Daniels. So while he was in Tallahassee for the pardon board hearing, the Leesburg police chief paid a visit to Attorney General Richard Ervin and shared with him his concerns. He not only told Ervin that he thought Daniels was being "framed" for the rape of Blanche Knowles, but also divulged to him the confidential information that he had gleaned from his visit with Alfred Bosanquet at Fair Oaks—that "it would not look good in newsprint" that his daughter had been raped by a black man.

On his return to Lake County, Fisher received an irate phone call from Gordon Oldham, who delivered a stern warning: "Stay out of the case."

State attorney Gordon Oldham

CHAPTER TEN

Don't Talk to Me
About Conscience, Lady

By August 12, telegrams and letters from Odom's family, local black churches, black community leaders, the NAACP, civil rights advocates, capital punishment opponents, and concerned citizens from across the nation were pouring into Governor Collins's office, pleading for the boy's life. Bettye Odom, Sam's twenty-one-year-old sister, wrote, "If 4 white men can rape one colored of 16 and live, why can't a colored boy live after the woman herself says he did not hurt me? . . . He is my only Bro and oldest. Please don't let him die if you can help it please." Laura Cope, who had not pleaded for her child earlier, now did. "Governor, I don't ask you this favor because of those white boys," she wrote, "because I feel like those boys would not have done what they did if they hadn't been drinking"—and that, she believed, was also the case with her son.

In his response to Cope a few days later, Collins wrote, "I understand your grief but I have no power as Governor to grant the relief you are seeking. You are doubtless a person of great faith and I deeply hope that in that faith you may find some help in bearing this cross which understandably is beyond reason to any mother."

The black churches of Leesburg and Okahumpka appealed to the governor's "sense of righteousness," which should allow Odom the clemency granted the defendants in the Owens case. Likewise, the Tallahassee branch of the NAACP, "praying for equality under the law," urged the governor to "employ the power and full authority of your office to insure equality." Letters from black bishops and other leaders across Florida, as well as concerned white citizens, poured in, making the same case.

The flood of letters appeared to have some effect. Although the governor—despite his personal opposition to the death penalty, or "Florida's gutter of shame," as he'd called it—insisted that he had "no power" to commute Odom's death sentence to life imprisonment, he did ask his assistant to look into whether the case had been disposed of by unanimous decision of the Florida Supreme Court, "and what, if anything, was said which would indicate a consideration of leniency on Odom's behalf."

Mabel Norris Reese remained focused on the information Odom held that could clear the charges against Jesse Daniels. "Rape Attacks Have Stopped in Lake County" ran the headline of one of the pieces she'd written for the *Daytona Beach Evening News* that had so incensed McCall. But the sheriff refused to answer reporters' questions about the relevance of this fact to whatever evidence against Daniels, still largely undisclosed, his office had gathered. "It is in this evidence that the truth may be locked away from the public," Mabel asserted, and added, "Truth also is locked away in one of two other places—either in the death cell at Raiford . . . within the mind of a young Negro or in a ward of the hospital for the insane at Chattahoochee."

After much "knocking on doors" throughout central Florida, Mabel managed to find a lawyer—Orlando criminal attorney John Lenninger—willing to assist with Jesse's case, despite the near certainty he'd never get paid. She also managed to convince Lenninger to drive the hundred miles north to Raiford with her and Pearl Daniels, in the hope that the condemned youth would consent to a visit. If Chief Fisher was correct in his theory that Odom had been involved in the rape of Blanche Knowles, Mabel reasoned, the boy might want to clear his conscience before the State of Florida took his life—especially with the mother of Jesse Daniels sitting across the table from him.

On August 18, Mabel and Pearl were escorted into the interview room at Raiford; Lenninger waited outside. Odom, in handcuffs, was led in by a guard; he took a seat across from the two women. The three of them engaged in some small talk for a few minutes. Then abruptly Odom remarked that he had only six days to live, as he was scheduled to go to the electric chair on Monday. The utterance seemed to make him anxious and "bitter," Mabel noted. It also lent her the opportunity to steer the conversation toward her purpose. She suggested to Odom that he should not go to his death with a burden on his conscience.

"Don't talk to me about conscience, lady. I ain't got any," Odom riposted.

He was "twisting in his chair," Mabel jotted in her notepad, but after a minute or so, he seemed to settle down and said he would like to continue the conversation. "I'm not afraid to die. Everyone's got to go some time, ya know."

Mabel brought up the Kate Coker rape. "Sure, I did it," Odom admitted, "and I'm not proud of it. I had been drinking wine and 'shine, and it was the 'shine that told me to do it, and I did. I was foolish and I know it."

Mabel scribbled her notes. Pearl sat silent, her eyes fixed searchingly on the boy.

"I'd like to make a statement," Odom said to Mabel. "Would you print it?" Mabel nodded.

"I don't think Jesse Daniels is guilty," he said. "In fact, I know he isn't guilty."

At that, Pearl leaned in anxiously.

"Wiley Sam," she implored, addressing him as he was known in Okahumpka, "then who did it? You've got to help us."

Again, Odom shifted in his seat, but he answered cagily. "Can you come back up here just before?" he said. "If you come back just before they take me, I'll tell you about the Blanche Knowles case."

Mabel and Pearl pleaded that now was the time for him to tell them what he knew, but Odom replied only, "I didn't do it." Then he offered, "I'll confess if you want me to. Sure won't hurt me any now."

"No, Wiley Sam," said Mabel, emphatic. "We sure don't want that. We want only the truth."

But she'd been preempted. Deputy Yates, Odom disclosed, had paid his own visit to Raiford, just before Odom's case went to the pardon board in July. He'd asked Odom to write out a statement, which, as he recalled it for Mabel, read: "I am going to be electrocuted for raping Mrs. Coker but I did not rape Mrs. Knowles."

More than a year after Odom's conviction and death sentence, Yates had driven to Raiford to have him sign a statement asserting that he hadn't raped Blanche Knowles? That roused Mabel's suspicions. She asked Odom if he'd signed.

"Sure, I signed it," he said. "In fact, I wrote it out. It makes me laugh . . ." And laugh he did—"a deep, rolling chuckle," Mabel noted.

The two women urged Odom to tell more of what he knew, and he turned to the subject of the Coker rape. He remarked that another man had been with him that morning, a detail that startled Mabel, because in no accounts of the crime had the presence of a second person at the scene been mentioned.

"He got me to do it," Odom said. "And with all that 'shine I'd been drinking, I fell in with his idea. He was supposed to be the lookout while I went in, and then I was supposed to sit in the car while he went in. But he run out on me—when I came out, he was gone."

As Odom spoke, Mabel recalled how it had been reported that Blanche Knowles had waited until she heard a car leave before she called for help, out of fear that her attacker might return. Which was why deputies had initially searched for tire prints outside the Knowles home, only to let that point drop when they arrested Jesse Daniels.

"I tried to tell the law about him," Odom said, referring to his companion, who was always "boasting of attacks and attempted attacks on white women." But the officers were not interested. "They said, 'Boy, we got you—you're the one we want.'"

Mabel tried to pin Odom down. "Do you really think he's the one in the first case, Wiley Sam?"

Again, Odom was elusive. "You come back," he said, urging Mabel to return just before he went to the chair. "I'll really talk then."

Mabel and Pearl left the interview room, and John Lenninger took his turn with Odom. Initially he got no further. Odom told him, too, to come back on Sunday, the night before his execution, and said he would disclose everything. Lenninger, however, was not easily diverted or dismissed. An hour later, when he emerged from the interview room, he was, Mabel noted, "tense with excitement." Odom had given Lenninger the name of the man he claimed had raped Blanche Knowles and, afterward, "boasted of the crime."

"We worked fast then," Mabel noted. Back in Mount Dora, she put in a call to Governor Collins, and "the new development was turned over to him."

Collins issued a four-day stay of the electrocution. The official reason, according to prison superintendent DeWitt Sinclair, was the temporary absence of the governor from the state because of a light-plane crash in Maryland, in which his twenty-four-year-old son, LeRoy Collins Jr., a U.S. Navy lieutenant, had sustained serious injuries. Collins and his wife had thus flown to Maryland to be with their son. The governor, Sinclair indicated, "doesn't like to have an execution when he is out of state."

Mabel, however, believed from her conversation with Collins that the governor was likely to order an immediate investigation into Odom's possible involvement in the rape of Blanche Knowles. She contacted the offices of the NAACP in Tampa, which had vast experience and success with death-penalty appeals, and Robert Saunders agreed to lend his support. Still, a four-day reprieve would not allow much time to garner evidence to justify an appeal on Odom's behalf, in order then to be able to shape a case for the release of Jesse Daniels. And the next day brought setbacks. Collins's office sent word that the investigation would be "turned back to Lake County authorities," with state attorney Gordon Oldham—the man who had prosecuted Jesse Daniels—in charge of the probe.

Mabel now fully suspected that a conspiracy had been afoot to frame a young, white, mentally retarded youth for a rape that appeared to have been committed by a black man. Yet the question remained: Why?

That Sam Wiley Odom had "implicated a man in another rape case"—a rape case more infamous than his own—made front-page news across the state. Asked for a statement in response to Odom's reported claim that Jesse Daniels did not rape Blanche Knowles, Oldham said he had no comment. But the state attorney's casual dismissal of a reporter's question apparently masked a genuine concern. That night—August 21—a Florida Highway Patrol cruiser driven by Yates's friend Bryant "Hamp" Spears took Oldham, Yates, and court reporter Janice Burleigh back up to Raiford.

Just after midnight, a guard again led Odom into the interview room. Oldham sat at the table, with Yates and Spears behind him and Burleigh at her stenography machine. Odom sat down opposite Oldham. From the start, the interview had a decidedly antagonistic feel.

"Sam, I want to find out what you know about that rape at Okahumpka," Oldham said.

"I don't know anything I want to tell you," Odom said.

"You don't know anything about it?"

"I know about it," Odom answered, "but I don't want to talk about it."

"Well, if you don't know anything about it," Oldham suggested, "I will go ahead and report to the Governor's office and tell him you state you don't want to talk about it at all or don't know about it."

With that point apparently settled, to Odom's indifference, the young inmate turned his attention to Yates. He accused the deputy of falsifying a statement that Odom had made by making it seem that Odom had admitted to attempted rapes other than that of Mrs. Kate Coker, when, Odom contended, he had admitted only to breaking into the women's homes. That statement, Odom noted, had been presented to the pardon board.

"You were there, Mr. Yates," Odom said. "I didn't tell you that."

"Them's your words, aren't they?" Yates replied.

"No, sir, them ain't my words."

"You didn't sign that?" Yates asked, waving the statement before the boy. "That ain't your signature?"

"No," Odom said.

"That ain't your signature?"

"No."

"How come that notary public swore to that as being the truth and put her seal and signature right there?" Yates asked.

Odom was adamant. "That ain't my signature. When I signed my statement it was blue ink . . . I told you everything that I knew about it and I ain't told you anything about taking other women. I ain't told nobody that."

"You told Mr. Yates about that," Oldham interrupted. "That other house you went into before you went to Mrs. Coker's."

"I didn't try to take no other women," Odom insisted.

"What were you trying to do?" Oldham asked.

"Rob them," Odom replied. "I wasn't going to take no other women. That's what I told you in my statement. That hurt me. I don't mind dying for something, but nothing like that."

"You don't want to die telling a lie, do you?" Oldham asked.

"No."

Oldham did not want to revisit the Kate Coker rape case, or any other case in Lake County in 1958 for that matter. He had driven up to Raiford for one reason alone. He pulled from his briefcase a different statement. "You signed *that* paper," Oldham said, pointing to the document. "Now do you remember this paper?"

Odom scanned the document, his eyes settling on the signature. "I signed that, yes sir."

Oldham then had Odom read aloud the statement he'd told Mabel and Pearl about, in which he declared that he hadn't had anything to do with "the rape case in the Knowles house."

"Do you remember giving Mr. Yates that statement, Sam?" Oldham asked.

"Yes, I remember giving it to him."

"Do you remember being on the lie detector machine?"

"That's right," Odom said.

"And you stated you didn't have anything to do with this case?"

"That's right," Odom said, "on the lie detector, but . . ."

"But what?"

"Daniels, he ain't guilty," Odom said. "I will tell you that."

"Who is guilty?" Oldham asked.

Odom did not answer.

"Did you talk to Mrs. Reese yesterday?" Oldham asked.

"Sure, I talked to her," Odom replied. "But I didn't tell her who was guilty." He explained that he'd told only the lawyer, Lenninger, the name of the man who had raped Blanche Knowles.

"How come you say you know something about it?" Yates asked.

"I know something about it."

"How come you say that now?"

"You want to know about it?" Odom asked.

"Well," Yates said, "I know about it. I investigated it just like yours. Now, if you know something about it, you better tell me."

"I know about it," Odom said, "but I ain't telling you about it."

"I am the man to tell about it," said Yates.

"I told you too much the other time," Odom fretted. "That confession . . . the other thing."

"Look at me, Sam," Yates said. It wasn't a request.

"I ain't going to look at you," spat Odom. "You can listen to me. If you don't want to, you can take me back to the hole. I say I know about the case. I know about it."

With that, abruptly, as if he'd finished with the interview, Odom rose from his chair. The guard, his hands pressed firmly on Odom's shoulders, persuaded him back down. "The man is still talking to you," the guard reminded him.

"If you know something about this other case, you ought to let me know about it," Yates said.

Odom told Yates that he'd had second thoughts after signing the statement in which he'd professed ignorance about the Knowles case. "Didn't I tell you I started to write you a letter when I read that statement?" Odom asked.

"Yes," Yates replied, but noted that Odom hadn't said it was about the Knowles case.

"No, I was dumb when I wrote that," Odom said. "I was green when I went into the other room and I was dumb when I come up here. The death room wised me up."

"You been doing some thinking?" Yates asked.

"Yes, and some thinking I should have done. I am sorry that I did it," he said, referring to the Coker rape, "but that don't mean nothing."

"What about this Okahumpka case?" Yates asked.

"I will tell you what I know," Odom said. "Cat told me that he did it. That he raped that woman."

"Who?" Yates asked.

"I ain't going to tell you who told me that," Odom said, even though he'd given Lenninger the name of the man the day before.

"Well, if you don't tell me his name, what can I do about it?" Yates asked.

Odom hesitated a second or two, then said, "His name is Clarence. Clarence Stephenson." And Odom had been with him and two other men in a 1951 Chevrolet, he said.

"Tell me who else was there," Yates said.

"No, I ain't telling you," Odom snapped. He was willing, however, to talk about Clarence. "He said he was paid to do it. He wasn't paid to rape her. He was paid to go out there and get her out of the way."

Odom paused, and for a moment Burleigh's tap-tap-tapping halted as well.

"I don't know if it was talk or what," Odom continued. "But that's what he said. That's why I started to write you that letter but Cat told me not to do it."

Yates clearly didn't like what he was hearing. "Now, we drove over a hundred miles to come up here tonight—"

"Sure you did. I did too when I come up here," Odom noted, not without irony. He repeated his disinclination to cooperate with the deputy who had played him false. Once more he sounded a note of betrayal. "You said I had a record," Odom said, again invoking Yates's statements to the parole board and sounding injured, like someone who'd been promised one outcome and given another.

"Now, I ain't done nothing to you, have I?" Yates asked.

"You could explain to them. I had a lot of respect for you and I told the ladies"—referring to Mabel and Pearl—"that I had you pegged as one of the best men that worked there in Tavares. I figured you was on the level."

Again, Yates tried to steer the conversation back to the names of the other men who, Odom was claiming, were in the car the night Blanche Knowles was raped. He didn't succeed.

"When you said I had a record, that hurt me," Odom continued on his own track. "I ain't scared to die, but I didn't even harm the woman," he said, meaning Coker. "I didn't hurt the lady. That guy told me to do it and I did it. That 'shine I was drinking, it told me to do it, and that's what happened."

Once more Yates pressed Odom for names, and once more Odom refused to divulge them, except to say, "You pick up Clarence Stephenson. You might get something . . . The guys, if I tell you their names, they could get messed up."

"How could they, just for telling something they knew?" Yates asked.

"For holding out like that." Lenninger, Odom explained, had thought that "Mr. Joe paid me to go in there and do that."

That got Yates's attention, and Oldham's. "Paid you?" Yates asked. "He tried to get you to say that?"

"He said nobody would believe that," Odom replied. Then he shared another of Lenninger's theories—that maybe Joe Knowles "wanted to marry another woman."

"He told you to say that Mr. Joe paid you?" Yates asked.

No, Odom answered, that was what Lenninger thought, not what he'd told Odom to say.

"You mean he suggested that might have happened?"

"Yes, he asked me if I knowed him and I said yes." Odom also knew Joe Knowles's brother, Tim, he'd added, and the lawyer had asked him a second time if Joe had paid him. "I said no, if he paid me I would say so," Odom told Yates.

"This would be a mighty late time for you to take pay for that, wouldn't it?" said Yates.

Blanche's statement to Gordon Oldham—in which she'd mentioned that her attacker had told her, "I was paid five thousand dollars to kill you. Wouldn't you like to know who paid me that?"—had never become public, but Yates was aware of it. Yet neither Yates nor Oldham now pursued Odom's lead, which, however speculatively, tied the crime to a financial transaction and possibly tied Odom himself to the crime.

"But you believe Daniels is guilty?" Odom asked.

"That is not the point, what I believe," Yates said.

"Yes it is," Odom countered.

"No," Yates snapped, "what I believe and what the court believes might be two different things."

"I am telling you," Odom said. "He is not guilty."

Yates strove again to get Odom to admit that the lawyer was putting words in his mouth, but Odom insisted that he himself had done most of the talking and Lenninger "did the listening."

"He asked me did I know Mr. Joe real good," Odom said, "and I said, 'Sure, I worked for him.' And he asked me did I know how he stood, and I said he was real nice. And he said they would pay to have Daniels convicted. They wanted him."

"They can't burn him," Yates said of Daniels. "Did this woman suggest that you say anything? The newspaper woman?"

"She told me to tell the truth, was all she told me," Odom said.

"What did she mainly do?" Yates asked. Had Mabel told him that Jesse had been home all night?

"She said she know he didn't do it," Odom said. "And she ain't the only one that knows."

At that point, Yates and Oldham resumed pressing Odom for the identities of the other men in the Chevrolet that night, and Odom finally complied. He gave them two names—Willie Jones and J. C. Washington—as well as the names of the places where he said they worked.

"Do you believe the Daniels boy guilty or do you believe Clarence Stephenson?" Yates asked.

"I know he isn't guilty," Odom replied.

"What do you base that on?" Yates asked.

"Base it on my case."

"Your case and his case ain't got nothing to do with one another," Yates told him.

"Same kind," Odom said.

"You are guilty?"

"Sure I am," Odom said. "I told you I was."

"What makes you think he was not?"

"That boy ain't got enough sense to do that."

"Do you know him?"

"Sure, I know him. I seen him every day," Odom said. Jesse Daniels would sometimes come into the Quarters and sell fresh perch that he had caught to Sam and his mother.

"He goes hunting," Yates submitted, "and he's got sense enough to do everything else. He's just childish, that's all."

"He ain't got that much sense," Odom disagreed. "I see him riding down the road, cars blowing horns at him."

Still, Yates argued, it took hardly any sense at all to steal into a house like the Knowleses'. "How did he get in the house?" Yates asked. "Do you think it takes much sense to open a screen lock?"

"No, but another thing about that house," Odom said—Clarence knew a lot about it, and Odom wanted Yates to explain how that could be.

"What do you mean?" Yates asked.

"He went in there," Odom said.

"What did he tell you about the house?" Yates asked. "If he went in there, how did he say he went in?"

"In the front door."

"Then how did he go?"

"He didn't say," Odom answered vaguely. "He said something about some stairs. That's what he said and then I don't know but I believe he is guilty. He might not be, but it appears like he did [it]."

Was that the only basis for Odom's opinion? Yates asked.

"Daniels, I will tell you if you want to know," Odom said, "he ain't smart enough."

"Ain't it a fact that he got pretty good sense, but it takes him a long time to think?" Yates asked.

"Might be like that."

"You ask him a question and give him a long time to answer and he will answer, won't he?"

"I don't know about that," Odom said. "I ain't had too much sense my-self. I didn't know how to use it. But that cat know about it."

"This newspaper woman," Yates said, "did she suggest you say any-thing to us different than what you have said?"

"She told me to tell what I know to her."

"Did she suggest any bad thing to tell?" Yates asked.

"Just what I know, that's all."

Yates paused, and after a moment returned to the matter of Odom's conversation with John Lenninger, particularly the lawyer's suggestion that Joe Knowles might have been involved in the crime against his wife. "He said that Joe Knowles paid you to do that?" Yates asked.

"No," Odom replied, "he said that's what it look like."

"So, in other words, you are going to die without . . . that attorney, what he was suggesting . . ."

"No," Odom interrupted. "I said I asked him, 'Do you believe I did it?' and he said, 'I know of only one suspect,' and he said I was the number-one suspect."

"Have I ever said I believe you did it?" Yates asked.

"No," Odom answered. "He said you wouldn't believe I did it."

"You didn't, did you?" Yates as much asserted as he asked.

"No," Odom said. "I could tell you something. I wasn't going to tell you nothing about that and was going to die with it, but they kept after me . . ."

"You don't want to leave here with people thinking you did it," Yates said.

Pleased with the direction that the interview had at last taken, Yates prepared to wrap up the session. There was another point, though, that Odom wanted to clarify further. He reiterated that the break-ins, to which he had confessed, were attempted robberies only; he'd had no intention to rape either Amelia Rutherford or Opal Howard. "I ain't ever tried to take no other women," Odom insisted, "and I been working in the fields right around them, and I ain't tried to take them. I can't understand why they said I did."

"Well," Yates responded with alacrity, "I believe that statement right there."

"Sure, that statement is true," Odom affirmed.

"In fact, I believe everything you told me."

"You do?" Odom asked.

"I did."

"How about now?" Odom asked.

"I don't know. Are you telling the truth?"

"I am," Odom said. "I was jawing you about not knowing nothing about it."

"About the Okahumpka case?"

"Yes, I am telling you now." He told Yates that he didn't think Clarence Stephenson had been lying about the rape. Nor should Yates disbelieve him now, because "I ain't got nothing to lose. No good lying."

By then, more than a couple of hours had passed. "I ain't intended to talk to you all night long," said Odom, and he readied himself to leave. But if they picked up Clarence Stephenson for questioning, he assured them, they'd learn a lot more about the Knowles case. He had started to rise from his chair when he thought of something else he wanted to ask, and sat back down.

"You check with that woman to see what she say?"

"What woman?" Yates asked.

"Knowles," Odom answered, as if confident that he was familiar with facts about the case shared by only a few. "Did she tell you anything about what I told you here?"

"No," Yates said. "One of the troubles with the other people is that they don't know what Mrs. Knowles told me."

"I don't know what she told you either," Odom noted. "All I know is what Clarence told me and I don't know whether it's talk or not, but he say he got paid to do that. He got paid to kill her."

"That attorney didn't suggest you say that, did he?" Yates asked.

"He said, 'Sam, maybe Mr. Knowles paid some guy to kill her,' and he say, 'Do you think he did?' And I said, no, I didn't think he did. I know Mr. Joe pretty good while I was working and he seemed like a nice man. I don't think he would do anything like that."

Now the interview seemed to be over. Gordon Oldham asked Sam if he had anything else on his mind. If so, he said, "I would like to hear it before we go."

"I ain't got nothing on my mind," Odom said.

And with that, a guard led him back to his cell on death row.

Before the others left Raiford, Gordon Oldham spoke with the guard who had attended Odom the day before, during his interviews with Mabel and Pearl, and then with Lenninger. The guard confirmed that he had been present for both interviews and that none of the three had pressured Odom into making statements or admissions. Nor had they made the prisoner any promises. Odom had spoken freely, he told them, when he said that Jesse Daniels hadn't raped Blanche Knowles, but he knew who had.

LAKE COUNTY WASN'T quite finished with Sam Wiley Odom. Gordon Oldham returned with Yates to Okahumpka to continue his investigation, but the next day he dispatched assistant state attorney James W. Kynes Jr. up to Raiford. Like Sam Buie, Jimmy Kynes had been a football legend at the University of Florida; he'd been drafted by the Pittsburgh Steelers but chose instead to play in Canada. After a season, however, he'd returned to Florida to study law at Gainesville, and by 1959, his promising legal mind had brought him to the state attorney's office. He interviewed Odom in the presence of prison superintendent DeWitt Sinclair and a stenographer.

Once again, with a four-day stay of execution and his life on the line, twenty-one-year-old high school dropout Sam Wiley Odom would attempt to steer his way through an aversive interrogation without the aid of counsel.

Odom appeared to be more at ease with the hulking former football star than he'd been with the duplicitous Deputy Yates. Oldham had not shared with Kynes transcripts of Blanche Knowles's statement in his office the previous winter, or of his own prison interview with Odom of the day before. Without the benefit of any prior briefing, then, Kynes set out to construct with Odom a timeline of his whereabouts and actions in the hours leading up to the attack on Blanche Knowles.

Earlier in the evening of December 17, Odom said, he and his uncle had attended a night class at Carver Heights Negro School, after which he had gone back to North Quarters and watched the fights on NBC with a friend who lived a few houses down from the Hawkins family. Then, Odom said, he'd gone out to visit a cousin, Joe Smith, at the snack shop he ran in the Quarters. There, some neighborhood men were trying to get a game of whist going when Clarence Stephenson and a man Odom identified only as "Bill" showed up. The pair were looking for "entertainment" and something to drink, they said, so the three of them—Odom, Clarence, and Bill—had driven to Leesburg, where Clarence and Bill were "drinking pretty heavy." Odom, having indulged only in soda pop, had driven Clarence's 1951 Chevrolet back to Okahumpka.

When Kynes asked for more information about Bill, Odom said, "I don't know anything about Bill." Not being privy to the details of the previous day's not-yet-transcribed interview, Kynes was unable to press Odom about a number of other discrepancies Odom introduced. He now told Kynes that only three men were in the car on the night of the Knowles rape, whereas he'd included a fourth man—J. C. Washington—in the Chevrolet when he'd been questioned by Oldham and Yates. Nor did Odom mention a Willie Jones to Kynes, although it was possible that "Willie" was the same person as "Bill," whose surname he had perhaps forgotten or was intentionally withholding.

On their return to Okahumpka, Sam recounted, Clarence had said that he wanted to talk to Joe Knowles, who'd promised him a job, and asked Odom if he knew where Joe lived. That was how it happened that Odom had driven Clarence and Bill over to the Knowles house, alongside of which he'd parked the Chevrolet.

"How long had you known Joe Knowles?" Kynes asked.

"Well, I have worked for Mr. Knowles," Odom said, "but he don't know me personally from anyone else."

"What kind of work did you do for him?"

"I have worked in watermelons for him. Watermelons, and I have picked fruit for the company."

"Did you know his wife?" Kynes asked.

"Not personally," Odom said.

"Ever seen her?"

"Yeah, I have seen her," Odom said. "Round and about. Going from Okahumpka to Leesburg, I guess."

Odom recounted how Clarence had first gone around to the back door of the house but had ended up entering in the front; and how he and Bill had listened to music on the radio until Clarence came back out—about forty-five minutes later, Odom thought. "His arm was scratched up," Odom had noticed.

"Where was his clothes?" Kynes asked.

"His clothes was under his left arm," Odom said. "Didn't have on anything. He had his shoes there under his arm."

"Barefooted?" Kynes asked.

"Bare feet," Odom replied, then corrected himself. "He wasn't exactly in his bare feet. He had a pair of socks on."

"Get moving," Clarence had ordered Odom, so he'd started the car and driven "down the road a little piece." That was when Clarence realized that he'd lost his shorts. He wanted Odom to drive back to the Knowles house to get them, but Odom had refused.

Clarence said he'd "raped a woman in there." The reason he'd gone to the house in the first place, he told Odom and Bill, was "that he had got paid to murder this woman."

"That he got paid to murder this woman?" Kynes asked.

"That's right."

"Who did he tell you paid him?"

"He didn't say," Odom said.

"Did he show you any money?"

"Yeah, he showed me some money," Odom said. "I don't know exactly the amount but he had a pretty good sum of money."

Kynes asked Odom if he'd told anyone else about the incident, and Odom said that he'd told no one. The attorney pressed Odom for details about Clarence's intents and actions. "Did he say he had gone in there to kill her?"

"Yes sir," Odom replied. "Said that after he'd seen this baby there, that he couldn't go through with it. Said that he couldn't kill her on account of that baby was there."

"So his intents were to go in there and kill her, is that right?"

"That's right," Odom said.

"What was he gonna kill her with?" Kynes asked. Did Clarence have a gun or a knife? Odom said he didn't know.

"And he saw the baby in there," Kynes said. "Where did he say the baby was?"

"He didn't exactly say where it was."

"Said the baby was there and he changed his mind about killing her and raped her instead, is that correct?" Kynes asked.

"Yes."

Kynes flipped through the pages of his notepad, then paused. "Now what else do you know about the Knowles case that you haven't told me?"

"Well, that's about all," Odom said. Except for what he had not yet mentioned: "I told you about having that money," he said. "Got $5,000.00 to do that, but he didn't tell me who gave him this money."

The amount Clarence had claimed he was being paid to kill "this woman" was significantly higher than the five hundred dollars that Pearl had heard rumored in the melon patch—but unbeknownst to Kynes, it was exactly the same as the dollar figure in Blanche Knowles's statement to Gordon Oldham.

"This lawyer that came up here," Kynes said, "suggested that you are the one that raped Mrs. Knowles, is that right? Is that what he told you?"

"He didn't tell me that I did it," Odom explained. "Said that's what he heard. He said that he heard people say that Mr. Joe gave me some money to rape his wife and afterwards kill her." Or rather, Odom said, the lawyer had heard that a girlfriend of Knowles might have done so.

Kynes did not pursue this wrinkle in the story either, but instead turned his questions to the rape of Kate Coker. Odom related how he and Clarence, as well as J. C. Washington and "Bill," had been having conversations about what it might be like to have a white woman; and Clarence had told them "it was different between a colored woman and a white woman. Said you get more feeling out of a white woman." Seeing Odom's keen interest, Clarence had mentioned to him that he knew where he and Odom could find two women in Leesburg. "But he told me that if we got caught," Odom said, "we would go to jail. He didn't tell me nothing about no death sentence or nothing like that." As it happened, Clarence—if there was indeed a Clarence—had not got caught; he had driven off and abandoned his accomplice.

Like Oldham and Yates, Kynes took a stab at determining the influence of Mabel Norris Reese on Odom's story. Had she herself fed him the killer-for-hire tale verbatim, or had she planted details about the case in Odom's impressionable mind?

"What did Mrs. Reese tell you about the Knowles case?" he asked.

On this point, Odom did not budge. "She didn't tell me anything about the Knowles case," he insisted. "Ask me did I know anything about it. I told her I did."

"And what did you tell her?"

"I told her I had to talk to my mother first before I tell either one of them"—them being Mabel and Pearl—"anything."

OLDHAM'S INVESTIGATION CONTINUED. He had Lake County deputies dispatched to round up the three men Odom had named, and the Florida Sheriffs Bureau dispatched a special agent to Okahumpka as well. But the search for Odom's purported cohorts proved mostly fruitless.

Oldham himself interviewed Odom's cousin, who denied that Odom had visited him at the snack bar on the night of the Knowles rape and stated categorically that he'd never seen or met anyone named Clarence Stephenson—nor did he know a Willie Jones or a J. C. Washington. With the special agent present, Oldham spoke with Odom's parents, Laura and Frampy Cope, neither of whom recalled having seen or heard Sam speak of a Clarence Stephenson, a Willie Jones, or a "Bill." When the state attorney and the special agent tracked down Robert "Son" Nelson, the picking crew foreman who, Odom had claimed, was Clarence's employer, Nelson said he'd never hired a picker named Clarence Stephenson.

Neither had the owner of a Florida nursery ever employed a Willie Jones, contrary to what Odom had told Oldham and Yates.

Over the next few days, the Florida Sheriffs Bureau searched state records for any trace of a Clarence Stephenson's military service, driver's license, or automobile tags, but it found no Stephenson who fit the description Odom had provided. Bill Fisher did find an arrest record for a J. C. Washington, but this Washington was known to have left the area more than a month before the Knowles rape.

With news swirling about Odom's information regarding the rape, Laura Cope drove to Raiford to speak with her son. She advised him not to admit involvement in any crime other than the one for which he'd been convicted, in the hope that the governor might spare him the death sentence for his first and only crime. She suggested that he write to the governor himself.

Odom's letter opened with an admission of guilt. He had raped Kate Coker on March 31, 1958, he said, and explained that he hadn't known that he could die for the crime. "This is the first time I ever been in trouble and it was the first woman I ever attack," he asserted, and noted that in all the time he had worked around white women in Okahumpka, "they will tell you that I never made advances toward them and that I always have respect for any of them." He was "willing to pay for my crime, but not with my life but with my labor." He placed his fate in the hands of the governor, who, whatever his decision, Odom believed to be a "righteous man"; and he hoped that the governor's son would "recover well."

On August 25, Francisco Rodriguez of the NAACP in Tampa delivered a letter to Collins, advising the governor that he was now representing Sam Wiley Odom and that he had filed a petition for a stay of execution so that he might have "sufficient time" to file an appeal. He was, he said, of the "firm conviction that there might be a basis for reversal of the guilty verdict rendered" in Odom's case, though Rodriguez did not elaborate.

That same day, Jimmy Kynes returned to Raiford, not to interview Odom but to help him construct a statement regarding the rape of Blanche Knowles. In essence, the statement repudiated everything Odom had alleged in his interviews with Mabel and Pearl, John Lenninger, Oldham and Yates, and Kynes himself over the previous week. "I don't know nothing about that Knowles case," Odom now said, and what he'd said he knew was "all wrong." He confessed that "the reason I told you that story is that I knowed I only had one straw out of a million and I grabbed that straw." He admitted that his acquaintance with Clarence Stephenson and Bill was "just a bunch of fictitious stuff," a story he'd invented to get a reprieve—and he "didn't know what a reprieve was until I went back to my cell and looked through my dictionary." Finally, he denied having any idea as to who actually had raped Mrs. Knowles. "The main reason I came up with this story was to prolong my execution . . . I didn't get what I wanted, but I did get four days more to live . . . I'm strictly against Capital Punishment."

Gordon Oldham was wrapping up his investigation for Governor Collins when he received word from Kynes that Sam Wiley Odom had recanted his prior statements regarding his involvement in and knowledge of the Knowles rape, and had signed a statement to that effect. His report to the governor, which included the statement along with affidavits from seven witnesses, concluded Odom had lied about the actions of "Clarence Stephenson" and other accomplices on the evening of December 17, 1957. Odom's final statement, the state attorney affirmed, "is a true one."

The governor received Oldham's report on August 26. By then he had already answered Odom's letter, assuring Odom that he had read it but declaring that, under the law, he must pay for his crime with his life. Collins said he would pray that God grant Odom "mercy and forgiveness."

Odom's execution was scheduled for the morning of August 28. Francisco Rodriguez and the NAACP lawyers would have no time to prepare an appeal. The night before, DeWitt Sinclair attended to Odom's last meal: "a good dinner" capped off with "about a quart of ice cream." At about eight p.m., Odom asked permission to make one last telephone call. Sinclair consented, and he led the prisoner, in handcuffs, to a desk down the hall from his cell.

Gordon Oldham answered the phone when it rang in his Leesburg home; it was a call he'd "remember for the rest of my life."

"I'm guilty of what I did, Mr. Oldham," Odom said, "but all I want to do is live. I don't want to die."

Oldham tried to explain that the case was out of his hands.

"You can call the governor," the boy pleaded. "I don't want to die tomorrow."

The state attorney explained again that there was nothing he could do. Then, quietly, he hung up the phone.

It might have appeared to the public that Sam Wiley Odom had only been grasping at straws in his final days. Certainly he was out of his depth. Without a lawyer at his side, he'd been unable to navigate the political quagmire surrounding the case, and his attempt to save Jesse Daniels from punishment for a crime that he seemed to know Jesse did not commit had backfired. But what was it he'd been so "green" and "dumb" about when he'd first "come up here"? And what was it he'd wised up to in "the death room"? Rumbling under his interviews with Pearl and Mabel, with Oldham, and especially with Yates was that undercurrent of betrayal—as if he had been promised something that he had not received. But what? What had he given (and to whom), and what had he failed to get in return? And however much he'd invented, was there perhaps, among the straws he'd grasped in vain to forestall his fate, an attempt to tell the actual truth?

On the morning of the 28th, the newspapers were full of Odom's repudiation. "Odom Admits Hoax to Delay Death," trumpeted the *Orlando Sentinel*. Collins again postponed the execution, but only for five hours; he was traveling back to Tallahassee and wanted a little more time to absorb Gordon Oldham's report. By the time he arrived at the capital, he had made his decision. "I will expect the penalty of the law to be enforced by those responsible at such time they find proper."

McCall and Yates made the long drive up to Raiford to serve as witnesses to Odom's execution through three glass windows that provided a clear view into the death chamber. A handful of other witnesses were already seated when they arrived.

Odom appeared to be calm when the guards led him to the chair and as they fastened leather straps to his arms, his legs, his waist. He made no statement. "He even smiled," Yates recalled, "when the hood was placed over his head." At 1:38 p.m., the switch was thrown; at 1:44 p.m., Sam Wiley Odom was pronounced dead, and his convoluted accounts of the night Blanche Knowles was raped, along with whatever truths might lie within them, were silenced forever.

In Okahumpka, a heartbroken Laura Cope could barely talk to reporters. She recalled the day that Sam had been arrested by Lake County deputies after the rape of Blanche Knowles; how the meal she'd set out on the table for him was still there when she came home from work. She told one reporter, "I think they like to railroad some and let others go." She thought "a person like that . . . doesn't have much of a chance." She said that she was against capital punishment, and that she never believed her son was guilty of the rape for which he'd been executed. But, she added, "he might have been."

PART TWO

Mabel Norris Reese and daughter Patricia, 1959

CHAPTER ELEVEN

Way of Justice

THE SUN WAS JUST BEGINNING to set on December 5, 1959, when Officer Jack Hyde of the Mount Dora Police Department responded to a call regarding a domestic incident in East Town, the black section of the city. A woman named Mamie Lee Floyd, it appeared, had been removing some old furniture from her former home when she'd discovered that an itinerant yard worker named Joe Henderson had been squatting in the abandoned house. He had threatened her, and she had called the police.

To Hyde, a veteran police officer who'd retired after twenty-two years with the overburdened Baltimore Police Department and relocated to tranquil, slow-paced Sylvan Shores, the call seemed to be routine. He was standing with Floyd outside the house and taking down her statement when the front door was flung open, and Joe Henderson fired on Hyde with a twelve-gauge shotgun. Hyde crumpled to the ground, dead.

Within minutes, other patrolmen and the fire department had arrived. Henderson greeted them, too, with his twelve-gauge; one of the shots struck fireman George Hall in the head. Next on the scene was Hyde's partner, twenty-nine-year-old Tommy "Buddles" Ledford.

Grabbing his buckshot-loaded Browning automatic, Ledford ran around to the back of the house. Darting between cars parked in the yard, he crept closer to the house, then took cover behind a ramshackle shed. Henderson spotted him and fired three times from a first-floor window, just missing his target but not the chickens in the coop behind Ledford. Feathers flew. Ledford scooted out of Henderson's line of fire and was hiding behind a hedge when the back door of the house cracked open. Ledford didn't hesitate. One shot from his Browning felled his quarry. Warily, he crossed the yard to the back door, put his foot on the barrel of Henderson's shotgun, and, grabbing the dead man by the collar, dragged him to the street. "I wanted that bunch of niggers to see him," Ledford remembered.

By the time Mabel Norris Reese arrived on the scene, two dead men lay on the ground in front of the Floyd house, and an ambulance was rushing George Hall to the hospital.

Mabel cornered Ledford. "Did you have to shoot him?" she asked.

Dumbfounded, Ledford replied, "Yes, ma'am."

"Did you try to talk to him?" she asked.

"No, ma'am. He was shooting at me."

Ledford knew Mabel by reputation as a "hell of a newspaper woman"—but "crazy." He recalled that "she belonged to the NAACP or something, and she hated Willis McCall with a purple passion." Indeed, when McCall appeared at the crime scene that evening, the reporter slipped away.

McCall soon heard from witnesses about the heroics of the young policeman who had brought the incident in East Town to an end. "You come work for me," he said to Ledford. It was more an order than an offer.

Thomas Lloyd Ledford had been born in Missouri to "a poor dirt farmer and sharecropper who got tired of cotton and corn" and decided to give citrus a try. The family moved to Mount Dora and settled on Grandview Street, "in the last house in the white section," Ledford recalled, adding pointedly, "but we wasn't in Pistolville"—Pistolville being the "cracker district" where Mount Dora's poor white laborers lived. The Platt family had settled in the Pistolville neighborhood for a spell until the Klan chased them out, and so had James Yates.

After high school, Tom Ledford joined the Army, where he trained as a medic, and was sent to Korea. He was attached to the 2nd Battalion, 5th Cavalry Regiment, which, in October 1951, fell under attack on Pork Chop Hill, north of Yeoncheon. For seventy-two hours, surrounded by the enemy, Ledford and thirty-four other men braved heavy fire. Ledford's automatic rifle got shot out of his hands. Desperate for weaponry, he ran the fifty yards to the nearest bunker, where he found a machine gun in a canvas bag, along with ammunition and a tripod. "I weighed two hundred twenty pounds and was all muscle then," Ledford said, "so I had to run the gun back up the hill"; three others carried the ammo. By the time they had set up the gun the enemy had mounted a counterattack, and hundreds of Chinese troops, many of them bearing no arms, were charging half-blind up the hill. A wounded line medic fed the five-hundred-round belts into the machine gun as Ledford fired steadily into the enemy troops—"a seventy-five-yard-long train, caught in the open with no place to go." By his hand, Chinese fell by the dozens.

After his discharge in 1953, Ledford returned to Lake County, where he took a job and married Ora Mae Knight of Eustis, who chose as her maid of honor none other than Emily "Apache" Brown—the skinny girl who would later set up the two black airmen for arrest at Willis McCall's cabin in the Scrub. Around the same time, Ledford joined the Dunkers Club, a front for the Mount Dora chapter of the Ku Klux Klan. He was recruited by his father, a longtime member, who lamented, "It ain't the same as it was. It's more politics now."

The Dunkers met at a clubhouse built by a cattleman in the woods on Lake Jem, some fifty yards off the road. Its members, "usually about thirty men, standing in the dark," came from Lake, Orange, and

Seminole counties. The meetings, as Ledford's father had complained, focused mostly on politics and "situations." "A big citrus man came in, running for state senator," Ledford recalled. "He wanted our support. But we didn't like him." "Situations" had included the Platt family's moving into Pistolville and putting their children in the public school, or "if a nigger raped a white woman . . . or there was breaking into homes." As Ledford saw it, the Dunkers Club worked with law enforcement, not against it, unless the police and sheriff's departments failed to deal properly with a situation. "If it was handled by the police, it would be ignored. But if it wasn't handled right, we'd do it ourself."

By the late 1950s, Mount Dorans had gotten used to seeing the cavalcade of cars carrying men in white robes and hoods through the town's streets at night, bound for East Town. There the hooded Klansmen would burn crosses at the corner of Grandview and Grant Streets, to keep "niggers in line." Ledford recounted the process. "You build the cross at the location. You take a posthole digger and go two feet down. It's already wrapped with cheesecloth. Then you pour gas and soak the cloth, stand it up and burn it."

Ledford recalled it was the Dunkers who'd burned a cross on the front lawn of the Reeses' home, because Mabel had been "stirring up a ton of trouble" with her newspaper and the club had decided she needed some lessoning. He admitted knowing some of the men responsible, and noted that it was his brother, Roy, who'd painted the cross on the sidewalk in front of the *Topic*'s office. And although Ledford himself had not thrown the bombs that exploded in Mabel's yard, he had supplied the materials— munitions that he'd taken from Camp Blanding, the training base for the Florida Army National Guard just east of Raiford, which were "probably equivalent to a half stick of dynamite." He had ended up giving them to Ty Parker, a boy he'd known in high school. "Ty liked me and he hated Mabel," Ledford said. "The whole town had turned against her. Integration did not take well in Lake County." Parker wasn't in the Dunkers

Club, Ledford noted. "He just wanted to scare her. I saw him later and asked, 'Did you scare her?' and his eyes lit up. 'Hell, yes!'"

Ledford had been working at the Lake County Sheriff's Department for only a few months when he responded to the report of a prowler in Eustis. On his arrival, two Eustis police officers, Captain Jesse Burrow and auxiliary patrolman Harold Blumenberg, were questioning a "slightly intoxicated" fifty-three-year-old black man named William Bowen, known to the officers as Neckbone. Neckbone was in high spirits, joking with one of the officers about having been drunk earlier in the evening. A splotch of blood had dried under his nose, and his clothes looked as if he might have been lying on the ground. The Eustis policemen were about to release him, but Ledford, in an "extremely authoritative" manner, advanced on Bowen and shoved him toward his cruiser. Ledford pushed Bowen into the rear seat and then drove away.

At about one a.m., Burrow and Blumenberg were summoned to the Lake County jail in Tavares. William Bowen's body was lying on the hallway floor between the booking desk and the cellblock; "a large smear of blood" discolored the right hallway wall and blood had pooled on the floor next to the body. Bowen's face and head appeared to be badly bruised, bloody, and cut up. Glover Johnson, who owned a funeral home in Eustis, took Blumenberg aside and pointed out the skull fracture on the left side of Bowen's head as well as a severe trauma to the back of his head, which caused a deputy to snap at Johnson to "stop meddling and take that nigger away."

Elmer and Delmer Wilkinson, teenage brothers who were locked in the cellblock at the time, told Blumenberg that during the night they'd heard what sounded to them like an older black man "begging not to be locked in a cell." In a small shaving mirror that Delmer held through the bars, he'd seen two deputies, one of them Tom Ledford, "supporting a Negro male by the arms." The commotion got louder—the black man protesting, the deputies swearing—and then the brothers had heard "three loud slapping noises" before everything went silent. After a few minutes, they'd heard voices, at once animated and hushed, and flashbulbs popping. A black trusty—a prisoner given special privileges—told the brothers that "a man had been beaten to death in the hallway."

A brief article in the *Orlando Sentinel* reported that William Bowen had "collapsed and died while being booked" at the jail. McCall told the paper that in a few days, after an autopsy had been performed, the results would be turned over to a coroner's jury. Deputy William Hamner, who photographed the body, said that "there was nothing to indicate the death was not from natural causes."

Ledford later stated that he and two other deputies were escorting Bowen to a cell when Bowen "gave out a small cry, threw his arms out, and started to fall to the floor." Ledford caught him, he told investigators, and "lowered him to a sitting position on the floor leaning against the wall." He said that Neckbone was prone to seizures, and he recalled that in the jail that night Bowen had had a "fit," and that he had "grabbed him until his fit was over." He denied striking, or seeing anyone else strike, the prisoner. The coroner's jury concluded that Bowen had died of natural causes. No charges were filed, and the case was closed. The results were not surprising; as Ledford admitted, McCall controlled the coroner's juries by filling them with "people Willis knew."

Kiser Hardaway's family owned Superior Cleaners in Leesburg, which provided uniform dry-cleaning services for the Lake County Sheriff's Department. It wasn't uncommon, he said, for a deputy, or even McCall himself, to drop into the store and request his service on a coroner's inquest. What was expected of the jurors was clear, he said, recalling one such case, a homicide inquiry involving a deputy's use of force. "Let me say it this way. I wouldn't want my sons pulled over by McCall's men."

Bowen's wasn't the only case in which a suspect or detainee met with questionable behavior on Ledford's part. He himself later recounted how, answering a call at a Lake County public housing unit, "I went in and a guy raked me down the back with a linoleum knife. I grabbed him, slammed him, and played 'pop-the-whip' with him against the wall. *Pop! Pop! Pop!*"

Not only had the suspect "died on me," Ledford recalled, but when deputies called to the scene searched for the linoleum knife, none of them could find it until one of them spotted it "hanging in my wallet in my back pocket." No investigation ensued, and no stories about the man's death appeared in the local newspapers. "The nigger was a nobody," Ledford recalled. "No family. He was just buried and that was that." Willis McCall, when he heard about the mess of blood at the scene, told Ledford, "You should have just shot him."

THE DISTANCE and the price of bus tickets allowed Pearl and Charles Daniels only one visit a month to Chattahoochee. Pearl usually made the trip alone, and she'd return home with more questions than answers about her son's condition. Letters to the institution would follow. The drop in Jesse's weight alarmed her; wasn't there "something in the way of a tonic or medicine" the doctors could provide to "help build him up"? She worried about his medications, though she had been assured by Jesse that the pills (Tofranil) he'd been given for depression had "helped his feelings quite a lot." She fretted that the gifts, supplies, and dollar bills she sent as regularly as she could afford weren't reaching him.

Mabel, meanwhile, wrote again to Governor Collins regarding Jesse's case, which prompted Collins to write to Florida State Hospital superintendent W. D. Rogers and ask for further clarification as to Jesse's mental competence and his ability to aid in his own defense, were he to stand trial on rape charges. Rogers replied that Jesse could not be released without the consent of the Fifth Circuit Court.

Not satisfied with the response from Chattahoochee, Mabel again sought out a lawyer to assist in the case. Her friend Walker Kennedy, who had unsuccessfully defended Odom, and his young associate Tom Champion devised a legal strategy that focused on a Florida statute allowing the court to commit defendants verified as "insane." In a letter to a psychiatrist at Chattahoochee, Champion argued that while physicians at the hospital had found Jesse to be mentally deficient and "retarded," nowhere in the hospital's report to the court had he been deemed "insane." The aim of this strategy was not to free Jesse, but to get him transferred to another institution "which might be more in line with his disability."

Virtually any institution might have been less worrisome for Jesse than Chattahoochee. Kenneth Donaldson was forty-eight years old when he was committed to Chattahoochee in 1957, the year before Jesse Daniels arrived. The Philadelphia native had been visiting his elderly parents in Florida, and they had become alarmed when he'd voiced his suspicion that a neighbor up North had been poisoning his food. Donaldson had been treated for paranoid schizophrenia at a Philadelphia hospital earlier that year, and his father had feared that he was once again suffering delusions and fostering dangerous, irrational thoughts. His parents had thus signed an "inquisition of incompetency," which authorized deputies to place Donaldson under arrest. When Donaldson attempted to explain to a cellmate at the Pinellas County jail that his arrest was due to a misunderstanding and that officials would soon see "that I'm not nuts," the cellmate replied ominously: "You don't know these people. They'll put you in Chattahoochee. You can't get out."

Sure enough, lacking legal representation, Donaldson was committed against his will to Florida State Hospital, where he spent every waking day engaged in a Kafkaesque battle to prove that he was being illegally imprisoned. Throughout his hospitalization, he kept meticulous diaries, which he successfully hid from hospital staff. He also managed to smuggle out letters—to newspapers like the *Tampa Tribune*, to lawyers and

politicians—where he described the squalid conditions, institutionalized abuse, scarcity of staff, and lack of medical treatment at the facility.

The patients on Ward 1, where Jesse Daniels was also housed, were
particularly affected by constant noise, Donaldson wrote. "We lived in
aimless pacing *plus* stress." When Donaldson complained about the severely limited access to doctors and treatment, Dr. J. B. O'Connor, the
physician who had also been charged with Jesse's care, told him that he
was receiving "milieu therapy"—"a euphemism for confinement in the
'milieu' of a mental hospital." Donaldson recalled telling a morning attendant shortly after his arrival how he wasn't "nuts" and didn't belong on
the ward. In a rare moment of candor, and even of empathy, the attendant
commented, "We're getting tired of having so many railroaded here."

Donaldson didn't think that Jesse Daniels belonged at Chattahoochee
any more than he did. Donaldson saw Jesse as a "slow, timorous individual" who was "neither retarded nor crazy." For both patients, though, the
years were passing, and the warning from Donaldson's former cellmate
was proving true.

In the fall of 1959, a letter written by a patient in the colored male
department at Florida State Hospital was smuggled out and delivered to
the NAACP. Signed "Patient X"—out of fear of "retaliatory action"—the
letter described the hospital's treatment of black patients as, in effect,
institutionalized slavery. They were forced, for instance, to clean up the
white patients' dining room and do their laundry, and if they failed to
comply, on the orders of white supervisors they were "beaten with metal
chains, leather belts, rubber hoses and boards," sometimes to the point of
unconsciousness. The conditions described by Patient X got front-page
coverage in black newspapers like the *Chicago Defender*, which bannered
its exposé "Bare Florida Slavery." White newspapers picked up the story,
and the *Tampa Tribune* carried out its own investigation, taking the hospital to task for its brutal treatment of patients.

The negative publicity spurred the Committee on State Institutions to conduct a thorough study of the conditions at the hospital. Its report, released in early 1961, was grim in its discoveries of cruelty, abuse, violence, and extremely low morale among both patients and staff. It found especially troubling the white male department, which had become a dumping ground of sorts: "Criminal patients, sexual psychopaths, elderly feeble and helpless patients and teen-age boys" were crammed in there together, in wards that were maintained more as "detention wards for inmates than hospital wards for the sick."

The study cited testimony from present and former patients, who voiced complaints about "terrible" food—powdered eggs for breakfast, prunes at lunch, nearly inedible "bone stew" for dinner—and about over-medication. Many of the patients were "so doped up" they could hardly converse with investigators. If patients resisted medication, attendants forced the pills down their throats.

Attendants, many of them illiterate or alcoholic, were said to have no qualms about going through packages sent to patients, especially at Christmas, and routinely taking whatever they wanted before passing on the remainder. One patient in the white female department told how she'd been "thrown in a cage" with her clothes ripped off and then forced to sleep naked on a bare concrete floor. Another patient, in the colored male department, recounted random beatings and indignities like being required to work barefoot or insufficiently clothed.

John Epright, a patient in the white male department, testified that he had seen "patients being given shock treatment and packed in ice, or put in steel handcuffs for six months at a time, not for treatment but because these men tried to escape or did escape." Some of the attendants "make patients have homosexual relations," Epright said, and related how problem patients were put on "the Squad" and kept there for weeks. "That is where most of the beatings and brutal treatment occurs. Ask any patient at the hospital—he can tell you how he fears the Squad."

Kenneth Holloway was one of those patients. In June 1959, when he got into an altercation with another patient, three attendants beat him and choked him, then strapped him "upside down from the bars for one hour" as punishment. An attendant named Joseph Craig confirmed such brutality, and disclosed that "attendants could beat the patients on the Squad as much as they wanted to" without fear of retribution from staff officials.

Mail got lost. Theft abounded. Suicides, suicide attempts, and self-mutilations occurred in all the wards. Medical treatment was, at best, inadequate, but narcotics, smuggled into the wards by attendants, were rife.

Because of the rape charge against him, Jesse was locked in the criminal ward with the most violent offenders. Doctors described him as "disoriented" when he first arrived at Chattahoochee, where his "docile" and compliant nature made him an easy target for other patients as well as for attendants. One patient punched him in the face. In the event of such altercations, the attendants usually punished both parties, often by placing them in handcuffs for whatever period of time they chose. Sometimes, Jesse recalled, "the guards would take towels and try to choke us, just out of pure meanness." It was the guards whom Jesse feared most. "They made me crawl on my knees and clean the commodes and do all sorts of things to earn tokens to pay them, so I could sleep on my bed," he said. "Otherwise, we slept on the floor."

The report corroborated this kind of abuse as common practice, and noted that attendants who "choke down disturbed patients for the purpose of subduing them" could always "fall back on a fabricated alibi that the patient was violent." The problems created by overcrowding and incompetent attendants were compounded by a shortage of physicians. Before 1960, in the white male department, the report noted, "there was only one doctor responsible for the care and treatment of approximately 1,000 patients in wards one through ten and the maximum security building." Because doctors were forced to devote "a large portion of their working day to answering court correspondence" as well as correspondence with the families of each patient, it was not uncommon, the report found, for patients to go years without seeing a physician.

Jesse endured the cruelty of the attendants and the arbitrary violence of other patients. Moreover, because he had been committed to the hospital by court order and in the face of criminal charges, he was housed on the criminal ward and under constant lockdown. To discourage escape attempts and attacks on attendants, the hospital administration had prohibited use of the yard for "patients with charges." By March 1960, it had been two years since he had been outside the gloomy hallways of Chattahoochee. The most he could capture of Florida's sun were the rays strained through a steel-grated ward window; it was his favorite place.

In early 1960, Tom Ledford was assigned a new partner in the sheriff's department: Evvie Griffin. Griffin proved to be a calming influence at a time when the new deputy much needed it: Ledford was having marriage problems; Ora Mae was sleeping around on him, he knew, and they had a young son to consider. Although by nature a man of few words, Griffin shared some of his own marital experience with his new partner. A decade before, at twenty, Griffin had married sixteen-year-old Nancy Driver. Barely a year later, she left him a note saying she'd gone to New York to pursue a career as a fashion model. She succeeded: Her image soon graced the covers of magazines like *Vogue, Mademoiselle,* and *Harper's Bazaar,* and over time she landed parts in television shows and in movies like *Blue Hawaii,* starring Elvis Presley. She and Griffin had officially divorced in 1951, and Nancy Driver Griffin had changed her name to Nancy Walters.

Around midnight on March 10, Griffin and Ledford stopped for coffee at the Dona Vista Drive Inn just outside Umatilla. They were shooting the breeze with a few Eustis policemen when a report came in over the radio about a breaking-and-entering case in Fruitland Park, not far from the Bosanquet place. Also a "possible rape," the radio operator added, and requested assistance from the Lake County Sheriff's Department. The two deputies jumped into Griffin's car, picked up the department's tracking dogs, Buck and Red, and sped on to Fruitland Park.

When they arrived at the scene, they learned that the victim, a fifty-six-year-old white woman named Charlotte Wass, had stumbled, blood-ied and disheveled, to a neighbor's home, and had since been taken to Durham Young Hospital in Leesburg, where she was treated for a frac-tured skull and other injuries. Griffin and Ledford secured the area to prevent valuable evidence from being destroyed, including three partial footprints in the sandy soil that they covered with buckets and pots. Thunder rolled in the distance; rain was imminent.

With police and other deputies taking statements from neighbors, Griffin harnessed up the bloodhounds in hopes of getting them on the scent before the rain began. A handkerchief that Ledford found at the scene led the dogs and the two deputies to the home of "an elderly Ne-gro" about a mile and a half away. Inside, increasingly eager, Buck and Red pulled the deputies into a bedroom where two twenty-year-old black citrus workers, Robert Shuler and Levi Summers, lay sleeping. The bloodhounds, Griffin said, would normally identify suspects in this situ-ation by putting "two front paws on the bed and then smelling," but in-stead the dogs excitedly jumped into both beds.

After the deputies had placed Shuler and Summers under arrest and transported them to the Leesburg city jail, they proceeded to the hospi-tal in order to question Charlotte Wass about the attack. Wass was still under sedation, a doctor informed them, though he was otherwise vague as to her condition and the nature of the attack. He would not state that the victim had been raped, so Griffin and Ledford treated the crime as an assault and battery. The two deputies returned to the crime scene at Fruitland Park, but by 3:30 a.m. the rain had become so intense that they could not continue their investigation. They picked up the two prisoners in Leesburg and moved them to the Lake County jail, where James Yates and another deputy, Lucius Clark, began questioning them. The interrogation led to the capture of a third suspect, twenty-three-year-old Jerry Chatman—arrested at Fain Theater later that evening.

Later, when Griffin ran into McCall and attempted to brief him on the case, the sheriff groused, "You got the wrong niggers."

"They the right ones," Griffin insisted. "Buck and Red jumped in bed with 'em."

McCall huffed. He'd already had three suspects arrested in Oklawaha; now he'd be forced to release them and tell reporters they had only been "wanted for questioning." Whoever the three were, it was clear to Griffin that McCall had intended, for whatever sinister reason of his own, to charge them with the crime, and he was upset that he had to let them go. To Griffin's mind, this was yet another instance of McCall's abuse of authority, and it added another to his growing list of questions about the integrity of the Lake County Sheriff's Department.

On Friday, March 11, assistant state attorney John W. McCormick interviewed Charlotte Wass, the victim in what became known as the Fruitland Park rape case. The press described Wass as a "spinster," although her neighbors referred to her as "the funny-acting lady" down the road. She was as gentle and "harmless as she was eccentric," they said; and poor—so poor that she had no electricity or running water in her tarpapered shack. Every morning she'd show up at a neighbor's home with a pail to "borrow" some drinking water.

Wass recounted for McCormick how on the previous Saturday evening, a few nights before the attack, some men standing outside her house had been tapping on her windows, pestering her.

"Say, let us in," one of the men said.

"No, you can't come in," Wass replied. "It is bedtime."

When the men persisted, Wass told them that a Negro woman down the road kept a shack for laboring-camp people. "I am sure she will take you in and give you something to eat and a place for the night," she said.

The men left, but on Tuesday night they returned.

Again a voice said, "Let us in. Let us in."

"Why, no, you can't come in," Wass answered, warning, "I will throw a pan of water at you if you don't go on."

At that, Wass said, one of them "ripped off" the back door, and a boy of maybe seventeen broke the window glass and hit her over the head—with what, she wasn't sure, but she thought it might have been a hammer. Then an older man grabbed her.

"Twenty, twenty-one years old?" McCormick asked.

"Oh, no," Wass said. "He must have been in his forties or close to his fifties." The older man began strangling her, she said, while the younger one started rummaging through her house, looking for money.

"Whether he raped me or not, I don't know," Wass admitted, "because all I know is he kept strangling me, strangling me and strangling me."

"Could you have blacked out?" McCormick asked.

"I don't know," Wass told him, "but he never left my throat."

Wass did know the boy, she said; she'd seen him around Fruitland Park, she was certain, and she'd recognize him if she saw him again. It was the older man, though, who concerned her: "I just begged him not to touch me and take his hands off me," she recalled. "Now, I believe then he raped me, I really do."

"Do you think you were unconscious when he raped you?" McCormick asked.

"Well, I think I was just so . . . he had his hands right here on my throat, right up under here," she said. "Well, if a person would bend over you this way, he would have his hand right there, wouldn't he?"

Wass thought it over, and focused on the older man. It occurred to her that she might have recognized him as well; she thought he might be a man who lived behind her and had bought a couple of turkeys from her. His build was similar.

"What is that man's name?" McCormick asked.

"That is Mr. Glenn. He works for the dairy and he is a very good friend of mine."

The older man was "about this fellow Glenn's age?" McCormick asked.

"Yeah . . . he was probably younger, but he moved so quickly."

"How old is this Mr. Glenn?"

"He must be about forty-five," Wass said. "He has been very, very kind to me."

"You think this man would be about forty, is that right?"

"Yes," Wass said. "He was much older than this younger boy."

Wass told McCormick that she'd had a look at the two suspects that morning at the hospital when Yates and Clark brought them by for identification purposes.

"Did you recognize either of those boys?" McCormick asked.

"No," Wass said. "Not especially. But they could have been those boys."

But neither Shuler nor Summers resembled either of the men she'd described. Of course, the lighting in the hospital was different from that in her home at night, Wass said, and at any rate one's sense of sight might not be the most reliable means of identification. The statement left McCormick confused. "I know the smell of Mr. Glenn's voice or breath," Wass explained. "I have been around him enough that I can tell, just the same as you can tell that girl's breath." (She indicated the stenographer.) "It was real dark, but couldn't you tell the smell of her complexion and the smell of her body if she was two feet in front of you?"

"No, I couldn't," McCormick said.

"Oh, I think you can tell," Wass said. "Everybody has skin that is different."

McCormick left the interview convinced that the case was in trouble. Wass could not identify either Shuler or Summers, and worse, their ages did not match her description of her attackers. McCormick arranged to have Gordon Oldham meet with the victim. The state attorney emerged from his interview with the same opinion. He found Wass "completely incompetent," unfit for the witness stand. In fact, to eliminate the risk of her testimony ever being heard in court, he had her committed to Florida State Hospital at Chattahoochee. Without an eyewitness, the state would have to take its chances with the physical evidence found at the scene of the crime.

By March 12, word about the confusion around the identities of the rape suspects had reached a group of Klansmen in North Florida, and Willis McCall had heard murmurs of a planned lynching. At a meeting of the Mount Dora Dunkers Club, McCall asked J. T. "Bud" Huett—the club president and a longtime police officer who'd recently been promoted to police chief—to take a ride up to Jasper, close to the Georgia border, and have a talk with the men who were making noise up there.

"Okay," Huett told the sheriff. "I'll take Tom Ledford with me."

McCall peered into the darkness as Ledford stepped forward. "Willis's eyes got big as silver dollars," Ledford recalled. "That's when he knew about me." Dunkers Club leaders didn't want anyone getting involved in situations of this sort if they weren't "in the unit." (Huett himself would gain notoriety a few years later when he testified before the House Un-American Activities Committee on Klan activities. He offered testimony about the Dunkers Club and its possible Klan affiliations without benefit of an attorney—unlike previous witnesses—until, apparently recognizing that he was getting in deep, he refused to answer further. "I didn't know you were going to give me the third degree here," he said.)

"Okay," McCall told Huett, now that he understood about Ledford. "Take him and go."

They went, and the two placated their fellow Klansmen up north with assurances that McCall would bring the "right niggers" to justice.

Two months later, the trial began, with circuit judge D. R. Smith presiding (Truman Futch having passed away in March). The state attorney's office had worked out a deal for Levi Summers on the condition that he testify against Shuler and Chatman, both of whom claimed that they had been forced into giving "involuntary confessions." Shuler said that he had been physically abused and that deputies had "threatened to turn me over to a mob if I did not cooperate," whereas Chatman attested that he'd been kept in a "steel-enclosed cell with no windows and nothing but a mattress to sleep on for two days" and that he'd been told he would not be allowed to see his wife until he confessed. Both Shuler and Chatman were represented by Francisco Rodriguez of the NAACP, who argued that the confessions had been obtained through use of brutality and therefore should not be introduced at trial. Judge Smith disagreed; he allowed the two signed confessions to be introduced as evidence.

Also introduced into evidence were casts of a dozen or so perfect footprints. Griffin knew that Yates and Clark had collected all three suspects' shoes. Yet when he'd asked Yates about the condition of footprints he and Ledford had attempted to preserve at the crime scene by covering them with buckets and pots, Yates had told him that the prints hadn't been complete enough to make plaster casts. In May, however, as Oldham was rehearsing the state's witnesses in preparation for the trial, Griffin had mentioned the hard rain that had fallen in the early hours of the investigation. "Don't mention the rain," Oldham had interrupted him. "It will mess things up." At trial, Ledford had testified about covering the footprints at the scene with pots to protect them, but when asked if the plaster casts in evidence had been taken from those he'd covered at the scene, he'd replied truthfully that he could not say, since he hadn't been present when the casts were made.

On July 7, 1960, after deliberating only slightly more than an hour, the

all-white male jury convicted Shuler and Chatman of rape, with no recommendation for mercy. Judge Smith sentenced them to death by electrocution in September at Raiford.

Outside the courtroom, Griffin ran into Lucius Clark. Where, he wondered, had Clark found those perfect footprints Oldham had introduced
into evidence? He and Yates had poured the casts in Clark's backyard, the
deputy answered without hesitation, elaborating with some pride on the
process by which they had made a more pronounced hole in the cast so
that it would better match the sole of one of the defendants' shoes.

That gave Griffin pause. He recalled talk around the department
about the footprints in the Groveland case, and the perfect plaster casts
of them that had likewise been entered into evidence after Yates had
confiscated the shoes of the defendants, and how the casts had been mysteriously broken before the defense had had a chance to examine them.
He recalled how, after Jesse Daniels had been sent off to Chattahoochee,
Yates had bragged of discovering a guitar pick on the floor of the Knowles
home. As it turned out, all the physical evidence Yates had collected—
the undershorts, the footprints, the guitar pick—had proved to be im-
material, because Jesse Daniels had not had his day in court, and it
appeared he never would. Still, it all pointed up why Willis McCall had
made Yates his chief criminal deputy: "Yates got shit done for Willis."

BY AUGUST 1960, the Reeses had no choice but to sell the *Topic*. It was no
longer economically feasible for Mabel to devote the time necessary to
meet the *Topic*'s editorial demands while also writing for the *Daytona Beach
News-Journal*, and she couldn't afford to hire help. The competing *Mount
Dora Herald* itself survived only a year, but that was long enough to do
permanent damage to the *Topic* by luring away advertisers who never returned. "McCall eventually did get to me financially," Mabel admitted.

Paul had always been supportive of Mabel's crusades for justice in

Lake County, despite the economic consequences. "He never said quit," Mabel recalled. But the financial stress generated by the decline and eventual failure of the *Topic* had taken its toll on their marriage. With Patricia off at college, she and Paul had talked about moving to Daytona Beach together, but by September that prospect had become tenuous. Paul relocated to South Florida to be closer to his daughter from a previous marriage. Mabel left Lake County for Daytona Beach, where the editor of the *News-Journal*, Herbert Davidson, and his wife, Liliane, welcomed her on board full-time.

The couple had met at the Pulitzer School of Journalism at Columbia University and graduated together in 1918. When Herbert's father, Julius, had purchased majority interest in the *News-Journal* in 1928, the Davidsons had moved to Daytona, and they had been working at the paper ever since. The Davidsons and Mabel shared a similar journalistic vision, and mission. In assuming her new position, Mabel promised to continue her pursuit of justice through journalism while also reporting and writing editorials on important civil and governmental issues in Daytona Beach. "I feel the newspaper has to take this sort of leadership," she said. "It's a newspaper's responsibility to the community."

TOM LEDFORD'S MARITAL PROBLEMS had deepened. Gossip brought to Evvie Griffin's attention that Ora Mae was sleeping with another deputy on the force and that the lovers were planning a rendezvous at Willis McCall's cabin in the Scrub. Griffin felt he had to tell his partner. Ledford made up his mind to confront his wife there. Bud Huett agreed to accompany him, to ensure that the situation, and his friend's quick temper, didn't get out of control. "Bud wouldn't let me take my gun," Ledford recalled.

The scene that greeted them on their arrival at the cabin confirmed the rumor Griffin had heard. Yet to his own surprise, Ledford realized that the sight of his wife and her lover did not enrage him. He was simply depressed by what his eye could not deny, and dismayed when he saw that his young son was also present. He told Ora Mae on the spot that he wanted a divorce, which a court granted to him a few months later. He got custody as well, but his son did not want to live with him.

Gordon Oldham was also dealing with adultery issues—his own. The state attorney had been carrying on an affair with Audrey Dillard, the socialite wife of Charles Dillard, a prominent businessman and member of the Leesburg Quarterback Club. In the fall of 1960, Charles caught them together in St. Petersburg. The strain this put on the Dillards' marriage extended to the family's social dealings with Gordon Oldham, and the acrimony intensified when it became clear that Audrey was not interested in patching up her marriage to Charles but wanted to leave him for Oldham. Charles decided to grant her wish. With Audrey in tow, he confronted Oldham at his Leesburg office and announced that he'd gladly divorce her so that the two could continue their relationship. Oldham was stunned. "Oh, no," he told Dillard. "I'm married."

The confrontation in Oldham's office aggravated the already bitter relations between the Dillards and Oldham. Indeed, there was a rumor afoot of a plan to have Oldham killed, when McCall waded into the conflict. The sheriff, who knew the Dillard family well, intervened on Oldham's behalf, it was said, and "smoothed the thing over."

Only then Charles Dillard failed to show up for a Quarterback Club trip to Baton Rouge, where the Gators were playing the Louisiana State University Tigers. A Dillard family member said Charles had canceled because Gordon Oldham was also going, but it soon became apparent that Charles Dillard had in fact disappeared. A search was mounted, and his body was eventually found in a cabin in the Ocala National Forest, "the top of his head blown off." When a family member notified Audrey of the gruesome discovery of her husband's body, he felt "from the way she acted" that she "might have already known about the death."

What you believed about how Charles Dillard died depended on whom you listened to. Jack Hooten, a grove service operator and Lake County commissioner from 1956 to 1958, had joined the Klan "mainly to find out who were in the Ku Klux Klan and what was going on," as he later told investigators. What he found out was that Sheriff Willis Mc-Call was the "main power" behind the Klan in Lake County—that he "controlled it." Hooten also stated McCall "has either killed a lot of people or had something to do with people being killed in Lake County," more often than not to his personal advantage. Since Dillard's death, Hooten noted significantly, McCall had "been able to control Gordon Oldham" as if the two were "bed partners." "No one should underestimate the power of Willis McCall in Lake County," Hooten asserted, "and his capability of doing dirty work to anyone who opposes him."

Tom Ledford, however, claimed to have seen Dillard's suicide note, which, he recalled, was "mostly about how he wanted his estate split up." Dillard family members were convinced that Charles's death "wasn't anything but suicide," as evidenced by a two-page handwritten note on a table in the cabin and by "a high powered rifle between his legs." One said, "I know Charles took his life over a piece of tail. It was his pride that got in the way." And the same family member professed fondness for the "firm but fair" sheriff of Lake County: "Tell it straight about McCall. He was a good man."

PEARL DANIELS was worried about her husband. "We have just got to do something," she wrote to Mabel, or Jesse's father was going to "go out of his mind. He's like a wild frantic thing." Pearl herself was feeling desperate. By the end of 1960, her hope that the state attorney's office would bring her son to trial, and so free him from Chattahoochee, was just about gone.

Mabel, however, perceived a new opportunity for Jesse's release. W. Troy Hall, who had run unopposed for county judge on the Fifth

Circuit Court after Truman Futch's death in March 1960, seemed in general to have resisted the pull of Willis McCall's influence. The judge had become friendly, too, with Pearl, and Mabel believed that he had also become convinced of Jesse's innocence. The lawyer Tom Champion agreed, and in February 1961, he filed a petition in Hall's court requesting that Jesse Daniels be transferred from Florida State Hospital at Chattahoochee to Sunland Training Center in Gainesville, where Jesse's needs would be more suitably met. He provided correspondence indicating that the Gainesville facility would approve of such a transfer. All that was needed was a court order.

One week later, Gordon Oldham filed a motion to dismiss the petition on behalf of Jesse Daniels, and a few days after that, he filed a motion to disqualify Judge Hall from the case. In June, Oldham filed a third motion, in which he called for the state to "delay further hearing on said petition of the Defendant." The court found Oldham's motions "without merit," but the state attorney did succeed in one respect: Judge Hall was removed from the case and replaced by circuit judge Carroll W. Fussell.

At a March 1961 hearing, Champion argued that Jesse Daniels was, according to the Florida State Hospital psychiatrists' report, a "mentally defective child" who should never have been sent to Chattahoochee. Nowhere in the report, Champion noted, had Jesse been diagnosed as "insane." Futch alone, speaking for the court at the sanity hearing in 1958, had deemed him so without any kind of corroborating assessment. Oldham quickly pointed out that Jesse's attorney at the time, Sam Buie, had waived the need for such corroboration. The court agreed, and the legal setbacks mounted. Pearl Daniels was running out of options, and Charles Daniels, his health failing, was running out of time.

By August 1962, time was also running out for Robert Shuler and Jerry Chatman. Since the close of their trial, the NAACP had appealed their convictions, made their case to the Florida pardon board, and filed petitions to stay their executions, all to no avail. They were scheduled for the electric chair at Raiford in less than a week when, out of the blue, according to Robert Saunders, a man from Lake County showed up unannounced at NAACP headquarters in Tampa and asked to speak with an attorney there. "He says that it involves the two black men who are supposed to die in the chair," Margie Johnson, Saunders's secretary, informed him.

Waiting in the reception room was a white man wearing cowboy boots and blue jeans held up by a belt with a big silver buckle, and carrying a Stetson. He looked, Saunders thought, uncomfortably out of place. No one would ever have imagined the day that Evvie Griffin would turn up, hat in hand, inside NAACP headquarters. But he had a story he'd decided finally to tell.

Saunders summoned a colleague, attorney Francisco Rodriguez, to his office. The three men shook hands. Then Griffin launched into a tale of unparalleled corruption and bigotry, Saunders recalled. "He confessed that Chatman and Shuler had been accused intentionally and fraudulently and that the convictions had been attained based upon trumped-up evidence," and recounted what he had learned from Deputy Lucius Clark about the plaster casts. Griffin "had decided that he could no longer stand idly by and see injustice continued," Saunders said.

Rodriguez moved quickly. That afternoon he petitioned for stays of execution, citing the new evidence. As quickly, Judge Hall stayed both executions for forty days, to allow the NAACP attorneys time to prepare an appeal. Then Judge Hall made a phone call.

Fifty miles away in Daytona Beach, a reporter hung up the phone, sharpened a few pencils, and picked up her notepad. Then she drove west, back to Lake County, to confront her old nemesis once again.

James Brock, manager of the segregated Monson Motor Lodge in
St. Augustine, pouring muriatic acid in the motel pool near protesters

CHAPTER TWELVE

If It Takes All Summer

Tom Ledford had known his days in the Lake County Sheriff's Department were numbered once he refused to "play along" with Gordon Oldham's line of questioning and vouch for the integrity of Deputy Yates's footprint casts during the Fruitland Park rape case trial. Before Ledford's appearance in court, Oldham had summoned the deputy to his office and told him, "This is what you're going to testify to: You covered the prints and Yates and Clark poured them." Ledford was dumbfounded. "I'd get twenty years if they caught me lying," he recalled.

McCall, too, had turned on the deputy. "I was Willis's fair-haired boy for a while," Ledford said. "Not after that." Sure enough, McCall soon dismissed Ledford from the department for his "overbearing tactics," but Bud Huett quickly hired him for Mount Dora's police force.

Evvie Griffin's fall from McCall's grace occurred in a moment of naiveté. He was riding with McCall in the sheriff's Oldsmobile when he felt compelled to share some disturbing information he'd learned: A fellow deputy, Doug Sewell, was taking payments from moonshiners in Volusia County and also running "chicken fights" in Pine Lakes. The disclosure was not appreciated. McCall responded with a cold stare, and they passed the rest of the ride in stony silence. The next day, Griffin was suspended for a week without pay.

Ten days after his disquieting ride with McCall, Griffin, along with Ledford and three other men, was arrested in Volusia County. The five of them had been caught hunting wild hogs in the St. Johns River area and were charged with theft. McCall fired Griffin on the spot and ordered him to turn in his uniforms. With similar efficiency, Mount Dora mayor Jesse Wilmott suspended Ledford indefinitely. Little did it matter that a Volusia County judge cleared the five men of the charges after a preliminary hearing established that a wildlife official had given them permission to hunt in the area. "Willis had it out for me," said Griffin, who went back to work on the family ranch.

More serious harassment of the former deputies soon followed, however. Both men began to receive anonymous, threatening phone calls at all hours of the night. When Griffin's wife answered a call one afternoon, a voice warned, "If your husband goes hunting tomorrow he won't come back." Griffin took to strapping a sawed-off shotgun to the steering column of his pickup truck. "I was never more than three feet away from a gun," he said.

Griffin and Ledford decided they were not about to go down quietly. Together, they engaged in a campaign to expose fraud and corruption in the Lake County Sheriff's Department and in the state attorney's office. Although Griffin's letters to the governor and the Florida Sheriffs Bureau elicited little response, his insider's story won the full attention of Tom O'Connor, a reporter with the *Tampa Tribune*. It was O'Connor who'd advised Griffin to meet with the NAACP lawyers, as Shuler and Chatman stood only days away from execution.

As Saunders and Rodriguez took action, O'Connor reported every explosive detail of the case in the *Tribune*. The Department of Justice opened a civil rights investigation, and FBI agents once again descended on the Lake County Sheriff's Department. Judge Hall ordered that the controversial plaster casts be turned over to the FBI, and agents took soil samples from the backyard of Lucius Clark's house as well as from the crime scene. Hall announced that he was referring "falsification of evidence" charges to a grand jury; however, as he believed it would be "impractical and inexpedient" to impanel a grand jury in Lake County "on account of undue excitement or prejudice among the people," he was forwarding his order to the circuit court in Orlando. In effect, he was returning the favor Gordon Oldham had once done him and taking the case out of the state attorney's hands.

In early December, after comparing the soil outside the home of the victim with the soil in Lucius Clark's backyard, the FBI presented the results of its report before an Orange County grand jury. The footprints, agents testified, "could not have been made at the crime scene." Furthermore, the casts themselves had been constructed from footprints made by "empty shoes," the same conclusion that had been drawn by a forensic expert regarding Yates's plaster casts in the Groveland trial a decade before. The Orange County grand jury was persuaded by the testimony of the FBI agents, and on December 21, a sealed envelope was sent to Judge Hall in Tavares, who announced the indictments of James Yates and Lucius Clark on the grounds that they "did unlawfully conspire, combine and confederate to gather to commit a felony, punishable by imprisonment for life." Hall ordered their immediate arrests. The two deputies were free on bond later that afternoon, but Sheriff Willis McCall, who had himself been granted a waiver of immunity in exchange for agreeing to testify, had no choice but to suspend both Yates and Clark from the department.

News of the indictments spread quickly in the national press. "Fake Footprints Case Due . . . History Repeated in Florida," read the headline to the article in the *Pittsburgh Courier*, which opened provocatively:

Any time a white woman claims she was raped in Lake County, Fla., the safest thing for all Negro males between the ages of 13 and 82 to do is burn all their shoes.

If they don't, a deputy sheriff is mighty apt to come along, throw them into the clink, borrow their shoes, and turn up in court with plaster casts of footprints he says he found at the scene of the crime.

In which case, the hapless victim of a frame-up is consigned to burn in the electric chair.

It happened here before, and came awfully close to happening again.

An editorial in the *Tampa Tribune* deplored the "cloud of doubt" that had arisen over the justice process in Lake County, given that two men had nearly been sent to the electric chair on the strength of evidence that, "in an important element, appears to have been deliberately faked." This, the editors affirmed, "is the cloud that hangs over Lake County. No newspaper can remove it. Only the court and the people of Lake County can."

Asked by reporters if he had any comment, McCall said only, "It will all come out in the wash." Evvie Griffin was disappointed that neither the sheriff nor Oldham had been indicted for their roles in the conspiracy. He struggled with the notion that his promising career in law enforcement had been curtailed while the sheriff carried on business as usual. Still, Griffin remained patiently convinced that one mistake too many would eventually bring McCall down.

Ledford told the *Tribune*, "I now feel vindicated," but the feeling did not last. "After Willis fired me, he hired my ex-wife," Ledford recalled. The Lake County Sheriff's Department began paying bonus checks of hundreds of dollars each to Ora Mae and other employees, which they quickly cashed and contributed to a fund for the legal defense of Yates and Clark.

Added to that, McCall was sleeping with Ora Mae. When Ledford discovered this, he made up his mind: He was going to murder Willis McCall. "That's the only man I set up to kill purposely," he recalled. "He'd just done so damned much to me that I thought, life ain't worth it if I got to put up with him."

After learning McCall was planning a trip to his cabin in Alexander Springs, Ledford grabbed his Browning, drove to the Scrub, and parked near the bridge at Spring Creek. His plan was to "bust a windshield" in McCall's face with his shotgun and, when the car came to a stop in the woods, to finish the sheriff off with another blast, if necessary.

But Willis McCall didn't show up at the bridge. "I went there three or four nights," Ledford recalled, insisting that had the sheriff driven up to the Scrub the way he'd planned, he'd have been as good as dead. "I done took all of him I was gonna take." Evvie Griffin concurred: "Willis was a lucky man. Tom would have killed him."

Lake County held no further surprises for Mabel. She'd hoped against hope the indictment of Yates and Clark would expose the corruption in the Lake County Sheriff's Department and finally bring down Willis McCall, and that authorities would be spurred into investigating some of the sheriff's most suspect cases—especially that of Jesse Daniels. None of that happened. In fact, the two-year statute of limitations on perjury expired before the deputies even faced trial, whereupon McCall rehired both men at full pay. (In their absence, McCall had deputized the suspended officers' brothers, at the same salaries.)

Nor did the stay of execution bring to pass the hopes of the defendants in the Fruitland Park rape case. In early 1963, Florida Supreme Court chief justice B. K. Roberts, who had written the majority opinion denying Virgil Hawkins admission to the University of Florida College of Law, appointed retired Hillsborough County circuit judge L. L. Parks to

review testimony in the case of Robert Shuler and Jerry Chatman in order to decide whether the two were entitled to a new trial. In his ruling
against Shuler and Chatman, Parks stated that he was not persuaded by
the testimony of Griffin and Ledford, nor did he accept as fact the
conclusion of the FBI's lab report, signed by J. Edgar Hoover, that the
footprint evidence had been falsified.

Neither did a letter written to Governor LeRoy Collins by the victim's sister, Sally Wass, hold sway. In it, she asserted that Charlotte Wass
"does not wish . . . to see these young men pay the supreme penalty."
More particularly and pertinently, she noted, "our sister is also troubled
by doubts whether one of the men was guilty as charged. That is Robert
Shuler. His family had been known to her and kind to her, and she says
she did not recognize him as one of her assailants." Charlotte Wass herself wrote a letter to Sheriff McCall in which she stated, "Robert Shuler
did not rape me and I wonder why he has been in the condemned row of
men." McCall simply filed the letter away.

In spite of Francisco Rodriguez's efforts to win a new trial for his clients, the Florida Supreme Court upheld Parks's ruling. Willis McCall
had again prevailed; with the assistance of an entrenched judiciary,
Shuler and Chatman would remain on death row at Raiford, awaiting
their execution. As usual in Lake County, the wash had come out dirty.

BY THE EARLY 1960s, the United States had narrowed the gap in its
Space Race with the Soviet Union. NASA had launched astronaut Alan
Shepard into space and John Glenn into orbit around the earth. President
John F. Kennedy announced in a speech before Congress that America
"should take a clearly leading role in space achievement," and he challenged politicians, scientists, engineers, and civil servants to commit to
"a new course of action" to accomplish a lofty goal by the end of the decade. "I believe we should go to the moon," Kennedy said. Assassinated

in Dallas on November 22, 1963, the thirty-fifth president of the United States did not live to see the achievements of the American space program that he had envisioned.

On the day that Kennedy was killed, Walt Disney was flying above the swampland of central Florida, secretly scouting locations for an East Coast version of his Disneyland theme park in Anaheim, California. It was the Space Race, however, that thrust a new, modern Florida into record economic growth. In Brevard County, where Cape Canaveral was located, the unemployment rate in mid-1964 was an extraordinarily low 1.6 percent. By the end of the summer, though, economic optimism in the state would be eclipsed by an explosive racial conflict in America's oldest city. St. Augustine would be the final battleground in the long fight for what would become the Civil Rights Act of 1964.

In the spring of 1963, Vice President Lyndon Johnson attended a dinner in St. Augustine announcing a commission to organize the city's upcoming four-hundredth-anniversary celebration. "There was one flaw in plans for the dinner," wrote Dan Warren, the state attorney in Daytona Beach at the time. "It failed to include blacks." The "deliberate exclusion of a major segment of the city's citizens," he noted, "doomed the celebration from the start."

Mabel covered the developments in St. Augustine for the *News-Journal*. She reported assiduously on the activities of Dr. Robert Hayling, who would become known as the father of the St. Augustine Movement. One of the first black dentists in Florida, Hayling had founded the NAACP Youth Council, which organized a sit-in at the local Woolworth's lunch counter. The sixteen young protesters were arrested and imprisoned—among them four teenagers, two boys and two girls, ages fifteen to seventeen, who were deemed delinquents by the court, sentenced to six-week stints in the county jail, and then dispatched to state reformatories for six months.

Undeterred, Hayling and his followers continued to protest. As a result, he was continually receiving death threats from the Ku Klux Klan, which had a growing presence in St. Augustine. After his NAACP associate Medgar Evers was gunned down in Jackson, Mississippi, in June 1963, Hayling made a statement that garnered headlines across the country. "Passive resistance is no good in the face of violence. I and others of the NAACP have armed ourselves, and we will shoot first and answer questions later. We are not going to die like Medgar Evers," he announced.

The militant threat from an NAACP official sparked a white backlash around St. Augustine. KKK night riders began terrorizing residents of the city's black neighborhoods, and Hayling and his cohort at the NAACP answered by driving the Klansmen off with gunfire. By the end of the summer, the Klan's membership had swelled, and KKK chapters were holding meetings throughout the city. When Hayling and three activists confronted the Klan at one of its gatherings, they were seized and severely beaten with clubs and fists. The Florida Highway Patrol rescued them and arrested four whites in connection with the beatings. The charges against the whites were dismissed; Hayling was convicted on charges of assault against the KKK.

Because of her reportorial commitment to issues of race and justice, Mabel was asked to serve on the Florida Advisory Committee to the U.S. Commission on Civil Rights. Its 1963 report concluded that the city of St. Augustine was "too timid" in its support of civil rights and that it harbored conditions worse than any city in the state, as "Negroes are excluded entirely from the white power structure." It described St. Augustine as "a segregated super-bomb aimed at the heart of Florida's economy and political integrity," warning direly, "the fuse is short."

The fuse was shorter by midsummer 1963. The heat had become so stifling during the day that black protesters, Hayling's NAACP Youth Council among them, took to marching at night. Klansmen from the city and surrounding counties responded by attacking demonstrators from their cars or by driving through black neighborhoods and harassing residents, often shooting at them in their homes, as they did in Lincoln-ville that October. On one such occasion, blacks returned fire on a car driven by the son of Halstead "Hoss" Manucy, the local Klavern's Exalted Cyclops, and killed twenty-five-year-old William Kinard, who was in the backseat. Kinard's wake was teeming with Klansmen when state attorney Warren arrived at the funeral home to question the young men who had been riding with Kinard at the time of the shooting. The reason they were driving around the city with loaded guns that evening, they told Warren, was that it was "dove season." Warren left the wake convinced that "trouble was in the offing and it would not be long in coming."

The circle of Klansmen descending on St. Augustine grew wider that fall. Connie Lynch, a fundamentalist preacher from California, teamed up with Hoss Manucy to hold Klan meetings in the city. Fond of mis-quoting the Bible to promote white supremacy, Lynch implored his white audiences to "remember the words of Jesus Christ, who said, 'You can't love two masters. You love one . . . and you HATE the other . . .' Now it may be some niggers are gonna get killed in the process, but when war's on, that's what happens."

The NAACP stood by the three men who were charged with killing William Kinard; however, they also maintained that the organization "does not believe in violence as a course for achievement of our rights." Robert Hayling, finding himself increasingly at odds with the nonviolent stance of the NAACP, resigned. The black protest movement in St. Au-gustine found both its focus and its forces divided. Its potency was not restored until the following spring, with the arrival of Martin Luther King Jr. and the Southern Christian Leadership Conference (SCLC).

King's timing could not have been better. Lyndon Johnson, now presi-dent of the United States, was intent on passage of the Civil Rights Act. Mary Parkman Peabody, the seventy-two-year-old mother of Massachu-setts governor Endicott Peabody and a cousin of Eleanor Roosevelt, was an avid supporter. In March 1964, at the invitation of the SCLC,

Peabody joined the protests in St. Augustine. The presence of "northern scalawags" at the SCLC demonstrations inspired mostly resentment among city authorities, and she, along with a dozen other white women, was arrested during a sit-in. Newspapers across the country ran images of the elderly doyenne being escorted by deputies to the county jail.

When Mabel went to interview Peabody, she found her "undimmed" by two nights in the cell she'd shared with the other white female protesters. Despite making bond, Peabody told Mabel she wasn't going anywhere: "I want to stay with them. We're in it together now." She also expressed to Mabel her shock at the depth of hatred and violence she'd observed in the city—a comment that caused St. Augustine's mayor, Joseph Shelley, to charge that Peabody had done "irreparable harm to race relations" in the city. The *Orlando Sentinel*, angered by the efforts of northerners like Peabody to "blacken the South," ran an editorial titled "She Should Have Stayed in Boston." For, indeed, Peabody's arrest had "fueled the flames of civil disobedience that had been smoldering for more than a year in St. Augustine." The racial crisis escalated; increasing numbers of protesters, as well as national news organizations, poured into the Ancient City. In early June, when King was scheduled to go back to Florida from California, he received an "explicit death threat" to the effect that night riders in St. Augustine were vowing to "hang a Negro." Undeterred, King returned to St. Augustine, where he discovered that the Crescent Beach cottage in which he'd been planning to stay had been shot at "from all four sides" the night before. On the evening of June 4, at a black church in the city, King told the crowd of congregants and protesters that if the death threat had been successfully executed, "It would be the price I would have to pay to redeem my brothers from spiritual death—both White and Negro." He vowed not to allow such threats to divert him and his followers from their purpose, and reasserted his determination to protest in St. Augustine until the battle was won. He praised the courage of blacks in recent demonstrations, telling them they showed "beauty and dignity" in the struggle for justice "You confronted the totality of the Klan," King declaimed, "and you stood up to say eloquently you would not be turned around. You are the heroes of St. Augustine."

Mabel was sitting in the church audience that evening, and after the speech, while King was autographing paper fans and high school yearbooks for admirers, she managed to score an interview with him. "We want desegregation of all public facilities," he asserted, then cited three other pressing demands: merit employment, a biracial committee to address segregation, and dismissal of all charges against peaceful demonstrators. As to how to achieve these ends, he told Mabel, "We will be negotiating, if they will meet with us. If not, we will have to continue in the streets so we can keep the issue before the conscience of the nation."

Mabel's story and interview with King ran under the headline "What Manner of Man Is Leading America's Negro Revolution?" "To his lowliest followers," Mabel wrote, "he is virtually a saint." The saint's battle for St. Augustine, though, was only just beginning. Shortly after King left the city, vandals again attacked the Crescent Beach cottage, this time breaking windows, smashing furniture, and pulling cabinets from the walls before setting the house on fire.

On June 11, Martin Luther King returned to the Ancient City. When he and a small group of activists appeared on the steps of the Monson Motor Lodge to challenge policy in what King had described as "the most segregated city in America," motel manager James Brock informed them, "We're segregated at this time." When they refused to leave, Sheriff L. O. Davis had them arrested and locked up in the St. Johns County jail. Interviewed in his cell, King renewed his vow to desegregate St. Augustine, "even if it takes all summer."

Tirelessly, King continued to call the nation's attention to the Jim Crow laws and their fervent enforcement by city officials. Southern senators, meanwhile, had spent the past two months filibustering the civil rights bill, which was being protested with increasing frequency and virulence in St. Augustine's Old Slave Market, a site chosen as a KKK meeting place for its symbolic significance. Racial diatribes assailed the summer air on a nightly basis, and violence constantly erupted, as when the Klan assaulted white civil rights activists and journalists who'd converged on the city. The *Daytona Beach Morning Journal* covered, and condemned, the attacks, and Mabel pleaded for peace and cooperation between factions in the escalating racial fray. She pleaded in vain.

King rallied his supporters: "We're preparing for a long, hot summer, and we see our push here in St. Augustine as a purifying prelude." The Klan dug in. Connie Lynch ranted at meetings in the Old Slave Market; posters displayed King's portrait with the caption "Martin Luther Coon." Jackie Robinson, who had broken baseball's color barrier in 1947, traveled to St. Augustine to encourage the protesters in their struggle.

Two days later, King organized a "swim-in" at the Monson Motor Lodge. As black demonstrators in bathing suits jumped into the motel pool, dozens of newsmen and photographers were present to witness James Brock pouring jugs of muriatic acid into the water. The next day, Hoss Manucy and the Klan arrived with several alligators, which they promised to dump in the pool should any blacks decide to test the city's segregation laws again. Later in June, at the segregated St. Augustine Beach, black protesters began staging "wade-ins," singing hymns and walking arm in arm as they made their way into the ocean—or attempted to, as they were invariably assaulted by whites at the water's edge. Ultimately, troopers had to be dispatched to form protective wedges between the protesters and their adversaries. Indeed, the situation in the city had become so combustible that Governor C. Farris Bryant, who had been in office since 1961, invoked emergency powers to create a special police force to supplement the troopers.

On one occasion, Lynch was joined on his platform at the Market by J. B. Stoner, a Klansman who would eventually be convicted of conspiring in the 1958 bombing of the Bethel Baptist Church in Birmingham, Alabama. Stoner's incendiary diatribe—"Niggers want to integrate because they want our white women," and when black demonstrators appeared on the north side of Cathedral Plaza, "There they come! The niggers are coming now!"—sparked a riot, as roaming packs of whites set upon the black demonstrators and left nineteen of them inert on the pavement.

For their part, blacks stood undaunted and undeterred. At mass meetings in black churches, impassioned speakers asked, "Are you willing to get beat up and go to jail for freedom?" Their audiences responded with their actions, marching, shouting, wading in, and clashing with their oppressors in near-nightly violence. Footage of blacks being beaten on the beach and assaulted on the streets of St. Augustine was broadcast nightly on the news across the nation. Three weeks into June, the racial turmoil in St. Augustine was sharing headlines with the disappearance of three civil rights workers who had been arrested by local police in Neshoba County, Mississippi. The FBI as well as hundreds of U.S. Navy sailors descended on the area; swamps were dredged and woodlands combed in the search for Andrew Goodman, Michael Schwerner, and James Chaney. Not until August would their bodies be found.

In an effort to calm the "racial war of nerves" in St. Johns County, Governor Bryant—again claiming broad emergency powers granted to him by state law—banned nighttime demonstrations. Tobias Simon, representing the SCLC, challenged the ban in federal court, and Judge Bryan Simpson ordered the governor to appear in his Jacksonville courtroom to show cause for the suspension of rights. Flouting a charge of contempt, the governor refused to appear himself and instead sent Attorney General James W. Kynes, who was also named in the contempt proceedings.

Mabel had been following the case closely. She had written critically of Kynes five years before, when, as an assistant state attorney to Gordon

Oldham, he had interviewed Sam Wiley Odom at Raiford. She remained convinced that powers in Lake County and beyond had been responsible for Odom's reversal, and she was certain that Kynes had been instrumental in effecting it. Mabel's congenial relationship with the state attorney, a fellow Volusia County resident, ensured that she'd have a seat in the federal courtroom for Kynes's appearance.

Among the first witnesses to be called was Officer Jerry Harris, who arrived with Kynes and who testified that his shirt had been torn by a knife in a scuffle with a demonstrator. As state attorney Warren pointed out, a crisis was brewing. If Harris's assertion was true, the credibility of King's claim that the demonstrations were peaceful, and therefore protected under the First Amendment, would be in jeopardy. Still, Warren noted, in all his experience with the St. Augustine protests, "discipline among the demonstrators was excellent," and he had never witnessed a single incident of one of them "fighting back or engaging in disruptive conduct or abusive language of any kind," even when assaulted verbally and physically by the Klan "and other hoodlums."

Judge Simpson ordered the officer to produce the torn shirt as evidence, but Harris demurred. He claimed that he had sent it to his wife in Tampa "to be mended," whereupon Simpson ordered federal marshals to "proceed immediately to Tampa and retrieve the torn shirt, without alerting the wife or allowing the officer to place a phone call." Warren, too, suspected foul play, and requested the court's permission to speak with the officer in the judge's chambers. Under Warren's questioning, and with Kynes also present, the officer admitted that he had lied—there was no torn shirt. Displeased that a witness in his courtroom had testified untruthfully in a crucial federal case, Judge Simpson proposed the officer be held in contempt of court, but SCLC attorney Tobias Simon "made an impassioned plea on King's behalf that the young man not be punished." Aware of the "intense pressure the witness was under," King "would be satisfied," Simon averred, "if he recanted his testimony in open court."

Accustomed though Mabel had grown to corruption in Lake County, she was incensed by the blatant willingness of a witness in federal court to derail a vital battle in the civil rights movement by committing perjury. But she restrained her indignation in reporting the story for the *News-Journal*, in light of Martin Luther King Jr.'s position. Still, she took heed of every instance that Judge Simpson clashed with Kynes or admonished him for attempting to introduce new testimony with his questioning. What might be routine in Lake County was not necessarily standard procedure in federal court.

"The Ku Klux Klan is not going to take over St. Augustine," King had said, "even if we must offer our bodies as sacrifices." That sacrifice was at least temporarily averted on July 2, when President Johnson signed the Civil Rights Act of 1964 into law, the Senate having finally voted in favor of the bill. King called for a truce and shut down demonstrations for two weeks. He was ready to "declare victory" and leave the city.

On July 16, in an interview with Mabel, King said, "I pray that I shall never have to demonstrate in St. Augustine again. I would like to get out from under the tension." Expressing dismay that the city, unlike Birmingham, had not yet desegregated, he remarked that Governor Bryant had not made good on his promise to form a biracial committee and that, as a result, "the Ku Klux Klan—or call it what you will" had indeed "taken over the city." Still, he did not favor bringing federal troops to St. Augustine, because their presence would summon up thoughts of Reconstruction—"We don't want to inflict this on our Southern Brothers." After reaffirming his desire to work out the conflict in accord with the law, King ended the interview by turning to Mabel with a request: "If you know of any other channels we can explore to bring this thing to an end, please let me know. If anyone can reach the power structure here and persuade it to call off the Klan, we will welcome it."

Mabel spoke highly of King to state attorney Warren, whom she praised in an editorial for his efforts "to settle the racial crisis" in St.

Augustine and whom she encouraged to bring the Civil Rights Act of 1964 to bear on the city's tense racial situation. Mabel never relented in her own efforts to stand up to and editorially challenge white supremacists like Hoss Manucy, even as he continued to baldly assert that his "boys" intended "to fight niggers."

In August, King held a press conference in St. Augustine to claim a victory for his movement. He held in his hand an order from Judge Simpson declaring that fifteen local restaurants must begin serving Negroes immediately and prohibiting Hoss Manucy's Ancient City Hunting Club from interfering with their peaceful compliance with the law.

Generally, Manucy did not suffer from bad press. As he remarked, reporters for the local newspapers often themselves "donated" to his hunting club. He did note one exception: the "Daytona paper," which "was the only ones that give us a rough time."

MABEL HAD CLEARLY REGAINED her professional footing in Daytona, and she had regained peace and pleasure in her personal life as well. In November 1960, Patricia Reese, while still a student at Florida State, had married Sanborn Chesley, the son of Army Corps engineer and Mount Dora councilman Harrison Chesley. A year and a half later, Mabel married Harrison. They bought a modest ranch house on a thin peninsula between the Halifax River and the Atlantic Ocean, just south of Daytona Shores.

In August 1963, in the little house in Yalaha County, Charles passed away at the age of seventy-five; Pearl broke the news to Jesse in a letter. Bereft of her husband's companionship, and absent her fellow conspirator, strategist, and confidante now that Mabel had been driven from Lake County, Pearl found herself rudderless. She seemed to be tallying only losses, and added another when she returned to Yalaha from a visit with Jesse at Chattahoochee and discovered that her tiny shack had mysteriously burned to the ground. The fire had claimed her photos of Jesse and all the letters he'd sent her from Chattahoochee—the letters she'd read over and over, letting them dissolve the miles that lay between her and her son, as if the two of them were once again lying side by side beneath an Okahumpka pine, the way they had done before Jesse's illness, gazing at the clouds and laughing together at the shapes they took in the sky.

Heavy-hearted, Pearl called her old friend. When they hung up, Pearl did not hesitate to act on Mabel's advice: She packed her bag and moved to Daytona Beach. With Mabel's help, she found a job as a maid at the Princess Issena, an upscale historic hotel, and a small, affordable apartment near a city bus stop. The two women still found time to fish together along the Halifax River, Mabel chain-smoking her low-tar cigarettes as the pair waded in calf-deep water and planned Pearl's next trip to Chattahoochee. In the absence of any news from attorney Thomas Champion, the possibility of Jesse's transfer had dimmed.

Attorney Richard Graham

CHAPTER THIRTEEN

Troubled by It

THE SKIES OVER THE ATLANTIC were quiet that autumn evening in 1969 as the middle-aged woman from Okahumpka made her way along the shoreline of Daytona Beach. Three months earlier, on July 20, the United States had met President Kennedy's challenge when Apollo 11 landed on the moon; America could declare a victory in the Space Race. The woman on the beach could boast no triumphs. Her husband had died "a bitter man," as her friend Mabel had observed, "his hopes of seeing his son freed dashed on the rock of judicial injustice." Pearl, too, had married again, to a Lake County man, Thomas Eisentrager, but he'd died of cancer in 1968. And Jesse, now thirty-two, was still locked up in the criminal ward of the state hospital.

Pearl walked frequently along the shoreline, in part to save herself the cost of bus fare but also to lend herself hope for her son and his future. She still wrote to Jesse twice a week, and he faithfully answered her. She carried his latest letters with her, and on her solitary walks she read and reread them. "My dearest Momie," they usually began, and they would continue with accounts of his day-to-day doings and simple requests, for new batteries for his radio or for coffee "and something to eat." "My sweet Momie," read one letter, "I sure do want two say that I thank you for being so good as two send me the dollar bil as it will sure come in handy."

But today Pearl was walking with purpose, to the Daytona office of Volusia County Legal Services (VCLS), where twenty-eight-year-old lawyer Richard Graham had a desk.

"Mabel Chesley recommended I come see you," she said.

Graham, like most residents of Volusia County, knew Mabel Chesley by her editorials in the *News-Journal*, but he'd never actually met her. And initially he found Pearl's account of Jesse's case hard to believe—"another mother who thinks her kid's innocent," he'd thought. Still, Pearl's sincerity affected him, and he was new enough on the job to be more intrigued by the case than skeptical of it.

"Does he have a lawyer?" Graham asked.

"Tom Champion," Pearl told him. "In Mount Dora."

Wary about encroaching on another lawyer's territory, Graham advised, "I need to talk to him first. If he's representing your son, I shouldn't be interfering."

Pearl explained that Champion could no longer work on the case. "The sheriff and the state attorney are just ruining him. He's going to have to leave the county if he doesn't get off this case because they've taken all the business he's got away from him."

The explanation puzzled Graham, who was as yet unfamiliar with the way justice operated in Lake County. But Champion confirmed what Pearl had said—his involvement in the Jesse Daniels case had "given him a hard time in Lake County." Willis McCall and Gordon Oldham, both of whom were still in office, had been exerting their power against him. Champion briefed Graham on the case and indicated that he'd be happy to have a lawyer from Legal Services step in.

"Do you think he's innocent?" Graham asked.

"I know he's innocent," Champion said. "The boy was railroaded."

Champion suggested that Graham speak with Mabel Chesley, as she knew more about the Daniels case than anyone. "She will not let this case go," he said. "She wants justice for this kid."

Richard Graham had grown up in nearby DeLand, where his father was a partner in Landis Graham French, the oldest law firm in Volusia County—circumstances that made Graham, as he said, "probably programmed a little bit" toward a career in law. When he joined the firm after he'd finished military service, however, he quickly realized that real estate law wasn't what he wanted to practice. "I wanted to see some action."

The Office of Economic Opportunity, which had instituted a federally funded program to provide legal assistance for Americans in low-income neighborhoods as part of Lyndon Johnson's War on Poverty, had opened a small Legal Services office in Daytona Beach. In 1969, Graham heeded the call for young attorneys. Still, there were tensions. "The OEO wanted us to do impact cases, but the local bar wanted us to do divorces," Graham recalled. "They didn't want us to be fooling around with constitutional cases." After only a few months, the director of the office left, and Graham moved up. But he'd had very little practical lawyering experience behind him when Pearl walked through the door.

After he spoke with Tom Champion, Graham spoke with Mabel Chesley, who gave him a detailed and impassioned account of Jesse's case and the McCall-Oldham power axis that had thwarted her and Pearl so many times. In researching the relevant case law, Graham and his young associates came across a 1966 case, *Baxstrom v. Herold*, that seemed pretty much on point: The U.S. Supreme Court had ruled that a prisoner who had been certified insane by a prison physician and detained for a period of time beyond his original sentence had been denied equal protection under the law. He discovered, too, that he could file a petition for writ of habeas corpus in a court at any level in the state, which would allow him to bypass the hopeless Lake County court and to file directly with the Florida Supreme Court.

Mabel found Graham to be not only bright but also committed, inexperienced though he and his staff were, and for the first time in a long time she was moved to write an update on the Daniels case in the *Daytona Beach Morning Journal*, noting that the sheer amount of "judicial water" that had passed over the dam had opened up some new options. In addition, the passage of the Civil Rights Act and the creation of poverty programs—including Legal Services itself—had altered the tenor of the times enough that the courts might be more receptive to Graham's petition.

The petition argued that there had been insufficient basis for the indictment, and that Jesse's due process and equal protection rights had been violated. The Florida Supreme Court agreed to hear the case, and it ordered J. B. O'Connor, M.D., as superintendent of Florida State Hospital, to show "the lawful cause and authority for the detention and imprisonment of the petitioner."

In reporting Graham's trip to Tallahassee to argue before the court in early July 1970, Mabel dared to wonder, "After 12 long years in a mental institution, is justice finally on the horizon for mentally retarded Jesse Daniels?" But as soon as Graham stood before the bench to present his oral argument, he encountered the judicial resistance that Tom Champion had met with eight years earlier. When Graham attempted to make the point that the only treatment Jesse had received at the hospital was his daily vitamins, Justice B. K. Roberts—the same judge who had bridled at Virgil Hawkins's admission to the University of Florida College of Law—cut him off. He seemed to take umbrage at the suggestion that his friend O'Connor had done anything wrong.

"He hasn't done anything wrong," Graham responded. "He just hasn't done anything."

By the time he'd finished his argument, Graham sensed that he'd not be winning the day in Tallahassee. Still, there was reason for hope. Richard Ervin, who as the Florida attorney general had filed with the U.S. Supreme Court the famous amicus curiae brief supporting gradual integration in schools ("by all deliberate speed"), had been appointed to the Florida Supreme Court in 1964 by Governor Bryant, and in 1969 he'd been named chief justice. Unbeknownst to Richard Graham, this was the same Richard Ervin whom Leesburg police chief Bill Fisher had met with a decade before, to brief him about the Daniels case and to convey his suspicion that it was the soon-to-be-executed Sam Wiley Odom, not Daniels, who had been responsible for the rape of Blanche Bosanquet Knowles. It was that conversation that had prompted Gordon Oldham's call warning Fisher to "stay out of the case," and while Richard Graham had no way of being aware of this history, it was unlikely that Ervin had forgotten it.

Still, a decision was slow in coming, and as Christmas drew near, Pearl urged Graham to call the court to see if there was any news. To his great surprise, he found himself on the phone with Ervin himself.

"Sorry to tell you this," Ervin said, "but we ruled against you." By a 4–1 vote, the court had ruled not to review the case evidence against Daniels and, in effect, not to overturn the state's insanity law. However, Ervin said, he himself had written the sole dissenting opinion, arguing for an evidentiary hearing and proceedings "to determine the merits both as to law and facts." He buoyed the young lawyer's hopes with a few words of encouragement. "You're right and we're wrong," he told Graham. "Don't let this stop you." Even the majority opinion reflected O'Connor's concession that Jesse Daniels was "entitled to a hearing on the question of whether his sanity has now been restored before the court under whose order he was committed and is being detained."

Mabel Chesley, too, sounded an optimistic note in her coverage of the court's decision, remarking that Graham was planning to ask for a hearing in Lake County's Circuit Court in order to present new psychiatric evidence and ask for a trial. Graham, in fact, had other plans. Having challenged a state statute in Florida's highest court and lost, he could now file a direct appeal to the U.S. Supreme Court; a hearing in Lake County was his backup plan if the Supreme Court refused to hear the case.

Unfortunately, the future of Volusia County Legal Services by this point had become uncertain. Funding was being withheld by the OEO because the organization's board had not yet agreed to follow the OEO's Legal Services Division guidelines, which prohibited the office from participating in criminal cases. So Graham returned to his father's law firm, on the condition that he'd be able to continue working on the Daniels case. He estimated the cost of moving forward with the hearing, which would require hiring expert witnesses such as doctors, psychiatrists, and criminologists, at ten thousand dollars, and he won the support of a partner, Ted Husfeld—and, in turn, of the firm itself—to take the case on a pro bono basis.

Husfeld did not want for experience or expertise; his work on major corporate and medical cases had won him a reputation for aggressiveness and persistence. As soon as they began working on the case, Graham realized that he would have been at a loss without the older man. "Ted became a mentor," Graham said. "He was a bulldog, and he had a better understanding of the politics in Lake County than I did."

While waiting to hear from the U.S. Supreme Court, they tried to subpoena McCall's files on the case, but the sheriff claimed they couldn't be located, due to the "moving of offices." Next, Graham and Husfeld drove to Tavares to meet with circuit judge E. R. Mills Jr. in order to arrange for the sanity hearing Jesse had been promised. As soon as they'd agreed on a date in late February, the lawyers presented Mills with an order that would allow them access to Jesse's records at Florida State Hospital. Mills signed the document, the clerk's office certified it, and Husfeld told Graham to get in the car.

"Where are we going?" Graham asked.

"We're going to Chattahoochee," Husfeld told him.

"Now?"

"Yeah, now," Husfeld said. "Those records won't be there tomorrow."

Chattahoochee was "a hellhole," Graham recalled, and Jesse, now twelve years into his time there, was treated like "a convicted rapist" as he was brought from lockdown to see his visitors. Graham waited until just before the administrative office closed for the day to present the signed order allowing them access to Jesse's records.

"Well, we'll have to talk to our attorneys," an official told him.

"There's nothing to talk about," Graham replied. "This is a certified copy of a court order telling you to immediately make those records available to us."

Reluctantly, the hospital officials complied, and the two lawyers retreated to a nearby hotel, where they made copies of every note, letter, report, and evaluation in Jesse's file.

Graham continued to consult with Mabel on the case, and the attention that she paid to it in print caused his friends and associates some puzzlement. "Everybody was asking me, 'What are you doing hanging around with Mabel Norris Chesley?' You know, because I'm a Republican," Graham recalled. "I'd say, 'I'm not hanging around with her! I'm trying to get an innocent guy out of the nuthouse.'" Graham's wife, Bunnie, was more worried than puzzled. She had been hearing stories about Lake County, and with her husband involved in a case that questioned the actions of authorities there, she feared for his safety, especially since they would soon have a child to care for; she was eight months pregnant. "These guys are rough," Bunnie told him. "How do you know they're not going to come after you?"

Jesse learned about the hearing and his new lawyer in a letter he received from Pearl. He wrote back immediately, expressing his excitement at getting out of his dreary ward at last, even if it was for a drive to a jail cell in DeLand, and his hope that Pearl might be able to visit him there. The straight-shooting Volusia County sheriff, Ed Duff, urged Graham to be careful in Lake County and volunteered to drive Jesse from Chattahoochee to Tavares for his court date. Mindful of the fate of the Groveland Boys and others while in transit with McCall, Graham requested a court order allowing Duff to transport Jesse to the Volusia County jail, where Graham and Husfeld could have psychiatric experts evaluate their client before the hearing. Duff had a gift for Graham as well—a card certifying the lawyer as a Volusia County special deputy. "Now don't go arrest anybody with it," Duff told him, "but if you're pulled over in Lake County, you put that right next to your driver's license. Just hand them both over."

Two days before the hearing was scheduled to begin, Mabel discovered that she would not be allowed to attend it, let alone write about it: Oldham intended to subpoena her as a witness for the state. It was not only a profound disappointment for the reporter, who had followed the case from the beginning and "written a virtual book in news stories and editorials on the injustice it represents," but also a clever move on Oldham's part, ensuring that Jesse Daniels's most committed partisan in the press would be denied her voice. Mabel made sure that the two reporters from the *Daytona Beach News-Journal* who were assigned to cover the hearing in Tavares in her stead were thoroughly briefed on the case—by her.

The hearing was held on February 24, 1971, in an ordinary conference room at the Lake County Courthouse, with Jesse and Pearl in attendance along with Graham and Husfeld, and Oldham representing the state. Richard Graham was new to Lake County, but not to Judge Mills. He and Graham's father had worked together representing Greyhound bus lines, "and maybe a railroad or two," and initially Mills was friendly enough. Graham found Oldham arrogant and uncooperative, brushing the young attorney aside "like I didn't know what I was talking about."

The session brought him his first taste of McCall as well. Graham was standing by the stairs in the courthouse when the sheriff walked straight toward him, glaring and "trying to intimidate me" before he abruptly turned and mounted the stairs.

Graham could tell that Mills was intimidated by Oldham and McCall. As a native not of Lake but of nearby Marion County, and a new judge in the Fifth Circuit Court who was coming up for reelection, perhaps Mills had reason to be concerned.

Husfeld began by calling as a witness Dr. Ray Mulry, a clinical psychologist at the University of Texas. Mulry testified that he had examined Jesse at the Volusia County jail a few days earlier and found him to be "extremely cooperative, considerate, appropriate in every way." He noted, too, that Jesse had responded to all his questions "clearly and intelligently."

"Do you feel that he needs hospitalization in the State insane asylum?" Husfeld asked.

"Absolutely not," Mulry said.

On cross-examination, Oldham established that Mulry was not licensed in the State of Florida and then introduced a theme he'd repeat in his questioning of all the defendant's witnesses. "Do you believe if you had the benefit of all of the other doctors over a period of thirteen years . . . you would be in a better position to give an opinion in this case than you would just talking to this man for an hour without all the benefit of the other psychiatrists, psychologists and all of the test results?"

"No," Mulry replied. "I'm in equally good, if not better position because I'm unbiased."

Next, Graham called Reverend Robert Jenkins, a Methodist minister in DeLand who had done graduate work in clinical psychology at Emory and at a mental hospital near Cleveland. Jenkins testified that he had questioned Jesse at the Volusia County jail about presidents, geography, counting, and math. Jesse "didn't miss a question," Jenkins said, and in his opinion, the defendant sufficiently understood the nature of the charges against him to assist counsel during trial.

A third witness, Robert T. Miller, a public defender who claimed to have represented thousands of indigent defendants, had found Jesse to be "slow but cooperative" and "very anxious to stand trial."

"Now in your years of practice as a criminal lawyer," Husfeld asked, "how many times have you seen the State of Florida attempt to keep a defendant from standing trial over the objections of the defendant?"

"I don't think I've ever seen the problem arise," Miller said.

"Have you ever heard of a defendant wanting to stand trial and the State attempt to prevent a trial by saying the defendant was insane when the defendant claimed to be sane?"

"Not that I can remember offhand," Miller said.

Oldham then set forth a series of hypotheticals in which "insanity" might be used as a defense in the Jesse Daniels case—to which Miller replied that he was unqualified to answer because he had not evaluated the defendant's case history.

On redirect, Graham kept being stalled by Oldham's objections, but finally he broke through.

"Mr. Oldham has been posing hypotheticals," he said to the witness. "Let me give you one: Assuming this was your case, you had an independent investigation, and [you] convinced yourself that there was no evidence against your client. [You] hired two licensed psychiatrists and had a Ph.D. psychologist to examine the defendant and were told that he is ready to go to trial, he can understand the charge, he can help you defend himself. Would you go ahead with this defense?"

"If it was his desire to go to trial," Miller said, "yes."

Graham next called Warren Cobb, the former director of Volusia County Legal Services, who had also interviewed Jesse in the county jail. Graham inquired, "Did you ask him questions about his arrest and the events surrounding his first being taken into custody?"

"Yes," Cobb replied. "He was able to give me an account of his arrest, [and] the conditions under which he signed the statement. He was even able to describe the gun that he stated was held on him by Sheriff Willis McCall. I asked him what caliber it was. He felt it was a .32 or .38 . . . He described it as being a revolver as opposed to an automatic. He described the way he was held from behind, and his neck vised by the deputy."

"Did he advise you that he had signed a statement?" Graham asked.

"Yes, he expressed great apprehension and concern," Cobb said. "He seemed to think that would be very damaging to him, the fact that he had signed a statement that McCall had asked him to sign."

"Did you discuss any other evidence, or potential evidence with him, or any evidence of this case?"

"Yes," Cobb said. "We discussed the question of whether or not . . . the victim would identify him, and he seemed to feel very strongly that she would not, in open court."

"And why did he feel this?" Graham asked. "Did he explain that?"

"He felt that he was innocent and that when it came to open court," Cobb said, "he did not feel Mrs. Knowles would be untruthful in that respect, and would not falsely identify him in court."

Gordon Oldham, who had been objecting avidly throughout the hearing, now stared at his notes in silence. He chose not to "correct the record" regarding a confession allegedly made at gunpoint, nor did he address Jesse's speculation that Blanche Knowles would not testify against him at trial. He confined himself to trying to establish that the doctors at Chattahoochee, having observed the defendant for more than thirteen years, were more qualified to evaluate his psychiatric condition than the witnesses called by the defense attorneys. Oldham pointed out, too, that it was the defendant's own court-appointed attorney, Sam Buie, who had requested the psychiatric evaluation of Jesse Daniels, not the state.

At that point, Judge Mills closed testimony for the day. As the lawyers filed out with the witnesses, Pearl "rested her arm gently on her son's shoulder and spoke to him quietly." The two remained seated until a deputy approached to return Jesse to the Volusia County jail for the night.

On the second day of the hearing, Richard Graham presented to the court a copy of a recent opinion from the Florida Supreme Court upholding the conviction of a man with an IQ of 35—roughly half that attributed to Jesse Daniels—who had been deemed fit to stand trial. Judge Mills agreed to enter the document into the record.

Ted Husfeld called the day's first witness, Dr. Merton L. Ekwald, a physician and surgeon in Tallahassee who was board-certified in psychiatry and who had testified in court more than three hundred times, for both the prosecution and the defense. He had evaluated Jesse twice at Chattahoochee and found the patient to be "an intensely ingratiating person," who "stammers occasionally when he's under emotional pressure." Dr. Ekwald stated, too, that he'd been under the impression that Jesse was "mentally retarded" until he'd actually met with him. "I was rather surprised when I talked with him, about how well he could communicate, how good his vocabulary was," Ekwald said.

Over the years of his incarceration, Jesse's reading and writing skills had improved dramatically. Although his intellectual development had mostly stagnated and he still struggled with the concept of numbers and dates, he was able to memorize objects and events that appealed to him, such as the year, make, and model of automobiles, the Apollo missions to space, the names of presidents, and an impressive collection of lyrics to what he called "antique country" music songs.

"He gave me the names of all the past presidents in rotation," Ekwald said. "I thought he was wrong and I checked later and found he was right, and I'd forgotten about Mr. Truman."

Ekwald addressed the issue that had bedeviled nearly every evaluation of Jesse's mental condition over his thirteen years of institutionalization at Chattahoochee. Despite all the notations in Jesse's files about his being cooperative, nonaggressive, compliant, and in no need of any psychiatric medications or shock-treatment therapy, doctors had unfailingly pointed to his "delusional" insistence that he was being framed for a crime he did not commit. The proof of delusion lay, for the doctors, in the signed confession taken by Willis McCall and in the letter from Buie stating, "There is no question in my mind . . . he is the man." The patient's "proven" delusion and paranoia in turn became grounds for determining that Jesse was not capable of assisting counsel at trial. But at one point, Ekwald said, he'd just been talking with Jesse generally "about why he was there; he felt he sort of had been railroaded into being there, and I had to wonder, is this a delusion or not?"

On cross-examination, Oldham elicited an answer he was not expecting. Had O'Connor told Ekwald, he asked, the results of his own initial evaluation of Jesse?

Yes, he had, Ekwald replied. O'Connor had used just a single word: "Hold." He spelled it out, "H-O-L-D." Oldham did not explore the response. He simply reprised his theme that the doctors at Chattahoochee had had the benefit of observing Jesse Daniels over thirteen years. But Richard Graham knew what "H-O-L-D" meant. It spelled out the acquiescence of the medical evaluators to the favor asked of them by the powerful men of Lake County.

Next, Dr. Herbert C. Anderson, a board-certified psychiatrist with an impressive pedigree and a private practice in both Miami and Tallahassee, not only concurred that Jesse did not belong at Chattahoochee but also mentioned that a Dr. Gumanis there, with whom he had spoken extensively, was of the same opinion and had in fact brought Jesse before the staff "with the hope of gaining his release, and each time he was outvoted."

"You disagree with the diagnosis at the hospital, I take it?" Husfeld asked.

"That's a hard question to answer," Anderson said. "I am under oath. I agree with his physician; his physician says he has repeatedly brought him before the . . . I think the phrase was 'staff for release,' and he had repeatedly failed to obtain his release. I have searched my brain and I guess my heart. I guess that's what you do when you are in a situation like this, and I can't understand, based on my experiences in Tallahassee, why this man is a patient at the Florida State Hospital. I am troubled by it."

Husfeld next called Gumanis himself. He testified to Jesse's obedience and excellent conduct over his years at the hospital. When asked about any delusions Jesse might suffer, Gumanis acknowledged that Jesse had been known to express "paranoid ideas that he was framed and all of that, if that is a delusion." But he was clear that Jesse had never been "actively psychotic." Again, the only evidence of his delusion seemed to be the fact that he denied the crime of which he had been accused. Oldham, on cross-examination, got the Chattahoochee doctor to admit that the hospital considered Jesse Daniels "medically" insane and that his low IQ rendered him incompetent to stand trial. But Husfeld pushed the point: Had Jesse been found mentally incompetent by the doctors at Florida State Hospital because of his low IQ, or "because he was psychotic, because he denied committing a crime?"

"I don't know," Gumanis admitted. "It could be."

And so they came to Jesse himself. Oldham declared his approval of the proposal to have him testify, and although he refused to offer Jesse immunity, he did agree to limit his cross-examination to the issue of sanity rather than questioning the witness about the crime itself. Mills, however, voiced concern that Jesse might inadvertently volunteer information during questioning. "I want to be very careful that none of us violate any of his rights," he said. After a brief recess, it was decided that Jesse would not be called as a witness. Instead, Graham called Pearl. He had her explain the financial need that had brought her to Volusia County Legal Services, and the limits it had placed on her long struggle "to try to get the boy cleared and get him home where he can be with me."

And if Jesse were to be released, Graham wondered, what would he do?

"I have a promise of a job," Pearl said, and she explained that the Princess Issena Hotel had agreed to put Jesse to work in the kitchen. "If he was to go home tonight, he could go to work tomorrow."

"Do you think Jesse needs to be committed and confined in the mental institution?" Graham asked.

"Definitely not," Pearl answered, "because there is no program there that will build up the mind. It's just to eat and sleep and be a living vegetable. I have been there."

"Jesse can't even leave the building he's in, is that true?"

"That's true," Pearl said. "He cannot get out in the sunshine at all."

Oldham had no questions for Pearl, and Graham had no further witnesses, so Oldham now called his one witness for the state. Dr. Julian C. Davis, a psychologist at Chattahoochee, stated that the evaluations of Jesse Daniels that he had reviewed (he had not himself performed one) "have consistently shown him to be mentally retarded." Under cross-examination by Husfeld, Davis affirmed that Jesse had been evaluated by doctors only eight times over a period of thirteen years and acknowledged that Jesse had scored a 74 on one of his most recent IQ tests—a score within the range of persons "who did not function as retarded."

Graham and Husfeld called one final expert to testify as a rebuttal witness: Frank Nibbler, a lieutenant detective with the DeLand Police Department, who had trained with the FBI in "interrogation and voice investigation and interviews." At the request of Jesse's lawyers, he had interrogated the defendant about his possible involvement in the rape of Blanche Knowles.

Husfeld asked the detective if he was satisfied with the information and answers he had received from Jesse.

"I interrogated him quite lengthily," Nibbler said.

"Was he able to withstand the interrogation?"

"He didn't crack, as the saying goes," Nibbler said.

On cross-examination, Oldham suggested that Nibbler, as a detective, did not qualify as an expert to evaluate the defendant's mental capacity. "Do you feel that psychiatrists or psychologists are more qualified than you are?" Oldham asked.

"Much more," Nibbler said.

"No further questions," Oldham said.

Testimony ended at 4:35 p.m. Judge Mills indicated that he would need about an hour to "digest" the evidence before making a ruling, and he asked the attorneys if they would be willing to wait. "We would like to wait," Graham said, "if we can get a ruling tonight." Oldham did not object. Nor did Judge Mills object to Graham's request to make a "thirty second argument on the law in this case" before the recess.

Graham said, "I would just like to urge the Court to keep in mind that this is not an irreversible decision. If the Court says Daniels can stand trial now, later on you could change your mind, if it turned out he were making a spectacle of himself in Court, or obviously didn't understand the proceedings." But if they simply sent him back to Chattahoochee, "chances are, he's going to stay there the rest of his life, and without having had the chance to stand trial on this charge."

Mills responded judiciously. "I will soul search, and I will do my best to apply the facts to the law fairly and impartially."

Ted Husfeld added that the evidence they had presented showed a "sane man" who did not need "to be locked up in a building where he cannot walk in the sun or do occupational therapy, or to be locked up with insane people." In thirteen years, he reminded the court, he had exhibited "no behavioral problems whatsoever." No one had said that he was "psychotic or suffering from delusions, and no one has presented a picture of anyone other than a man with a low IQ."

Asked if he, too, would care to comment, Oldham was brief. "The Court must decide as it feels it should," he said, "but by taking a defendant out of the State Hospital when the people at the Hospital feel that he's not ready to be out, I think, could possibly be a bad precedent. That's all I have to say."

The court recessed. Ted Husfeld had to return to DeLand, so Graham waited alone for the court's decision. When word came down that Mills was ready to issue a ruling, McCall strode back into the courthouse that for nearly three decades had been his domain, his Stetson his crown. In every courtroom Graham had been in, the bailiff would have made him take his hat off. But in Lake County, "No one was going to mess with McCall."

Graham took a seat beside Jesse and Pearl. The court came to order, and Judge Mills began to read from the bench. "It is an awesome decision for me to reach," he said. "However . . . the Court finds that the defendant has failed to prove by a preponderance of the evidence that the defendant is at this time competent to undergo trial, to cooperate with his attorneys, to assist them in his trial; and so that counsel might have the benefit of the reasoning in which this decision was reached, it was done on the basis that the witnesses who testified favorably for the defendant only saw him on several occasions and for very short periods of time, in most cases under an hour; whereas the witnesses who testified that in their judgment and expert opinion the defendant was incapable of going to trial, have had an opportunity of being with, treating, administering tests to the defendant over a period of years, and therefore in weighing the evidence, I've put more weight on those who, in the judgment of this Court, had a better opportunity for a longer period of time to observe and arrive at their opinions."

Oldham wasted no time in offering to prepare the order to have Jesse Daniels returned to Chattahoochee, adding that he would be glad to arrange for the sheriff of Volusia County to be responsible for Jesse's transportation.

Stunned though he was, Graham asked to approach the bench. "May

I make one comment, Your Honor?" he said. "I have a very definite opinion myself that the statute and the rule which provides that the defendant can be committed involuntarily because he has been charged with a crime without showing that he is dangerous or needs treatment, is unconstitutional. I would ask this Court not to change its ruling that he is insane, but to not return the defendant to Chattahoochee, [and] to release him to the custody of his mother, because automatic commitment to an institution without showing of need or dangerousness or potential danger to himself or to society, is a denial of his due process of law and equal protection of the laws."

Gordon Oldham quickly responded. "To that I would object, Your Honor."

Mills stated that he did not have the authority to grant the allowance Graham had requested, but Graham had not yet given up. He asked the judge if he could "get a ruling based on the evidence," which, he said, "was uncontradicted in this one respect . . . that Jesse Daniels does not constitute a danger to himself or society. All the doctors from Chattahoochee or defense doctors agreed on that one point."

Mills had no objection, but Oldham did. "That was not the purpose of the hearing," he reminded the judge, who'd been fixed in McCall's cold, steady glare.

At that, Mills changed his mind. "Well," he said, "I'm going to stick with my original ruling."

Without Ted Husfeld to support him, Graham sensed that the power in the courtroom had shifted—back to where it always did, toward the sheriff of Lake County. "Your Honor," Graham pleaded, "I'm asking you to do that as an act of humanity toward a defendant. No one thinks he is dangerous. Where he is, he's not allowed to go outside in the sunshine. He's not allowed to play pool because he's got charges on his head, and the defendants with charges on their heads are treated in one way at the institution." And he again emphasized "the gross Constitutional inequities of the commitment statute."

Judge Mills, however, had heard enough. "You'll have to make that argument to the Supreme Court, not me," he said. "I'm merely the trial court." And with that he rose from the bench. "Court's in recess."

Volusia County deputies led Jesse toward the elevator, with Pearl following closely behind. In the hallway they passed Willis McCall, who was holding court with Gordon Oldham outside his office—the office where Pearl had begged, thirteen years before, for permission to visit her son in jail; the office where Jesse had, "like a parrot," at McCall's prompting, confessed to the rape of Blanche Knowles.

Once the elevator doors had closed, Pearl could no longer contain herself. She had been convinced that at long last her son would be coming home to Daytona Beach, free on bail while he awaited trial. She'd told a reporter how she'd fixed up his room and laid out clothes for him. Now she clasped Jesse in her arms and sobbed. "Thirteen years shut up for something he didn't do. May God have mercy on those who put him there."

Richard Graham climbed into the blue 1965 Dodge Dart that he'd been driving since his law school days. He pointed the car east, away from Tavares. Behind him, the sun had begun to set over Lake Dora. He started his drive home slowly, as in his mind he reran—and tried to make sense of—what had just happened in court. Everything Mabel had warned him about had come to pass. He'd been steamrolled by Gordon Oldham, and Willis McCall had lent his own intimidating touch to the afternoon's proceedings by arriving in court for the verdict and hard-staring Judge Mills into complicity with the state attorney. Nothing in Graham's law classes at Stetson had prepared him for this. Nothing in his experiences with the U.S. Army JAG Corps, with Volusia County Legal Services, or at his father's firm, either. He'd requested nothing more than a fair trial—the right of his client to defend himself in court. Yet the request had been denied.

Graham put his foot to the gas pedal. Bunnie was waiting at home and he wanted to be with her. As he sped by the pastures outside Mount Dora, a wave of remorse rose from his gut. He'd failed Jesse Daniels. Pearl and Mabel, too. Overcome by emotion, Graham pressed his foot down on the brake. He brought the Dodge to an abrupt halt, off the road, on a long, thin stretch of Bahia grass. The sickly sweet aroma of orange blossoms hung in the air. His hands covering his face, the lawyer broke down in heaving sobs. Dusk turned to dark on the quiet road out of Lake County.

Blanche Bosanquet Knowles on her wedding day, 1948

CHAPTER FOURTEEN

Faith in Blanche

By 1971, Florida was growing by leaps and bounds. In the years that Jesse Daniels had been locked away at Chattahoochee, the state's population had ballooned to more than seven million—an increase of about 70 percent since 1957. Though Walt Disney himself had died five years before his vision for an East Coast theme park was realized, Walt Disney World opened in Kissimmee in October 1971, bringing nearly eleven million visitors to central Florida in its first year of operation. To capitalize on the surge in tourism, the Florida Citrus Commission named a popular singer and former beauty pageant queen, Anita Bryant, as its spokesperson, and in a highly successful promotional campaign she reminded Americans that "breakfast without orange juice is like a day without sunshine" and beckoned consumers to "come to the Florida Sunshine Tree." Citrus production, up 14 percent from the previous year, reached a record high of two hundred million boxes of fruit.

Social progress came more slowly to Lake County than economic progress, however. It wasn't until 1970, sixteen years after the U.S.

Supreme Court's landmark decision in *Brown v. Board of Education*, that the last black schools in Lake County finally closed. And tensions at the newly integrated high schools, already running high, mounted further when Willis McCall paid one of his frequent visits, with his vicious German shepherd police dog, Maggie, in tow to remind black students what county they were in.

With Jesse Daniels packed off to Chattahoochee again, Gordon Oldham was hoping that his victory in Judge Mills's courtroom would finally dispose of the case once and for all. The state attorney had succeeded not just in court but in the media as well. The two-day hearing in Tavares had garnered only scant newspaper coverage in Lake County, and Blanche's name had been kept out of newsprint from the beginning. A Florida statute made it unlawful to publish the identity of a victim of a sexual offense, but it was no doubt Joe Knowles's standing in the community that ensured that "journalistic discretion" would keep his wife's name and also the latest legal maneuverings and hearings in the case from being trumpeted in the papers, as the Leesburg Quarterback Club counted several local reporters and editors among its members. Norma Padgett, the alleged rape victim in the Groveland case, who lived among the truck farmers and citrus pickers in the swampland of south Lake County, had not been able to count on similar discretion, and her name had eventually found its way into print.

And the Knowleses' social status had only risen. At the beginning of the year, the Leesburg city manager had ceremoniously handed Joe a gavel and a Bible and sworn him in as mayor. Joe could count on a much busier social calendar in the upcoming year, whether he was signing certificates issued for the city's utility bonds or pushing discs for a newspaper photographer at the opening of a new shuffleboard court. Yet despite his new responsibilities, he would continue to devote time to the Melon Patch Players. The very next month he would be directing a lighthearted piece titled *The Man in the Dog Suit*, in which he cast first-timers beside veteran performers. The combination, Joe said, was "just what we need to put this comedy across."

Blanche Knowles had long participated in social activities of her own, with the Leesburg Women's Club and the Bertha Hereford Hall Chapter of Daughters of the American Revolution, which had appointed her Good Citizenship Chairwoman. Once her three children were enrolled in grade school, however, she'd gone back to work, taking a job teaching English and math at Leesburg High School. The role of first lady of Leesburg put additional demands on her already busy schedule, requiring that she appear at various public events with her husband. "He is pretty good about giving me a few days' notice," she told a reporter from the *Orlando Sentinel* who profiled her in 1971. "Although sometimes things do become hectic. I become a short-order cook, or I may plan a meal, then serve it two or three evenings later." Nonetheless, she found the time to make the dog suit for her husband's play.

If Blanche was keeping up appearances, it was a social skill she'd been schooled in from the cradle, by virtue of her time, place, and class. Rape in the South was still viewed largely as a violation of a man's property rather than an act of violence against a woman. And adultery was a fact of life among the citrus elite. Mary Alice Herlong Pattillo, daughter of citrus baron and congressman Syd Herlong, grew up close to the Knowles family, and her family had vacationed with the Bosanquets in Ormond Beach each summer. One of her sorority sisters at the University of Florida was "Kat" Robinson, soon to become Mrs. Gordon Oldham. Like others, she recalled Joe Knowles as a good-looking ladies' man around town—a town where men ruled the roost and the women understood their place. "There was a lot of womanizing then," she said. "It was the custom, and the wives knew that the men fooled around. They just turned their backs on the affairs. The big thing was, don't get caught." Author Florence King explained this ability to look the other way as a relic of antebellum life that endured in "the cult of Southern Womanhood." It was the same deliberate blindness that had "enabled the white woman to maintain her sanity when she saw light-skinned slave children, who were the very spit of Old Massa, running around the plantation."

Blanche's cousin Priscilla Newell knew this dynamic firsthand. Her mother, Frances Bosanquet, had married a dashing outdoorsman, David Newell—he hunted with the legendary sharpshooter Annie Oakley, who wintered in Leesburg until her death in 1926, and he went on to become the editor of *Field & Stream*. David's work in media necessitated that he live in New York for a large part of the year, and it was no secret in the Bosanquet and Newell families that he shared an apartment there with his girlfriend, a photographer who traveled with him. When the girlfriend eventually became terminally ill, David brought her to his home in Leesburg, and Frances ended up caring for her until her death, while David continued to travel for work.

The economic displacement that affected women and children after divorce was as clear to the wealthy Episcopalians in Leesburg as it was elsewhere, but among them there was an extra element of social stigma to divorce that made it the solution of last resort to marriage problems. "Your daughter would be disgraced if she was divorced," Priscilla said. "When somebody got divorced it was shocking news and you just didn't do it." The women of the citrus elite of Lake County were exactly the ones for whom *Ladies' Home Journal* and other influential mass market women's magazines of the day pumped out stories with headlines like "Divorces Are Not Crimes: They Are Tragedies."

So if Blanche Knowles's marriage was hard, she did not let on. She was a mother first, and as Dr. Durham Young had observed in the hours after her rape, she was also "a rather stoic type of person . . . quite herself and very well composed under the circumstances."

JUDGE MILLS'S RULING at Jesse's competency hearing had disappointed Richard Graham, but it had not daunted him. As he told Mabel, he was not done trying to rescue his client just yet. He filed a motion for discovery with the court, which, if granted, would allow Jesse's legal team to take depositions from the other participants in the case. More specifically, Mabel elaborated, discovery would allow them to question the alleged rape victim about her initial description of her attacker, and to interrogate McCall about the circumstances under which he'd obtained Jesse's confession. They'd also have the opportunity to question the deputies who took Jesse in for questioning and searched his home, collecting his personal property without a warrant.

On March 1, the *Daytona Beach Evening News* ran an editorial about Jesse's case, asking, "Do the Mentally Retarded Have Civil Rights, Too?" On March 2, in a letter to newly elected Governor Reubin Askew, a liberal with a strong civil rights stance, Mabel praised Richard Graham for "virtually making a life cause of this man's release" and pointed out how plainly Judge Mills was in McCall's pocket. The more pressing concern, though, was justice, for "his mother and he have suffered enough."

Ted Husfeld went way back with Askew. Both of them had adopted children through the Children's Home Society of Florida, and they had long sat together on the organization's board. Husfeld, too, wrote the governor to ask for an investigation into the Jesse Daniels case. "On his behalf I would call upon the power of your office to afford this man humane relief; and even to the effect of pardoning him for a crime that I am firmly convinced he was wholly incapable of committing, and for which he has never been tried." Although Husfeld had always abided by the decisions of the court, in this case he could not let the matter rest, for it concerned "a benign, timid, quiet, friendly and pathetic soul who has no friends in high places."

The letters from Mabel Chesley and Ted Husfeld caught Askew's attention, and his general counsel, Edgar Dunn, promptly submitted a request to the clerk of the circuit court in Lake County for all transcripts and pleadings in the case. He contacted the executive director of the Florida Department of Law Enforcement, the newly formed government agency (formerly the Florida Sheriffs Bureau) that served as the state's investigative arm, much as the FBI did for the U.S. Department of Justice. Dunn requested that the FDLE immediately share any information on the charge against Jesse Daniels.

Graham, meanwhile, appealed to another Fifth Circuit Court judge, John Booth, who offered a deal: If Jesse Daniels pleaded guilty, Booth would put him on probation. Graham refused to bite. "For Jesse to plead guilty would have let all those people off the hook neatly," he said, "all those people who had kept Jesse tucked away without a trial."

On April 10, in an effort to keep Jesse's story in the news, Mabel wrote again about Richard Graham's appeal to the U.S. Supreme Court, likening Jesse's plight to that of an indigent Florida drifter named Clarence Earl Gideon. Arrested for breaking and entering in 1961, Gideon, unable to pay for an attorney, had defended himself in court, where he'd been convicted and sentenced to five years at Raiford. From his cell, in a five-page petition handwritten in pencil, Gideon appealed to the U.S. Supreme Court in what ultimately became the landmark case *Gideon v. Wainwright*. The Court ruled that under the Sixth Amendment, states must provide counsel in criminal cases for defendants who cannot afford an attorney. "Gideon had no attorney to write his brief," Mabel wrote. "Daniels does." Graham himself, she noted, had described Jesse's situation as "being sentenced to life imprisonment without proper judicial findings."

One month later, Mabel at last received reason for hope. The United States Supreme Court had handed down an order to show cause, compelling the State of Florida to legally justify Jesse Daniels's confinement at

Chattahoochee—a sign that it was considering Graham's case. As Mabel reported in a front-page story for the *Daytona Beach Morning Journal*, the justices "strongly questioned the statute under which Daniels is being held which permits incarceration without a legal determination of insanity." In their order, they cited a previous case in which a similar statute had been overturned. The Court gave Florida attorney general Robert L. Shevin until the end of the month to respond. It was a remarkable development, and, Graham said, "the biggest day of my legal life."

The news was remarkable for another reason. After the Groveland Boys rape case and the Virgil Hawkins integration case, the Jesse Daniels appeal would become the third civil rights suit rooted in Okahumpka, with its population of about three hundred, to reach the United States Supreme Court. The previous two cases had at length effected some measure of progress, if not true justice for the defendants. Walter Irvin, after having his sentence commuted to life by Governor Collins in 1955, was paroled in 1968. In the case of Virgil Hawkins, the State of Florida, after throwing up roadblock after roadblock, had had to read the legal writing on the wall and bow to the inevitable: It would no longer be able to keep black students from attending the University of Florida College of Law. In acceding, however, the state managed to inflict an additional indignity on the long-suffering petitioner. In June 1958, it agreed to begin accepting qualified black applicants without delay, on condition that Hawkins would withdraw his own application. Selflessly, and unwilling to deprive other black students the opportunity of a higher education, Hawkins accepted the deal, and in September of that year, the College of Law admitted its first black applicant. Hawkins "opened the door but he never walked through it," said W. George Allen, the first black man to earn a law degree there, in 1962. "He was my hero."

Now, in 1971, legal momentum was building for Jesse Daniels for the first time in more than thirteen years. Upon receiving the Supreme Court's order, Graham had driven to the *News-Journal* to show the letter to Mabel, who'd persuaded the editors to banner the story on the paper's front page. "She'd done her best to keep this story alive," Graham said. "Until then, many people in the community thought Mabel was just pushing another liberal cause." But now that the U.S. Supreme Court was showing interest in the Daniels case, Graham said, "it turned those thoughts around. They don't issue an order to show cause unless they mean business."

Graham had another appeal pending—the February ruling in Judge Mills's court—with the Second District Court of Appeal of Florida, so that, as Mabel optimistically put it, "it may be a race to see which court finally disposes of the Daniels case." Meanwhile, Governor Askew had taken a critical step: He'd removed J. B. O'Connor as superintendent of Florida State Hospital and replaced him with Dr. Milton J. Hirshberg, giving him explicit instructions to investigate the Daniels case.

Hirshberg, a graduate of the United States Naval Academy, had served in the Iwo Jima and Okinawa operations during World War II and had gone to flight school before resigning from the Navy and attending medical school at Yale. Now, in his new position at Chattahoochee, he opened the patient file that had been marked "H-O-L-D" by Dr. O'Connor nearly fourteen years earlier. It contained the signed confession to rape as well as the correspondence from Sam Buie assuring O'Connor that Jesse was indeed guilty of the charge and urging the doctor not to hurry to evaluate the new patient's fitness for court. Hirshberg, however, didn't just read the file; he also got to know Jesse. By the end of the summer, they'd formed a bond.

On September 10, in a letter to Husfeld and Graham, Hirshberg stated that, as it was his intention to operate the hospital "in accordance with high professional standards," he did not feel that justice was being served by keeping Jesse locked up, and he wanted to do whatever he could to get him released. With the letter, Hirshberg enclosed several scholarly articles on the topic of determining mental competency for trial. "I see the man in an impossible bind, just as other people do," Hirshberg wrote, "that he is denied a trial because of an alleged mental defect which would serve as his adequate defense if he were ever to go to trial. This cannot be justice by any sense of the word." In short, he added, "I personally believe he is competent to go to trial."

Already, Hirshberg had had Jesse moved to less restrictive quarters, despite the criminal charges against him. That summer, Jesse had at last been permitted to walk the grounds and feel "the sun on his face, and the fresh air, and the shade of live oak trees."

Word of Hirshberg's assessment of Jesse Daniels made its way to the Office of the State Attorney in Lake County, of course. Gordon Oldham, in a letter to the new hospital superintendent, criticized his meddling in Jesse's case and hinted that the doctor "should be careful if he ever had to come to Lake County." Soon thereafter, Hirshberg began receiving anonymous telephone calls reminding him of the hospital's regulations, whether he supported them or not. He was forced to move Jesse back to the criminal ward. In October, in an interview with a reporter about the challenges he was facing at Chattahoochee, Hirshberg indicated that "foot-dragging" in the courts had kept some patients institutionalized for unacceptable lengths of time. "But," he added, perhaps out of concern over Oldham's thinly veiled threat, "I don't want to get into a hassle with state attorneys. I just want to do a good job."

On November 17, 1971, the race to see which court would rule on *Daniels v. State* was decided: The Florida Second District Court of Appeal in Lakeland sent Graham a telegram informing him that the court had reversed the Lake County Circuit ruling. "It doesn't get any faster than that," Graham said, observing that "the Judges were not pleased with this version of Lake County Justice."

Contradicting the lower court's finding, the ruling found that testimony showed "conclusively that Jesse Daniels is now properly oriented as to time, place and person, and could aid his lawyers in the defense of his case." In closing, the court noted, "In a case such as this, where the evidence is overwhelmingly contrary to the findings of the trial court, the appellate court has the authority to enter a reversal . . . Accordingly, we reverse the order of the trial court and remand with directions to enter an order declaring Jesse Daniels competent to stand trial."

Martin Dyckman, one of the best-known political reporters in Florida, wrote a feature story for the *St. Petersburg Times* titled "He Was Sentenced to a Living Death." Dyckman interviewed everyone from Gordon Oldham to Mabel Chesley, and Jesse himself, who told him, "It's been nothing in the world but pure torture since I've been here in this place." Dyckman wrote critically of Sam Buie, holding him partly responsible for Jesse's incarceration at Chattahoochee. It was his interview with Gordon Oldham, however, that proved to be the most revealing.

Oldham admitted that the case against Jesse Daniels hinged on a confession that he, as state attorney, was not certain would stand up in court. Pushed about the specifics of Jesse's confession, particularly his statement that he had told the victim who he was—"Is that you, Joe?" "No, it is me, Jesse Daniels"—Oldham replied that the confession was wrong, without elaborating. "He didn't identify himself to the victim," Oldham said. "That was never said to her." Then, distancing himself further from the substance of Jesse's statement, Oldham made clear that he had not been present at the confession, which, the boy claimed, had been taken from him at gunpoint. "I've never talked to Jesse Daniels in my life, other than to say hello in a courtroom," Oldham said. "I don't talk to defendants. Confessions are the jobs of law enforcement agencies, not the state attorney." As for Blanche Knowles's identification of her attacker initially not as a nineteen-year-old white boy (with a stutter) but as a black man, Oldham explained, "It was dark in the house. Her basic identification was on the voice—that of a person she felt was 'ignorant country' or black."

The state attorney was noncommittal as to whether he would continue to oppose a trial for Jesse Daniels. "I'm inclined offhand to feel that should be determined by the judge, and we would probably have a hearing," Oldham said. He did acknowledge, though, that Supreme Court rulings since Jesse's arrest, like the 1964 *Miranda* decision limiting the use of confessions in criminal trials, "could wash out his case." Oldham noted, "I would have to see if I had sufficient evidence in light of those cases."

When Dyckman remarked that Oldham "sounded rather eager" for Graham to have Jesse Daniels plead insanity, Oldham replied, "That is a good defense since he's been legally insane for thirteen years. That would place a more terrific burden on me."

"Hell, no!" declared Graham on learning of Oldham's suggestion. Having already stated plainly that he was not going to entertain a guilty plea in order to free Jesse Daniels, Graham was not in any way disposed to afford Oldham the opportunity to "close the file with a solved crime." He hoped that the Second District Court's ruling would prompt Oldham to assume a professional level of cooperation with the defense in its preparation for Jesse's day in court. He tried to appeal to Oldham's sense of decency. "Just let him go," Graham pleaded with the state attorney, pointing out the length of time that Jesse Daniels had already been locked up. But "there was no talking to him." Oldham stood firm in maintaining Jesse's guilt. He even fought Graham's motion of discovery, which was routinely employed in criminal cases, to force the state to produce the evidence relevant to the case. "Oldham fought us every step of the way."

He was "forcing us to gamble," Graham recalled. "Here we are fighting for trial without being able to know whether they have any evidence." In his brief before the District Court, Graham charged that key documents had vanished mysteriously from Jesse's hospital file, including the transcript of the victim's testimony that Oldham had sent to Dr. O'Connor—Oldham's accompanying cover letter to O'Connor was there, but not the transcript itself. Along with the transcript had vanished

Blanche's acknowledgment that she had known Jesse as the boy on the bike. Missing, too, were details of the process by which she had identified the voice of her attacker. Nor could Graham see how she had previously failed to characterize the voice as 'ignorant country' or black, as Oldham was claiming, or to link Jesse Daniels to the attack at all.

Apparently lost, too—when "moving offices," according to McCall—were the Lake County Sheriff's Department files on the Knowles rape case, in which the deputies had recorded, presumably, that Blanche's first description of her rapist was of a "young, husky Negro." With the files missing, Graham did not expect to gain any helpful information by deposing McCall or Yates, who had been tasked with the investigation. Furthermore, "No one in Lake County would talk about this case," Graham said. "One of my best friends from law school was from Lake County, and when this Daniels case came up, he never spoke to me again."

Nonetheless, Graham pursued his motion for discovery, because, even lacking the missing materials, he suspected that Oldham did not want him taking depositions from Blanche or Joe, or from Willis McCall or any of his deputies, even though the sheriff's department had successfully weathered so many inquiries and investigations in the past.

He also suspected that the Knowleses themselves were not eager to go to trial. He knew that Oldham really needed only one witness to convict Jesse Daniels at trial, and should someone of Blanche's stature take the stand and, before a jury, point to her former Okahumpka neighbor as her attacker, it would be difficult for any lawyer to make a winning case for the defense—especially in Lake County. But, Graham said, "I had more faith in Blanche, that she wouldn't testify against Jesse and commit perjury. She'd had enough of that lie." Moreover, a spokesman for the Florida attorney general's office had told Martin Dyckman that Jesse would "probably not have a trial. He probably will get out." That led Graham to believe that he was right in his hunch that Oldham was not going to be able to bring Jesse's case to trial because Blanche Knowles was refusing to testify to his guilt. On his faith and on that hunch, Graham had decided not to force Oldham's hand by seeking a subpoena for Blanche Knowles.

Before preparing a defense in the event of a trial, Graham had another, more pressing matter at hand. The Second District's ruling allowed the state fifteen days to appeal. Absent an appeal, because Dr. Milton Hirshberg had certified his patient to be "harmless to society," Jesse Daniels could be released on his own recognizance while he awaited trial. True to form, Oldham took all fifteen days to determine that he'd not appeal the ruling. Then a circuit judge further delayed the application that Graham had filed for Jesse's bail. The delays did not faze Pearl. "I've waited nearly fourteen years," she said. "I can wait a little longer if I have to, and so can the boy."

On December 4, 1971, Frank J. Doughney, an ex-cop from New York whom Graham had previously employed as an investigator at Volusia County Legal Services, arrived at Chattahoochee with a court order authorizing him to transport thirty-three-year-old Jesse Daniels home to his mother.

"You should have seen the parting," Doughney told Mabel Chesley. Jesse's ward mates had brought him "a huge bag of candy," and "black and white together," they "hugged him and cried with joy over his release." Jesse told them, "It's the happiest day of my life. The best day I've ever had."

Kenneth Donaldson was not among the patients bidding Jesse goodbye. Since he'd had no charges filed against him, and thus no court order holding him, Donaldson had been released a few months earlier by Dr. Hirshberg, along with the secret notes and diary entries he'd compiled from his fifteen years at Chattahoochee. One of the first things Donaldson did upon being freed was to meet with an attorney in order to prepare a lawsuit against Dr. O'Connor and Florida State Hospital for confining him against his will.

The first thing Jesse Daniels did upon being freed was fill his stomach. Because it was late afternoon when they'd left Chattahoochee,
Doughney decided they'd spend the night in a Tallahassee hotel and
drive to Daytona Beach early the next morning. Doughney took him out
to a restaurant that was a politicians' favorite, and Jesse regaled him with
stories about the food at Chattahoochee—"hard as a rock," and the rumor on the wards was that the bacon came from cadavers—as he cut into
his steak. "I hope I can forget about those fourteen years," he told the
former New York cop.

Jesse passed the next morning's drive by identifying the make and
provenance of passing cars; despite his long incarceration, he could un-
erringly peg each license tag's serial number to the correct county. Jesse
had also been following developments in the U.S. space program. "He
recited to me the sequences of space shots, right up to Apollo 15 and all
the way back to Gemini," Doughney said. Newspapers had kept him
abreast, too, of the war in Vietnam.

Jesse Daniels's reunion with his mother at Pearl's tiny apartment on
North Oleander Drive in Daytona Beach was documented by Mabel and
a photographer. Dressed in a dark suit, white shirt, and tie, Jesse was carrying a suitcase and his guitar as he walked down the driveway. Spotting
him, Pearl burst into tears and hurried out to meet him, her arms extended to embrace the "lost boy" who'd finally come home to his "Momie." The camera clicked; Mabel scribbled in her notebook. "It was as
bad as a toothache when Jesse was gone," Pearl said. "When my boy
walked up to me I didn't recognize him—his hair was thinner and he was
so much older. All these years I was waiting to get my little boy back . . .
and he came home a man."

Inside his new home, Pearl showed Jesse "the furniture she had reup-
holstered herself, the quilts she had made for their beds, the gifts she had
squeezed out of her $87-a-month take-home pay." In Jesse's small room,
Mabel inventoried "tie clasps, cufflinks and a wristwatch. Seven dress

white shirts and several sport shirts and a suit she had been given for him." Pearl had also fashioned for him a quilted beach coat; Jesse modeled it, and the photographer snapped another few photos.

A few other gifts lay wrapped beneath a small Christmas tree—gifts that Pearl and Charles had brought to the Lake County jail in 1957 before being turned away by a heartless sheriff, and that had thus never been opened. There was a wallet, a belt, and a pair of shoes, slightly scuffed, that Jesse hadn't been able to wait for Christmas to wear fourteen long years ago, just before he was picked up by Deputy Yates. Pearl had saved the gifts a second time, from the fire that had destroyed the Yalaha home. Now Jesse contemplated them, and all the time that had passed. "I'd like to be eighteen again," he stuttered.

Jesse had something for his mother as well. Seated on Pearl's bed, he pulled a wad of bills from his pocket. "Mom," he said, "I want to take you downtown and buy you the prettiest dress we can find." He'd sold his radio to get the money.

Mabel stole a moment of her own with the boy whose story she'd been following for fourteen years. His cheeks had hollowed and his hairline had receded, and he sported a two-day stubble. His "quiet voice," though, had not changed, and he'd not lost his stutter. He'd also remained impeccably polite, with "ma'am" punctuating his responses to Mabel's questions. Although it had been years since Mabel had last visited Jesse at Chattahoochee, Jesse recalled that her daughter had once accompanied her there, and he described Patricia in detail.

At thirty-three, Jesse still had a future, and he had plans. "I want to be an auto mechanic still," he told Mabel, and she noted in her story that working on cars had been his dream ever since he was a young boy in Okahumpka, painting and assembling tiny model automobiles in South Quarters, "before his world was shattered." As a mechanic, Jesse reasoned, "I'm going to earn a lot of money some day so I can pay Mr. Graham for all he's done for me."

"And I'm going to be a musician too," he said, pulling the guitar from its case. He opened his impromptu concert for Mabel, Pearl, and the photographer with one of his favorites: "Oh, Lonesome Me," a country song written and recorded by Don Gibson in December 1957, the same month that Jesse was apprehended for the rape of Blanche Knowles. Looking his mother in the eye, he rested the guitar on his thigh, and in a deeper voice unaffected by his stutter, he crooned.

Well, there must be some way I can lose these lonesome blues
Forget about the past and find somebody new

After she'd bade Pearl and her boy good-bye, Mabel returned home to her typewriter. "For now, I close my own personal book on the Jesse Daniels case," Mabel wrote, "a book I began those fourteen years ago as the editor of the weekly *Mount Dora Topic*. I smelled something fishy in the arrest, and I dug into the circumstances. I campaigned with that awfully limited power of the press that is a weekly. I campaigned still more with the *News-Journal*. Then the *St. Petersburg Times* also took up the cause. At last, a bewildered man-child is free now to develop his capabilities."

A few weeks after Jesse's release, Gordon Oldham did what Richard Graham had predicted he would have no other choice but to do. He quietly dropped the fourteen-year-old rape charge in the hope that the sordid story would once again disappear from the newspapers and public memory. It didn't work out that way. In the weeks and months that followed, light would be cast into the darkest corners of Lake County, and uncomfortable, long-buried truths would emerge. Mabel would have no choice but to reopen her personal book on the case of Jesse Daniels.

Pearl and Jesse Daniels in Green Cove Springs

CHAPTER FIFTEEN

Someone Should Write a Book

"WE'LL START OFF a brand new year with happiness." With that resolve, Pearl Eisentrager ended 1971. On December 31 she had learned that Gordon Oldham had filed a formal nolle prosequi in Lake County Court, officially discontinuing all action in the prosecution of Jesse Daniels for the rape of Blanche Bosanquet Knowles. The state attorney did not, however, in any way acknowledge the defendant's possible innocence; rather, he stated it to be "pointless" to proceed, in that Supreme Court rulings like the 1964 *Miranda* decision, which limited the use of confessions in trial, posed difficulties in the prosecution of this case, as did "a lack of availability of witnesses." Further, Oldham noted, a trial "would be a considerable cost to the taxpayers." The state attorney expressed his confidence "that if I'd have tried Jesse Daniels at the time he was indicted, I would have convicted him," although he acknowledged that, had Jesse been convicted with a life sentence in 1958, "he probably would have been paroled before now."

Oldham's decision disappointed Richard Graham, who had been looking forward to "taking everyone's dirty underwear out of the closet

BENEATH A RUTHLESS SUN

in a trial." And Oldham's statement that should Jesse become involved in another crime, he "would not be so fortunate to be found not guilty by reason of insanity," offended Graham, as Jesse had been adjudged to be sane. In Graham's assessment, Oldham had behaved like a coward.

Still, the nolle prosequi brought unequivocal relief to the Daytona Beach household where Pearl and her son had been attempting to fashion life anew for Jesse in the two weeks since he'd returned home. Carl Warner, the chef at the Princess Issena, where Pearl still worked as a maid, had given Jesse a job as a cook's helper, and Pearl had only praise for her son's new boss. "He has several retarded employees," she noted. "He's just as kind to them as their own mothers could be."

On the same day that Oldham dropped the rape charge against Jesse, Graham indicated to reporters that he had prepared a relief bill, in which he accused the state of negligence in illegally confining his client and, therefore, sought compensation for both Jesse and his mother. "The mental anguish and deep hurt [Daniels] suffered, through no fault of his own, have damaged him in a manner for which he could never be compensated and which could never be erased from his mind," read the bill, which, Graham hoped, would be introduced in the next legislative session. The bill proposed compensation in the amount of $122,640, a figure based on loss of earnings at the rate of a dollar an hour for the time Jesse was held at Chattahoochee, and a smaller amount for Pearl, based on the time she had spent trying to free Jesse and on the amount she had saved the state by doing so. The very idea of compensation, though, caused Graham some ambivalence. "I don't know," he reflected. "How do you put a monetary value on what he went through?"

When asked to speak at the Business and Professional Women's Club in Daytona Beach on January 6, Mabel invited Jesse and Pearl to accompany her, as she'd chosen to address the role of the press in justice and civil rights cases. "Because a weekly newspaper speaks with a small voice," Mabel told the gathering, "my role actually became that of buoying the faith of Jesse's parents. They came to know that someone with at least some voice believed in their son's innocence; that someone was unafraid to challenge McCall. It was after I came to Daytona Beach that the voice grew, eventually interesting the *St. Petersburg Times* and the Associated Press in an obvious miscarriage of justice. The combined voices of an angry press reached Governor Askew and the courts, and things really started moving toward the day of Jesse's release and clearance." Mabel applauded Pearl's courage and tenacity, and she spoke glowingly of the dedication to Jesse's case shown by Graham and Husfeld.

Unlike Oldham, who had attempted to resist or delay every effort by Graham to grant Jesse Daniels his day in court, the Florida legislature acted on Graham's relief bill with a sense of urgency. Graham had persuaded three lawmakers from Volusia County to sponsor the bill, and Senator Frederick Karl from Daytona Beach had agreed to introduce a claims bill in the legislature in January 1972. The Florida House of Representatives' Committee on Retirement, Personnel and Claims appointed Thomas F. Woods as special master to oversee investigations and hearings related to the Jesse Daniels bill. Once he had taken sworn testimony, reviewed the documents in evidence, and weighed the attorneys' written and oral arguments, he would submit a final "Master's Report," which would include recommendations on compensation. "There has never been a trial," Senator Karl explained to a reporter. "So in considering the bill, the Legislature must decide guilt or innocence. We are in the position of rewarding a guilty person or refusing to grant damages to an innocent man who was confined for fourteen years of his life."

Like Richard Graham, Mabel Norris Chesley was disappointed that Jesse Daniels would not have the opportunity to clear his name in a Lake County courtroom. Still, the legislative hearings, over which Woods would preside, would become, in effect, Jesse's trial, and they would have the advantage of taking place outside the jurisdiction of the Fifth Judicial Circuit and Oldham's prosecutorial influence. For that, Mabel was ecstatic, and she looked forward to the day that Willis McCall would be subpoenaed to testify. As it happened, Mabel, too, was subpoenaed as a witness and ordered to appear in the Orange County court on the same day—March 2, 1972—as McCall.

Jesse, in a navy blue suit and tie, arrived at the Orange County Courthouse with Pearl, who admitted to a reporter that Jesse was "terrified" and added, "I'm trembling a little myself." Graham and Husfeld opened the hearing by calling Jesse's former attorney, Thomas Champion, who provided background on the case. Graham next called a psychologist from Daytona to testify to Jesse's sanity and then a psychiatrist from Florida State Hospital at Chattahoochee, who told Special Master Woods that the hospital had determined Jesse to be "sane although somewhat mentally deficient."

The next witness was Deputy James Yates, who testified that Jesse had become a suspect "after a pair of underwear was found near the rape victim's home." Under questioning by Graham, Yates appeared to have forgotten that after Deputy Leroy Campbell discovered the much-trumpeted size-34 underwear outside the Knowles house in the early morning hours of December 18, 1957, it was Bubba Hawkins who had been arrested for the crime. Not until five days later was Jesse Daniels taken into custody—no matter that his size-26 underwear had not been discovered at the scene of the crime but confiscated by Yates, without a warrant, from the Daniels house while no one was at home. Yates also testified that Jesse Daniels had made "a verbal confession, describing how he had entered the raped woman's home."

Yates's testimony as to when and where Jesse's underwear had been discovered was disputed by McCall himself, who was called by counsel representing the office of the attorney general. The sheriff, however, could not support his dispute with proof, because he could not fully remember, hard as he tried, many details about the alleged rape and Daniels's subsequent arrest. Nor could he refer to departmental records on the case, as he told Special Master Woods with regret and apology, since "all notes taken by investigators," Jesse's purported confession, "and all other records regarding the case" had disappeared either by "misplacement or a loss in moving from one office to another." When Graham finally had the opportunity to confront in court the man in the big hat who had stared him down outside Judge Mills's Lake County courtroom the previous year, McCall responded with docility and apology. The experience was deflating, as McCall feigned regret upon regret: The case was so old, the records had gone missing, his memory was lacking. "He just brushed me off," said Graham.

Mabel took the stand late in the afternoon. She recounted for Graham how she had "conducted her own investigation, waged a campaign for Daniels' release and agreed with professional opinions that Daniels was too nonaggressive to have committed a rape." She bore no sympathy for the sheriff's memory lapses or his office's inadequacies. "She apparently had a green light from her paper to go after him," Graham recalled. "McCall would try to intimidate everyone, but she'd look him right in the eye. She was not afraid of him." For, as Mabel herself remarked, "I'm my own best protection. If anything ever happened to me, everyone in the state would know who did it."

On March 3, the second day of hearings, Graham and Husfeld called Pearl to the stand. She detailed her son's whereabouts on the day and evening of the rape for which he had been charged. Then the lawyers called Jesse Daniels, who had been waiting outside the courtroom so he'd not hear his mother's testimony. Jesse "verified his mother's story." Stuttering, he testified to Woods, "They told me I had to sign a confession. At gunpoint." He said the piece of paper was "already typed," but he wasn't allowed to read it. "They said it was none of my business."

At the close of the hearings, Thomas Woods told reporters that he would evaluate the case back in Tallahassee, although he plainly expressed concerns about Jesse's confession and indicated his intention to collect further testimony, particularly from Gordon Oldham and Margaret Hickman, the secretary who'd allegedly witnessed Jesse's signing of the confession.

Woods planned to return to court in Orlando within a matter of weeks, but new events in Lake County brought the proceedings to a temporary halt. Anyone who'd thought Willis McCall had grown docile by his twenty-eighth year in office didn't know Willis McCall.

In April 1972, a thirty-eight-year-old black man named Tommy J. Vickers was arrested and taken to the Lake County jail for failure to respond to a summons he'd received for driving a vehicle with an invalid inspection sticker. At the jail, Vickers, who had a history of mental illness and, possibly, brain damage from an injury he'd sustained in a motorcycle accident five years earlier, began kicking the door of his cell. As the ruckus continued through the night, the jailers ordered two trusties, Jack and Bobby Huffman, both serving a year's sentence for aggravated assault, to move Vickers into a fourteen-by-fourteen-foot "tile tank" without bars or windows. Vickers resisted, and in the tussle that followed the two trusties bloodied the new inmate's nose. They confiscated Vickers's shoes to deter further kicking and threw a mattress into the tank. The jailers locked the door.

The next morning, on their arrival at the jail, Willis McCall and Deputy Lucius Clark, along with the Huffman brothers and a third trusty, Willis June, went to check on the unruly inmate. What happened next is uncertain, but in the scuffle that ensued, the three trusties managed to subdue Vickers. Both Jack and Bobby Huffman later stated that while they pinned Vickers to the floor, Willis McCall repeatedly kicked the prisoner hard in the stomach, shouting, "This damn Nigger ain't crazy! This damn Nigger ain't crazy!" Willis June corroborated that account.

After the scuffle, Vickers was carried to the "creech tank"—a "six foot square stainless steel cell," which had no toilet or running water—and put on a "punishment diet" of peas and carrots. For seven days, however,

Vickers did not, or could not, eat. Then the jailers began to detect a "bad smell" outside the tank: "It was not a jailhouse smell," one of them said. Another of them noticed that Vickers was vomiting up "black foam." The inmate was removed to Waterman Memorial Hospital, where he died.

At the coroner's inquest, all three trusties testified to a version of events in the jail that corresponded with McCall's account, in which the sheriff claimed only to have "popped" Vickers a few times on the back of the head. The cause of death was determined to be "acute peritonitis as a result of a blow to the lower abdomen incurred by mischance or accident, said blow inflicted by person or persons unknown." In announcing the verdict, the presiding judge stated that Vickers "was mistreated somewhere . . . but that the jury had no testimony to point to anyone."

Since assuming the governorship, Reubin Askew had received numerous letters from Mabel Chesley in which she'd urged the removal of Sheriff Willis McCall from office. Unlike the cowed or politically apprehensive governors whom the sheriff had outplayed over his twenty-eight-year reign, Askew needed no urging. Unconvinced by the verdict, and reluctant to allow Gordon Oldham to conduct his own investigation, Askew dispatched officials from the FDLE "to assist" the state attorney. In addition, he sent his general counsel, Edgar Dunn, to Tavares, where he met with Judge Troy Hall—no friend of Willis McCall—to request that a grand jury be impaneled outside Lake County, because Askew suspected that the county sheriff might be "a principal suspect" in the death of Tommy Vickers. Judge Hall moved the case to Orange County, infuriating McCall. The governor also requested that ten material witnesses in the Lake County jail be immediately transferred to Orange County "for their safety."

While McCall was waiting for the grand jury on the Vickers case to convene in Orange County, Thomas Woods returned to central Florida to proceed with his investigation into the matter of Jesse Daniels's reparations. The hearing resumed on May 31, with Graham and Husfeld calling several residents of Okahumpka's North Quarters, who testified that they were among the dozens of black men initially rounded up for questioning in the rape of Blanche Knowles. Primary among them was Melvin Bubba Hawkins, who had since, on a football scholarship, gone on to Bethune-Cookman College, where his uncle Virgil had worked and studied. Bubba told Graham that on the night he was taken into custody by Lake County deputies, he stood over six feet tall and weighed 210 pounds, every bit the star halfback he'd been for Carver Heights Negro High School. Jesse Daniels, Graham noted, had at the time weighed only 130 pounds.

Oldham's testimony took up most of the court's first day back. Unperturbed, nearly yawning at times, the state attorney maintained that he was "still convinced Daniels is guilty," although he conceded, "If someone could prove to me that he is not guilty, I would be the first to admit it." Daniels's guilt or innocence, however, had "nothing to do" with Jesse's confinement at Chattahoochee. "I think he would have been there anyway," Oldham contended.

When Graham asked Oldham why he'd initially told reporters that law enforcement was seeking a "young Negro," Oldham responded that he was "often misquoted in the press."

"Did you ask for a retraction of the story?" Graham asked.

"No," Oldham admitted.

Finally, to Special Master Woods, Oldham voiced his objection to Blanche Knowles's being subpoenaed, on the grounds that "she still suffers from the experience and testifying would be too upsetting."

Bill Donaldson, the polygraph expert on whom McCall and Oldham had relied to administer lie detector tests on several suspects in the days following the Okahumpka rape, testified that in his report on Jesse Daniels, he'd noted that the subject had responded "intelligently" and appeared to be "no different than anyone else" he'd examined. The boy had not impressed him as "being mentally retarded" but, rather, had "seemed like a normal human being"; nor had he detected a stutter in the subject's speech. Reviewing the test results on Jesse Daniels, Donaldson had concluded that the subject was being deceptive and that he had "either committed the rape or knew who had." When Donaldson had finished his tests, he said, he had communicated his findings to Sheriff McCall and to Joe Knowles—both of whom had been present at the polygraph examination.

Damaging though Donaldson's testimony was to Jesse Daniels, its significance would fade after Graham questioned the next witness, Leesburg native Margaret "Sis" Hickman, the secretary and notary public at the Lake County Sheriff's Department. Efficient, candid, and matter-of-fact, Hickman claimed to remember clearly the occasion of Jesse's confession. She certainly related details. It had taken place in the ID room of the Lake County jail, with deputies James Yates and Leroy Campbell standing behind Jesse Daniels as he "orally"—and "calmly and clearly, without a stutter"—described his rape of Blanche Knowles. When he'd finished, she'd left the ID room to type the statement. On her return, she'd read the confession back to Jesse Daniels, who was sitting "slouched in a chair." In her presence, he'd signed the confession. She'd notarized it.

At that point, Richard Graham handed Hickman a photograph of Jesse Daniels at age nineteen and asked if the picture helped her recall any other details about that December 1957 day in the ID room of the jail. Hickman considered the image of the boy and without hesitation replied, "I've never seen him before in my life."

Graham then asked Margaret Hickman to describe the man who had confessed to rape fifteen years ago in the ID room of the Lake County jail.

"He had kinky black hair," she said, and a murmur rippled across the hearing room. Turning toward the special master, she added, "He was a dark Negro—that is, dark brown."

Abruptly, Woods called a recess. As Margaret Hickman, confused by the reaction, was ushered from the room, Woods retreated into the jury room with the attorneys representing Jesse Daniels and the counsel from the attorney general's office, "all gasping in utter astonishment." Pacing the jury room, Woods let the implications of Hickman's testimony settle into comprehensibility. "Someone should write a book," he said.

The special master and the attorneys all agreed that the surprise testimony of the notary public demanded further investigation outside the hearing room, and that agents from the FDLE should also be involved. The attorneys decided that they would take both Jesse Daniels and Margaret Hickman, in separate cars, to a lounge on the outskirts of Lake County. There, Richard Graham and Mabel Chesley observed the proceedings. Jesse was seated on a stool at the counter, and on her arrival, Hickman was escorted to a table. Then, brought face-to-face, they were asked if they'd ever seen each other before. Both responded that they had not.

Immediately Hickman grasped the point of their meeting. "Is this Jesse Daniels?" she asked.

The attorneys nodded. Hickman stared at the man whose face bore the strain of fourteen long years in Chattahoochee. Overcome with emotion, she began gasping for breath. Graham watched in astonishment as a devastated Hickman practically collapsed in her chair.

"But it was a Negro whose confession I took," she sobbed. "I WATCHED a Negro sign that confession."

No one in the lounge doubted the notary public's memory. Jim Mahorner, counsel for the attorney general, sent word of the stunning development in the case to Ed Dunn at Governor Askew's office. The attorneys left Hickman to the FDLE agents, who questioned her more specifically about the confession. The agents noted that Hickman "stoutly maintains that the Jesse Daniels who made the confession under scrutiny was black." The agents determined, too, that Hickman's memory was clear on this because of a particular moment in the confession, when the suspect "sneered" at Hickman, stating: "When I was through I asked her if she enjoyed it, and she said 'Yes.'" The implication had offended Hickman; she told the FDLE agents that she "became most angry at this because the Negro looked at her as if to imply that she would also enjoy having intercourse with him." She was sure that her memory of his remark and her reaction was accurate, for it had been etched in her mind, agents noted, not least because Margaret Hickman had attended Leesburg High School with Blanche Bosanquet and knew her well. "I'm a personal friend of the victim," she told the agents. "I would not get this crime confused."

When presented with the actual confession document, Hickman readily acknowledged that the notary signature on it was hers. As she realized what had occurred in the ID room at the Lake County jail, she was affronted, the agents observed, by the now evident fact that "Deputy Yates tricked her in some manner." Of that she had "no doubt in her mind."

Margaret Hickman's revelatory testimony prompted the FDLE agents to follow up with Tampa polygrapher Bill Donaldson. The FBI report from the January 1959 investigation had included Donaldson's signed statement in which he claimed that he'd interviewed Blanche Knowles in the sheriff's office five days after the rape. According to his statement, he had also been present with Yates when Jesse Daniels was brought in for questioning later that night, and he had spoken with Jesse's parents and with Jesse himself before administering the lie detector test, which had quickly led to Jesse confessing to the rape.

When the FDLE agents interviewed Donaldson after his testimony before the Florida Legislature and Special Master Woods, however, they heard a very different version of events. He had never been allowed to interview Blanche Knowles, Donaldson told the agents, because Joe Knowles would not allow it—he'd simply declared it "could not be done" and any information Donaldson needed he'd have to get from Joe. (Had he been allowed to speak directly with Blanche, Donaldson later noted, he would have been able to frame his questions to the suspects more specifically.)

Donaldson then produced his own, more muted version of Hickman's courtroom surprise. He was certain that the only suspects he had questioned were black, and only one of the subjects had evidenced deception in his tests—"a seventeen- to eighteen-year-old Negro." When shown the alleged Jesse Daniels test results, Donaldson was at a loss to explain why the letters "W" and "M," indicating the subject was a white male, were circled next to Jesse's name, because he had not questioned any white suspects. Donaldson made clear that his only responsibility in the Daniels case was administration of the polygraph tests and that, contrary to what both Oldham and McCall had asserted in the special master's hearings, he was "in no way in charge of the investigation."

Once he'd confirmed for Sheriff McCall and Deputy Yates that his lie detector test of "Jesse Daniels" had shown deception, Donaldson had returned to Tampa. A few days later, he now confessed to the agents, he'd received a white sport coat in the mail. The note accompanying it read, "Thanks. Willis V. McCall." Donaldson estimated the coat to have cost about one hundred dollars.

Recognizing that his responses to the FDLE's questions were significantly discrepant from the signed statement he'd provided to FBI agents fourteen years earlier, Donaldson admitted, in his FDLE interview, to being "most concerned with his reputation as a polygraph examiner." Whether because of fear of facing perjury charges or the wrath of Willis McCall, Donaldson, the FDLE agents noted, "displayed extreme reluctance to modify his testimony before the legislature."

Clearly, the Jesse Daniels case had been riddled with both fraudulent evidence and falsified documents. In addition, with so many machinations by James Yates, the deputy who'd "investigated" both the Groveland and the Fruitland Park rape cases, some details never got considered at all. For example, there was this seemingly innocuous sentence in Jesse's alleged confession: "I then started out of the bedroom but I heard something fall on the floor that sounded like a little piece of wood and I got down on the floor to see what it was and felt around with my hands, but could not find anything."

"A little piece of wood"? Was this detail meant to refer to Jesse's guitar pick, the piece of crime-scene evidence that Yates had bragged to Deputy Evvie Griffin about confiscating from the Daniels home without a warrant and planting at the Knowles house? Perhaps, then, it was more script than coincidence that a similarly worded "search" for an object on the Knowleses' bedroom floor had appeared in the now missing statement Gordon Oldham claimed to have taken from Blanche in March 1958: Her assailant had gotten "down on his hands and knees and started hunting for something on the floor, and it was not in a particularly intelligent manner, because he kept hunting over exactly the same spot . . . fanning out with his hand in front of him, patting the floor right hard, trying to find something that he apparently thought was there."

Griffin, for one, had believed that Yates was fraudulently "strengthening the case" against Jesse Daniels, should the case ever go to trial. But where would this "little piece of wood" have fallen from, if the suspect was wearing only socks when he entered the Knowles house?

MABEL CHESLEY TOOK Woods's comment regarding Hickman's revelations—"Someone should write a book"—as a cue for an editorial in the *Daytona Beach Sunday News-Journal*: "A Book There Should Be, and Its Title: 'McCall.'"

"Indeed, a book is due on the bizarre case of mentally retarded Jesse Daniels," Mabel declared, "nabbed in the little Lake County town of Okahumpka in 1957 by deputies for Sheriff Willis McCall and summarily packed off to the criminal ward of Chattahoochee." To the injustices in Jesse's case, Mabel added those in the cases of the Groveland Boys, the Platts, the black airmen who'd been entrapped and beaten in McCall's cabin in Big Scrub—all of them cases on which she had reported and by which she'd incurred the wrath of McCall. Her list was neither complete nor completed, for the long-reigning sheriff continued to terrorize blacks as he had in the Fruitland Park rape case and, most recently, in the case of the now deceased Tommy Vickers.

Yet, even as the details of the Daniels conspiracy, with the help of both intentional and unwitting participants, came to light, Mabel could not fathom what Willis McCall's motivations had been, and she seemed almost resigned that the truth might never become known in the case of the boy on the bicycle from the tiny hamlet of Okahumpka.

"It would take a Truman Capote" to capture Jesse's "years of bewilderment, the cruelties he suffered and those he witnessed," Mabel asserted. "A crack reporter with eons of time to spare needs to get at the core question: Why Daniels? Why did a white man suffer so, when it is the Negro that McCall hates?"

It wasn't a writer or crack reporter who found the answers to Mabel's long-pondered questions. It was a gray-haired, heavyset, fifty-year-old Army veteran from northern Mississippi who was still in his rookie year at the Florida Department of Law Enforcement. It was someone Willis McCall would never have imagined: the FDLE's first black special agent.

FDLE agent Al Albright

CHAPTER SIXTEEN

Whether They Be White or Black

ALFRED ALBRIGHT, the youngest of sixteen children, was born in By-halia, Mississippi, in 1921. Both his father and his mother, William and Alice, were listed as mulattos in the United States Census. Shortly after Alfred's birth, William, a farmer, deserted the family, and most of his sons moved north to Cincinnati in search of a better life. Alice became head of the household. "I am the product of a broken family," Alfred wrote on his FDLE employment application. "I was reared in a poor, depressed, female centered atmosphere. After the death of my mother . . . the entire family disintegrated."

At age seventeen, Al Albright followed his brothers to Cincinnati. In 1943, he joined the Army. He'd served in England, France, Germany, and Austria when he was selected to attend the U.S. Constabulary School for military police training. He'd also managed to take college courses during the time he was stationed overseas, which was most of his Army career. A reassignment to Omaha enabled him to complete his undergraduate courses for a bachelor's degree from the University of Nebraska. In 1969, when a new posting took him to Norman, Oklahoma, Albright began work toward a master's degree in public administration at the University of Oklahoma, but his progress was interrupted when he was reassigned overseas. In 1971, while stationed in Japan as an operations officer for the criminal investigation division of the U.S. Army, Albright applied for a civilian law-enforcement job with the FDLE, to which he would bring, as he wrote in his application, "twenty-three years of criminal investigation experience." In the spring of that year, Albright traveled back to the United States for interviews at the FDLE Tallahassee office.

"Although my life and the lives of my relatives have been turbulent," Albright noted in his personal statement, "my proficiency and efficiency in achievements in the past performance of law enforcement assignments have not been adversely affected, but rather enhanced." His FDLE interviewers concurred. In staff evaluations, Albright's initiative, drive, energy, and ambition were all scored "outstanding." The personnel director did not doubt his "very good potential," and on his file wrote: "Colored applicant—very impressive." Albright was offered a position as a special agent in the Orlando Field Office. He and his third wife, Marie, a Vietnamese woman he'd met and married in 1968, when he was stationed in Saigon, settled in Winter Springs, Florida.

The FDLE's investigation into the beating death of Tommy Vickers was ongoing when Al Albright joined the agency. Only months into his new job, he was assigned to Lake County—and plunged into the final throes of a Jim Crow South that he'd not experienced since his escape from Mississippi at the age of seventeen.

THE SAME WEEK that the coroner's jury was assembled to investigate Vickers's death in May 1972, Evvie Griffin received what felt like some long-overdue good news: U.S. District Court judge Charles R. Scott in Jacksonville overturned the guilty verdicts of Robert Shuler and Jerry Chatman. Griffin had been providing case assistance to attorney Tobias

Simon, Mabel Chesley's friend and fellow committee member from the Florida Advisory Committee to the U.S. Commission on Civil Rights. Simon had stepped in to take up the Shuler-Chatman appeal and had presented the case in federal court. Judge Scott concluded that the evidence against the men was "fraudulently manufactured" and that searches had been made without warrant. Reserving his harshest words for state attorney Gordon Oldham's office, Judge Scott ruled that the "suppression" of the alleged victim's statement regarding her inability to identify her attackers, as well as her conflicting answers about whether she'd actually been sexually assaulted, was "highly reprehensible," as it was "not solely for the prosecution to decide for the court what is admissible."

It was bad news for Oldham, but the following month brought worse news for Willis McCall. In June, a grand jury in Orange County indicted the Lake County sheriff on a charge of second-degree murder in the Tommy Vickers case. The prisoner's death, the jury said, was caused by an act "evincing a depraved mind regardless of human life." Governor Askew immediately suspended McCall from office, and Judge W. Troy Hall appointed a former FBI agent as acting sheriff.

Rick Hernan was the FDLE case agent in charge of the Vickers investigation. Once the indictment had been handed down, he had to devise and execute a plan to remove Willis McCall from office and place the Lake County Sheriff's Department under new command. He decided to have FDLE agents drive in a multi-car caravan to Tavares and there arrest the sheriff. "We wanted Al Albright to read McCall his rights," Hernan said. "That was the plan. But Al had car problems en route and we had to keep the caravan moving."

The black special agent, however, did not arrive too late to be photographed while serving the sheriff his suspension—the sheriff who, only a few months before, and seven years since passage of the 1964 Civil Rights Act, had finally been forced by order of a federal judge to desegregate the jail facilities and to remove the "Colored" and "White" signs from the courthouse walls. McCall balked at signing the governor's suspension order and demanded that Albright "take your people and get out." Albright did not oblige, and the sheriff was subjected to the added humiliation of being photographed as he was being fingerprinted in his own jail. He then posted the thousand-dollar bail. "I am innocent," McCall told reporters, and vowed that Lake County had not seen the last of him. "Like MacArthur, I shall return."

As always, McCall played the victim and blamed his adversaries for trying to bring him down. "This is the NAACP, the Civil Liberties Union, and a few local enemies collaborating like they always have," he alleged. He also claimed that this new investigation into his conduct did not worry him. The Vickers case, he said, was the "forty-ninth time" he'd been probed. "My back is like a gator's hide," he bragged to reporters. "You just bend the needle when you try to stick it in."

A trial was set for August, and Governor Askew appointed Florida Supreme Court justice James Adkins to preside. Grand jury testimony is historically secret, but Adkins, in a highly unusual move, decided that, as McCall had signed a waiver of immunity, which allowed his own words to be used against him in court, the sheriff's grand jury testimony would be admissible in the Vickers murder trial, which was being moved to nearby Marion County. McCall's unflattering estimations of his enemies would thus be made public. One of the grand jurors, for instance, had asked the sheriff, "Sir, you ... kept saying ... 'they are out to get me.' Who are you referring to, Sir?" In reply, McCall had named a number of people, including Judge Troy Hall—"about the two-facedest man I ever saw"—before zeroing in on the "Daytona Beach newspaperwoman," Mabel Chesley, who, he'd averred, was waging an all-out war to bring him down. "I don't know whether she is a Communist," he'd elaborated, "but she surely writes like one in the newspapers. She is pro-Communism and anti-establishment [on] most everything, and the people that's against the establishment, whether they be white or black without any lawful purpose are usually the people that are out to get me."

In its report, the twenty-three-person grand jury was especially critical of the Lake County authorities who had conducted the coroner's inquest. Indeed, the report found the conduct so questionable that it called for a separate inquiry into the "operation of the jail." What disturbed the jurors even more was the fact that Sheriff McCall had met with the trusty witnesses prior to their testimony at the coroner's inquest and had made it clear that "they must testify according to the account stated to them by McCall." The report concluded, "Each prisoner believed that unless he so testified, he would be punished after returning from court to the jail."

In the testimony of the three trusty witnesses—Willis June and the Huffman brothers, Jack and Bobby—at McCall's murder trial, discrepancies with their grand jury testimony became crucially evident. Willis June's court appearance made headlines when he admitted that he'd lied before the grand jury. Asked why by the prosecutors, June "surprised the defense" by stating, "I was afraid of getting killed, that's what. I was a black man in Lake County." He and the other trusties were all "afraid of getting killed, man. Afraid of getting [our] brains beat out like a dog. If I was to tell you everything that happened, you'd sit down and cry."

As McCall's trial progressed, the scope of the FDLE's investigation of him broadened beyond the Vickers case. Rick Hernan had been discovering how justice worked in the sheriff's department—with payoffs for ignoring activities like distilling moonshine or running bolita games, a type of lottery popular but illegal in Florida—and how rehabilitation translated into free prison labor for work on Willis McCall's land in Umatilla. "There are lots of rumors of misconduct," Governor Askew's general counsel, Edgar Dunn, told reporters, and the governor was determined not to ignore a single one of them.

Al Albright was one of the agents poking around Lake County, and the Jesse Daniels case in particular roused his investigative instincts.

Everyone he questioned about Jesse and the Knowles rape was still, after fifteen years, hesitant or plain unwilling to speak about it, at least initially. But, with McCall now looking more vulnerable, and with a little Albright persuasion, some county residents were beginning to open up. Albright's investigative skills led him eventually to Leesburg, where he found a path into the circle of Willis McCall's decades-long and (mostly) loyal confidants.

"Al Albright was the greatest interrogator I've ever seen in law enforcement," Rick Hernan attested. "He had a conversational way about him that is hard to put a finger on. He'd start asking questions and people just opened up to him. It was something to see." One of those people was Carl Klaber, a longtime Lake County grovesman who'd known the sheriff since 1940, when McCall was working as a fruit inspector. "Willis McCall is a murderer," declared Klaber, who insisted that Albright keep his identity confidential, "and a lying, scheming, no good son-of-a-bitch." He estimated that McCall "has killed or has had killed between twenty-five or [*sic*] thirty people."

Albright and Hernan found one interrogation technique particularly useful in Lake County. "We would sit down with witnesses and look them right in the eye," Hernan recalled, "and we'd make it very clear that *they* were not the target of our investigation. Then we would remind them that lying to an agent is a criminal offense." Once the message landed, witnesses became cooperative, especially now that a perception was taking hold around the county that Sheriff Willis McCall might finally be taken down.

The more that Albright and Hernan explored the underbelly of Lake County, the more they realized that the fears of its citizens were not misplaced. They learned, for example, the fate of a fifteen-year-old black youth, James Farmer, who in 1969 was being held not for a crime but for competency hearings, as his parents had claimed he was "suffering from hallucinations and a fear that someone was trying to kill him." Two days before Christmas, Farmer, who'd begun having outbursts in the Lake County jail, was transported by a deputy and two trusties to Northeast Florida State Hospital at Macclenny for evaluation. After the deputy in charge had completed the paperwork for Farmer's admission, he returned to his cruiser, where he discovered two healthy trusties pointing to a dead boy in the backseat. The coroner's inquest determined the cause of death to be "sickle cell disease." An alarmed reporter notified the FBI of the suspicious death, but their investigation went nowhere.

Farmer's case, Albright and Hernan came to see, was not exceptional. Too common were the accounts of violence and brutality at the hands of the Lake County Sheriff's Department, and the investigators soon understood why Governor Askew had demanded the transfer of the inmate witnesses in the Vickers case to Orange County for their safety. Like Willis June, trusty Bobby Huffman, though white, had concerns about the authority—and virulence—of Willis McCall. Testifying in the murder trial as to why he'd lied to the grand jury, Huffman said that he'd felt pressure to protect McCall. Under cross-examination he told McCall's defense attorney, "I was scared of the sheriff."

"Are you nervous, Mr. Huffman?" the lawyer asked.

"I'm always nervous," the trusty replied, perhaps with good reason. Just weeks after testifying against McCall, Huffman was released from jail. After he'd had a celebratory drink with his teenage wife at a tavern in Fruitland Park, a stranger approached the couple outside and pointed a 20-gauge shotgun to Huffman's head. The police said he'd taken the "full load of a blast in his face, neck and chest" at point-blank range; he was killed instantly.

In June, Albright met with the Klansman Jack Hooten, who told him, as he had told investigators a dozen years before, that McCall was the "main power" behind the Klan, and that he "has either killed a lot of people or had something to do with people being killed in Lake County." Albright's questions about the Jesse Daniels case prompted Hooten to relate how

Leesburg police chief Bill Fisher had traveled to Tallahassee to present Attorney General Richard Ervin "with evidence of who raped Joe Knowles's wife"—and how, when Gordon Oldham learned of Fisher's trip, he'd told him to "stay out of the case." The Knowles family "was influential in Lake County and pressure was on to arrest and convict someone for the rape," said Hooten; so, he alleged, Oldham and McCall had conspired to charge Jesse Daniels. He urged Albright to continue his investigation and to speak with Bill Fisher, who "might reveal what he knows of the case" now that McCall had been suspended.

Albright interviewed Fisher, and the police chief related to him the details of his 1959 meeting with Ervin in Tallahassee. Fisher had told Ervin that Jesse Daniels had been framed for the Knowles rape, which, Fisher was convinced, had been committed by Sam Wiley Odom. Any doubt he'd had was eliminated by his conversation with Alfred Bosanquet at Fair Oaks: Because "it would not look good in newsprint that Blanche . . . had been raped by a Negro," as Alfred had put it, "emphasis was then placed on Jesse Daniels because he was a mentally deficient person who lived near Blanche Knowles."

To further his investigations into the Daniels case, Albright attempted to gain access to the sheriff's department files on the Knowles and Fruitland Park rapes. In that effort, Rich Hernan served two subpoenas on the interim sheriff, Frank Meech. Meech demanded that Deputy Malcolm McCall, the former sheriff's son, abide by the subpoenas; however, when Hernan arrived to claim the documents, the "visibly upset" deputy stalled. He called Oldham's office and spoke to him for a while, and after he hung up, he "made every effort to block the service of the subpoena." Eventually, Deputy McCall did release the Fruitland Park case files. The Daniels case files, he insisted, could not be located.

On August 15, Al Albright made sure that he arrived on time at the Marion County Courthouse in Ocala, where the trial of sixty-three-year-old Willis McCall for second-degree murder was set to begin.

Already seated in the gallery was former deputy Evvie Griffin, who did not want to miss the opportunity to see his longtime enemy led away in handcuffs to a jail cell of his own. "I wanted him to see my face every day in the courtroom," Griffin said.

What the former deputy saw on that opening day of the trial was a bulge in McCall's right-hand pants pocket as McCall proceeded to the table for the defense. Immediately, Griffin left his seat to speak to Al Albright, who was standing near the wall to one side of the courtroom. "Willis has got a gun in his pocket," Griffin told him.

Albright sprang to attention. "You gotta be kidding."

"He's got a Colt Cobra Airweight in his right pocket," said Griffin, who knew that McCall always carried a roll of bills in his left pocket and the pistol in his right.

Albright hustled over to a bailiff. Informed that he'd have to submit to a search of his person, McCall removed the Colt Cobra from his pocket and laid it on the table. Albright was dumbfounded. Carrying a concealed gun into a courtroom was a felony offense, but doing so while under indictment compounded the gravity of the violation. McCall was indifferent. He'd been carrying a gun in his pocket for years, he said; it was a habit, as natural to him as pocketing his keys or his wallet. (Evidently, it was a habit his sixteen-year-old daughter-in-law shared. In a courtroom search of McCall family members, a concealed handgun was discovered in her purse. She was arrested and turned over to juvenile authorities.)

Testimony in the Vickers murder case ran five days. Throughout the proceedings, McCall made a show of his lack of interest by yawning, feigning sleep, or chuckling at the funny pages in the newspaper. Not even testimony that after Vickers's death, Deputy Lucius Clark was overheard arguing with McCall, contending he "wasn't going to lie for you this time," seemed to ruffle the defendant. Apparently, he had no reason to be ruffled. It took little more than an hour for the all-white jury of four men and two women to acquit Willis McCall of second-degree murder.

After the verdict, supporters gathered around the defense table. There was laughing, backslapping, and talk about where they'd be dining that night. McCall threw an arm around his wife, Doris, and left the courtroom flanked by his son Malcolm and the sheriff of Marion County. "By the time they hit the ground floor," one reporter wrote, "it was just like Tommy Vickers had never lived."

Hernan had known that the Vickers case would not be easy to prosecute, given that the state's key witnesses were convicted felons who altered their grand jury testimony and thus were easy targets for the charge that they were habitual liars. Still, neither Hernan nor any other FDLE agent doubted that McCall had viciously kicked Vickers repeatedly in the stomach. In an interview after the trial, one jury member said he thought that McCall was "probably guilty," but, in acquitting the sheriff, the jurors had also to consider other, practical concerns. "We have to live here," he said, "here" being a county with a still "active Klan presence."

The not-guilty verdict concluded the sixth trial in which a Florida governor had failed in an attempt to oust the sheriff of Lake County from office. The acquittal, however, did not move Governor Askew to reinstate McCall, as the former sheriff had committed an additional felony by carrying a concealed weapon into court.

After his suspension from office and before his trial, McCall, undeterred by any prospects of bad publicity—or a possible guilty verdict—had been first in line at the Lake County Courthouse to register as a candidate for reelection. Asked by a reporter if he thought he could win an election in Lake County after being charged and tried for the murder of a black man in his jail, he'd said, "I don't know if it will hurt or help me." To another reporter, he'd observed, "I've done this eight times now. It's nothing new." Although his campaign had been hindered by the preparation for his trial defense and then his appearances in court, just weeks after his acquittal McCall emerged victorious in the Democratic primary for sheriff of Lake County. With only a month until the general election, he began campaigning for his eighth consecutive term.

WITH THE VICKERS CASE HAVING FAILED to bring down Willis McCall, the FDLE focused its attention on what it now considered its best alternative: the Jesse Daniels case. FDLE commissioner William Reed, all the more determined to see McCall and possibly other elected Lake County officials brought to justice, informed Governor Askew that "investigation of this matter has been assigned top priority status and is being closely coordinated with the United States Department of Justice." Reed had indeed already been in direct contact with John Briggs, the U.S. attorney for the Middle District of Florida, and DOJ attorneys. After they'd been briefed on the Daniels case, the FBI dispatched a team of agents to central Florida, where they launched the largest and most comprehensive investigation to which McCall had ever been subjected. But it was FDLE agent Al Albright who ultimately uncovered the secrets and lies that had lain buried in Lake County for more than fifteen years.

In August, after McCall's acquittal, Albright traveled to Green Cove Springs, the small town west of St. Augustine where Pearl and Jesse had moved into a trailer sitting just off a rural dirt road. Albright carefully walked Pearl through the days leading up to and immediately following the attack on Blanche Knowles. He fixed upon one small but important detail that Pearl had neglected to mention to Mabel Chesley or anyone else up to that point. On December 17, 1957, when Jesse had gone raccoon hunting with a neighbor, Lloyd Harrison, about the time the sun was setting, they'd come back sooner than expected, and without a coon, because they'd stumbled upon a skunk that had sprayed the three of them—Jesse, Lloyd, and Lloyd's hound. Pearl remembered the skunk smell on Jesse being so bad that she'd had him remove his clothes outside and straightaway take a bath. The odor from the skunk spray had nevertheless lingered for days. Lloyd Harrison corroborated Pearl's account of the hunt on the date in question. He told the investigators he had been sprayed many times while on coon hunts and "had never been able to get the smell off in one day's time." Yet in her statement to Gordon Oldham, it was noted, Blanche had detected no such smell.

Another detail arrested Albright's attention when he was combing through the interviews with Sam Wiley Odom that had been subpoenaed by Special Master Thomas Woods for the claims bill hearings. It was a detail that, apparently, Willis McCall, Gordon Oldham, and assistant state attorney James Kynes had considered to be of no particular consequence. But why, Albright wondered. Odom's statement that Blanche's rapist had been paid five thousand dollars to kill her, possibly by her husband, was, to Albright's mind, too significant to ignore.

Joe Knowles's affairs were no secret in Lake County, and agents were able to find people willing to talk in confidence about the Leesburg mayor's indiscretions. They set their sights on Mary Ellen Hawkins. The business venture she had set up when she'd first moved to Naples in December 1957 had failed, and Hawkins had decided to return to Washington, where she'd taken a job as an assistant to a Georgia congressman. Her subsequent marriage to the president of a savings and loan association in Georgia had ended in divorce after eleven years, and in 1972 Hawkins had once again settled in Naples, where she had become a political reporter for the *Naples Daily News*. She was blissfully unaware that her brief affair with Joe Knowles fifteen years earlier was about to bring two FBI agents knocking on her door.

BY THE SUMMER OF 1972, so relentless had the FDLE's investigation into the Tommy Vickers and Jesse Daniels cases become that Gordon Oldham was feeling more than the heat of the season. In June, Mabel Chesley had written an editorial praising Governor Askew for his good start in "ridding Florida of the long engrained blot on its reputation" by suspending Willis McCall from office. "The spotlight now should turn to State Atty. Gordon Oldham," she wrote, since it was Oldham who had prosecuted Shuler and Chatman on a rape charge based, as federal judge Charles Scott had ruled, on "tainted and falsified evidence." Mabel pointed to Judge Scott's strongly worded decision in which he'd characterized as "reprehensible" the prosecution's misconduct in the case and declared, "A strong and free nation can't abide this type of justice." Mabel concluded the editorial with a provocative flourish: "There is much, much more in [Scott's] opinion in condemnation of prosecution tactics and constitutional violations in Lake County to raise strongly the question: Why is McCall's sidekick, Gordon Oldham, still in office?"

Mabel sent a copy of the June editorial to Edgar Dunn (whom she was now addressing as "Ed") at the governor's office. In the accompanying letter, she answered the question her editorial had posed regarding Oldham still being in office. "Of course, he shouldn't be. He's next for removal," Mabel wrote, and as cause, she asserted that the state attorney "has been hand in glove with McCall down through the years."

By July, Oldham was trying to distance himself from the embattled sheriff of Lake County. To that end, he placed a "terse" call to the director of the FDLE, William Troelstrup. Oldham informed the director that he had "no interest in the Sheriff McCall investigation" and that he was "tired of getting phone calls from people in the area" saying FDLE agents had contacted them and made "possibly criminally libelous statements concerning him." If the governor wanted to investigate him, Oldham said, "that is fine," but he reminded the director that he would be state attorney for five more years. Then he hung up.

In August, after Willis McCall's acquittal in the Vickers case, Edgar Dunn met with civil rights attorneys from the Department of Justice to assure them Governor Askew's office and the FDLE "will be most happy to assist your investigation in whatever way we can." One month later, the DOJ stated that it was "very interested in the Jesse Daniels Case." In lieu of subpoenas, the governor himself formally requested all state records about the cases of Jesse Daniels and Sam Wiley Odom.

In a report based on a study of all the available evidence from the FDLE, the FBI, and the legislative hearings, attorney Ben Krage of the DOJ's Civil Rights Criminal Section cited four individuals for prosecution of civil rights crimes and concluded that the "named subjects"— Willis V. McCall, Gordon G. Oldham Jr., James L. Yates, and Leroy Campbell—had "sought the incarceration of Jesse Daniels knowing he was innocent of the crime charged. The subjects employed fraud, perjury, coercion and intimidation to further that end and for 14 years suppressed evidence of Daniels' innocence, thus maintaining his deprivation of liberty." Krage recommended that the case be "presented to a federal grand jury at the earliest convenience."

On January 15, 1973, a federal grand jury convened in Jacksonville. More than two dozen witnesses, including Joe Knowles and Mary Ellen Hawkins, had been subpoenaed to testify. In response to a letter Hawkins had thereupon written to Knowles, he had telephoned her and "expressed his sorrow for the trouble" he was causing her. Sam Powell, Joe's close friend and fellow Quarterback Clubber, had also called Hawkins to ascertain details about her interview with the FBI and the date she was scheduled to testify.

In preparing their notes for the grand jury, attorneys for the DOJ credited the FDLE for its "absolutely zealous and quite thorough investigation," but noted that some evidence, including the testimony of Blanche and Joe Knowles, could be uncovered only by the grand jury. Of particular concern to the DOJ attorneys was Joe Knowles's "sudden absence on the night of the rape," and then, upon his return to Lake County, the "active role" that he'd "assumed . . . in the investigation of his wife's rape." They advised that "Knowles can be expected to be hostile and uncooperative"—all the more so now that the attorneys had finally gained access to Blanche Knowles's interview with Gordon Oldham, which corroborated discussion of the alleged murder-for-hire plot put forth by Sam Wiley Odom. While FBI agents were examining the banking records of Joe Knowles and Mary Ellen Hawkins for any evidence to support the "rumors" of a five-thousand-dollar payment to kill Blanche Knowles, the evidence already in hand, the DOJ attorneys opined, "lends to the suspicion that [Joe] Knowles may have been involved."

Learning that the Daniels case would be going to a federal grand jury, Joe Knowles had informed his family, with dismay, "It's coming up again."

Former state senator Frederick Karl, now serving as a consultant for the state and still ramping up to introduce the Claims Bill for the Relief of Jesse Daniels in the legislature, had been fully briefed on the case by Richard Graham before he met with Gordon Oldham. Oldham assured Karl that Daniels was guilty of raping Blanche Knowles, but this did not entirely persuade Karl, who availed himself again of the investigative reports and remained troubled by the case. By mail, he requested Oldham's clarification on a key point; the state attorney did not reply. In a phone call, he pressed Oldham further as to "why the investigation shifted from a black suspect to a white one." Oldham's equivocal answer— the investigation had been conducted not by Willis McCall or James Yates but by an "outside expert," the polygrapher Bill Donaldson from Tampa—hardly satisfied Karl, who informed the state attorney he himself would have to interview Blanche Knowles.

For that purpose Karl traveled to Leesburg in February 1972. Up to that point, Blanche Knowles had never submitted a signed statement or affidavit describing what had transpired in her home on the night of December 17, 1957. Not since her testimony before a Lake County grand jury in January 1958 (conducted by Oldham) had she ever testified orally as to the events—ever raised her right hand and sworn to tell the truth and nothing but the truth under threat of perjury charges—because the case against Jesse Daniels had never gone to trial. At none of the hearings related to the case had Gordon Oldham ever called her as a witness, because, he professed, it would be "too upsetting" for her to have to recount, in public, details of a trauma still distressful in her memory. And Richard Graham had never pressed to have Blanche testify, on his hunch (correct, as it turned out) that if he didn't, Oldham would be more inclined to drop the rape charge against Jesse. Graham suspected, however, that Oldham had other, less empathetic reasons not to call Blanche as a witness. For one, it would open her up to troublesome questions about the evening of December 17, such as: Where was Joe Knowles on the night of the rape? Did the attacker tell you that he was paid five thousand dollars to kill you?

That Graham had chosen not to force Blanche to testify under oath as a strategy in the best interest of his client did not, however, impede or in any significant way affect Karl in his purpose. Neither did the aura of intimidation that hung in the air when he was introduced to the Knowleses in their Palmora Park home, where they were flanked by members of the Quarterback Club, among them an old friend of Karl's and a fellow state senator, Welborn Daniel. Also present were Oldham and assistant state attorney John McCormick, along with the Knowleses' attorney, Red Robinson.

From the outset the meeting was tense, as Karl was pressured by all parties to back off his demand to interview Blanche. Joe in particular, Karl recalled, "clearly indicated his displeasure." But Karl was determined that he'd not leave Leesburg without her statement, for the Jesse Daniels case was no longer a local matter. Governor Askew was watching its progress with keen interest, as were the commissioner of the FDLE, the Florida legislature, and the U.S. Department of Justice. If elected officials and powerful citizens had criminally conspired to frame an innocent man for a crime he did not commit, it was essential that the victim be put on record. The time had come for Blanche Knowles to speak.

THE DEPARTMENT OF JUSTICE, having decided its investigation required a follow-up visit with Mary Ellen Hawkins, dispatched FBI agents to Naples. Hawkins, entirely cooperative, told the agents that in January 1958, about a month after their December 17 rendezvous, Joe Knowles had come to Naples to tell her what had happened since. "Concerned that something may have happened to his children," Joe had driven at a speed well above the legal limit back to Lake County, where he'd learned his wife had been raped by "a white mentally retarded neighborhood boy," although "people in the neighborhood" did not believe he'd done it. Knowles also recounted to Hawkins that the rapist had "threatened the baby and told Blanche . . . he had been paid $5,000.00 to kill her."

On the morning after the attack, about the time when Knowles had been leaving the Tampa police station, a few members of the Leesburg Quarterback Club who'd heard about the rape had conferred and decided that one of them—Sam Powell, as it had turned out—should attempt to intercept Joe before he'd arrived back in Leesburg. A prominent building contractor, president of the Leesburg Chamber of Commerce, and one of Joe's closest friends, Powell had known exactly what "business" had taken Joe to Tampa. Hawkins could not recall if Joe had told her why Powell and the other Clubbers had thought it necessary to meet and speak with him before his return home. If, as the FBI agents suggested, it might have concerned "a plot to kill Blanche Knowles," Hawkins claimed ignorance and largely dismissed the possibility, but "if there was one, she does not believe Joe Knowles or Sam Powell had anything to do with it," said the FBI report. The report noted as well that at this point Hawkins had asked if she was being interviewed by the FBI as a possible suspect. She "denied that she ever had any hope of Joe Knowles getting a divorce and marrying her." Nor had she ever shared a joint bank account with Joe, and she had no objection to agents' examining her old bank records for any suspicious five-thousand-dollar transactions.

Hawkins admitted to still feeling "great remorse over the affair" and "blaming herself for what had happened to Mrs. Knowles." But for her, she reasoned, Joe "would have been at home, and the rape probably would never have occurred."

Horrified by the news of Blanche's ordeal, Mary Ellen Hawkins had terminated her relationship with Joe Knowles on that January day in 1958, although she told the agents, "Joe did try to renew it several times."

TAKING CUES FROM THE FBI REPORTS, Al Albright began to cultivate contacts inside the Lake County Sheriff's Department, and one deputy led him to Earle Fain Jr. According to the deputy, Fain, a longtime Leesburg resident and member of the Quarterback Club who owned a Cadillac dealership, supposedly had insider information about the rape of Blanche Knowles. (Earle's family had once owned the Fain Theater on Main Street, where young Blanche Bosanquet used to park the family Chevrolet while she spotted planes with her father on the roof of the Leesburg National Bank.)

Fain's nervousness was immediately apparent to Albright. As he began to feel more comfortable with the FDLE agent, Fain confessed that he'd long been and still was afraid to report what he knew about the Jesse Daniels case. Albright, though, had done his research. Since 1970, Earle Fain Jr. had been chairing the Lake County Retarded Children's Campaign, which encouraged contributions from business leaders and volunteers throughout the state. So, in his winning, easy way, Albright got to talking to Fain about the case of a Lake County retarded boy, Jesse Daniels, and Fain began to respond. He was "absolutely sure Jesse Daniels did not rape Blanche Knowles," he said, and then he related what had transpired on the morning of December 18, 1957. In effect, his story picked up where Mary Ellen Hawkins's had left off.

Joe Knowles was a "ladies' man," Fain said, and he and Blanche had been having "family problems." She did not like being left on her own in Okahumpka, as she was that night of December 17 while Joe "spent the night with a woman" in Tampa. On the morning of December 18, after Joe had returned to Leesburg and checked on his family, Oz Ferguson of the Leesburg Motor Company had picked Joe and Sam Powell up in his big Buick, along with Gordon Oldham, Red Robinson, and Fain himself. Then they'd driven around Leesburg, "discussing what to do about Blanche Knowles's report of having been raped by a Negro."

"I be goddamn if Blanche is going to be accused of being raped by a nigger," Joe sputtered in anger and frustration. Oldham had assured him that "he could handle the matter" and Joe was "not to worry about it." Together the men of the Quarterback Club considered and agreed upon the advisability of "moving Blanche Knowles from Okahumpka to Leesburg" for her safety and well-being. And, Fain told Albright, they decided, after further discussion, that it was essential for Blanche to "change the description of her attacker being a Negro."

Next, Fain said, Oldham and Knowles contacted Sheriff Willis McCall, who was initially hesitant to comply with a plan that deprived him of the opportunity to be "hanging a nigger" for rape. In light of Knowles's predicament, however, the sheriff acceded, and "arrangements were made to release the Negro suspects." Chief Criminal Deputy James Yates was told to refocus his investigation. The Lake County Sheriff's Department needed a white person that it could charge with the rape.

Fain was abashed. He avowed to Albright he had personally thought the arrest and confinement of Jesse Daniels at Chattahoochee constituted "a gross miscarriage of justice." Fain himself had later gone to Tavares to speak with Willis McCall about the measures taken against

Jesse. In Fain's view, the sheriff had rationalized his role in the conspiracy to frame an innocent white man for rape by asserting that Jesse "was from a poor family" and "would get better treatment in the State Hospital."

Fain told Albright that it was imperative for the agent to protect his identity at all costs, or Fain would be isolated "socially and business-wise." Of particular concern to Fain was Gordon Oldham. "As long as Gordon Oldham is state attorney," Fain said, he could cause him trouble. However, Fain added, if Albright could convince any of the other people in the car to tell what had happened, he himself would be willing to testify to the conspiracy.

The day after their meeting, Fain contacted Albright. Gordon Oldham had phoned him to learn about the officer who'd visited Fain's house. He'd wanted to know who the man was and if he was from the FDLE. He'd asked whether Fain had gotten the "tag number" on the man's car and whether "any questions were asked about the Knowles rape case." Fain told Albright how he'd responded; he did not know the officer's identity, he'd said, and had not told him anything about the case.

THE MEN of the Leesburg Quarterback Club were keenly aware that more than reputations and careers were at stake in the face of Frederick Karl's authority and his resolve to interview Blanche Knowles. Should Blanche now, after fifteen years, choose—or dare—to speak the truth, she might expose her husband and a cohort of county and state officials, including Gordon Oldham, to serious criminal charges. Influential though the Quarterback Club was, its members were powerless to spare Leesburg's first lady the indignity—or themselves the threat—of Karl's inquiry. Blanche would have to speak.

In response to Karl's questioning, Blanche acknowledged that she had initially said the man who'd attacked her was a Negro. The admission prompted the senator to ask Blanche to explain, then, "her inability to tell the difference between a black man and a white man."

"The room was completely dark," Blanche told him, and added that she "was unable to see the man at all."

It was apparent to everyone—to Oldham, to Knowles, to their fellow Clubbers, and to Blanche—that Karl wanted more, and that he was determined to get it. If the atmosphere in the room had been tense upon his arrival, it was now bristling with apprehensiveness and an edgy defensiveness. This did not deter Karl. He posed the critical question that Blanche had yet to answer in any public statement. Was she now confident as to the identity of the man who had broken into her Okahumpka home on the evening of December 17, 1957?

Blanche replied that yes, she was now confident.

Karl asked her to identify her assailant by name.

Standing next to her, ostensibly supporting her, was the man to whom Blanche had been married for almost a quarter of a century—the successful citrus and melon man, mayor of Leesburg, and Bull Gator of the Quarterback Club, Joe Knowles. Surrounding them both, expectant, was their coterie of long-loyal associates. To speak the truth? Mrs. Joe Knowles really had no choice. She answered the question.

"Jesse Daniels."

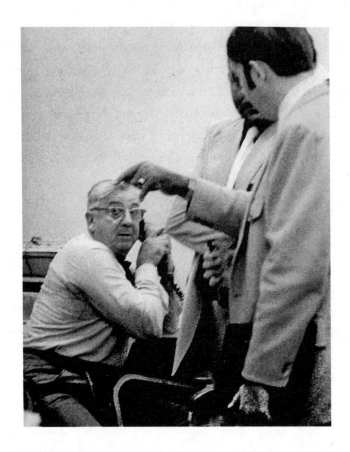

Sheriff Willis McCall being arrested by FDLE agents Al Albright and Rick Hernan

CHAPTER SEVENTEEN

A Newspaper Woman

"I believe the Fain statement may provide the break we have been seeking."

There was hope in the message, from FDLE commissioner William Reed to U.S. attorney John L. Briggs. Yet the hope was tempered by both men's awareness that under Karl's questioning, Blanche had identified her assailant as Jesse Daniels. If she were to give the same testimony before the grand jury, under oath, it would be difficult if not impossible to procure indictments on criminal conspiracy charges. Reed thus suggested, in his letter to Briggs, that it might be worthwhile to propose that "as an investigative tool" Blanche Knowles submit to a polygraph test. "I say this from the standpoint," Reed wrote, "that she appears to be a very strong willed woman and this might afford her a crutch to lean on and thereby excuse her truthful testimony against her husband and the other conspirators." Should Blanche fail a polygraph test, he reasoned, the U.S. attorney might have some leverage to persuade Joe Knowles, who was not a target of the investigation, to cooperate.

On the first day of grand jury proceedings in Jacksonville, Briggs told reporters, "It is fair to assume that any person who knows anything about this case will be called before the grand jury." "Any person" included Willis McCall and Gordon Oldham, deputies James Yates and Leroy Campbell, former attorney general James Kynes, former state senator Frederick Karl, Sam Powell, and the Lake County coon hunter Lloyd Harrison. Mabel Norris Chesley and Blanche Knowles were also called.

Notably absent from the witness list was Earle Fain Jr. But Sam Powell was on it, no doubt in order to provide Briggs with the opportunity to question a close friend of Joe Knowles's about his activities that long-ago morning and thereby to learn, with the witness under oath, if Fain's statements could be substantiated.

As Richard Graham learned from the DOJ attorneys who attended the proceedings, McCall and Oldham had attempted to negotiate for immunity, but the request had been denied, and so they were "sweating it out in the courtroom hallway." (McCall told reporters that he'd never sweated the charges, even for a second. "This has been a political harassment thing from the word go.")

Although testimony and proceedings in federal grand jury cases are sealed, the communications between investigative agencies shed light on the challenges that Briggs and the DOJ were facing. In one such communication, Ed Miller, who as legal counsel for the FDLE attended the proceedings, wrote to U.S. attorney Briggs that some of the witnesses' testimonies "strike me as excellent examples of the very real but incredible problems faced by the citizens of Lake County for many years." One witness, Miller noted, "quite calmly, in my considered opinion, perjured himself for reason that he seemingly has an abiding conviction that he can do so with impunity."

Presumably, Blanche Knowles testified before the federal grand jury, as in her statement to Frederick Karl, that she had initially misidentified

Jesse Daniels as a black man because the room was totally dark. Also, since Earle Fain was never called as a corroborating witness, it seems plausible that Sam Powell, and any other Quarterback Club man called to testify, denied that any conspiratorial conversation had taken place in that Buick on the morning of December 18. Even under oath, the Club men would not break their bond. With no conspirators, there was no conspiracy. As the focus of the investigation had been to prove the conspiracy, not to determine Jesse Daniels's innocence or guilt, DOJ attorneys notified the FDLE that "lack of corroborating evidence to support a conspiracy theory" had prompted them to close the case.

DOJ attorneys also pointed to the problems presented by the statute of limitations in prosecuting a fifteen-year-old criminal conspiracy case. Which raised the question: Had the violation of Jesse Daniels's civil rights occurred upon his indictment in 1958, or had criminal conspiracy defined the case for the entire term of Jesse's institutionalization at Chattahoochee? The question was never legally resolved, and that lack of resolution added another reason to end the inquiry. In the opinion of DOJ Civil Rights Division investigator Carlton Stoiber, the case would "not have been successful and would have detracted limited resources from more current civil rights cases." If still another reason not to pursue the Daniels case further was needed, there was this: Although he was "somewhat embarrassed to confess this non-legal perspective after forty years," Stoiber later recalled, "it could have shifted attention and blame to a black man, with all the negative and potentially violent reactions from the white community in Florida."

With the inquiry ended, Briggs acknowledged, "There are many conflicts that cannot be or have not been resolved. There are many questions still unanswered, which in all probability, may never be."

While the investigation into the Jesse Daniels case did not in the end produce enough clear and decisive testimony to warrant indictments on criminal conspiracy charges, the conclusions of the investigators themselves held little ambiguity. In a letter to Governor Askew, Reed baldly expressed disappointment that the DOJ had decided to close the case. "In spite of the very real legal and practical obstacles inherent in an investigation of a fifteen year old crime," Reed found good reason to take pride in the investigative work of his department's agents and in the co-operative effort of the DOJ's Civil Rights Division. He minced no words: "Although no competent substantial evidence sufficient for criminal prosecution could be adduced at this late date, there is absolutely no doubt in my mind that this crime was committed; there is also no ques-tion in my mind that those persons who perpetrated the offense of send-ing Jesse Daniels to the State Hospital at Chattahoochee for a crime which he did not commit are well aware that we know the extent of their guilt and that any such future actions which might be contemplated by them or their associates will not be tolerated by the State of Florida or the United States." The FDLE report on its investigation, which Reed submitted to Governor Askew on October 16, 1972, concluded, "There has now been collected and documented sufficient data to clearly and positively indicate a continuing and ongoing criminal conspiracy be-tween Gordon Oldham, Willis McCall, James Yates, and others which had as its main object the wrongful incarceration of Jesse Daniels."

Special Master Thomas Woods had decided to delay the Florida Leg-islature's investigation into the Jesse Daniels case until Briggs had com-pleted the grand jury hearings (which had been further delayed by Briggs's being tasked with the "dirty tricks" investigation of President Nixon's political operative Donald Segretti during the Watergate scan-dal). Now that the Daniels inquiry had ended, Woods filed a suit against the U.S. attorney, in which he petitioned for access to the grand jury transcripts on the grounds that they were essential to determine the merits of the Daniels claims bill. The suit came before federal judge Charles R. Scott in Jacksonville. A judge highly regarded by civil rights groups, as President Lyndon Johnson had noted on appointing him to the bench in 1966, Scott was already more than familiar with the names Oldham, McCall, and Yates. It was he who had recently overturned the verdict in the Fruitland Park rape case, citing "reprehensible" prosecutorial misconduct. In a rare decision regarding the disclosure of grand jury testimony, Judge Scott ruled that "the public interest in secrecy is outweighed by the public interest in limited disclosure"; he granted Woods access to the transcripts but put constraints in place so that their content would remain "inaccessible to the general public." In his ruling, Judge Scott declared that the case was "replete with indications that a tragic miscarriage of justice was perpetrated against Jesse Daniels . . . [by] persons cloaked with the awesome authority of the state."

For more than three years, Special Master Thomas Woods had been evaluating all of the evidence that, with the assistance of the FDLE and the FBI, he had accumulated through his legislative hearings, investigations, and interviews. His access now to the federal grand jury transcripts prompted him to interview anew witnesses called or referenced in the conspiracy case—among them Earle Fain Jr., Lloyd Harrison, and Mary Ellen Hawkins—who might have evidence pertinent to the claims case. Woods's charge as special master was to determine whether the state had been "negligent in charging the claimant with the crime of rape." As Governor Askew had requested, Woods had been assiduous.

In his final report, Woods held that the State of Florida "has placed the claimant in an almost impossible position of having to prove his innocence. However, after three years of hearings with this committee and investigation by the Federal Grand Jury, it would appear that the claimant may have done just that." Whereas in a criminal trial, a defendant must be proven guilty beyond reasonable doubt, Woods noted, the standard set for his investigation to prove the defendant's innocence had been more like "by absolute truth"—and "while 'absolute' truth is often unobtainable for mortal beings," in Woods's estimation, "at least 95% of the facts have been discovered in this case." Compelling among those facts for Woods were two details absent from Blanche Knowles's description of her attacker. She detected neither a "skunk smell" on his person nor, more remarkably, an impediment in his speech. Since Jesse "was well known for stuttering it would be reasonable to assume in an excited state of committing a rape," he would have stuttered. Not only did Woods believe Jesse Daniels to be innocent in the rape of Blanche Knowles, but he also found that "the evidence strongly indicates that the actual assailant was, in fact, Sam Wiley Odom." He had come to the conclusion that Odom would not have been able to describe the incident in so much precise detail if he had not been present at the scene.

The evidence Woods had collected unquestionably pointed to a criminal conspiracy. But there was one more discrepancy that had eluded everyone to date. Al Albright, himself a polygraph examiner, had analyzed the results of the polygraph test Bill Donaldson had administered. The test had been based on responses to a mere seven questions that made no specific reference to the crime—Donaldson, as he'd stated, had "no specific evidence about the crime"—so Albright had deemed the results "essentially worthless." Yet on closer examination, not entirely. The "Jesse Daniels" chart, particularly of the "breathing pattern," had clearly indicated to Albright deception on the part of the subject throughout the test. Recalling Donaldson's claim to have tested only black suspects, Albright understood the pattern in a new light. It signified "the fact that the person taking the test was lying about his identity."

That lie had eluded both Donaldson and Margaret Hickman, who had typed and notarized the confession of a black Jesse Daniels; or it had until the revelations at Special Master Woods's legislative hearings on May 31, 1972. The DOJ declared "the most prominent fact indicating a conspiracy to deprive Jesse Daniels of a Constitutional right, is the false confession obtained from a black male purporting to be Jesse Daniels."

The enlistment of that black male by Deputy James Yates and the Lake County Sheriff's Department to accomplish its deception had fooled not only the Tampa polygraph expert and the Leesburg notary but also quite possibly the Okahumpka rape victim herself. In her statement to Gordon Oldham, Blanche affirmed that she had identified the voice of her assailant at the Lake County jail both on a recording and from behind a closed door, when the suspect was "prompted" to recite specific sentences and phrases he had spoken to her on the night of the attack. On that occasion in the Lake County jail, Blanche, in fact, may very well have heard and recognized the voice of the man who'd attacked her back in 1957, but it was not the stuttering, hesitant voice of the real Jesse Daniels. Could the voice that Blanche identified behind that jailhouse door have belonged to Sam Wiley Odom, who was still in custody at the jail at the same time as Jesse Daniels? Could the young black man with "bushy hair" whom Blanche described to Yates as her attacker be the same young black man with "kinky hair" who confessed before Margaret Hickman?

In his appearance before the special master, Deputy Yates had testified that Jesse Daniels had confessed to the rape within "twenty or thirty minutes and upon Donaldson giving him a polygraph test," which, Yates claimed, Jesse had failed on the evening of December 23, 1957. However, the FDLE investigation found that Yates had not brought "Jesse Daniels" before Hickman until December 27. "It seems beyond reasonable belief," the FDLE report stated, "that it would have taken four days to procure a confession from a youth of Jesse Daniels' mental and emotional makeup." Special Master Woods agreed, as the testimony in his hearings had indicated that Jesse was "highly suggestible"—according to one Chattahoochee physician, the boy "could easily have been convinced that he was the King of England."

Even after Sam Wiley Odom, at Yates's bidding, had refused to finger his neighbor Bubba Hawkins for the crime, Yates had not released Odom from his cell in the Lake County jail; nor did Yates free him after Jesse

Daniels had been arrested for the rape. Pearl Daniels learned from Odom's mother, Laura Cope, that her son had confessed to raping Blanche Knowles and, from another source, that Sheriff McCall had told Cope the Knowles rape "would not be put on her son" but on Jesse Daniels. This left Richard Graham to wonder: Had the Lake County Sheriff's Department struck a deal with Odom whereby he, a confessed rapist, would be freed in exchange for his sworn and notarized admission to the crime, and a polygraph exam, not as Sam Wiley Odom but as Jesse Daniels?

Late in December 1957, with the rape of Blanche Knowles now assigned to the more socially acceptable white Jesse Daniels, Sam Wiley Odom was released from the Lake County jail, where Jesse was waiting to be indicted. Willis McCall, who'd originally expected to be "hanging a nigger" for the rape of Blanche Knowles, would have been of no mind to let Odom go unpunished for his admitted violation of a white woman. No less than any member of the Leesburg Quarterback Club, the sheriff had a reputation to uphold. But perhaps Odom's punishment would occur outside the legal system, as suggested by the rumors Pearl Daniels had told Mabel she'd heard in the melon patches of Okahumpka, of KKK plans to "get the Negro" who had raped Blanche Knowles. But that was after Odom had been taken into custody for the rape of Kate Coker. Couldn't McCall, or the Klan, have gotten to Odom sooner?

Had such a plan existed, it had apparently been scuttled, if unwittingly, by Odom himself. It had been only a few months between the time he had at last been released from jail as a suspect in the Knowles rape and the break-ins at the homes of Amelia Rutherford and Opal Howard. It was not until the break-in at the home of Kate Coker, however, that he had been shot and apprehended. Odom had subsequently confessed to the Coker rape, as well as the Rutherford and Howard break-ins; then, after a quick conviction and dispatch to Raiford, he'd waited to burn in the electric chair. It was thus that Sam Wiley Odom had ensured that his punishment for the rape of a white woman would not be delivered by

Willis McCall and the Klansmen of Lake County. That responsibility had fallen instead on the State of Florida.

Reed's report to the governor called attention to the "distinctly hostile" exchange between Sam Wiley Odom and Deputy Yates when the two of them spoke in August 1959 at Raiford, after Odom had told Mabel Norris Reese that he knew all about the Knowles rape. It's not cynical to assume that, with Gordon Oldham overseeing and documenting the interview, not every sentence spoken that evening had necessarily been transcribed by, or even been uttered in the presence of, the stenographer. Plainly, though, Odom believed Yates had betrayed him when, before the pardon board, he had characterized Odom's break-ins as attempts at rape. It seemed just as plain that the condemned youth was struggling, without legal assistance or experience, to use information about the Knowles rape as leverage in gaining the remission of his death sentence and, possibly, as a way to also save the life of Jesse Daniels. Odom's motives aside, Reed had found it "interesting to note" that when Odom had asked the deputy if his account of the post-rape conversation between Blanche and her attacker was corroborated by what Mrs. Knowles had reported, Yates had said, "One of the troubles with the other people is that they don't know what Mrs. Knowles told me."

What is certain is that Yates and Odom had conversations about the rape of Blanche Knowles after Odom was picked up in the initial sweep of the Quarters on December 18, 1957. Odom was, in fact, the last suspect to be released from custody. A year and a half later, with Odom awaiting the governor's signature on his death warrant and Jesse Daniels locked up in a sunless criminal ward at Chattahoochee, Yates had nonetheless felt compelled to drive the hundred miles to Raiford in order to secure from Odom a signed statement declaring that he was not responsible for the rape of Blanche Knowles. For what purpose? And why, after witnessing Odom's execution, could neither Yates nor McCall remember Odom's insistence, in that heated exchange with Yates, that Jesse Daniels was not guilty of the Knowles rape? It simply wasn't plausible. Indeed, as Reed remarked in the FDLE report, "this would appear incredible in light of the continuing notoriety attached to the Daniels case through the years."

Jesse Daniels might have seen freedom a dozen years sooner had Governor LeRoy Collins not depended on Gordon Oldham to investigate Sam Wiley Odom's claims. Oldham's report to the governor had neglected to mention Odom's account of the rapist's claims that he'd been paid five thousand dollars to kill Blanche Knowles, that men were waiting for him outside in a car, or that a baby lay asleep in the victim's bedroom—details that had been purposely kept from the public and that were corroborated in Blanche's own statement. In Reed's estimation, Gordon Oldham had failed to point out to Governor Collins or to anyone else any of "the discrepancies in the Daniels confession and none of the striking similarities in the Odom and Knowles statements."

Instead, Oldham had focused on the presumably false names of the rapist and his accomplices, which Odom had supplied, and, having quickly determined that no such persons existed, had reported to the governor that Odom must have been lying. Commissioner Reed believed that Odom put forward other untruths and deceptions, including what Blanche, in her interview with Gordon Oldham, had alleged her attacker to say—that he had decided not to kill her because "during the war I got all the killing I could want." Aside from being convinced that Jesse Daniels would never have uttered such a phrase, investigators initially assumed Blanche Knowles's attacker might have served in the military. That is, until Lester W. Thompson, a criminal investigator and polygraph expert with the Florida Sheriffs Bureau, advised that the statement "During the war I got all the killing I could want" should not necessarily be taken literally; it was a common expression, he explained, equating the phrase to cultural hyperbole: "That's a typical colored remark. It is the boasting of a Negro." In fact, Blanche's attacker had vowed not to harm her if she agreed not to tell anybody, ever, of the rape—the very same vow Odom had made to Kate Coker.

With his last-minute disavowal of the claim that Jesse Daniels was innocent, Odom seemed to have been grasping at his last straw—his "one straw out of a million"—in a gambit for his life that had played into Oldham's hand. Odom had sought mercy when he'd placed that final phone call to Oldham, in which he'd admitted to his "hoax" and begged for his life. Instead, he'd provided Oldham an advantage, for the state attorney had then recounted to the press how Odom had rendered his eleventh-hour plea and recanted. Mabel Chesley, with a skepticism bred by long familiarity with Lake County politicking, viewed the phone call as Oldham's final trick at Odom's expense, in that Odom had been encouraged to believe that a last-minute apology to the state attorney might stay his execution, just as he'd likely been duped into making a false declaration of his own innocence in the Knowles rape.

Whatever secrets the young man from North Quarters had withheld, however, they had expired with him at the turn of a switch one late-August afternoon in 1959. As Mabel wrote, "The truth died with Odom in that stiff-backed chair in Raiford State Prison."

Evvie Griffin was not the least bit skeptical of the possibility that under the circumstances, McCall and Yates would release a guilty black man to frame an innocent white one for the rape of a socially prominent woman. "Hell, yes . . . that would not surprise me one bit," he said. His former partner Tom Ledford agreed. "Yates did whatever Willis told him to do," he said. "He was one sneaky son of a bitch, and he got away with it every time." Ledford contemplated the scenario for a moment, then added, "They'da had that nigger killed, though."

IT WAS THREE YEARS since Special Master Thomas Woods had begun investigating the Daniels case, and he admitted to reporters that he'd been "very skeptical" of Jesse's innocence until he'd started to examine the evidence. By the end, though, he'd had no doubts. "Buttressed by . . . years of investigation and mountains of evidence," he noted, he and his staff had been "led to the inescapable conclusion that the claimant did not commit the rape for which he was charged." Jesse Daniels "has been victimized by our society," Woods contended, and was "entitled to some compensation to live out the remainder of his years without undue hardship." Having duly considered Richard Graham's proposed compensation of $122,640, he recommended, instead, that the State of Florida award $200,000, nearly twice the amount Graham had filed for. Woods recommended, further, that Pearl be compensated $30,000 for the pain and suffering she had endured. The Claims Committee agreed readily to those amounts. "But, more critical than monetary damages in this particular case," Woods pleaded, "would be the Legislature's declaration of innocence, which would mean more to this young man and his family than great wealth."

Even Richard Graham's opposing counsel, James G. Mahorner, who represented the State of Florida in the Special Master's investigation, agreed with Woods's decision, informing the legislature that in the case of Jesse Daniels, the evidence "substantially supports a finding of innocence." He found the amount of compensation appropriate. Pearl was overwhelmed by the recommendation. "Thank God for delivering Richard Graham," she told reporters. Graham pointed out that Pearl ought to thank God for delivering Mabel Norris Chesley. "It was all because of Mabel. She drove the case from the start and she never gave up on Jesse," Graham asserted, and Ted Husfeld concurred: Mabel's conscience "would not let her accept something she knew in her heart was wrong . . . She wouldn't give up the fight, even though crosses were burned in her yard and every other damn thing was done to intimidate her."

House Bill 2431, when it came finally to the floor of the Florida Senate, indeed declared the innocence of Jesse Daniels and agreed to compensate him for "the losses, damages and injuries he suffered through no fault of his own as the result of wrongful imprisonment." Citing "the mental anguish and deep hurt" he had endured by being wrongfully deprived of his freedom, the bill warranted that the State of Florida "has damaged him in a manner for which he could never be compensated and which could never be erased from his mind." Acknowledged, too, were the roles played by Pearl and Mabel in gaining Jesse's freedom. "But for the unfaltering belief in his innocence by his mother," the bill read, "and but for the exhaustive efforts of a newspaper woman who campaigned throughout the state for justice on behalf of Jesse Daniels, he would have languished in the criminal section of the Florida State Hospital, untried and unheard, in all probability for the remainder of his natural life."

THE APOLLO ERA WAS OVER. By 1974, the skies above the Atlantic coastline had grown mostly quiet. Economic stagnation and a recession had effectively ended America's post–World War II economic boom, rocket launches from Cape Canaveral had dropped off dramatically, and workers had been laid off by the thousands. Up the coast at the Princess Issena, the glory days, and nights, had ended. The resort hotel, now failing, had reduced its staff. Among the casualties was Jesse Daniels.

At thirty-six, Jesse was known around Daytona Beach, as he had been in Okahumpka seventeen years before, as the guy on the bike. Pedaling up and down the streets of the resort town with a cigarette dangling from his lips, he'd go looking for any kind of menial job that might be available. His history limited his prospects. As he later acknowledged to a reporter, "When they find out I was in an insane asylum, they tell me 'we have no work.'" Still, he found part-time employment as a dishwasher, a busboy, and a cook's helper while he waited, and waited, for the Florida Senate to approve his compensation.

While on his bike, Jesse would sometimes spot Mabel in her car. She never failed to honk her horn, and he would wave to Mrs. Reese, as he still called her. He and his mother dined regularly at Mabel's home, where Jesse enjoyed talking with Patricia about the old days when they were growing up in Lake County; they both remembered the good fishing there. "Sometimes," Jesse recalled, a sheepish smile on his face, "Mrs. Reese gave me a beer."

Astride his two-wheeled green cruiser, Jesse would frequently also see Richard Graham. In anticipation of a surge in urban development that never came, Graham had purchased a few small, run-down properties in Daytona Beach, one of which he'd allotted, rent-free, to the Volusia County Mental Health Association. It was there that he and Jesse were most likely to run into each other, as almost daily Jesse cycled by the offices to check in with the social workers—they helped people like him, people who had "problems with living"—and Graham would slip Jesse some cigarette money, to help tide him over.

Progress on the claims bill had apparently stalled in the Florida Senate, while Pearl and Jesse continued "to scrimp and set aside dreams." In the little town of Green Cove Springs, Pearl sold her hand-sewn quilts. She grew bell peppers, pumpkins, sweet potatoes, and cranberries in her small garden, and she kept a storage shed well stocked with canned preserves. "You never know what's going to happen in this world," she said. "Jesse and I might have to hide out some day and we'll have a lot to eat for a long time." Pearl was not being entirely fanciful. After all, she'd known what it was to lose a home to fire, and she continued to live in fear of reprisal for being on the wrong side of Willis McCall. So did Jesse. Whenever he caught sight of a car with Lake County license plates in the vicinity of Pearl's trailer, he'd come bursting inside, his chest heaving, and "furiously strum his guitar" to relieve his anxiety.

Meanwhile, Pearl was having fainting spells and severe headaches. "Oh, there are pains and not enough money to see a good doctor," she'd say, "but there are others who are worse-off." Others less fortunate, at least in Pearl's eyes, lived all around her in Green Cove Springs, and many were the neighbors she'd provide for with her canned preserves. In fact, Pearl had been "classed as 100 percent disabled," according to Mabel, and had been advised to avoid strenuous activity. That did not include fishing, and from time to time Mabel would drive north to St. Augustine and west to Green Cove Springs. She and Pearl would kick off their shoes and, once Mabel had lit up her low-tar cigarette, wade once again with their fishing poles into the shallow waters of the St. Johns River, the way they'd used to do nearly twenty years before, until a devil of a man in a tall white Stetson had run them both out of Lake County.

Reporters besides Mabel had been tracking the case of Jesse Daniels, and on occasion one of them would turn up in Green Cove Springs for a follow-up. With Pearl by his side, Jesse shared his modest dreams with one reporter: "I was looking forward to buying a camper and touring the country. The only wheels we have now is my bicycle. I'd like to buy the land next to our trailer, but we can't afford it. We won't starve, though . . . I've seen worser days. I spent the best years of my life in a place worser than death." The pauses in Jesse's responses grew longer when the reporter asked about Chattahoochee; much of what had happened there Jesse was still unable, or unwilling, to talk about.

Jesse's release from the institution and his exoneration gratified Pearl more than the delay in compensation disturbed her, the reporter noted. "I'm so thankful to God they finally admitted my young one didn't do it," she said. "You can bet there was lots of people that figured Jesse did it, seein' how he was locked up so long." Out of Jesse's earshot, she confided to the reporter that "Jesse really feels the loss. He knows he'll never make up for all those years. He came up to me the other day and said, 'You know momma, it just doesn't seem right that I'm 36 years old. It don't feel right. I don't feel like I should be any older than 19 or 20.'"

"I'm still not adjusted to society," Jesse himself confessed to the reporter. "I thought I'd never get out—that I was put there for the rest of my life. I don't like to think about bein' free because it reminds me of bein' locked up. I can't ever forgive for what's happened. It cost me fourteen long years and destroyed my teenage life . . . I still have nightmares about that place. I dream about it all the time. There wasn't a day went by that I wouldn't have minded dying right on the spot."

In April 1975, about the same time that Pearl was diagnosed with cancer, the Florida House of Representatives finally convened to vote on Special Master Thomas Woods's recommendation that she be compensated thirty thousand dollars for her pain and suffering, as well as for financial losses incurred by her son's incarceration. Representative Richard Langley of Lake County, a longtime friend of both the Knowles family and Gordon Oldham, took the floor to argue against the measure. "We don't owe her anything but our sympathy," he contended, because her son was in fact incompetent and insane. For proof, Langley circulated a copy of Jesse's original commitment order by Judge Truman Futch, which Gordon Oldham had delivered to the legislator hours before. The State of Florida had rightfully committed Jesse Daniels to Chattahoochee, Langley argued, and had otherwise in no way injured Pearl.

Frustrated by this last-minute turn of events, the chairman of the House Claims Committee urged his colleagues in the legislature to rely not on Langley's interpretation of the case but on the Special Master's Report. If they only took the time to read it, he advised, wielding his thick copy, they'd want "to investigate a lot of other people." Then, his voice rising in outrage on behalf of Jesse Daniels, he declared, "There ought to be a bunch of people in jail instead of him!"

There was one woman on the floor, however, who was not taken in by the Lake County contingency on that April afternoon in Tallahassee. Like Mabel Norris Chesley, she'd spent years as a reporter learning the ins and outs of local politics while she searched for truth. Her only political experience had been in serving as a congressional aide in

Washington, D.C., almost two decades earlier. But in 1974, the divorced single mother of three small children made the unorthodox choice to run for public office, even though some of her would-be constituents thought she was "not a good mother" because of her decision.

As the first female and first Republican state legislator to represent Collier County, Mary Ellen Hawkins listened to the chairman read "the most emotional bill we've ever had as far as the legislature goes." She had, of course, a different perspective on the case from that of her colleagues, having been drawn into it by her affair with Joe Knowles nearly twenty years before. After she had been questioned by the FBI as a possible conspirator in a murder-for-hire plot, had her banking and finance records scrutinized, and been called before the federal grand jury, no evidence had ever materialized that linked either her or Joe Knowles to a conspiracy to kill Blanche, and it was entirely possible that the mention of a five-thousand-dollar payment for murdering her was just another of Sam Wiley Odom's untruths. In any event, Hawkins insisted that her vote on the claims bill had nothing to do with her connection to the Daniels case. "I decided based on the merits and facts of the case," she said, and she rejected Langley's arguments and voted to compensate Pearl Eisentrager "for the loss of services and companionship of her only son, Jesse D. Daniels, as a result of his wrongful imprisonment."

Hawkins's vote was not enough to tip the balance. The House, "utterly misled by Langley," Mabel reported, had been "bamboozled" into believing Jesse's commitment legal and proper. After a "short but furious debate," she wrote, Langley had skillfully "maneuvered a 50–37 tactical vote" to kill Pearl's claims bill and deny any chance of compensation.

Jesse Daniels was waiting on the steps outside the Volusia County Mental Health building on U.S. 1 in Daytona Beach. He was wearing the same suit and tie he'd worn upon his release from Chattahoochee five years before. When the Volvo sedan pulled up, he slid into the backseat. Mabel Chesley was at the wheel, and in the passenger seat was Patricia, now thirty-five and an elementary school teacher in Volusia County. Conversation was muted, inconsequential, their minds roaming elsewhere, as they drove the eighty miles west to the funeral. In March 1976, at the age of sixty-one, Pearl had succumbed to her long illness.

She was buried between the graves of Jesse's father, Charles Daniels, and her second husband, Thomas Eisentrager, in Sumter County's Center Hill Cemetery. The funeral went largely unnoticed, but among the few who came to pay their respects were Richard Graham and his wife, Bunnie.

After the service, Mabel offered to drive back to Daytona Beach by way of Okahumpka, it being a day for good-byes. The late-afternoon light was dwindling by the time the sedan crept past the Okahumpka country store where once the boy on the bike had picked up the daily post and listened to Mayo Carlton play tunes on his fiddle. Jesse might not have been good at tallying sums or marking time by a calendar, but he wasn't wanting in memories of people and everyday events, and he remembered how Mayo used to promise he'd keep Jesse safe from those who said or did unkind things. "Don't you worry about one God blessed thing," he'd once told Jesse. "Won't nobody harm one hair on your head."

At the old depot, scrub grass and tiny saplings were sprouting between the station's long-idle tracks. One could barely see the rusted rails where, twenty years before, shirtless black men, their arms strained and torsos lustrous with sweat, stacked watermelons by the thousands onto scores of straw-padded railcars bound for the North. The melon business had since moved farther south, and trains no longer ran through Okahumpka. Jesse remembered when, and why, they had.

Many of the weather-beaten shacks alongside the sandy lanes of South Quarters were deserted, too. Dog pens and chicken coops sat empty on sandspur-patched lots. The hamlet had lost nearly half its population over the past two decades. Okahumpka had become a ghost town.

On Bay Avenue, the Volvo slowed in front of a small Cracker house. The porch wasn't bare in Jesse's memory. He could picture his daddy, set for the day on a rusty metal chair under the tin awning as he waved to his son pedaling away, a fishing pole fixed to his handlebars. Between the porch posts had hung the laundry line where Pearl would hang his rain-soaked clothes after another summer downpour had drenched the boy on his bike. Jesse stared at the old house. He'd not seen it since he'd left it, days before Christmas in 1957, when Deputy Yates had guided him into the backseat of the Plymouth Belvedere he'd parked there, on that sandy spot in front of the house. "I sure miss my mother and father," Jesse said.

Mabel turned the car toward the road that once, at summer's dusk, blazed a rust-colored trail into the torrid blood-orange sun hanging in the western sky over Sumterville. Now paved with asphalt, the county road took the sedan by a stretch of pasture, away from Bugg Spring, to the once grand Knowles home, long fallen into disrepair. The two-story Georgian frame house appeared vacant, and the grounds, overgrown with scrub and weeds, evidenced neglect. Mabel idled there for a moment, allowing Jesse a glance at the big house in the little town he'd called home. The sweet, juicy satsumas Blanche Knowles had placed in his hands . . . the fish he'd sell to Wiley Sam, the black boy he knew from the Quarters . . . whatever thoughts and memories ran through Jesse's mind, he'd kept to himself. His last moments in Okahumpka were his alone.

Mabel put her foot to the gas pedal. The sedan accelerated. The evening darkened on a ghostly reminder of a ruinous mid-December night.

Deputy Noel "Evvie" Griffin, 1957

Epilogue

THE DEBATE OVER HOUSE BILL 2431 to compensate Jesse Daniels for the damages he'd suffered by wrongful imprisonment proved to be just as contentious as the claims bill for his mother. To combat it, Gordon Oldham drove to Tallahassee, registered as a lobbyist, and, in the hallway outside the House chamber, coached Lake County representative Richard Langley on how to argue against the bill.

"When this boy was arrested, he was immediately appointed an attorney," Langley began, and the misstatements grew from there. "Not some twenty-four-year-old kid out of law school, but Sam Buie. Sam Buie had been a state's attorney for twenty-four years. He knew the law as it was in 1957 as good as anybody in this state. He talked with the parents before he represented the boy. They asked him to try to get the boy committed to Chattahoochee. They waived a hearing. He was examined by three medical doctors in Chattahoochee who said he is not competent to stand trial. How can a state's attorney bring him to trial if Chattahoochee has ruled he's not competent to go to trial? So where's the fault of the state's attorney for not bringing him to trial?"

Langley not only falsely summarized the Daniels case; he also mis-characterized the results of the federal investigation. "The grand jury in Jacksonville considered this case not two years ago," Langley asserted, "and found absolutely no fault. No fault whatsoever."

At that point, committee chairman Jerry Melvin, incredulous, inter-rupted. "Mr. Speaker, might I ask Mr. Langley, did you refer to the grand jury report, Mr. Langley, in your remarks?"

"Yes, sir," Langley admitted.

Melvin noted that Special Master Woods had been allowed to review the grand jury report "to determine certain facts but that if he revealed any evidence or any information contained in that special report . . . he would be prosecuted." How then, he asked the representative, "do you know the contents of that grand jury report?"

"Mr. Melvin," Langley responded, "my argument is [the jurors] were given all the information and all the investigatory product and they did not make any finding." Langley, in other words, had not in fact seen the grand jury transcripts. He had simply delivered the message that Old-ham wanted the legislature to receive: that Jesse Daniels belonged in a mental institution, and that no indictments had been brought in the case—although it was far from true that the U.S. attorney had found "no fault."

Immediately, several legislators rose to defend both Woods's investi-gation and his recommendation for compensation. "I'd like to say to you, Mr. Langley, that if I had my choice tomorrow between fourteen years in a regular prison or fourteen years incarcerated with the criminally in-sane, I would take the fourteen years in prison," one declared. Another agreed, and suggested that "the gentlemen who keep insisting that he wasn't imprisoned, he was in a mental institution" should go try out "the monkey cages up in Chattahoochee" for themselves.

Still, Langley persisted, arguing so stridently for a reduction in Jesse's compensation that one of his colleagues asked why he had introduced an amendment to give Jesse anything at all.

"Evidently, some members of this House need to salve their conscience," Langley replied. "I don't. Frankly, I'll vote for zero if you want to put an amendment up there."

Again Chairman Melvin rose, now apoplectic at Langley's repeated misrepresentation of the facts in the Daniels case. He admonished his colleagues to take a deeper look at the actual evidence in the report. "There's a lot more to it," Melvin said. "I ain't gon' give up, I'm gon' keep lookin' . . . Somewhere back there, there's something in that woodpile that I don't like. And all you've got to do is read this testimony word for word and you'll understand that it *is* the state, through the state's offices and the state's representative and other people, that did this person wrong."

Melvin had his supporters, but Langley did, too, including Vince Fechtel Jr., a friend of Joe Knowles and a fellow Lake County representative, who argued that the State of Florida would be setting a "dangerous precedent" if it fiscally compensated claimants like Jesse Daniels who purported they'd "lost their personal liberties." And in the absence of Special Master Woods, who, as a representative lamented, "could have answered very specifically many of the legal questions that have been glazed over and have been obscured" by "these two gentlemen from Lake County," Langley prevailed: The legislature voted to reduce Jesse Daniels's compensation from the recommended $200,000 to $75,000. "I don't believe that $125,000 is a bad day's work, frankly," commented a self-satisfied Langley afterward.

Indisputably, his success owed much to Gordon Oldham, whose influence in the case of Jesse Daniels extended beyond the Florida Legislature—even to the special master himself, who, despite having accumulated copious evidence pointing toward a criminal conspiracy, absolved, however faintly, the state attorney from Lake County. "Nothing in this report shall be considered, in any way, to be derogatory to the handling of this case by the State's Attorney, Gordon Oldham," Woods wrote. "The State's Attorney, working with the facts as given, handled the case in a reasonably prudent manner, and there is no intent by the Special Master to offer criticism of him or his office."

Journalist Martin Dyckman, who knew both men, considered Thomas Woods a man of character and ethics; he noted Woods had learned a sobering lesson a few years before, when a bill he had drafted to compensate families of prisoners killed in a work-camp fire started by inmates had been defeated by Pork Chop legislators because, they said, "had the men not broken the law, they wouldn't have been in prison." Dyckman believed that "experience may well have conditioned Woods to say what he needed to say to get a claims bill passed—always an uphill task in the Florida Legislature." And, he added, "what Woods did *not* need to say on Jesse Daniels's behalf was anything that might further antagonize Oldham, who had powerful friends throughout the political establishment."

Mabel Chesley outright blamed Oldham, first for having "railroaded" Jesse to Chattahoochee and then, with the help of his friends in the House, for sabotaging the claims bill. Richard Graham did not disagree. "If you're looking for . . . a culprit in this whole story, don't put it on Willis McCall," he told a reporter after the legislature's vote. Armed with his law degree, "Oldham is the most dangerous man in Lake County."

UPON HIS RELEASE FROM CHATTAHOOCHEE, Kenneth Donaldson sued Florida State Hospital in federal court for violating his constitutional rights by confining him against his will. "I'm so angry," he said. "I'll go anywhere to talk about this. I'm angry because it took fifteen years out of my life without any legitimate reason. I made hundreds of friends [who] died there. They weren't any crazier than I was." Donaldson won his suit and was awarded $38,000 in damages. The hospital appealed, and the case went ultimately to the U.S. Supreme Court. In *Donaldson v. O'Connor*, a landmark 1975 decision for mental health law, the Court ruled unanimously in his favor, on the grounds that "a State cannot constitutionally confine . . . a nondangerous individual who is capable of surviving safely in freedom by himself or with the help of willing and responsible family members or friends."

Seventy-two-year-old state representative Maxine Baker of Dade County had followed both the Daniels and Donaldson cases closely. As chair of the Subcommittee on Mental Health and Retardation, the matronly Baker, working the corridors of the state capitol in her cat-eye glasses and pearl necklaces, had long been outspoken about not only the conditions at Chattahoochee but also the "dignity and human rights for mentally ill persons." In 1971, she set out to comprehensively revise Florida's century-old mental health laws. To that end, she brought Richard Graham to Tallahassee to draft legislation that would protect the due process and civil rights of citizens admitted into the state's mental health facilities. The Florida Mental Health Act, more commonly known as the Baker Act, went into effect in 1972 and has since served as a model for many states undertaking similar reforms.

Graham himself went on to be elected to the Florida House of Representatives in 1988. In 2002, he was appointed judge of the Seventh Judicial Circuit by Governor Jeb Bush; he retired from the bench in 2012. He lives in Ormond Beach, Florida, with his wife.

Al Albright was later promoted to special agent in charge of the FDLE's Orlando office. Afterward, he taught criminal justice and sociology at Florida Southern College in Lakeland. He died in 2005.

Like Mabel Chesley and Pearl Daniels, Allen Platt and his family were chased from Lake County. "I wouldn't have treated a dog the way they treated me," Platt later said of his experiences there.

Robert Shuler and Jerry Chatman were within hours of being executed by the State of Florida in August 1962 when Evvie Griffin revealed that deputies Yates and Clark had manufactured evidence against them. To this day, Griffin insists that his tracking dogs, Buck and Red, had correctly identified Charlotte Wass's attackers. Yet despite the medical testimony presented at trial, Griffin, like Wass herself, was never convinced a rape had taken place that night in 1960. By ensuring that Shuler and Chatman were tried for rape, a capital crime, McCall and Oldham could seek and win death sentences, which surely would have been carried out had Griffin not gone public with his accusations.

In 1972, the U.S. Supreme Court ruled death penalty statutes unconstitutional, a decision that commuted the sentences of hundreds of death-row inmates nationwide, including Shuler and Chatman. Their convictions were upheld in 1974 when a federal appeals court ruled that Griffin's testimony "could not be believed," and that his and Ledford's accusation of manufactured evidence was "overwhelmingly refuted" by Gordon Oldham and other Lake County officials on the scene. In a familiar refrain, the decision read, "The evidence clears Mr. Oldham of any reflection on his professional integrity." Ultimately, Judge W. Troy Hall resentenced Shuler and Chatman, effectively securing their release, as they had by then spent more than two decades in prison. Their commutation had ensured that Sam Wiley Odom would be the last person in Florida executed for nonhomicidal rape.

From his family's ranch in Eustis, Evvie Griffin continued to speak out about corruption in the Lake County Sheriff's Department, and in the late 1970s, he campaigned actively against Sheriff Malcolm McCall, which earned him a wooden cross and a mock grave on a sandy lot not far from his home. In 1980, Griffin himself ran for the office and unseated McCall; he served two terms as sheriff of Lake County. One of his most vocal critics was Willis McCall, who wrote countless letters to the editors of local newspapers, criticizing the new sheriff's policies, and Griffin himself. "There was no love lost between the two of us," McCall told a reporter. Griffin still lives in the same Eustis house where he was born. He keeps a gun always within reach.

Tom "Buddles" Ledford passed away in Tallahassee in 2016 at the age of eighty-six.

Mary Ellen Hawkins, "the grand dame of Collier County politics," served ten consecutive terms in the Florida House of Representatives. The Republican from Naples was known as a fierce advocate for women's rights, the environment, and the arts. She lives in Tallahassee.

Sheriff Willis McCall died in 1994, and remained adamant until the end that Jesse Daniels had raped Blanche Knowles. "He was just as guilty as he was a moron," McCall said. In 2007, Lake County commissioners voted unanimously to remove the road signs on Willis V. McCall Road, which ran past the former sheriff's home in Umatilla, and to rename it County Road 450A. "He was a son of the old South," his son Douglas said at the time. "He was investigated more times than the Kennedy assassination and they never found anything."

After twenty-nine years at the Lake County Sheriff's Department, James Yates became police chief of Fruitland Park, where he spent another decade in law enforcement. He died in Orlando in 2000.

Gordon Oldham was state attorney for the Fifth Judicial Circuit for twenty-eight years; he retired in 1984. By then he had personally prosecuted more than two hundred capital cases and sent at least fifty defendants to death row in Florida. "I thought it was great," Oldham said months before his death in 1998. "A lot of them thought they'd get life [in prison]. They didn't." In 2000, the Lake County Bar honored Oldham by erecting a granite monument and dedicating an oak tree to his memory; the oak shades a stone bench outside the Lake County Courthouse.

In 1976, twenty-seven years after Virgil Hawkins was denied admission to the University of Florida College of Law because of his race, he returned to Lake County bearing a law degree. After abandoning his fight to enter the University of Florida so that other black students might gain entrance there, he had instead sought a legal education up North. But his application for admission to the Florida Bar was rejected, on the grounds that the New England School of Law was not accredited when he'd graduated in 1964. Hawkins fought the decision, and once again his case reached the Florida Supreme Court. The debate was heated, but the court finally ruled in his favor. After a thirty-year struggle, Virgil Hawkins was sworn in to the Florida Bar as a member in good standing.

"This is the proudest day of my life," he said, indicating that he would return to Leesburg and Okahumpka to represent indigent clients. But, at seventy and in poor health, Hawkins was not equipped to begin a law career, and the pace of high-stakes criminal defense work soon overwhelmed him. One client, convicted of assault and sentenced to prison, argued in his appeal that Hawkins had botched his defense. It was Hawkins's first felony case. The bar agreed with the client. Hawkins was also reprimanded for ethical complaints over client billing and placed on probation. In tears, he resigned from the bar.

In 1988, Hawkins suffered a debilitating stroke. With his wife, Ida, unable to care for him in Leesburg, he languished in an Ocala hospital, where he died penniless. "I know what I did," he said before his death. "I integrated schools in Florida. No one can take that away from me."

A Florida attorney named Harley Herman, one of the few whites to attend Hawkins's funeral, was appalled by the state's treatment of the Okahumpka native. At his own expense, and against considerable resistance from the legal community, Herman began pressing for Hawkins's posthumous reinstatement to the Florida Bar. In October 1988, the Florida Supreme Court complied, noting that Hawkins's heroic struggle for equality under the law should be recognized and apologizing for its "great mistake" in having barred Hawkins in his efforts to gain admission.

Herman ultimately led an effort to persuade the University of Florida

College of Law to name its library for Hawkins. What gratified Herman most, though, was the seven-foot granite monument commemorating Hawkins that was unveiled in 1991, at the edge of the Knowles family property on North Quarters Road. The monument, in effect, marks the gateway to the tiny Florida town where three significant civil rights cases that would reach the U.S. Supreme Court—those regarding Hawkins, the Groveland Boys, and Jesse Daniels—were ignited.

By the 1990s, Lake County was trying to move on from the racially charged past, but by burying discomfiting truths rather than confronting them. No one talked openly about the rape of Blanche Knowles, not even in Leesburg or Okahumpka, and none except those involved in the case knew of any conspiracy, but rumors fueled by the puzzling particulars of the case circulated. "I always heard that Jesse Daniels painted his face black, and Mrs. Knowles scratched him and the paint came off," said Virgil Hawkins's niece, Gloria Hawkins Barton. "That's how they found out it was a white person." The actual sequence of events was much more complicated and bizarre, but to anyone familiar with the county's social constraints, it would not have seemed implausible for the most powerful men of Lake County to falsely incarcerate a vulnerable white boy to protect the reputation of a white woman. "Blacks were seen as less than human, and Blanche was one of life's flowers," said longtime citrus grower William "B.G." Floyd. "People would have looked at her differently. It kept Blanche from being a pariah."

IN THE DECADES after his release from Florida State Hospital, Jesse Delbert Daniels experienced more than his share of life challenges. From the outset he had difficulties holding on to steady employment, and the death of his mother in 1976 radically destabilized his living situation. He never became homeless, but the various residences he subsequently shared with other marginalized Floridians did not afford him adequate structure or supervision, and post-release counseling was virtually non-existent in Florida at that time. The traumatic years he had spent at Chattahoochee without any treatment, and the "bad influences" Pearl Daniels had alluded to in her letters to physicians, had taken their toll, and not surprisingly, behavioral problems arose as he aged. Transfixed by bikini-clad women on Daytona Beach, he was arrested for exposure and lewd and lascivious behavior in 1986, and twice again in 1998.

Reverend David Troxler, the minister at First Christian Church in Daytona Beach, took a protective interest in Jesse. "He'd been exposed to and experienced inappropriate sexual behavior at Chattahoochee," Troxler said. "As time passed he became more out of touch and confused, and he didn't have the mental ability to adjust to behavioral norms and expectations outside that asylum."

Jesse's record would be purged, a judge ruled, if he agreed to move into a facility where he could be more closely supervised. Once the trust fund from his claims bill settlement ran out, he began receiving small disability payments, and was able to move into an assisted living facility in Daytona Beach, where he now lives. He has had no further behavioral incidents. His hearing and vision are failing him, and he recently broke his hip. Now he gets around not on a bicycle but with a walker.

"I've had a pretty good life," Jesse says with a stutter, his face lighting up with a friendly smile. "So far."

BLANCHE BOSANQUET KNOWLES never spent another night at the house in Okahumpka after she left it in the early-morning hours of December 18, 1957. As her mother, Ruth, had long desired, Blanche and Joe resettled in Leesburg, where they built a new house in Palmora Park and rejoined the city's lively social set. Still, Blanche was fearful whenever her husband was away overnight; she insisted that all the windows in their new home be reinforced and that double bolts be installed on all the doors, including a door to the hallway outside the bedrooms. In the months after the attack, she often awoke in a panic, convinced she'd heard someone or something outside the house, especially when Joe was not at home. Immediately, she'd call the police, and with flashlight in hand and her sleepy children in her arms, she'd huddle in the darkness until help arrived. Once, she reported seeing a man with a flashlight approaching her home in the middle of the night. When the Leesburg Police Department investigated, they discovered bottles of fresh milk in the box by the door—the dairy man had delivered. As the years passed, police responded to her panicked, late-night phone calls more with patience than with alarm.

Blanche's daughter, Mary—the baby in the room on the night of her mother's rape—spent two years at a local community college before she decided to finish her schooling at the University of Florida in Gainesville. She did not make the move alone. Nearly thirty years after graduating from Florida State College for Women, Blanche returned to school, to pursue a master's degree in special education. She and Mary roomed together in the summers. "She had a heavier course load than me," Mary recalled, "and we got along just fine." Blanche resumed her Leesburg teaching job in the fall, and continued to make the weekly seventy-plus-mile trip to Gainesville to attend night classes at the university.

When she'd completed her degree, Blanche devoted herself to working with the mentally disabled students at Leesburg High School; she taught young men and women like Jesse Daniels in the classroom and helped them prepare for useful lives outside by assisting them in practical matters like job applications, driver's licenses, and personal finances. The new focus of her work wasn't coincidental, according to her son Steve. "There's more than one victim in this story," he said.

A few years after Blanche and Joe celebrated their twenty-fifth wedding anniversary, Joe Knowles decided to throw his hat into the ring and run for the House of Representatives. The Leesburg Quarterback Club rallied around its founder, providing endorsements for billboards and newspaper ads. "Rarely do men of the caliber, character, and ability of Joe Knowles seek public office," Sam Powell declared. "Joe Knowles will give us honest, efficient, and effective representation," Gordon Oldham promised. Voters evidently agreed. Joe breezed to victory in the 1976 Democratic primary, but he lost the general election by a narrow margin to his Republican opponent—none other than Vince Fechtel Jr., who had joined Richard Langley in arguing against compensating Jesse Daniels. Joe served for a number of years more on the city commission and as mayor of Leesburg, and Blanche dutifully played the politician's wife, standing by his side at ribbon cuttings, donning a visor and a campaign T-shirt to hand out flyers, and attending balls and country club events. The Leesburg Watermelon Festival had largely passed into history after the Freeze of 1957, however, and the Knowles Trophy, once awarded to the grower of the season's largest melon, had been gathering dust in Joe's office. Nor did the mayor's wife, or any wife, any longer meet her husband at the train depot when the Quarterback Club returned from its annual autumn jaunt, as the Seaboard Coast Line had stopped routing trains through Leesburg. The Quarterback Club now chartered flights for its yearly trips to Florida Gator football games, and the club-car revelry that an aging generation of Lake County princes had enjoyed was relegated to memory.

In 2006, after more than half a century of marriage, Blanche laid her husband to rest. She herself passed away in Leesburg in 2012, and silenced at last were the ugly whispers in the dark ("I was paid five thousand dollars to kill you . . . Wouldn't you like to know who paid me that?") that had long haunted her memory.

Mabel Norris Chesley retired from the *Daytona Beach News-Journal* in 1977. She spent her remaining years in Volusia County, fishing and reading until her vision and her health began to fail. She died of cancer in 1995. Despite her award-winning coverage of the St. Augustine Movement in 1964, she always considered her reporting in Lake County on the Jesse Daniels case, as well as the Platt and Groveland cases, to be her most important work. "Those were the three really big stories I was involved in," she said. "And eventually, they all worked out for the best."

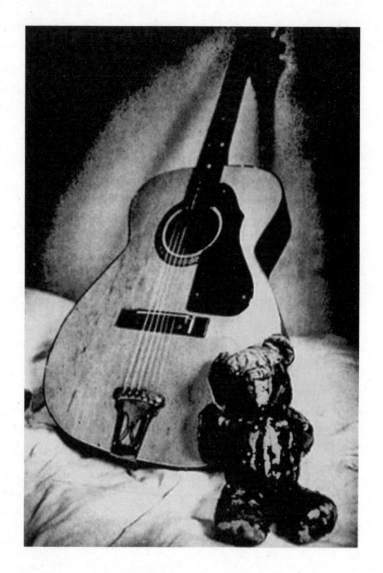

Jesse's guitar and teddy bear

ACKNOWLEDGMENTS

I am grateful to everyone who generously contributed to this project over the years, and none more so than Jesse Daniels, who patiently sat with me on several occasions, tolerated my countless questions, and entrusted me with his story. Jesse's caretaker, the Reverend David Troxler of First Christian Church in Daytona Beach, graciously arranged my meetings with Jesse and facilitated my Freedom of Information Act requests to the FBI for Jesse's personal files and reports. David was a godsend, and Jesse is fortunate to have him in his life. I am eternally thankful to Richard Graham and his wife, Bunnie, who welcomed me into their home and met with me many times for interviews and conversations. Richard was always in reach when I needed him (frequently) to guide me through the complexities of Jesse's legal journey, and this book is infinitely better because of him.

The book never would have been written had Evvie Griffin not brought Jesse's story to my attention when I visited Groveland in 2012. Since then, I've met with Evvie dozens of times—usually before sunrise, over biscuits and gravy, at the Mason Jar in Umatilla. There, Evvie ceremoniously gave up his seat at the head of table 13—the same seat where Sheriff Willis McCall used to hold court—and we would talk for hours. He toured me around Lake County in his pickup truck, and he introduced me to insightful people, including his former partner, the late Tom Ledford. Evvie also gave me correspondence, photographs, reports, and other documents that were indispensable over the course of my research. I am deeply grateful for his friendship and trust.

My trips to see Priscilla Newell in Connecticut were invaluable for understanding Leesburg and Fruitland Park from her perspective. Priscilla guided me with grace, wisdom, and candor, and I'm proud to consider her a new friend. I am eternally thankful to other family members as well. Bud Bosanquet and his wife, Janine, welcomed me into their home in St. Louis, where they shared stories, answered questions, and shined light on the life of Blanche Bosanquet Knowles, and on growing up at Fair Oaks. Bob Gilchrist was also extremely informative and helpful.

I would like to express my gratitude to the Knowles family—David, Steve, and Mary Elizabeth, the children of Joe and Blanche Knowles—who agreed to talk with me and who shared memories relating to a painful part of the family's past. And Mary Ellen Hawkins was kind enough to speak candidly with me about her involvement in this case.

Cindy Chesley and her mother, the late Patricia Chesley, were supportive from the start of my work on this book, describing to me Mabel Norris Chesley's life and career in both Mount Dora and Daytona Beach. I will never forget a conversation with Cindy, midway though the project, when she casually said, "Oh, I found a box in Mom's attic. Seems to be Mabel's old newspaper files."

Rick Hernan, the former FDLE agent, contacted me out of the blue to tell me he had read *Devil in the Grove* and wanted me to know that in 1972, he and his partner, Al Albright, arrested Willis McCall. I'm most grateful for all of Rick's assistance in the preparation of this book. Glorianne Fahs at the Leesburg Heritage Society was also particularly informative, granting me access to whatever I needed and helping track down people and documents. Legendary Lake County reporter and columnist Lauren Ritchie of the *Orlando Sentinel* was essential to my research, and I'm always happy when she shares with me her vast Lake County knowledge over a bottle of wine. Martin Dyckman, the great political writer, reporter, and columnist, was generous with his time throughout the research and writing of this book. And whenever I had a question about the Florida Supreme Court, it was reassuring to know that I could count on Justice James E. C. Perry for fast and precise answers.

Over the course of the past eight years, I've spoken to hundreds of people in Lake County and beyond who were most generous and helpful. I could never list them all, but among them, I'm thankful to Tom Ledford, Mardie White, Donna Bott, Anne Pattillo Kail, Mary Alice Herlong Pattillo, Chops Hancock, Jerry Melvin, Hyatt Brown, Ann Dupee, Wayne Campbell, Robert Yates, David Bishop, and Sally J. Ling. In Okahumpka, I'm grateful to Gloria Hawkins Barton, Joseph Branham, Carlton "Red" Fussell, Carolyn Waller, and Lorenzo Coffee; and in Leesburg, Gordon Oldham III, Billy Bob Polk, Rudolph Berry, and Larry King.

I relied heavily on the expertise of journalists, authors, librarians, and historians, including Lucy Morgan, Diane Roberts, Rachel Swarns, Janny Scott, Betsy West, Morris Kennedy, Craig Pittman, Dr. Eugene Huskey, Skip Horack, Pete Gallagher, Lisa Lindquist Dorr, Susan Carol McCarthy, Robert Bowie, Deborah Shafer, Kathy Kelly, and Mark Lane. Among the attorneys who guided me were Harley Herman, Barbara Peterson, Judge Emerson R. Thompson Jr., Mike Glazer, Mark Caramanica, Sandra Baron, Ira Feinberg, Joel Motley, Carlton Stoiber, Ben Krage, Jim Purdy, Christina Swarns, Tom Palermo, John Q. Barrett, Jimmy Crawford, and Lawrence T. King.

This book benefited from a group of bright researchers whose talents, and company along the way, were always inspiring. Thanks to Matthew Boylan, Lindsay McGrath, Jaclyn Dwyer, Matthew Plunkett, Hannah Kaplan, Clay Daniel, Anna Llewellyn, Lane Turkel, Eleanor Roy, David Cohea, Jaime Coyne, Ebony Nichols, Amanda Hurley, Allie Conti, Charles Vojta, Kathryn Adams, Dusty Matthews, and my late mother, Dorothy King, who loved a good crime story and was as research-obsessed as her son. Her enthusiasm for this project continually spurred me on.

I asked a lot of Karen Abbott, Emma Garman, Scott Smallwood, Greg Diskant, and Samantha Thompson LoCoco, who looked over an early draft of the book, and I'm ever grateful to them for helping me see things more clearly and offering invaluable advice and encouragement. The indefatigable Jim Wohl read several drafts, and his guidance was extraordinarily helpful to me throughout this project. And once again, my longtime friend Joe Hamilla and his wife, Cheryl, provided countless nights of hospitality and friendship on my Florida trips, as did my good friend Tom Schmidt. A special thanks to Elizabeth Prats, Bev Aoki, and Samantha Thompson LoCoco for everything they've done to keep me organized and in the right places.

I couldn't be more fortunate to be a part of Team Riverhead, beginning with my genius editor, Rebecca Saletan, who was handed a complicated and unwieldy manuscript and somehow managed to bring it under control. I'll be forever grateful for her diligence and wisdom, and I'm honored to be working with Geoff Kloske, Karen Mayer, Elizabeth Hohenadel, Glory Anne Plata, Michelle Koufopoulos, Anna Jardine, Grace Han, Jynne Dilling, and everyone else at Riverhead.

This is the third time I've had the pleasure of working with the inimitable Peter Skutches, whose contributions to this book are simply immeasurable. Thank you, Peter.

And my agent and friend Farley Chase has been with me from the beginning. Wise beyond his years, he's been a steady source of encouragement and sage advice, and I'm grateful to have him in my corner.

Finally, my wife, Lorna, and daughters, Maddie and Liv, had to put up with another five years of dinner table stories about Lake County history. I'm not sure how they survived, but I love them deeply, and I'm glad we all made it through.

NOTES

This book is based extensively on primary sources and unpublished materials, including thousands of pages of court documents and transcripts, hospital records, legislative records, and testimony. For all this I am indebted to the State Archives of Florida in Tallahassee, as well as the Lake County Clerk of the Circuit Court Records in Tavares. In addition, I relied on files from the Florida Department of Law Enforcement and the Federal Bureau of Investigation, as well as Department of Justice memos and reports located at the National Archives and Records Administration in College Park, Maryland, many of which were acquired through the Freedom of Information Act.

I also benefited from access to the personal files of Mabel Norris Chesley, courtesy of Mabel's daughter, Patricia. The most important of these were Mabel's files on the Jesse Daniels case, which included correspondence, unpublished articles, and original drafts of her stories for the *Mount Dora Topic*, of which nearly the entire year 1958 is missing from all collections of the paper's microfilmed archives. I also relied on Mabel's reporting, columns, and editorials in the *Daytona Beach News-Journal*, as well as reporting and feature stories by journalists Martin Dyckman and Pete Gallagher.

I conducted dozens of interviews for this book and relied most heavily on conversations with Richard Graham and Jesse Daniels, as well as interviews with members of the Knowles, Bosanquet, Newell, and Gilchrist families. Also invaluable to me were the many conversations I had with former deputy and eventual Lake County sheriff Evvie Griffin, former FDLE agent Rick Hernan, and Lake County deputy Tom Ledford.

I gleaned much of the historical context for this book from my many visits to the Leesburg Heritage Society, where Glorianne Fahs kindly granted me unlimited access to the extensive archives and photo collection. Historian Donna Bott generously shared a great deal of her research on the Chetwynd area of Fruitland Park, as well as her extensive files on the Bosanquet family history. Also extraordinarily helpful to my understanding of the relevant Florida history were D. R. S. Bott's *The Chetwynd Chronicles: The British Colony of Lake County, Florida, 1882–1902*; Dan R. Warren's *If It Takes All Summer: Martin Luther King, the KKK, and States' Rights in St. Augustine, 1964*; Gary Mormino's *Land of Sunshine, State of Dreams: A Social History of Modern Florida*; Frederick B. Karl's *The 57 Club: My Four Decades in Florida Politics*; Robert W. Saunders Sr.'s *Bridging the Gap: Continuing the Florida NAACP Legacy of Harry T. Moore*; John McPhee's *Oranges*; Lisa Lindquist Dorr's *White Women, Rape, and the Power of Race in Virginia, 1900–1960*; Danielle L. McGuire's *At the Dark End of the Street: Black Women, Rape, and Resistance—a New History of the Civil Rights Movement from Rosa Parks to the Rise of Black Power*; and Robert Bowie's *A Roast for Coach Dan Spear*. Sally J. Ling's *Out of Mind, Out of Sight: A Revealing History of the Florida State Hospital at Chattahoochee and Mental Health Care in Florida* and Kenneth Donaldson's *Insanity Inside Out: The Personal Story Behind the Landmark Supreme Court Decision* were also indispensable sources.

ABBREVIATIONS

NARA-FBI: Department of Justice Records Group 65, Federal Bureau of Investigation/DOJ Reports 44-HQ-11050, 44-HQ-13930, DOJ 144-18-855, National Archives and Records Administration, College Park, Maryland

FSH-SAF: Florida State Hospital, State Archives of Florida, Tallahassee

LEG-SAF: Florida Legislature Committee Records, Florida Department of State, State Archives of Florida, Tallahassee

FDLE: Florida Department of Law Enforcement Records, Tallahassee

LHM: Leesburg Heritage Society and Historical Museum, Leesburg, Florida

LOC: Library of Congress, Washington, D.C.

MNC: Mabel Norris Chesley files

FHWP: Franklin H. Williams Papers, Schomburg Center for Research in Black Culture, The New York Public Library

LCC: Circuit Court of the Fifth Judicial Circuit of the State of Florida for Lake County, Lake County Clerk of the Circuit Court Records

LDF: NAACP Legal Defense and Educational Fund Files, Library of Congress, Washington, D.C.

Unless noted otherwise, all interviews were with the author.

CHAPTER ONE. A KILLING FREEZE

3 **In Okahumpka he was known:** My descriptions of daily life in Okahumpka are drawn primarily from interviews with Jesse Daniels, as well as Okahumpka residents Carlton "Red" Fussell, Carolyn Waller, and Joseph Branham.

4 **He was "not educable":** FSH-SAF.

4 **She'd remind him:** Interview, Jesse Daniels.

4 **Joe Knowles sometimes hired Jesse:** NARA-FBI.

4 **The fifty-pound Garrisons:** Interviews, Noel Griffin Jr., Lawrence King, Jesse Daniels.

5 **His meager monthly welfare benefits:** FSH-SAF; U.S. Census; Florida State Census.

5 **Jesse's mother, Pearl:** FSH-SAF.

5 **The second attack, at age ten:** Ibid.

6 **the institution adhered to a classification system:** Steven Noll, "Care and Control of the Feeble-Minded: Florida Farm Colony, 1920–1945," *The Florida Historical Quarterly* 69, no. 1 (Jul. 1990), pp. 57–80.

6 **By 1956, however, the Colony:** FSH-SAF.

6 **The Danielses "kept to themselves":** Interview, Carolyn Waller.

6 **Another neighbor, Carlton "Red" Fussell:** Interview, Carlton "Red" Fussell.

7 **"Don't let the bear get you":** Interview, Jesse Daniels.

7 **One long-range missile:** *Logansport Press* (Ind.), Nov. 1, 1957.

7 **"The character of east central Florida":** *New York Times*, Dec. 22, 1957.

8 **Market centers were mushrooming:** Glenn Rabac, *The City of Cocoa Beach: The First Sixty Years* (Cocoa Beach, FL: Apollo Books, 1986).

8 **Scores upon scores:** *Jackson Clarion-Ledger* (Miss.), Dec. 22, 1957.

8 **"the grip of a giant fist"; "some of the old-line":** *New York Times*, Dec. 22, 1957.

8 **Lake County alone took in:** *Orlando Sentinel*, Jan. 20, 1957.

8 **It was a time and place:** *Orlando Sentinel*, Mar. 30, 2014.

9 **The flight, broadcast live:** Michael D'Antonio, *A Ball, a Dog, and a Monkey: 1957—The Space Race Begins* (New York: Simon & Schuster, 2007).

10 **Ice, as every Florida grove owner:** Dorota Z. Haman, ed., *Frost and Freeze Protection Workshop Manual*, sponsored by the University of Florida Southwest Florida Management District, and Alafia River Board, Hillsborough River Board, and Manasota Basin Board. Also Lawrence R. Parsons, "Cold Protection by Irrigation: Dew Point and Humidity Terminology," University of Florida, Florida Cooperative Extension Service Fact Sheet HS-76, Nov. 1995 (included in Haman, *Frost and Freeze Protection Workshop Manual*).

10 **"Hard freeze in North and Central Districts":** *Orlando Sentinel*, Dec. 11, 1957.

10 **"The freeze killed the whole crop":** *St. Petersburg Times*, Dec. 13, 1957.

10 **"It was hard work":** Interview, Jesse Daniels.

11 **The temperature dropped:** *Fort Myers News-Press*, Dec. 14, 1957.

11 **The state had not imposed:** Interviews, Lawrence King, David Knowles.

12 **"I do not know what we can do":** *Pensacola News Journal*, Dec. 18, 1957.

12 **Late in the evening of the 17th:** This scene is drawn from interviews with Noel Griffin Jr.

13 **Jesse Daniels woke:** This scene is drawn from drafts of stories Mabel Norris Reese (Chesley) wrote in 1958, MNC, and one published in *Daytona Beach Evening News*, Oct. 22, 1958.

14 **Once Patricia had been seen off:** *Mount Dora Topic*, Aug. 7, 1957.

15 **But in the camps:** *Mount Dora Topic*, Dec. 18, 1957.

16 **Mabel was moved:** Ibid.

16 **"They woke me up":** *Florida Today*, Oct. 13, 1974.

16 **"They took in thirty-three":** *Daytona Beach Evening News*, Oct. 22, 1958.

17 **"A restlessness began to run":** Ibid.

17 **Ethel Cope, a fifty-three-year-old maid:** Interview, Carolyn Waller.

17 **He persuaded McCall:** NARA-FBI.

CHAPTER TWO. REAL SUNSHINE

19 **In the minutes:** This scene is drawn from the transcript of Blanche Knowles's otherwise undated interview with Gordon Oldham, from early 1958, which he sent to doctors at Chattahoochee, "in order to clear up all possible facts." In his cover letter, dated March 3, 1958, he made it clear he wanted the transcript to be "kept completely confidential."

20 **She told him she had been "raped":** *Florida Today*, Oct. 13, 1974.

20 **After leaving her bedroom:** Blanche Knowles statement to Oldham.

20 **In light of the information taken from the victim:** *Tampa Tribune*, Dec. 29, 1957.

20 **The piece of evidence:** NARA-FBI.

20 **As more deputies appeared:** Interview, Noel Griffin Jr.

20 **Upon observing that Blanche:** FSH-SAF.

21 **He also observed "no bruising":** Ibid.

21 **Behind them hulks Joe:** LHM.

21 **Outside, on the dozens of acres:** Interview, Steve Knowles.

21 **On the morning of December 18:** Ibid.

21 **By then she had been informed:** NARA-FBI.

22 **The eldest of five children:** D. R. S. Bott, *The Chetwynd Chronicles: The British Colony of Lake County, Florida, 1882–1902* (Clowder Publishing, 2013).

22 **The Bosanquets traced their pedigree:** Ivan Ford, *Coming Home: The History of Holy Trinity Episcopal Church, Fruitland Park, FL* (Fruitland Park, FL: Chetwynd Church Press, 2013).

22 **They dedicated twenty acres:** Bott. Also Ford.

22 **In her novel:** Marjorie Kinnan Rawlings, *Golden Apples* (New York: Macmillan, 1935).

23 **"The young men who came here":** Alfred Bosanquet, "The English Colony in Fruitland Park," speech written in the early 1960s, Bosanquet family records, LHM.

23 **They worked and studied hard:** Bosanquet.

23 **However their courtship started:** Bott. Also *Orlando Sentinel*, Dec. 25, 2002.

23 **Louis proved to be a "horticulturist extraordinaire":** Bott.

24 **He would in time hybridize:** Ford.

24 **The heat could be relentless:** Ibid.

24 **"This is a nether region":** Quoted ibid.

24 **An unseasonably warm, wet January:** Ford.

24 **"The disaster is overwhelming":** Draft of story by Lee King, Sept. 11, 2000. Also Diary of C. H. Longstreet, quoted in Gary McKechnie and Nancy Howell, *A Brief History of Mount Dora, Florida* (Charleston, SC: The History Press, 2016).

25 **With no government or state aid:** Stetson Kennedy, "'Root, Hog or Die' Days," in *A Florida Treasure Hunt*, Florida Folklife from the WPA Collections, 1937 to 1942, Library of Congress.

25 **The Bosanquets stayed on:** Bott. Also Ford.

25 **Virtually overnight Chetwynd became:** Bott. Also Ford.

26 **"An English gentleman always has a garden":** Interview, Bud Bosanquet.

26 **Dozens of tables would be:** Ford.

26 **"Who's going to kindergarten":** Interview, Bud Bosanquet.

26 **She was remembered:** Bosanquet family records, LHM.

26 **But the prosperity did not last:** Interview, Bud Bosanquet.

27 **The boys helped with deliveries:** Ibid.

27 **"Swear to secrecy":** Interview by Jacqueline Ecoff, Blanche Bosamquet [*sic*] Knowles Collection (AFC/2001/001/07096), Veterans History Project, American Folklife Center, LOC.

27 **Then she'd begin to climb:** Interview, Bud Bosanquet.

27 **"I was honored":** Ecoff interview, Veterans History Project, LOC.

28 **"There was one short serviceman":** Ibid.

28 **The girls crept up to the edge:** Interview, Priscilla Newell.

29 **Blanche was amused:** Ecoff interview, Veterans History Project, LOC.

29 **There he was, reclining:** "United Nations: My War Effort": Photo album of Blanche Bosanquet, Bosanquet Collection, courtesy Donna Bott.

30 **"Hello, Darling, wish we could spend":** Bosanquet Collection; Bott.

30 **In a letter Ted had written:** Bennett Family Records, courtesy David Bishop.

30 **According to Bud; The news of Ted's death:** Interview, Bud Bosanquet.

30 **When she came back home:** Interviews, Priscilla Newell, Bud Bosanquet; Ecoff interview, Veterans History Project, LOC.

31 **It was Ruth who took notice:** Interview, Bud Bosanquet.

31 **"We may starve to death":** Interview, Steve Knowles.

32 **It was Blanche, home from college:** Interview, Bud Bosanquet.

32 **"He wanted to play":** Ibid.

33 **They set a wedding date:** Interview, Priscilla Newell.

33 **They took a driving tour:** Undated clipping, *Leesburg Leader*, [Jul. 1948], personal collection of Bud Bosanquet.

34 **"What a trip":** *Orlando Sentinel*, Oct. 8, 1953.

34 **"She didn't like":** Interview, Bud Bosanquet.

34 **"Everybody knew Joe had affairs":** Interview, Priscilla Newell.

35 **Once the children came:** Interview, Steve Knowles.

35 **Blanche assured her mother:** Interview, Bud Bosanquet.

36 **Jesse Daniels was one of nearly sixty thousand people:** Interview, Jesse Daniels.

36 **During it, Joe starred:** *Leesburg Daily Commercial*, Mar. 12, 1957.

36 **"Joe taught me how to kiss":** Interview, Cynthia Schumacher.

36 **The centennial also included:** *St. Petersburg Times*, Feb. 21, 1957. Also *Leesburg Daily Commercial*, Feb. 24, 1957.

37 **State senator J. A. "Tar" Boyd:** *Leesburg Daily Commercial*, Jan. 30, 1957.

37 **Kourt proceedings culminated:** *Leesburg Daily Commercial*, Feb. 25, 1957.

37 **A tongue-in-cheek letter:** Undated clipping, *Leesburg Daily Commercial*, [1957], LHM.

37 **Alabama-born-and-bred, Hawkins had moved:** Interview, Mary Ellen Hawkins.

38 **She had apparently also:** Ibid.

38 **She'd decided to relocate:** Interview, Mary Ellen Hawkins. Also NARA-FBI.

38 **The couple went to dinner; The couple said hasty good-byes:** NARA-FBI.

CHAPTER THREE. SMOKED IRISHMAN

41 **And hadn't Mrs. Knowles been seen:** Pearl Daniels to Mabel Norris Reese, undated, MNC.

41 **"I thought it was a bit of heaven":** *St. Petersburg Times*, May 20, 1956.

42 **She diligently reported:** Undated clipping, *Mount Dora Topic*, LHM.

42 **In his opinion, Justice Robert Jackson:** *Shepherd v. Florida*, 341 U.S. 50 (1951).

43 **What Irvin described:** Gilbert King, *Devil in the Grove: Thurgood Marshall, the Groveland Boys, and the Dawn of a New America* (New York: HarperCollins, 2012).

43 **Judge Futch, who was known:** Ibid.

43 **When Justice Jackson:** Interview, Mabel Norris Chesley, FHWP.

44 **"He hated me from then on":** Ibid.

44 **Indeed, McCall took to ridiculing her:** NARA-FBI.

44 **In August, she again took:** *St. Petersburg Times*, Nov. 28, 1954.

44 **Not long after, one night:** *Mount Dora Topic*, Sept. 16, 1954.

45 **At first she thought:** Chesley interview, FHWP.

45 **Later, unable to sleep . . . "See why I shall not":** *Mount Dora Topic*, Sept. 16, 1954.

45 **Mabel's story, with Patricia's photo:** Ibid.

45 **On September 16, Mabel's weekly column:** Ibid. Also FHWP.

46 **The killing of the family pet:** *Mount Dora Topic*, Oct. 28, 1954.

46 **That did not stop McCall:** Undated clipping, *Mount Dora Topic*, MNC.

46 **"We had telephone calls":** FHWP.

46 **One night she and Paul:** Interview, Patricia Chesley.

47 **At a recent rally:** Brian J. Daugherity and Charles C. Bolton, eds., *With All Deliberate Speed: Implementing Brown v. Board of Education* (Fayetteville: University of Arkansas Press, 2008).

47 **At another rally:** Robert L. Hayman Jr. and Leland Ware, eds., *Choosing Equality: Essays and Narratives on the Desegregation Experience* (University Park: Pennsylvania State University Press, 2009).

47 **"By whatever name it is called":** *Mount Dora Topic*, Dec. 9, 1954.

47 **The sheriff, who had sponsored:** *Philadelphia Tribune*, Jul. 31, 1954.

47 **However, Bowles, who had boasted:** *Jet*, Sept. 9, 1954.

48 **"I will get even":** *Washington Post*, Nov. 28, 1954.

48 **She visited Allen and Laura Platt:** Interview, Tom Ledford.

48 **They explained to Mabel:** *Chicago Defender*, Dec. 25, 1954.

48 **Mabel spoke with the Platt children:** *Mount Dora Topic*, Nov. 25, 1954.

48 **"Denzell favors a nigger":** FHWP. Also *Time*, Dec. 13, 1954.

48 **"He like to gave my wife a heart attack":** *St. Petersburg Times*, Nov. 28, 1954.

48 **Once McCall had dispensed:** *Time*, Dec. 13, 1954.

49 **"If you are a parent":** *Mount Dora Topic*, Nov. 25, 1954.

49 **"I'm protecting this town":** *Daytona Beach Morning Journal*, Jun. 13, 1972.

49 **"Well, you're missing a lot of sleep":** FHWP.

49 **"There must have been":** *Ebony*, April 1955.

49 **And Mabel continued:** *Mount Dora Topic*, Nov. 25, 1954.

49 **Mabel tried to keep:** Mabel Norris Reese, "Crusades Are Not Cheaper by the Dozen," in *Main Street Militants: An Anthology from* Grassroots Editor, ed. Howard Rusk Long (Carbondale: Southern Illinois University Press, 1977).

49 **"I know what company":** *Mount Dora Topic*, Dec. 9, 1954.

50 **"Don't you dare go out":** Ibid. Also *Mount Dora Topic*, Dec. 9, 1954.

50 **_Time_'s story focused as much on the feud:** *Time*, Dec. 13, 1954.

50 **"We would like to correct that statement":** *Mount Dora Topic*, Dec. 16, 1954.

51 **Mardie Bardwell had been present:** Interview, Mardie White.

51 "The Constitution says": *Mount Dora Topic*, Dec. 23, 1954.

51 "We weren't supposed to tell" . . . Finally the girl relented: Interview, Mardie White.

52 "The letter was about due process": Ibid.

52 She later defended her decision: *Mount Dora Topic*, Dec. 23, 1954.

52 Some, like June Bowie's father: Interview, June Bowie.

52 "People canceled gas business" . . . A chalk line appeared: Interview, Mardie White.

53 "My wife and I and our children": *Mount Dora Topic*, Dec. 23, 1954.

53 "I have no other course": *Mount Dora Topic*, Jan. 6, 1955.

53 "You are getting a look": *St. Petersburg Times*, Oct. 10, 1955.

53 The school board countered: FHWP.

54 The Platts' landlady: *Orlando Sentinel*, Feb. 10, 1991.

54 Admission of the Platt children: Undated clipping, *Mount Dora Topic*, MNC.

54 "This school will": Pete Gallagher, "The End of an Era," *Florida Today*, Dec. 31, 1972.

54 In October 1955 . . . "Much as I hate it": *St. Petersburg Times*, Oct. 19, 1955.

55 "I swore I would never": *Mount Dora Topic*, Oct. 19, 1955.

55 McCall was as livid: Isaac M. Flores, *Justice Gone Wrong: A Sheriff's Power of Fear* (New York and Bloomington, IN: iUniverse, 2009).

55 Hesitant though McCall was: *Mount Dora Topic*, Nov. 3, 1955.

56 To the reporters on the scene: *Evening Independent* (St. Petersburg), Dec. 14, 1962. Also *Mount Dora Topic*, Nov. 17, 1955.

56 "I've got more justice": *St. Petersburg Times*, Nov. 13, 1955.

56 "My boy, Denzell, is due": *Mount Dora Topic*, Nov. 17, 1955.

57 "I saw the suffering": *Orlando Sentinel*, Feb. 10, 1991.

57 The riots charged the racial atmosphere: Helen L. Jacobstein, *The Segregation Factor in the Florida Democratic Gubernatorial Primary of 1956* (Gainesville: University of Florida Press, 1972).

58 "Declaration of Constitutional Principles": *St. Petersburg Times*, Mar. 3, 1956.

58 As one newspaper reporter observed: Jacobstein.

58 "Something very much like panic": C. Vann Woodward, *The Strange Career of Jim Crow* (1955; Oxford and New York: Oxford University Press, 2002).

58 The Southern outcry: Jacobstein. Also *Torrington Register Citizen* (Conn.), Feb. 20, 2002.

58 Collins had come into office: Jacobstein. Also John W. Johnson, ed., *Historic U.S. Court Cases: An Encyclopedia* (New York: Routledge, 2001).

59 When Jesse Hunter: *St. Petersburg Times*, Dec. 16, 1952.

59 McCall was so incensed: *Mount Dora Topic*, Oct. 13, 1955.

59 Sheriff McCall, who had left town: *Mount Dora Topic*, Oct. 13, 1955. Also *Sarasota Journal*, Oct. 25, 1955, and Flores.

60 Mabel reported that in the aftermath: *Mount Dora Topic*, Oct. 27, 1955.

60 Collins indicated that he had sent: *Baltimore Afro-American*, Nov. 5, 1955.

60 Assuring her readers: *Mount Dora Topic*, Oct. 27, 1955.

60 As the avowed "white supremacy candidate": *Ocala Star-Banner*, Dec. 31, 1956. Also Seth A. Weitz, "Bourbon, Pork Chops, and Red Peppers: Political Immortality in Florida, 1945–1968," Ph.D. dissertation, Florida State University, 2007.

61 In a statement to the press: Jacobstein.

61 Still, he had no choice: *Tampa Tribune*, Feb. 17, 1956.

61 Collins's explanation garnered merely "scant applause": *Ocala Star-Banner*, Feb. 22, 1956.

61 In addition to giving public support: *New York Times*, Feb. 25, 1956.

61 Mabel's neighbor Herbert K. Beiser: *Mount Dora Topic*, Mar. 1, 1956.

62 Two nights later: Ibid.

63 She arrived in Tavares: Ibid.

63 **While in Lake County:** Interview, Noel Griffin Jr.

63 **What he did not enjoy:** *Tampa Tribune*, Oct. 30, 1955.

64 **"You're the one who let out":** *Miami News*, Feb. 23, 1956.

64 **Collins mumbled something:** *Mount Dora Herald*, Feb. 29, 1956. Also Gary Corsair, *The Groveland Four: The Sad Saga of a Legal Lynching* (Bloomington, IN: 1st Books, 2004).

64 **Unsurprisingly, the sheriff denied:** Corsair.

64 **When Mabel inquired:** Undated clipping, *Mount Dora Herald*, [Mar. 1956].

64 **While Mabel continued:** *St. Petersburg Times*, Dec. 14, 1955.

64 **Despite the region's robust population growth:** *Washington Post*, Nov. 28, 1954.

65 **Why was not clear:** *Orlando Sentinel*, Jul. 21, 1955.

65 **The first issue:** Ibid. Also undated clipping, *Mount Dora Herald*, [1955].

66 **"I refused to listen"; "I blasted the sheriff":** Mabel Norris Reese, "Crusades Are Not Cheaper by the Dozen," in *Main Street Militants: An Anthology from* Grassroots Editor, ed. Howard Rusk Long (Carbondale: Southern Illinois University Press, 1977).

CHAPTER FOUR. MAKE TRACKS

69 **The boy answered, "Bubba Hawkins":** Interview, Gloria Hawkins Barton.

69 **Immediately the reverend:** Ibid.

70 **The deputies escorted Bubba:** Ibid. Also FDLE.

70 **The victim had "scratched the nigger who raped her":** FDLE.

71 **The next morning:** Ibid.

71 **"vast, untamed wilderness":** "Florida Cattle Ranching: Earliest American Ranchers," Florida Memory (State Library & Archives of Florida), https://www.floridamemory.com/photo graphiccollection/photo_exhibits/ranching/.

71 **The Indian Removal Act of 1830:** Larry O. Rivers, "'Leaning on the Everlasting Arms': Virgil Darnell Hawkins's Early Life and Entry into the Civil Rights Struggle," *The Florida Historical Quarterly* 86, no. 3 (Winter 2008).

72 **Though they maintained:** James M. Denham, *Florida Founder William P. DuVal: Frontier Bon Vivant* (Columbia: University of South Carolina Press, 2015).

72 **In what was essentially still "pioneer country":** Rivers.

72 **What most notably identified them:** Martha Nelson, "Nativism and Cracker Revival at the Florida Folk Festival," in *The Florida Folklife Reader*, ed. Tina Bucuvalas (Jackson: University Press of Mississippi, 2012).

73 **A day laborer:** Rivers. Also *Sarasota Herald Tribune*, Mar. 15, 2004.

73 **Between 1882 and 1930, Florida had:** Stewart Emory Tolnay and E. M. Beck, *A Festival of Violence: An Analysis of Southern Lynchings, 1882–1930* (Urbana and Chicago: University of Illinois Press, 1995).

73 **Like many Southern political leaders of the time:** Paul Ortiz, *Emancipation Betrayed: The Hidden History of Black Organizing and White Violence in Florida from Reconstruction to the Bloody Election of 1920* (Berkeley: University of California Press, 2005).

73 **"At that tender age":** Quoted in Harley Scott Herman, "A Tribute to an Invincible Civil Rights Pioneer," *The Crisis*, Jul. 1994.

74 **He promised God he would:** Rivers.

74 **When he let slip his ambitions:** Ibid.

74 **There he met and married:** *Orlando Sentinel*, Mar. 8, 1987.

75 **Predictably, the State of Florida:** Rivers.

75 **The Florida Board of Control:** Rivers. Also Herman.

75 **"We're older than you":** Rivers. Also interview, Gloria Hawkins Barton.

76 **Thurgood Marshall lambasted Florida's contempt:** Herman.

76 **Virgil Hawkins had no choice:** Ibid.

76 **On the drive down to Tallahassee:** Constance Baker Motley, *Equal Justice Under Law: An Autobiography of Constance Baker Motley* (New York: Farrar, Straus and Giroux, 1998).

77 **"It is doubtful that any institution":** Martin Dyckman, "After *Brown*, the Law Was on His Side, but the Florida Supreme Court Wasn't," *St. Petersburg Times*, May 16, 2004.

77 **Baker Motley was nonetheless astounded:** Herman.

77 **Once again Hawkins was denied:** Rivers.

77 **The Court determined that Hawkins:** *St. Petersburg Times*, Mar. 13, 1956.

77 **The Supreme Court's:** Seth A. Weitz, "Bourbon, Pork Chops, and Red Peppers: Political Immortality in Florida, 1945–1968," Ph.D. dissertation, Florida State University, 2007.

77 **"Every legal recourse":** *St. Petersburg Times*, Mar. 13, 1956.

77 **In a hastily assembled:** *Ocala Star-Banner*, Mar. 14, 1956.

78 **The conference produced a message:** Helen L. Jacobstein, *The Segregation Factor in the Florida Democratic Gubernatorial Primary of 1956* (Gainesville: University of Florida Press, 1972).

78 **Sumter Lowry's campaign:** Ibid.

78 **As if to prove it:** Ibid. Also *Daytona Beach News-Journal*, Oct. 20, 1991.

78 **The beatings, Warren contended:** *Chicago Defender*, Mar. 24, 1956.

78 **"It is regrettable":** *Orlando Sentinel*, Mar. 16, 1956.

79 **"A Negro is now sitting":** *Florida Flambeau* (Florida State University), Apr. 24, 1956.

79 **On December 19, 1957:** *Ocala Star-Banner*, Dec. 19, 1957.

79 **Oldham first disclosed that the victim:** *Burlington Times-News* (N.C.), Dec. 20, 1957.

79 **He then announced:** Ibid.

80 **The next day's local newspapers:** Ibid. Also *St. Petersburg Times*, Dec. 20, 1957.

80 **All Virgil Hawkins could learn:** NARA-FBI.

81 **Mabel, unaware that Hawkins:** *Mount Dora Topic*, Dec. 25, 1957.

81 **The Hawkins family was terrified:** Interview, Gloria Hawkins Barton.

81 **Melvin Sr. told Saunders:** Robert W. Saunders Sr., *Bridging the Gap: Continuing the Florida NAACP Legacy of Harry T. Moore* (Tampa: University of Tampa Press, 2000).

82 **Moore's killing had left the NAACP:** Ibid.

82 **"We needed to move fast":** Ibid.

83 **On December 23, true to his word:** *St. Petersburg Times*, Dec. 24, 1957.

83 **"We're still in the middle":** *St. Petersburg Times*, Dec. 23, 1957.

83 **Evvie Griffin had been on the job:** Interview, Noel Griffin Jr.

84 **On the ride up to the Scrub:** This scene at the cabin of Sheriff Willis McCall in the Big Scrub of Ocala National Forest is drawn largely from FBI file 44-HQ-11050 and FDLE file 531-25-5001, as well as from interviews with Noel Griffin Jr. and newspaper and magazine coverage where indicated. NARA-FBI, FDLE.

89 **The accompanying article accused:** *Tampa Tribune*, Nov. 3, 1956.

90 **Mabel Norris Reese joined:** *Mount Dora Topic*, Nov. 8, 1956.

90 **When McCall learned that Apache:** *Jet*, Nov. 22, 1956. Also interview, Noel Griffin Jr.

90 **Evvie Griffin knew:** Interview, Noel Griffin Jr.

90 **It was time for the sheriff . . . He told Marlene:** NARA-FBI.

91 **As his next-door neighbor:** LCP.

CHAPTER FIVE. SENSATIONAL LIES

93 **In rural Lake County:** Interview, Joseph Branham III.

94 **"They were very interested":** Ibid.

94 **In short order, Morhart's shoes:** Ibid.

95 **As it happened, Jesse:** MNC. Nearly all issues of the *Mount Dora Topic* from 1958 are missing from known bound and microfilm collections of the newspaper in Lake County and at the George A. Smathers Libraries of the University of Florida. Undated drafts of dozens of

stories that Mabel wrote in 1958 were discovered in a box by her granddaughter Cindy Chesley in the attic of her mother, Patricia Reese Chesley, after Patricia passed away in 2015. These stories were likely published in the *Topic* in 1958, as Mabel referred to them in later columns and stories she wrote for the *Daytona Beach News-Journal.*

95 **"Sure, I'll go":** MNC.

95 **When state attorney Gordon Oldham arrived:** Ibid.

95 **On December 24, Melvin Hawkins Sr.:** Interview, Gloria Hawkins Barton.

96 **He related how, despite the efforts of McCall:** FDLE.

96 **But with the story:** Interview, Gloria Hawkins Barton.

96 **She accused the governor:** *Daily Commercial* (Leesburg), Jan. 3, 1958.

96 **Alice refused to discuss:** MNC.

97 **She said the clerk first hesitated:** Ibid.

97 **When he discovered:** Ibid.

97 **Jesse Daniels had confessed:** *Saratoga Herald Tribune,* Dec. 29, 1957.

98 **"We haven't left many stones unturned":** Ibid.

98 **"What of the diamond-shaped heel print?":** *Tampa Tribune,* Dec. 29, 1957. Also *Daytona Beach Evening News,* Dec. 22, 1958.

98 **McCall was dismissive:** *Tampa Tribune,* Dec. 29, 1957. Also MNC.

99 **McCall merely shrugged:** MNC.

99 **She'd learned of the conditions:** This scene is drawn from Mabel's story "Lad in the Dungeon" and her same-day editorial, both published in the *Mount Dora Topic* on May 30, 1957.

100 **The former friends:** Pete Gallagher, "The End of an Era," *Florida Today,* Dec. 31, 1972.

101 **"The judge brought you here":** *Mount Dora Topic,* May 30, 1957.

101 **Mabel's exposé of the failings:** Ibid.

101 **"You can see him":** MNC. Also *Daytona Beach Evening News,* Oct. 22, 1958.

102 **"Son, I hate to see you here so bad":** Pete Gallagher, "His Sentence: 14 Years of Darkness," *Florida Today,* Oct. 2, 1974.

102 **"Kiss me, Jesse":** *Daytona Beach Evening News,* Oct. 22, 1958.

102 **As he hustled the Danielses:** Ibid.

102 **A news story in the *Daily Commercial:*** *Daily Commercial* (Leesburg), Dec. 28, 1957.

102 **"A white laborer has been arrested":** *Norfolk Journal and Guide,* Jan. 4, 1958.

102 **Black newspapers ran headlines:** Ibid.

103 **To bolster the case for Jesse's defense:** MNC.

103 **Then he told Pearl:** Ibid.

103 **"Governor Collins," Pearl wrote:** Ibid.

104 **Pearl's letter mentioned as well:** Ibid.

104 **Mabel incorporated quotations:** NARA-FBI.

105 **She was standing on the sidewalk:** MNC.

105 **A few days later:** Ibid.

106 **Called to the witness stand:** Ibid.

107 **"The powerful sheriff":** Ibid.

107 **Then the session commenced:** Ibid. Also *Daytona Beach Evening News,* Oct. 23, 1958.

108 **"What did she say?":** *Daytona Beach Evening News,* Oct. 24, 1958.

108 **If Jesse had given:** Ibid.

108 **In a second letter:** Ibid.

108 **Pearl wrote, too, of her visit:** MNC.

CHAPTER SIX. YOU WILL NOT TURN US DOWN

111 **On January 9, the grand jury:** LCC.

111 **In a letter to the governor:** MNC.

112 **"Is this to further trap":** Ibid.
112 **Judge Futch quickly issued:** LCC.
112 **When the Danielses:** MNC.
112 **"You may rest assured":** *Daily Commercial* (Leesburg), Jan. 19, 1958.
113 **"Dear Judge Futch":** MNC.
115 **When the letter was made public:** Gary Corsair, *The Groveland Four: The Sad Saga of a Legal Lynching* (Bloomington, IN: 1st Books, 2004).
115 **when the story reached:** Thurgood Marshall to Daniel E. Byrd, Nov. 29, 1951, LDF.
115 **On October 27, 1956:** *Lumberton Robesonian* (N.C.), Dec. 11, 1956.
115 **Many feared the incident would meet:** *St. Petersburg Times,* Nov. 1, 1956.
115 **"I believe they done killed him up":** *Orlando Sentinel,* Oct. 30, 1956.
115 **Robert Saunders from the NAACP:** Robert W. Saunders Sr., *Bridging the Gap: Continuing the Florida NAACP Legacy of Harry T. Moore* (Tampa: University of Tampa Press, 2000).
116 **By the time Saunders arrived:** Ibid. Also *Lansing State Journal* (Michigan), Dec. 11, 1956.
116 **All nine pleaded not guilty:** *St. Petersburg Times,* Nov. 1, 1956.
117 **Instead, Futch placed the blame:** *York Gazette and Daily* (Pa.), Dec. 17, 1956. Also *Leesburg Daily Commercial,* Dec. 12, 1956.
117 **The first words he spoke:** *Daytona Beach Evening News,* Oct. 21, 1958.
117 **He spoke confidently:** MNC.
118 **Three days later, Futch ordered McCall:** LCC.
118 **In a letter to the two doctors at Chattahoochee:** FSH-SAF.
119 **In closing, Buie commended:** Ibid.
119 **On her return home, Pearl wrote:** Ibid.
120 **a reply not from Dr. Eaton but from Dr. Benbow:** Ibid.
120 **Buie assured O'Connor:** Ibid.
121 **In late February, Dr. O'Connor submitted:** Ibid.
121 **O'Connor reported, too, that he had read a copy:** Ibid.
122 **Regarding Mrs. Knowles, Jesse admitted:** Ibid.
122 **Dr. O'Connor and another psychiatrist on staff had concluded:** Ibid.
123 **Mabel of course was there:** MNC.
123 **McCall then proceeded:** *Sarasota Herald Tribune,* Mar. 13, 1958. Also MNC.
123 **Upon returning to the bench . . . When the hearing formally began:** MNC.
124 **"This court," he declared:** LCC.
124 **In disbelief, Mabel wrote:** MNC.
125 **Furthermore, Mabel pointed out . . . In tears, she watched:** Ibid.
125 **Pained by his mother's anguish:** Interview, Jesse Daniels.
125 **Jesse liked Griffin:** Ibid.
125 **One time, he and the deputy:** Pearl Daniels to Mabel Norris Reese, undated, MNC.
125 **On the way from Chattahoochee:** Interview, Noel Griffin Jr.
126 **And he had seen Jesse's confession:** Ibid.
126 **"Rape case of Mrs. Joe Knowles":** FSH-SAF.
129 **"Then I got in bed":** Ibid.
129 **"The only thing that boy":** Interview, Noel Griffin Jr.

CHAPTER SEVEN. NO SUITABLE PLACE

131 **"You're a crazy son of a bitch":** Interview, Jesse Daniels.
131 **A Florida newspaper editorial:** *Sarasota Journal,* May 14, 1956.
132 **Eluding capture:** Brent Richards Weisman, *Unconquered People* (Gainesville: University of Florida Press, 1999).

132 **In 1861, when Florida:** Sally J. Ling, *Out of Mind, Out of Sight: A Revealing History of the Florida State Hospital at Chattahoochee and Mental Health Care in Florida* (CreateSpace, 2013).

133 **Notoriously cruel and corrupt:** J. C. Powell, *The American Siberia; or, Fourteen Years' Experience in a Southern Convict Camp* (1891; Andesite Press, 2015).

133 **With prison labor he not only built:** Joe O'Shea, *Murder, Mutiny and Mayhem: The Blackest-Hearted Villains from Irish History* (Dublin: The O'Brien Press, 2012).

133 **In a letter to Major General George B. Carse:** Powell.

133 **prompted Martin to advise . . . In support of the warden's plea:** Ling.

134 **In 1877, with the passage:** Ibid.

134 **Institutionalized mental health care in America:** Howard Sudak, M.D., "A Remarkable Legacy: Pennsylvania Hospital's Influence on the Field of Psychiatry," Penn Medicine, http://www.uphs.upenn.edu/paharc/features/psych.html.

134 **Many of them were also restrained:** Ling.

134 **The treatments for mentally ill patients:** Sudak. Also Ling.

134 **As America became a more populous, industrialized nation:** Ling.

135 **Because the determination of a person's insanity . . . When, in 1896:** Ibid.

136 **A subsequent investigation uncovered:** Marynia [Farnham], M.D., "Report of Inspection and Survey of Florida State Hospital, Chattahoochee," date unknown, http://freepages.genealogy.rootsweb.ancestry.com/~chattahoochee/Farnhan.htm.

136 **More hopefully, the 1930s also brought:** Ling.

137 **In 1951–1952 alone:** Ibid.

137 **After performing another sixty-four procedures together:** Ibid.

137 **Watts's diagnosis of "agitated depression":** Elizabeth Koehler-Pentacoff, *The Missing Kennedy: Rosemary Kennedy and the Secret Bonds of Four Women* (Baltimore: Bancroft Press, 2015). Also *Daily Mail*, Sept. 25, 2015.

138 **Dr. James Lyerly Sr., the only neurosurgeon:** Ling.

138 **Approximately 271,000 admissions:** Ibid.

138 **The pick (which was indeed taken from the doctor's kitchen):** Janell Johnson, "Thinking with the Thalamus: Lobotomy and the Rhetoric of Emotional Impairment," *Journal of Literary & Cultural Disability Studies* 5, no. 2 (2011), pp. 187–200. Also Ling.

138 **The surgery took only minutes:** Ling.

139 **By the mid-1950s, Dr. Lyerly:** Ibid.

139 **Their procedures, which were designed to pacify:** Johnson.

139 **One year after the Child Molester Act:** Ling.

139 **While doctors at Chattahoochee:** Ibid.

140 **It induced "disinterest without loss of consciousness":** Thomas A. Ban, "Fifty Years Chlorpromazine: A Historical Perspective," *Neuropsychiatric Disease and Treatment* 3, no. 4 (2007), pp. 495–500.

140 **Difficult patients became docile:** Richard L. Lael, Barbara Brazos, and Margot Ford McMillen, *Evolution of a Missouri Asylum: Fulton State Hospital, 1851–2006* (Columbia: University of Missouri Press, 2007).

140 **A patient in the white male department:** Kenneth Donaldson, *Insanity Inside Out* (New York: Crown, 1976).

140 **According to the patient:** *Somerset Daily American* (Pa.), Sept. 30, 1975.

141 **Nor was there any "segregation":** Ling.

141 **Overtaxed attendants—who themselves:** *Daily American*, Sept. 30, 1975.

141 **The attendants favored choking and beating:** Ibid.

141 **"At Chattahoochee, each of us stood alone":** Donaldson.

141 **Perhaps the most famous patient:** *Jet*, Feb. 20, 1958.

142 **Hurston's coverage of the trial:** C. Arthur Ellis Jr., "Paramour Rights and Reparations Issues," *The Black Commentator,* issue 68, Dec. 11, 2003.

142 **Since Jesse had undergone a psychological evaluation:** FSH-SAF.

143 **Dr. Eaton, in his evaluation of Jesse upon admission:** Ibid.

143 **Jesse also told Eaton:** Ibid.

144 **Jesse's memory seemed to Eaton:** Ibid.

144 **Still, Dr. Eaton noted:** Ibid.

145 **Jesse also told Dr. Eaton:** Ibid.

145 **In exploring Jesse's sexual history:** Ibid.

145 **When Eaton asked Jesse:** Ibid.

145 **In his summation of Jesse's admittance interview:** Ibid.

146 **An attendant escorted the new arrival:** Donaldson.

146 **More recent inmates, confused or in a haze:** Ibid.

146 **That night, nineteen-year-old Jesse Delbert Daniels:** Interview, Jesse Daniels.

146 **In late February, Gordon Oldham drove:** FSH-SAF.

146 **He informed O'Connor that "in order to clear up":** LEG-SAF.

147 **According to the transcript:** This scene is drawn largely from Gordon Oldham's interview with Blanche Knowles sometime before March 3, 1958. The transcript, an eight-page typewritten document that Oldham sent to Dr. O'Connor at Chattahoochee, was not discovered until the early 1970s, during Special Master Thomas Woods's legislative investigation into Jesse Daniels's claims bill.

154 **She strived to raise money:** Pearl Daniels to Mabel Norris Reese, undated, MNC.

154 **Understanding that Sam Buie:** Ibid., MNC.

155 **"And then," she tapped:** MNC.

CHAPTER EIGHT. WELL-LAID PLAN

157 **First, on March 11, days after:** *Daytona Beach Morning Journal,* Oct. 2, 1958. Also MNC.

158 **The night before, Odom related:** *Orlando Sentinel,* Apr. 2, 1958.

159 **A woman poked her head:** *Daily Commercial* (Leesburg), Apr. 1, 1958.

160 **McCall shrugged; the woman had made a phone call:** Ibid.

160 **Several times he recalled:** Ibid.

160 **McCall had worse news:** Ibid.

161 **Leery of seeming to play politics:** *Daytona Beach Morning Journal,* Oct. 2, 1958.

161 **"It would not look good":** FDLE.

162 **"Talking like an excited child":** MNC.

162 **Jesse described how Sam Buie:** *Daytona Beach Evening News,* Oct. 24, 1958.

162 **The sheriff, Jesse said:** *Florida Today,* Oct. 2, 1974. Also NARA-FBI, and MNC.

163 **It wasn't the first time:** Gilbert King, *Devil in the Grove: Thurgood Marshall, the Groveland Boys, and the Dawn of a New America* (New York: HarperCollins, 2012).

163 **That day, Pearl recalled:** Pearl Daniels to J. Edgar Hoover, undated, NARA-FBI.

163 **Mabel wanted to know:** Pearl Daniels to Mabel Norris Reese, undated, MNC.

164 **They'd barely gotten to their rooms:** Ibid.

164 **In the room where Jesse slept:** Ibid.

164 **Pearl recalled a few more details:** Ibid.

165 **And there was also the matter:** *Daytona Beach Evening News,* Oct. 23, 1958.

165 **"I think it is most important":** Vera Rony to Mabel Norris Reese, undated, MNC.

166 **Mabel tracked down Bill Fisher:** MNC.

166 **The uncharacteristic silence:** Ibid.

166 **Still, candid as he was:** NARA-FBI.

167 "Has politically powerful Sheriff Willis McCall": MNC.

167 And there was a shocking new detail: Ibid.

167 Mabel reported that, on her advice: Ibid.

168 By a county court order: LCC.

168 Kennedy mounted: *State of Florida v. Sam Wiley Odom*, LCC.

169 Later, in tears, he'd tell Mabel: Ibid.

169 Less convincing in Kennedy's closing statement: Ibid.

169 The tactic was not: Lisa Lindquist Dorr, *White Women, Rape, & the Power of Race in Virginia, 1900–1960* (Chapel Hill: University of North Carolina Press, 2004).

170 Oldham also called: *Santo Trafficante Jr. and Henry Trafficante v. State of Florida*, 92 So. 2d 811 (Fla. 1957).

170 With testimony and arguments complete: *State of Florida v. Sam Wiley Odom*, LCC.

170 Judge Futch ordered Odom: Ibid.

170 Despite being certain of his client's guilt: LCC.

171 What the reporter likely did not know: Office memorandum, SAC, Jacksonville to Director, FBI, May 29, 1958, Subject: Citizens' Council, Lake County, Florida, FBI 62-24240-1.

171 Approaching Futch outside the courthouse: MNC.

171 The response infuriated Mabel: Ibid.

172 "We haven't had any": William Peters, "'The Law' of Lake County," *Coronet*, Dec. 1958.

172 Settled back at his desk, McCall expounded: Ibid.

173 Going door-to-door: Pearl Daniels to Mabel Norris Reese, undated, MNC.

174 Along with clippings of Mabel's stories: Pearl Daniels to Agent Quinn Tamm, Nov. 17, 1958, NARA-FBI.

174 Pearl closed her letter: Ibid.

175 The FBI "is not able to be of help": J. Edgar Hoover to Pearl Daniels, November 26, 1958, NARA-FBI.

175 Pearl wrote back: Pearl Daniels to J. Edgar Hoover, Dec. 1, 1958, NARA-FBI.

175 Hoover wrote again: J. Edgar Hoover to Pearl Daniels, Dec. 4, 1958, NARA-FBI.

175 White did not hesitate: NARA-FBI.

CHAPTER NINE. SO MUCH RACE PRIDE

177 Prepared for a long day's work: Interview, Lawrence King.

178 Still, the Reeses managed to scrape by: Mabel Norris Reese, "Crusades Are Not Cheaper by the Dozen," in *Main Street Militants: An Anthology from* Grassroots Editor, ed. Howard Rusk Long (Carbondale: Southern Illinois University Press, 1977).

178 The information Pearl gleaned: MNC. Also FDLE. Cope was interviewed by FDLE agent Al Albright. Albright's report is dated July 19, 1972, fourteen years after Sam Wiley Odom's arrest. Cope's recollection does not appear to be accurate, or there was a misunderstanding in the conversation or transcription. She claimed the deal for her son to name Melvin Hawkins as Blanche Knowles's rapist occurred at Raiford while Odom was awaiting execution. At that time, Jesse Daniels was already locked away at Chattahoochee, and it makes little sense that McCall would be attempting to reshift blame to Hawkins at this point. Since Odom was being held in the Lake County jail at the same time as Melvin Hawkins just days after the rape, it makes more sense that McCall was trying to get Odom to finger Hawkins while the two young men were in custody in December 1957.

179 Pearl learned further: MNC.

179 When Cope had visited her son: FDLE.

179 "Why?" she beseeched: Pearl Daniels to J. Edgar Hoover, Nov. 25, 1958, NARA-FBI.

179 In a letter to him: Pearl Daniels to W. Wilson White, Dec. 13, 1958, NARA-DOJ.

180 She was surprised to learn: *Leesburg Daily Commercial*, Sept. 19, 1958.

180 **One of those agents was Ted Tucker:** NARA-FBI.

181 **She told him, "Both my husband and I":** Ibid.

181 **But the agents did include:** Ibid.

182 **Sheriff Willis McCall played his recording:** Ibid.

182 **McCall did furnish the FBI:** Ibid.

182 **McCall's own notoriety, he asserted:** Ibid.

183 **On February 4, W. Wilson White informed:** NARA-DOJ.

183 **"What are you doing believing that Communist?":** FHWP.

183 **In the motion, Kennedy argued:** *State of Florida v. Sam Wiley Odom*, LCC.

184 **the court upheld:** *Sam Wiley Odom v. State of Florida*, 109 So. 2d 163 (1959), FSH-SAF.

184 **In June, Kennedy petitioned:** LCC.

184 **On May 2, Betty Jean Owens:** Danielle L. McGuire, *At the Dark End of the Street: Black Women, Rape, and Resistance—a New History of the Civil Rights Movement from Rosa Parks to the Rise of Black Power* (New York: Vintage, 2011).

185 **Owens's companions, meanwhile, drove:** Ibid.

185 **The four intoxicated white men:** *Tampa Tribune*, May 3, 1959.

185 **Reportedly, one white woman:** *Ocala Star-Banner*, Jun. 12, 1959.

186 **A Florida A&M student:** McGuire.

186 **In advance of the trial:** *Pittsburgh Courier*, May 16, 1959.

186 **Ella Baker, director of the Southern Christian Leadership Conference:** McGuire.

186 **On June 11:** Ibid. Also *Baltimore Afro-American*, Jun. 20, 1959.

187 **The defense attorneys took advantage:** McGuire.

187 **The defense called friends and family:** Ibid.

187 **The presence of alcohol:** Ibid.

188 **Those watching from the Jim Crow balcony:** *Baltimore Afro-American*, Jun. 20, 1959.

188 **One of the defense lawyers:** *Pittsburgh Courier*, Jun. 27, 1959.

188 **After the trial, Betty Jean Owens told a reporter:** McGuire.

188 **After praising the jury:** *New York Amsterdam News*, Jun. 20, 1959. Also Aug. 8, 1959.

188 **Editorials in many national newspapers:** *New York Times*, Jun. 16, 1959.

188 **"True-to-tradition white men":** *Baltimore Afro-American*, Jun. 20, 1959.

189 **The *Pittsburgh Courier* called attention:** *Pittsburgh Courier*, Jun. 27, 1959. Also *Palm Beach Post*, May 27, 1926.

189 **The *Chicago Defender* mocked the adulatory tone:** *Chicago Defender*, Jun. 27, 1959.

189 **With racial tensions already running high:** *Ocala Star-Banner*, Jun. 14, 1959.

189 **Yet when he appeared:** *Ocala Star-Banner*, Jun. 17, 1959.

189 **As in the court trial:** Ibid.

190 **As for the six-minute deliberation:** Ibid.

190 **Nor did Leesburg police chief Bill Fisher:** Ibid.

190 **The Okahumpka youth would have:** LCC.

190 **On his return to Lake County:** NARA-DOJ.

CHAPTER TEN. DON'T TALK TO ME ABOUT CONSCIENCE, LADY

193 **Bettye Odom, Sam's twenty-one-year-old sister:** LCP.

193 **"Governor, I don't ask you":** Ibid.

193 **In his response to Cope:** Ibid.

194 **The black churches of Leesburg and Okahumpka:** Ibid.

194 **Although the governor—despite his personal opposition:** Ibid.

194 **Mabel Norris Reese remained focused:** *Daytona Beach Evening News*, Oct. 28, 1958.

194 **But the sheriff refused to answer:** Ibid.

194 **After much "knocking on doors":** MNC.

195 **On August 18, Mabel and Pearl:** This scene is drawn from Mabel's story in the *Mount Dora Topic*, Aug. 27, 1959.
197 **The governor, Sinclair indicated:** *Orlando Sentinel*, Aug. 25, 1959.
198 **Collins's office sent word:** *Mount Dora Topic*, Sept. 3, 1959.
198 **That Sam Wiley Odom had "implicated":** Ibid.
198 **Just after midnight:** This scene is drawn from an extensive transcript of an interview with Sam Wiley Odom taken by deputy court reporter Janice Burleigh, with Gordon Oldham, James Yates, Bryant Spears, and a prison guard present, beginning at 12:05 a.m. on August 21, 1959, at Raiford. LEG-SAF.
209 **Earlier in the evening of December 17:** This scene is derived from James W. Kynes's interview with Sam Wiley Odom on August 22, 1959, at Raiford. DeWitt Sinclair, Superintendent, Florida State Prison, was also present, as was an unnamed stenographer. LEG-SAF.
213 **Oldham himself interviewed:** LEG-SAF.
214 **Over the next few days:** Ibid.
214 **Laura Cope drove to Raiford:** Ibid.
214 **Odom's letter opened with an admission:** LCP.
214 **On August 25, Francisco Rodriguez:** LEG-SAF.
215 **"I don't know nothing":** *Mount Dora Topic*, Sept. 3, 1959.
215 **His report to the governor:** LEG-SAF.
215 **Collins said he would pray:** LCP.
215 **The night before, DeWitt Sinclair attended to:** This scene is drawn from a story in the *Orlando Sentinel*, Oct. 2, 1977.
216 **On the morning of the 28th:** *Orlando Sentinel*, Aug. 28, 1959.
217 **Odom appeared to be calm:** *Orlando Sentinel*, Oct. 2, 1977.
217 **In Okahumpka, a heartbroken Laura Cope:** Ibid.

CHAPTER ELEVEN. WAY OF JUSTICE

221 **The sun was just beginning:** This scene is drawn largely from interviews with Tom Ledford, as well as newspaper accounts where indicated.
225 **On his arrival:** FDLE.
225 **At about one a.m.:** Ibid.
225 **Elmer and Delmer Wilkinson:** Ibid.
226 **A brief article:** *Orlando Sentinel*, May 31, 1960.
226 **Ledford later stated:** FDLE.
226 **The results were not surprising:** Interview, Tom Ledford.
226 **"Let me say it this way":** Interview, Kiser Hardaway.
226 **Bowen's wasn't the only case:** Interview, Tom Ledford.
227 **The drop in Jesse's weight:** FSH-SAF.
227 **Mabel, meanwhile, wrote again:** LCP. Also FSH-SAF.
228 **In a letter to a psychiatrist:** Walker Kennedy to Dr. Charles H. Cronick, Dec. 3, 1960, FSH-SAF.
228 **Kenneth Donaldson was forty-eight . . . Sure enough, lacking legal representation:** Kenneth Donaldson, *Insanity Inside Out* (New York: Crown, 1976).
229 **"We lived in aimless pacing":** Ibid.
229 **Donaldson saw Jesse:** Ibid.
229 **In the fall of 1959:** *Tampa Tribune*, Oct. 15, 1959.
229 **The conditions described:** *Chicago Defender*, Oct. 24, 1959.
229 **The negative publicity:** "Conditions at Florida State Hospital and the Alleged Mistreatment of Patients," Committee on State Institutions Report, 1961.
230 **The study cited testimony:** Ibid.

230 **John Epright:** Ibid.
231 **Mail got lost:** Sally J. Ling, *Out of Mind, Out of Sight: A Revealing History of the Florida State Hospital at Chattahoochee and Mental Health Care in Florida* (CreateSpace, 2013).
231 **Doctors described him as "disoriented":** FSH-SAF.
231 **"the guards would take towels":** Interview, Jesse Daniels.
231 **The report corroborated:** "Conditions at Florida State Hospital."
232 **The most he could capture:** Interview, Jesse Daniels. Also Donaldson.
232 **A decade before, at twenty:** Interview, Noel Griffin Jr.
232 **Around midnight on March 10:** Ibid.
233 **When they arrived at the scene:** FDLE. Also NARA-FBI.
233 **The bloodhounds, Griffin said:** Interview, Noel Griffin Jr.
233 **He would not state:** FDLE.
234 **Later, when Griffin ran into McCall:** Interview, Noel Griffin Jr.
234 **He'd already had three suspects:** *Ocala Star-Banner*, Mar. 13, 1960.
234 **The press described Wass:** FDLE.
234 **Wass recounted:** This scene is drawn from John McCormick's interview with Charlotte Wass, FDLE.
237 **The state attorney emerged:** Ibid.
237 **At a meeting of the Mount Dora Dunkers Club:** Interview, Tom Ledford.
237 **Huett himself would gain notoriety:** Transcript, House Un-American Activities Committee, 89th Congress, Activities of the Ku Klux Klan in the U.S., 3739.
237 **"Okay," McCall told Huett:** Interview, Tom Ledford.
238 **The state attorney's office:** FDLE.
238 **Also introduced into evidence:** FDLE. Also interview, Noel Griffin Jr.
239 **Outside the courtroom:** FDLE. Also interview, Noel Griffin Jr.
239 **"McCall eventually did get to me":** Chesley interview, FHWP.
240 **"He never said quit":** Ibid.
240 **"I feel the newspaper":** *Daytona Beach News-Journal*, Sept. 14, 1958.
240 **"Bud wouldn't let me":** Interview, Tom Ledford.
241 **Gordon Oldham was also dealing:** Agent Al Albright interview with Jack Hooten, FDLE. Details of the account are also based on an author interview with a Dillard family member who preferred to remain anonymous.
241 **The confrontation in Oldham's office:** FDLE.
241 **Only then Charles Dillard:** Ibid.
242 **Tom Ledford, however, claimed to have seen:** Interview, Tom Ledford.
242 **Dillard family members:** FDLE.
242 **"I know Charles took his life":** Interview, anonymous Dillard family member.
242 **Pearl Daniels was worried:** Pearl Daniels to Mabel Norris Chesley, undated, MNC.
243 **In June, Oldham filed:** LCC.
243 **At a March 1961 hearing:** Ibid.
244 **Waiting in the reception room:** It should be noted that despite Saunders's detailed account of this meeting, Griffin denies that he ever set foot into an NAACP office. He claims he only wrote letters to government officials before alerting the *Tampa Tribune* about manufactured evidence in the Fruitland Park case.

CHAPTER TWELVE. IF IT TAKES ALL SUMMER

247 **Tom Ledford had known his days:** Interview, Tom Ledford.
247 **He was riding with McCall:** Interview, Noel Griffin Jr.
248 **When Griffin's wife answered:** Ibid.
249 **Judge Hall ordered:** FDLE. Also *Tampa Tribune*, Sept. 6, 1962.

249 **The footprints:** *Daily Commercial* (Leesburg), Dec. 21, 1962.

249 **The Orange County grand jury:** Ibid.

249 **News of the indictments:** *Pittsburgh Courier*, Feb. 23, 1963.

250 **"After Willis fired me":** Interview, Tom Ledford.

250 **The Lake County Sheriff's Department:** FDLE.

251 **"That's the only man":** Interview, Tom Ledford.

251 **"Willis was a lucky man":** Interview, Noel Griffin Jr.

252 **In his ruling against Shuler and Chatman:** FDLE.

252 **Neither did a letter:** Ibid.

252 **Charlotte Wass herself wrote a letter:** Gary Corsair, *The Groveland Four: The Sad Saga of a Legal Lynching* (Bloomington, IN: 1st Books, 2004).

252 **President John F. Kennedy announced:** "Special Message to the Congress on Urgent National Needs," speech before joint session of Congress, May 25, 1961, https://www.nasa.gov/vision/space/features/jfk_speech_text.html.

253 **In Brevard County:** *Orlando Sentinel*, Jul. 2, 1964.

253 **"There was one flaw":** Dan R. Warren, *If It Takes All Summer: Martin Luther King, the KKK, and States' Rights in St. Augustine, 1964* (Tuscaloosa: University of Alabama Press, 2008).

253 **The sixteen young protesters:** *Pittsburgh Courier*, Sept. 21, 1963.

254 **"Passive resistance is no good":** Warren.

254 **The militant threat:** Ibid.

254 **Its 1963 report:** Ibid.

255 **The reason they were driving:** Ibid.

255 **Fond of misquoting the Bible:** David R. Colburn, *Racial Change and Community Crisis: St. Augustine, Florida, 1877–1980*, quoted ibid.

255 **The NAACP stood by:** Ibid.

256 **When Mabel went to interview Peabody:** *Daytona Beach News-Journal*, Feb. 3, 1991.

256 **She also expressed to Mabel:** Warren.

256 **The *Orlando Sentinel*, angered:** *Orlando Sentinel*, Apr. 2, 1964.

256 **For, indeed, Peabody's arrest:** Warren.

256 **In early June:** Taylor Branch, *Pillar of Fire: America in the King Years 1963–65* (New York: Simon & Schuster, 1998).

256 **Undeterred, King returned:** *Orlando Sentinel*, Jun. 9, 1964.

256 **On the evening of June 4:** *Daytona Beach Morning Journal*, Jun. 5, 1964.

257 **"We want desegregation":** *Daytona Beach Morning Journal*, Jun. 7, 1964.

257 **Mabel's story and interview:** Ibid.

257 **When he and a small group:** Warren.

258 **"We're preparing for a long, hot summer":** *Los Angeles Times*, Jan. 16, 2011.

259 **Stoner's incendiary diatribe:** Branch.

259 **At mass meetings:** *Plainfield Courier-News* (N.J.), Jun. 29, 1964.

259 **In an effort to calm:** *Daytona Beach Morning Journal*, Jun. 15, 1964.

259 **Tobias Simon, representing:** *Daytona Beach Morning Journal*, Jun. 23, 1964.

260 **Among the first witnesses:** During the riots, Florida beefed up the state police force by assigning state beverage agents to active duty in St. Augustine. Jerry Harris was a beverage agent from Tampa.

260 **As state attorney Warren pointed out:** Warren.

260 **Still, Warren noted:** Ibid.

260 **He claimed that he had sent it:** Ibid.

261 **But she restrained:** Ibid. Also *Daytona Beach Morning Journal*, Jun. 27, 1964.

261 **"The Ku Klux Klan is not going":** "Racial and Civil Disorders in St. Augustine," Report of the Legislative Investigation Committee, Feb. 1965, University of Florida Libraries.

261 **King called for a truce:** Warren.

261 **On July 16, in an interview:** *Daytona Beach News-Journal,* Jul. 18, 1964.

261 **"the Ku Klux Klan—or call it":** Warren.

261 **"If you know of any other":** *Daytona Beach News-Journal,* Jul. 18, 1964.

261 **Mabel spoke highly:** Warren.

262 **even as he continued to baldly assert:** Larry Goodwyn, "Anarchy in St. Augustine," *Harper's Magazine,* Jan. 1965.

262 **In August, King held:** Warren.

262 **Generally, Manucy did not suffer:** Halstead "Hoss" Manucy, interview with Edward Kallal Jr., St. Augustine, Florida, Feb. 21, 1976, Civil Rights Library of St. Augustine, http://cdm16000.contentdm.oclc.org/cdm/singleitem/collection/p15415coll1/id/1042/rec/7.

CHAPTER THIRTEEN. TROUBLED BY IT

265 **The woman on the beach:** *Daytona Beach Sunday News-Journal,* Jun. 28, 1970.

265 **"My dearest Momie":** FSH-SAF.

266 **"Mabel Chesley recommended":** This scene is drawn from an interview with Richard Graham.

268 **Mabel found Graham:** *Daytona Beach Morning Journal,* Jun. 28, 1970.

268 **The petition argued:** *Daniels v. O'Connor,* Supreme Court of Florida, July Term, 1970, LEG-SAF.

268 **But as soon as Graham:** Interview, Richard Graham.

269 **"Sorry to tell you this":** Ibid.

269 **Even the majority opinion:** *Daniels v. O'Connor,* Supreme Court of Florida, July Term, 1970, LEG-SAF.

270 **"Ted became a mentor":** The following scenes are derived from interviews with Richard Graham.

272 **Two days before the hearing:** *Daytona Beach News-Journal,* undated [Feb. 1971].

272 **He and Graham's father:** Interview, Richard Graham.

273 **Husfeld began by calling:** The hearing scenes are drawn largely from the transcript of proceedings before Judge Mills. LEG-SAF.

276 **Pearl "rested her arm":** *Daytona Beach Morning Journal,* Feb. 25, 1971.

276 **On the second day:** LEG-SAF.

281 **In every courtroom:** Interview, Richard Graham.

281 **"It is an awesome decision":** LEG-SAF.

283 **Once the elevator doors had closed:** *Orlando Sentinel,* Feb. 26, 1971.

283 **Richard Graham climbed:** Interview, Richard Graham.

CHAPTER FOURTEEN. FAITH IN BLANCHE

287 **By 1971, Florida was growing:** Stanley K. Smith, "Florida Population Growth: Past, Present and Future," Bureau of Economic and Business Research, University of Florida, June 2005, https://www.bebr.ufl.edu/sites/default/files/FloridaPop2005_0.pdf.

288 **And tensions at the newly integrated high schools:** Interview, Noel Griffin Jr. Also, Isabel Wilkerson, *The Warmth of Other Suns: The Epic Story of America's Great Migration* (New York: Random House, 2010).

288 **At the beginning of the year:** *Orlando Sentinel,* Jan. 5, 1971.

289 **The combination, Joe said:** *Orlando Sentinel,* Jan. 21, 1971.

289 **"He is pretty good":** *Orlando Sentinel,* Nov. 28, 1971.

289 **If Blanche was keeping up appearances:** Kelly McBride, "Rethinking Rape Coverage," *Quill,* Nov. 20, 2002.

289 **"There was a lot of womanizing then":** Ibid.

290 **Author Florence King attributed:** Florence King, *Southern Ladies and Gentlemen* (New York: St. Martin's Press, 1975).

290 **When the girlfriend eventually became:** Interview, Priscilla Newell.

290 **"Your daughter would be disgraced":** Ibid.

290 **pumped out stories with headlines:** Dorothy Thompson, "Divorces Are Not Crimes: They Are Tragedies," *Ladies' Home Journal*, Aug. 1951.

290 **"a rather stoic type of person":** FSH-SAF.

291 **On March 1:** *Daytona Beach Evening News*, Mar. 1, 1971.

291 **On March 2:** Mabel Norris Chesley to Office of Reubin Askew, Mar. 2, 1971, LEG-SAF.

291 **"On his behalf":** Ted Husfeld to Reubin Askew, Mar. 22, 1971, LEG-SAF.

292 **"For Jesse to plead guilty":** Interview, Richard Graham.

292 **"Gideon had no attorney":** *Daytona Beach Morning Journal*, Apr. 10, 1971.

293 **As Mabel reported:** *Daytona Beach Morning Journal*, May 10, 1971.

293 **It was a remarkable development:** Interview, Richard Graham.

293 **Hawkins "opened the door":** *Orlando Sentinel*, Sept. 16, 2008.

294 **"She'd done her best":** Ibid.

294 **"it may be a race":** *Daytona Beach Morning Journal*, May 28, 1971.

294 **Hirshberg, a graduate:** *Lowell Sun* (Mass.), Dec. 22, 2013.

294 **On September 10, in a letter:** Milton Hirshberg to Ted Husfeld and Richard Graham, Sept. 10, 1971, FSH-SAF.

295 **That summer, Jesse had:** *St. Petersburg Times*, Oct. 24, 1971.

295 **Gordon Oldham, in a letter:** William Reed to Reubin Askew, describing Oldham's letter to Hirshberg, Oct. 16, 1972, FDLE.

295 **In October, in an interview:** *St. Petersburg Times*, Oct. 24, 1971.

295 **"It doesn't get any faster":** Interview, Richard Graham.

295 **Contradicting the lower court's finding:** District Court of Appeal of Florida, Second District, Nov. 17, 1971, *Daniels v. State* No. 71-233, LEG-SAF.

296 **Martin Dyckman, one of the best-known:** *St. Petersburg Times*, Oct. 24, 1971. Also FDLE.

297 **"Hell, no!":** *St. Petersburg Times*, Nov. 19, 1971.

297 **Having already stated plainly:** Interview, Richard Graham.

297 **He tried to appeal:** Ibid.

298 **Nor could Graham:** *St. Petersburg Times*, Oct. 24, 1971.

298 **"I had more faith in Blanche":** Interview, Richard Graham.

298 **Moreover, a spokesman for the Florida attorney general's office:** *St. Petersburg Times*, Oct. 24, 1971.

299 **"I've waited nearly fourteen years":** *St. Petersburg Times*, Nov. 19, 1971.

299 **"You should have seen the parting":** *St. Petersburg Times*, Dec. 5, 1971.

300 **Doughney took him out:** Ibid.

300 **"It was as bad as a toothache":** *St. Petersburg Times*, Dec. 1, 1974.

300 **Inside his new home:** *Orlando Sentinel*, Dec. 25, 1971.

301 **A few other gifts:** Ibid.

301 **Seated on Pearl's bed:** *St. Petersburg Times*, Dec. 5, 1971.

301 **Mabel stole a moment:** *Daytona Beach Sunday News-Journal*, Dec. 5, 1971.

302 **"And I'm going to be a musician":** *St. Petersburg Times*, Dec. 5, 1971.

302 **"For now, I close":** *Daytona Beach Sunday News-Journal*, Dec. 5, 1971.

CHAPTER FIFTEEN. SOMEONE SHOULD WRITE A BOOK

305 **"We'll start off a brand new year":** *St. Petersburg Times*, Dec. 31, 1971.

305 **The state attorney did not:** William Reed to Reubin Askew, Dec. 16, 1972, FDLE.

305 The state attorney expressed: *Florida Today*, Oct. 13, 1974.

305 Oldham's decision disappointed: Ibid.

306 "He has several retarded employees": *St. Petersburg Times*, Dec. 31, 1971.

306 "The mental anguish": *Florida Today*, Oct. 13, 1971.

306 "Because a weekly newspaper speaks": *Daytona Beach Morning Journal*, Jan. 7, 1972.

307 "There has never been a trial": *Naples Daily*, Feb. 19, 1972.

308 Jesse, in a navy blue suit: *Daytona Beach Morning Journal*, Mar. 4, 1972.

308 Graham and Husfeld opened: Ibid.

308 The next witness was Deputy James Yates: Ibid.

308 Nor could he refer: *Daytona Beach Morning Journal*, Mar. 3, 1972.

309 "He just brushed me off": Interview, Richard Graham.

309 She recounted for Graham: *Daytona Beach Morning Journal*, Mar. 3, 1972.

309 "She apparently had a green light": Interview, Richard Graham.

309 "I'm my own best protection": *Florida Today*, Oct. 13, 1974.

309 Then the lawyers called Jesse: *Daytona Beach Morning Journal*, Mar. 4, 1972.

310 In April 1972: FDLE.

310 Both Jack and Bobby Huffman later stated: Ibid.

310 After the scuffle, Vickers was carried: Ibid.

311 At the coroner's inquest: Isaac M. Flores, *Justice Gone Wrong: A Sheriff's Power of Fear* (New York and Bloomington, IN: iUniverse, 2009).

311 Unconvinced by the verdict: *Tallahassee Democrat*, May 20, 1972.

312 Unperturbed, nearly yawning: *Daytona Beach Morning Journal*, Jun. 1, 1972.

312 When Graham asked Oldham: Ibid.

312 "Did you ask for a retraction": Interview, Richard Graham.

312 Finally, to Special Master Woods: *Daytona Beach Morning Journal*, Jun. 1, 1972.

312 Bill Donaldson, the polygraph expert: FDLE.

313 It had taken place: Ibid.

313 Richard Graham handed Hickman: Interview, Richard Graham.

313 "He had kinky black hair": FDLE.

314 Margaret Hickman, confused: *Daytona Beach Sunday News-Journal*, Jun. 4, 1972.

314 The attorneys decided: Interview, Richard Graham.

314 "But it was a Negro": FDLE. Also *Florida Today*, Dec. 31, 1972.

314 Jim Mahorner, counsel for the attorney general: FDLE.

314 The agents determined: Ibid. Also *Florida Today*, Oct. 13, 1974.

315 When presented with the actual confession: FDLE.

315 When the FDLE agents interviewed Donaldson: Ibid.

316 Donaldson then produced: Ibid.

316 Once he'd confirmed: Ibid.

317 For example, there was this seemingly innocuous sentence: LEG-SAF.

317 Griffin, for one, had believed: Interview, Noel Griffin Jr.

317 Mabel Chesley took Woods's comment: *Daytona Beach Sunday News-Journal*, Jun. 4, 1972.

318 "It would take a Truman Capote": Ibid.

CHAPTER SIXTEEN. WHETHER THEY BE WHITE OR BLACK

321 Alfred Albright, the youngest of sixteen children: U.S. Census, 1920. Also FDLE.

323 Judge Scott concluded that the evidence: *Palm Beach Post*, May 5, 1972.

323 The prisoner's death: *Tallahassee Democrat*, Jun. 13, 1972.

323 "We wanted Al Albright": Interview, Rick Hernan.

324 McCall balked: FDLE.

324 "I am innocent": *Orlando Sentinel*, Jun. 13, 1972.

324 **"This is the NAACP":** *Orlando Sentinel*, May 18, 1972.
324 **The Vickers case, he said:** *Orlando Sentinel*, Jun. 13, 1972.
324 **One of the grand jurors:** *Florida Times Union*, Aug. 18, 1972.
325 **In its report, the twenty-three-person grand jury:** *Orlando Sentinel*, Jun. 13, 1972.
325 **Asked why by the prosecutors:** *Palm Beach Post*, Aug. 19, 1972.
325 **"There are lots of rumors":** *Orlando Sentinel*, Jun. 14, 1972.
326 **"Al Albright was the greatest":** Interview, Rick Hernan.
326 **"Willis McCall is a murderer":** FDLE.
326 **Albright and Hernan found:** Interview, Rick Hernan.
326 **They learned, for example:** *St. Petersburg Times*, Jan. 14, 1970.
327 **The coroner's inquest:** FDLE.
327 **Testifying in the murder trial:** *Palm Beach Post*, Aug. 27, 1972.
327 **The police said he'd taken:** *Orlando Sentinel*, Nov. 12, 1972.
327 **In June, Albright met:** FDLE.
328 **Albright interviewed Fisher:** Ibid.
328 **Meech demanded:** Ibid.
329 **Already seated in the gallery:** Interview, Noel Griffin Jr.
329 **Albright hustled over:** Ibid. Also *Orlando Sentinel*, Sept. 1, 1972.
329 **Not even testimony:** *Palm Beach Post*, Aug. 27, 1972.
330 **"By the time they hit":** Ibid.
330 **In an interview after the trial:** Interview, Rick Hernan. Also FDLE.
330 **Asked by a reporter:** *Florida Today*, Sept. 30, 1972.
330 **To another reporter:** *Florida Today*, Jul. 12, 1972.
331 **With the Vickers case having failed:** FDLE.
332 **He told the investigators:** LEG-SAF.
332 **They set their sights:** NARA-FBI.
332 **In June, Mabel Chesley:** *Daytona Beach Morning Journal*, undated clipping, MNC.
333 **"Of course, he shouldn't be":** Mabel Norris Chesley to Edgar Dunn, undated, MNC.
333 **To that end, he placed:** William Troelstrup to William Reed, Jul. 26, 1972, FDLE.
333 **In August, after Willis McCall's acquittal:** Edgar Dunn to Ben Krage, Sept. 8, 1972, NARA-DOJ.
334 **the DOJ stated that it was:** NARA-DOJ. Also Reubin Askew to Florida Parole and Probation Committee, Oct. 9, 1972, NARA-DOJ.
334 **In a report based on a study:** Ben Krage to David L. Norman, Oct. 22, 1972, NARA-DOJ.
334 **In response to a letter:** NARA-FBI.
334 **In preparing their notes:** NARA-DOJ.
334 **Of particular concern to the DOJ attorneys:** Ibid.
335 **While FBI agents were examining:** Ibid.
335 **Learning that the Daniels case:** Interview, Bud Bosanquet.
335 **Oldham assured Karl:** LEG-SAF.
335 **At none of the hearings:** Ibid.
336 **That Graham had chosen:** Ibid.
336 **From the outset the meeting was tense:** Ibid.
337 **The Department of Justice:** NARA-FBI.
337 **On the morning after the attack; Hawkins could not recall:** Ibid.
338 **Hawkins admitted to still feeling:** Ibid.
338 **Horrified by the news:** Ibid.
338 **Fain's nervousness was immediately apparent:** FDLE.
338 **Since 1970, Earle Fain Jr.:** *Orlando Sentinel*, Mar. 24, 1970.
338 **He was "absolutely sure":** FDLE.

339 Joe Knowles was a "ladies' man": Ibid.
339 "I be goddamn": Ibid.
339 Next, Fain said, Oldham and Knowles: Ibid.
339 He avowed to Albright: Ibid.
340 Fain told Albright: Ibid.
340 The day after their meeting: Ibid.
340 In response to Karl's questioning: LEG-SAF.
341 "The room was completely dark": Ibid.
341 She answered the question: Ibid.

CHAPTER SEVENTEEN. A NEWSPAPER WOMAN

343 "I believe the Fain statement": William Reed to John Briggs, NARA-DOJ.
344 On the first day of grand jury proceedings: *Ocala Star-Banner*, Feb. 21, 1973.
344 Notably absent from the witness list: NARA-DOJ.
344 As Richard Graham learned: Interview, Richard Graham.
344 McCall told reporters that he'd never sweated: Isaac M. Flores, *Justice Gone Wrong: A Sheriff's Power of Fear* (New York and Bloomington, IN: iUniverse, 2009).
344 In one such communication: Ed Miller to John Briggs, NARA-DOJ.
345 As the focus of the investigation: NARA-DOJ.
345 In the opinion of DOJ Civil Rights Division investigator: Carlton Stoiber, correspondence to author, Mar. 22, 2016.
345 "There are many conflicts": *St. Petersburg Times*, Aug. 16, 1973.
346 "In spite of the very real": William Reed to Reubin Askew, NARA-DOJ.
346 The FDLE report: LEG-SAF.
347 In a rare decision: Ibid.
347 In his final report: Ibid.
348 But there was one more discrepancy: FDLE.
348 Yet on closer examination: Ibid. Also LEG-SAF.
348 The DOJ declared: NARA-DOJ.
349 The enlistment of that black male: LEG-SAF.
349 In his appearance before the special master: Ibid.
349 However, the FDLE investigation: FDLE. Also LEG-SAF.
351 Reed's report to the governor: LEG-SAF.
351 Reed had found it "interesting": Ibid.
352 "this would appear incredible": Ibid.
352 In Reed's estimation: Ibid.
352 "That's a typical colored remark": Ibid.
353 "Hell, yes": Interview, Noel Griffin Jr.
353 "Yates did whatever Willis told him to": Interview, Tom Ledford.
353 It was three years: LEG-SAF. Also *Daytona Beach Morning Journal*, Mar. 17, 1974.
354 "Buttressed by . . . years of investigation": *Daytona Beach Morning Journal*, Mar. 17, 1974.
354 "But, more critical than monetary damages": LEG-SAF.
354 Even Richard Graham's opposing counsel: James Mahorner to Terrell Sessums, Speaker of the House of Representatives, Mar. 25, 1974. LEF-SAF.
354 "Thank God for delivering": *St. Petersburg Times*, Nov. 17, 1975.
354 "It was all because of Mabel": Interview, Richard Graham.
354 Mabel's conscience: *Daytona Beach Morning Journal*, Mar. 17, 1974.
354 House Bill 2431: LEG-SAF.
355 As he later acknowledged: *St. Petersburg Times*, Nov. 17, 1975.
356 "Sometimes," Jesse recalled: Interview, Jesse Daniels.

356 **Progress on the claims bill:** *St. Petersburg Times*, Nov. 17, 1975.
356 **"Oh, there are pains":** Ibid.
357 **With Pearl by his side:** *St. Petersburg Times*, Dec. 1, 1974.
357 **"I'm so thankful to God":** Ibid.
357 **"I'm still not adjusted":** Ibid.
358 **Representative Richard Langley:** *St. Petersburg Times*, Apr. 26, 1975.
358 **Frustrated by this last-minute turn:** LEG-SAF.
359 **"I decided based":** Interview, Mary Ellen Hawkins.
359 **Jesse Daniels was waiting:** This scene is drawn from interviews with Patricia Chesley, Jesse Daniels, and Richard Graham.

EPILOGUE

363 **"When this boy was arrested":** This scene is drawn from the audio recording of the legislative debate on House Bill 2431. LEG-SAF.
365 **special master, who . . . absolved . . . "Nothing":** LEG-SAF.
366 **Journalist Martin Dyckman:** Martin Dyckman to author, Jul. 20, 2017.
366 **"If you're looking for . . . a culprit":** *Florida Today*, Oct. 13, 1974.
366 **"I'm so angry":** *New York Times*, Jun. 27, 1975.
367 **In *Donaldson v. O'Connor*:** Ibid.
367 **"I wouldn't have treated":** *Orlando Sentinel*, Feb. 10, 1991.
368 **Their convictions were upheld:** *Shuler v. Wainwright*, 491 F. 2d 1213, 1223 (5th Cir., 1974).
368 **"There was no love lost":** Harold Rummel, "'Caboose' McCall's Law: He Runs the Railroad in Lake County," *The Floridian* (*St. Petersburg Times*, Feb. 23, 1969).
369 **"the grand dame":** *Naples Daily News*, Nov. 26, 2014.
369 **"He was just as guilty":** *Florida Today*, Sept. 7, 1980.
369 **"He was a son of the old South":** *Orlando Sentinel*, Oct. 3, 2007.
369 **"I thought it was great":** *Orlando Sentinel*, Nov. 2, 1998.
370 **"This is the proudest day":** Harley Herman, "A Cause Worth Fighting For: The Story of Civil Rights Pioneer Virgil Darnell Hawkins," https://acauseworthfightingfor.wordpress.com.
370 **"I know what I did":** Tabitha Young, "Virgil Hawkins' Righteous Fight to Become a Lawyer," *Tallahassee Magazine*, Jan.–Feb. 2009.
370 **In October 1988:** *St. Petersburg Times*, May 16, 2004.
371 **"I always heard":** Interview, Gloria Hawkins Barton.
371 **"Blacks were seen as less than human":** Interview, William "B.G." Floyd.
372 **"He'd been exposed":** Interview, David Troxler.
372 **"I've had a pretty good life":** Interview, Jesse Daniels.
372 **Still, Blanche was fearful:** Interview, Steve Knowles.
373 **"She had a heavier course load":** Interview, Mary Elizabeth Knowles.
373 **"There's more than one victim":** Interview, Steve Knowles.
374 **"Rarely do men of the caliber":** *Orlando Sentinel*, Sept. 26, 1976.
375 **"Those were the three really big stories":** *Orlando Sentinel*, May 3, 1979.

INDEX

Italicized page numbers indicate illustrations.

PHOTO CREDITS